All the great thinkers who have set the intellectual tenor of our times – Hegel, Marx, Tylor, Spencer, Durkheim, Weber, and Freud – had a lifelong and abiding interest in the nature and significance of religion, and many of their crucial works were in fact devoted to explicating its origin and function. In this important, scholarly, wide-ranging, and readable text, Brian Morris provides a lucid outline of the nature of the explanations of religious phenomena offered by these writers, together with an account of the historical and cultural context in which they were developed, and of their relationship to the thinkers' broader social theories. In so doing, he also unravels the many theoretical strategies in the study of religion that have been developed and explored by later anthropologists, cogently discussing functionalist, intellectualist, symbolist, interpretive, structuralist, psychological, and ideological approaches. As well as covering the classical authors and the debates surrounding their work, Dr. Morris offers perceptive discussions of more contemporary scholars, such as Jung, Malinowski, Radcliffe-Brown, Eliade, Lévi-Strauss, Evans-Pritchard, Douglas, Turner, Geertz, and Godelier.

Written from the standpoint of critical sympathy, and free of jargon, this book – the first of its kind since Evans-Pritchard's pioneering *Theories of Primitive Religion* – is an invaluable guide to the writings on religion of all the major figures in anthropology. It will be indispensable for all students of anthropology and of the social sciences generally as well as for those interested in comparative religion.

Anthropological studies of religion

Anthropological studies of religion

An introductory text

BRIAN MORRIS

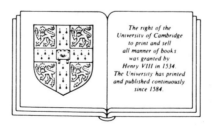

CAMBRIDGE UNIVERSITY PRESS

Cambridge

New York   Port Chester

Melbourne   Sydney

Published by the Press Syndicate of the University of Cambridge
The Pitt Building, Trumpington Street, Cambridge CB2 1RP
40 West 20th Street, New York, NY 10011, USA
10 Stamford Road, Oakleigh, Melbourne 3166, Australia

First published 1987
Reprinted 1987, 1988, 1989, 1990

Printed in the United States of America

Library of Congress Cataloging-in-Publication Data
Morris, Brian.
Anthropological studies of religion.
Bibliography: p.
Includes index.
1. Religion – Study and teaching – History.
2. Religion, Primitive – Study and teaching – History.   I. Title.
BL41.M63   1987   306'.6   86–18851

British Library Cataloging-in-Publication Data
Morris, Brian, 1936–
Anthropological studies of religion: an introductory text.
1. Religion
I. Title
306'.6   GN470

ISBN 0 521 32794 6 hardback
ISBN 0 521 33991 X paperback

To my friends
George and Helen Welsh

Contents

Contents

Acknowledgments

I should like to express my thanks to friends and colleagues who have warmly supported and critically reviewed my anthropological endeavors over the past decade: James Woodburn, Maurice Bloch, Ioan Lewis, Jacqui Morris, Pat Caplan, David Parkin, and Olivia Harris. Thanks are also due to Maggie Freeman, who deciphered and competently typed my scribbled manuscript.

For your teachers, they must be nature and history.

William Morris, *The Lesser Arts* (1887)

Introduction

"All mankind, Greeks and non-Greeks alike, believe in the existence of gods." So said Plato more than two thousand years ago. Few would deny that some form of religion is universal among mankind. We have yet to discover any society that does not articulate some notions about the sacred and about spiritual beings. Apologists for religion, in advocating a religious or theistic view of the world, have naturally tended to stress the universality of religion, but it is well to remember that skeptical attitudes toward religious beliefs have probably been expressed in all cultures and that a naturalistic conception of the world also has a long history. Indeed Radcliffe-Brown went so far as to assert that

> in every human society there inevitably exist two different and in a certain sense conflicting conceptions of nature. One of them, the *naturalistic*, is implicit everywhere in technology, and, in our 20th century European culture, has become explicit and dominant in our thoughts. The other, which might be called mythological, or *spiritualistic* conception, is implicit in myth and in religion, and often becomes explicit in philosophy. (1952: 130)

Mary Douglas, who in *Purity and Danger* was concerned to portray the "primitive world view" as essentially religious and symbolic, was later to question this notion of "primitive piety" and to suggest that there may be many tribal cultures that have a secular bias. She cites Barth's study of the Basseri nomads of Persia (1964), who, though Moslems, take their religion about as seriously as members of a typical London suburb, and she suggests that anthropologists should "ditch the myth of the pious primitive" (1975: 81). This seems to me preferable to the approach that assumes that all preliterate people are totally enmeshed in conceptual categories that are essentially religious. We have only to look back to Greek thought, which many have seen as the fountainhead of the Western intellectual tradition, to see the coexistence of several distinct conceptions of nature, society, and the world.

The anthropological study of religious beliefs and institutions, which

1

it will be my purpose to explore in the following chapters, has suffered unduly from the effects of the unnecessary schisms and specialisms that have developed within academia. The founders of social science – Spencer, Durkheim, and Weber, in particular – all of whom had an abiding interest in religious institutions and ideologies, had, it can be safely asserted, a world-historical outlook. These scholars were interested in social institutions both from a comparative perspective and in terms of historical change and development, so that in their studies we find not only incisive analyses and theories relating to the rise of industrial capitalism but also reflections on preliterate cultures. Herbert Spencer's *Principles of Sociology* is crammed with data drawn from a wide range of cultures; Weber's *Sociology of Religion* has volumes on all major religious systems; and even the studies of Marx, devoted as they are almost exclusively to a critical analysis of capitalism, nonetheless contain ample comparative material relating to the social life of preliterate and "ancient" communities.

The rise of sociology and anthropology as independent academic disciplines has, I think, had unfortunate consequences for it has led to rather parochial perspectives. A cursory examination of the basic textbooks in both subjects will prove my point, especially if consideration is given to religious beliefs and organization. On the whole, sociological texts deal almost exclusively with Christianity and secularism and treat religion as a rather peripheral issue, notwithstanding the fact that in a world context religious ideologies have played a fundamental role in human affairs. Anthropological texts, on the other hand, largely focus on the religion of tribal cultures and seem to place an undue emphasis on its more exotic aspects. There is invariably a chapter on magic or witchcraft. Thus, between them, a good deal of data on historical religions is left out of account, although recent scholars in both disciplines have made important theoretical contributions in subject areas that are normally neglected by the introductory texts. But, more important, an unnecessary conceptual division has arisen between tribal religion (as studied by anthropologists) and historical religion (as studied by sociologists and area specialists), and they have been accorded differential theoretical treatment. That the advent of literacy and state systems has had important implications with respect to the nature and organization of religious systems no one would deny; that it merits a different theoretical approach is questionable. But this is what has occurred.

Two instances are worth noting. First, in general discussions of religion, theories concerning the origins and functions of religion are invariably addressed to the religious systems of preliterate cultures. Freud, in *Totem and Taboo*, significantly links psychoanalytic theory to tribal religion, and Evans-Pritchard's important text is entitled *Theories of Primitive Religion*, though he suggests that the dichotomy between "natural and revealed religion is false and makes for obscurity" and argues that the data derived from tribal cultures is essential for a comparative analysis aimed at determining the earlier characteristics of religion generally (1965: 2). Similarly, discussions of the "savage mind" or of so-called primitive thought and its contrast with scientific understanding equate the former mode of thought not with religious thought generally but only with the traditional thought of preliterate cultures. Durkheim's suggestions as to the "generality" of primitive or symbolic classifications and the metaphorical nature of Christian concepts are significantly ignored. A seemingly sharp and unnecessary line of demarcation is maintained between folk and historical religion.

Second, whereas historical world religions are treated as conceptual entities by students of comparative religion, the religion of tribal cultures is dismembered and treated piecemeal. Thus most general texts on comparative religion devote a chapter respectively to Islam, Buddhism, and Judaism, which are treated both as belief systems and as solid historical phenomena, whereas "primitive" religion is discussed under a series of headings: mana, taboo, totemism, magic, shamanism, myth, and the sacred. The conceptual ideas that these terms embody are, of course, by no means restricted to tribal cultures but may be an aspect of any religious system. Surprisingly, some anthropologists have tended to follow this approach, for although there have been a number of excellent monographs on tribal religion, the general tendency has been to concentrate on one aspect of the ideological system. Symbolism, spirit possession, myth, and witchcraft, for example, are often treated as an autonomous set of beliefs and activities, almost independent of other aspects of the culture, and theoretical perspectives are directed specifically to one facet of religious life. Such studies may be ethnographic, as in Evans-Pritchard's classic account of Azande witchcraft, or they may be of a general nature, as exemplified in the works of Lévi-Strauss on totemism and Lewis on spirit-possession cults.

The essential Marxist premise, Lévi-Strauss remarked, is that "the way people live conditions the way they think." This issue is perhaps the only guiding thread of the present study, which is designed as an introduction to the writings of a number of scholars who have made theoretical efforts to understand or explain religious phenomena. It is written, I hope, from the standpoint of critical sympathy, and thus does not present any thesis of my own. I have interpreted both anthropology and religion in the broadest sense. Anyone who studies the human condition is, for me, an anthropologist, whereas the rubric "religion," to me, covers all phenomena that are seen as having a sacred or supraempirical quality: totemism, myth, witchcraft, ritual, spirit beliefs, symbolism, and the rest. In discussing each scholar I first outline in broad terms the nature of his or her social theory and then go on to describe and critically examine the theory of "religion." The organization of the work is roughly chronological and attempts to broadly situate scholars within currents of thought, reflecting the various approaches to the critical understanding of religion. The first two chapters deal essentially with the German historical tradition and examine the work of Hegel, Marx, Engels, and Weber. Chapter 3 outlines the work of those writers who have had an important influence on academic anthropology: Müller, Spencer, Tylor, Frazer, Durkheim, and Radcliffe-Brown. In the fourth chapter the work of those writing from a psychological standpoint is explored: Malinowski, Freud, Jung, and Eliade; and in the following one I examine the work of those writers who have developed the implications of Durkheim's thought: Lévy-Bruhl, Evans-Pritchard, Douglas, and Turner. The final chapter looks at the recent work of Lévi-Strauss, Geertz, and Godelier.

A final word needs to be said about my approach to the subject. Some years ago Alasdair MacIntyre (1964) posed the question as to whether understanding religion is compatible with believing it. He came to the conclusion that a skeptic has to explain the meaning of religion in order to reject it, whereas in order to maintain that understanding a religion is dependent on believing it one has to ignore the social context, which, given the widespread diffusion of naturalistic explanations, is rather difficult to do. Such philosophical issues I leave aside and can only plead, as an atheist, that I have tried to follow in my studies the approach that Bertrand Russell advocated with respect to philosophy, namely that the right attitude is neither one of reverence nor contempt, but rather an attitude of critical sympathy. In my own approach to religion and to the many scholars whose writings I review in this study, I have tried to reflect this attitude. Needless to say, this leads me to question whether Evans-Pritchard's belief that religion "can be firmly grasped only from within" is a valid one.

FROM: BRIAN MORRIS. 1987. ANTHROPOLOGICAL STUDIES OF RELIGION. CAMBRIDGE: CAMBRIDGE UNIVERSITY PRESS.

1

Religion as ideology

Hegelian metaphysics

"All the great philosophical ideas of the past century – the philosophies of Marx and Nietzsche, phenomenology, German existentialism, and psychoanalysis – had their beginnings in Hegel; it was he who started the attempt to explore the irrational and integrate it into an expanded reason, which remains the task of our century." So wrote Merleau-Ponty (1964: 63). Only two decades later, as Descombes observes (1980: 12), opinion seems to have shifted among French philosophers, and Foucault was to note that "whether through logic or epistemology, whether Marx or Nietzsche, our entire epoch struggles to disengage itself from Hegel." In truth these statements reflect not simply the changing fashions of French intellectual life, but the paradoxical and ambiguous influence that Hegel has had on modern thought. On the one hand he heralded the attempt to go beyond the mechanistic paradigm of the Enlightenment. He articulated a mode of thought that attempted to transcend the dualisms that he had inherited from this tradition, while remaining faithful to its insights, particularly Kant's stress on the radical freedom of human subjectivity. Hegel thus conceived of the world as a kind of organismic process and attempted to unify the various dualisms of positivistic science: spirit and nature, freedom and necessity, subjectivity and objectivity. In this sense his influence has been important, indeed profound, and Capra's recent (1982) plea for a "new" paradigm – a "holistic conception of reality" – simply expresses ideas that Hegel had mooted more than a century ago. On the other hand, Western scientific tradition has largely developed in reaction, or even in opposition, to Hegelian metaphysics and has thus sustained and developed the thought and premises of the Enlightenment (cf. Popper's critique of Hegel, 1945: 1–80). Such a philosophy, as Charles Taylor noted, was "utilitarian in its ethical outlook, atomistic in its social philosophy, analytic in its science of man, and . . . looked to a scientific social engineering to reorganize

5

man and society and bring men happiness through perfect mutual adjustment" (1979: 1). This positivistic vision, with its mechanistic and dualistic world view, is still in fact the dominant paradigm, and, as Capra has suggested, it permeates the human sciences, particularly economics and psychology. Foucault's suggestion that contemporary thought is struggling to disengage itself from Hegel's philosophy is misplaced; social science has been evading the implications of Hegel's thought since its inception, as Marcuse suggested in examining the theories of Auguste Comte, whom many have regarded as the founder of sociology (1941: 340–60). Both anthropology and sociology have largely followed the positivist tradition of the Enlightenment, and Hegel's influence has been a diffuse or muted one, largely communicated through the German idealist tradition rather than through Marx. Indeed Gillian Rose (1981) has recently argued that both Weber and Durkheim follow a neo-Kantian paradigm, and even those Marxist theorists who appear to be critical of empirical sociology – Lukacs, Adorno, Habermas, and Althusser – also tend, she suggests, to follow the positivist tradition. Likewise Bottomore and Nisbet have stressed the neo-Kantian trend in the general development of Lévi-Strauss's thought (1979: 581–4). The only tradition that has explicitly acknowledged the importance of Hegelian philosophy has been Marxism, although, as we shall see, Marx and Engels radically revised the tenor of Hegel's thought.

Hegel's writings have had an enormous impact on the modern world, yet almost everyone has acknowledged that they are obscure and difficult to understand. Hector Hawton admitted that he found them "almost completely incomprehensible" and went on to suggest that Hegel was a scholar who was clearly struggling "with the limitations of language in an agonizing attempt to communicate his vision" (1956: 94). And in an important sense Hegel is a visionary. He was a romantic, and was strongly influenced by the writings of Goethe and Schiller, but he would not renounce reason nor did he venerate the medieval age. He had a vision of a universal harmony, but he sought to convey this unity through the rational understanding of a cosmic process that he, like Aristotle, clearly believed was moving toward perfection. He had an abhorrence of mystical intuitions and sensed that this harmony would be achieved only through the creative activity of human beings. Because his writings are complex and obscure, Hegel is easily misunderstood, and I cannot pretend to have fully understood the subtlety of his thought. But my purpose here is only to outline some of Hegel's basic premises and his interpretation of religious culture. And I can do this best, I think, by quoting from his *Lectures on the Philosophy of History*, the introduction to which presents, in summary fashion, some of his basic ideas.

Hegel was born in 1770 in Stuttgart, the son of a minor civil servant, and for most of his life worked as a private tutor or university teacher. Though an "exuberant genius" and visionary, he was, as Copleston put it, "very much the honest bourgeois university professor" (1963: 197). The date of his birth is important, for it meant that Hegel came to maturity at a crucial period: The end of the eighteenth century was a period of social and intellectual turmoil. In 1781 Immanuel Kant had published his masterpiece, *The Critique of Pure Reason*; in 1789 the French Revolution had broken out, and in Germany the writings of Schelling, Goethe, and Schiller had ushered in the Age of the Imagination, which was to crystallize as the Romantic Movement. The Age of Reason was coming to an end, and many of the essential premises of the Enlightenment – and even reason itself – were increasingly being challenged. At this time, too, there was a revival of interest in the philosophy of Spinoza, a rationalist scholar and recluse who had been neglected for the past century. The essence of Hegel was that he absorbed, and attempted to unite, all of these conflicting trends. As Gray writes,

> Hegel's deepest longing – amounting to a passion – was for a reconciliation of all the conflicting forces which in his age the Enlightenment and subsequent Romanticism had set in motion. His passion for a synoptic view that would reconcile reason and reality, the real and the ideal, or mind and nature could be satisfied only by a comprehensive system in which every legitimate source of conflict and division was incorporated as an organic part of the whole. All his life he struggled against alienation – giving first currency to this term and its psychological and philosophical origins. (1970:1)

All the dualisms that mechanistic science and Kantian philosophy had generated, and that for Hegel were essential and necessary for the progress of human thought – spirit (mind) and nature, knowledge and passion, reason and morality, freedom and necessity, ideal and reality, human subjectivity and sociality – Hegel sought both to encompass and transcend. And he aimed to do this by reason alone. In doing so he tried to combine in one comprehensive system the following: Kant's critical philosophy and his stress on freedom and human subjectivity; the Enlightenment emphasis on empirical knowledge and reason; the view expressed by the Romantics (the poet Hölderlin was a close friend of Hegel's) that nature was an organic totality; the philosophical monism of Spinoza; and the holistic, cosmological world view of the Greek philosophers, for whom he had a lasting admiration (particularly Heraclitus and Aristotle). What a vision – and what a task. (For general accounts of Hegel's life and philosophy, see Stace 1955, Kaufmann 1965, P. Singer 1983.)

The first thing to be said about Hegel is that he is, in a fundamental sense, a historical thinker. All his basic notions – *Geist* (spirit), reason, freedom – have meaning and significance only within a historical context, or rather within a cosmic process. If we cast a glance over the world's history, he wrote, we "see a vast picture of changes and transactions; of infinitely manifold forms of peoples, states, individuals, in unresting succession ... The general thought – the category which first presents itself in this restless mutation of individuals and peoples, existing for a time and then vanishing – is that of *change* at large" (1956: 72). Hegel praises the oriental view of the universe (the Hindu concept of karma), with its recognition of endless cycles of change. But in making, like Plato and Heraclitus, a distinction between the phenomenal world of change and the infinity of spirit or the "eternal repose" of Buddhism, Hegel felt that such doctrines had presented a limited viewpoint. For Hegel all reality – spirit and nature – was ever-changing. "The abstract conception of mere change," he wrote, "gives place to the thought of spirit manifesting, developing and perfecting its powers in every direction which its manifold nature can follow" (73). The nature of the spirit, however, can only be learned from its products and formations – human culture – not from mystical insights. Moreover, the spirit fulfills its destiny or aim only in relation to its "entanglement" with nature. Thus Hegel saw history in general as a process, the development of the spirit, and this process was rational, necessary, and dialectical. As he put it,

> It is only an inference from the history of the world that its development has been a rational process; that the history in question has constituted the rational, necessary cause of the world spirit – that spirit whose nature is always one and the same, but which unfolds this its one nature in the phenomena of the world's existence. This must, as before stated, present itself as the ultimate *result* of history. But we have to take the latter as it is. We must proceed historically – empirically. (1956: 10)

Truth, for Hegel, unfolds itself through the course of history, and to obtain knowledge of the world as a cosmic process one can neither begin with axiomatic truths nor can one assume that there were, at one time, primeval people who had been taught by god and were thus "endowed with perfect insight and wisdom, possessing a thorough knowledge of all natural laws and spiritual truth" (10). Rather, to understand the nature of the spirit, which, Hegel suggests, manifests itself in ever-changing historical phenomena, one must study culture empirically – or at least one must begin understanding with empirical knowledge.

In his *Lectures on the Philosophy of History* Hegel attempted to indicate the various "grades of development" of the spirit, seeing the principles underlying different cultures as simply "steps in the development of the one universal spirit, which through them elevates and completes itself to a self-comprehending totality" (1956: 78). Taking a world-historical perspective, Hegel outlines four major cultural epochs: the oriental (Egyptian and the Asiatic civilizations), the Greek, the Roman, and the German (the latter encompassing essentially western European culture). There is no doubt that Hegel was influenced by the writings of the Scottish Enlightenment thinkers, particularly Adam Ferguson (Cullen 1979), and like his contemporaries Hegel had a rather Eurocentric bias. Tribal and African cultures are thus seen as outside history, as "unhistorical, undeveloped spirit," a viewpoint still implied by some historians (e.g., Toynbee 1976). Hegel has some disparaging things to say about African peoples, echoing missionary reports that they live in a "completely wild and untamed state," without any conceptions of god, law, or subjectivity (93). Hegel also held the belief that certain key people – "world-historical individuals," as he describes them – unconsciously embody the world spirit. It is of interest that they are all military heroes: Alexander, Caesar, Napoleon.

Hegel therefore made a distinction between historiography, which could be either descriptive or reflective, and the philosophy of history. Only practitioners of the latter were concerned, in studying the empirical data, to delineate a universal history – that is, the process by which the spirit comes to have a knowledge of itself. And like Aristotle, Hegel conceives of a world spirit developing itself "actually to what it was always potentially." As in growth of an organism, the "principle of development involves also the existence of a latent germ of being – a capacity or potentiality striving to realize itself." But whereas the development of natural organisms, Hegel suggests, is direct and unhindered, the development of the spirit is mediated by human consciousness and will (55). And this means that whereas the sphere of natural growth is "peaceful," in the development of the spirit it is dialectic and involves a "mighty conflict with itself " (55). Several important points emerge from this conception of "spirit" divided against itself.

The first is that Hegel draws a distinction between natural and cultural processes. Nature, he felt, exhibited only a "perpetually self-repeating cycle," whereas the realm of the spirit (culture) has an "altogether different destiny," creatively giving rise to all things new. Spirit has "a real capacity for change, and that for the better – an impulse of perfectability" (54). But this destiny is a germ, an idea pointing to something that is destined to become actual. Hegel therefore makes the famous distinction, taken up by Sartre in *Being and Nothingness*, between matter and spirit, between being *an-sich* (in itself) and *für-sich* (for itself). It is difficult,

⤷ analogy to class-in-itself + class-for-itself

9

therefore, to argue that Hegel was an evolutionary thinker. But it is important to realize that since "spirit is the consciousness of an objective real world" (1977: 295), it (as human culture) continually strives to achieve a unity of being-in-itself and being-for-itself, the unity of freedom and necessity, mind and nature. Unlike religious mystics such as Sankara, Hegel sees this unity in relation to nature, not as some transcendental realm of being.

Second, and linked with this, Hegel saw world history as "none other than the progress of the consciousness of freedom." He summed up this progressive development in this way: "The Eastern nations knew only that one is free (the theocratic ruler); the Greek and Roman world only that some are free (the aristocracy); while *we* know that all men ... are free" (1956: 19). But the destiny of the world, he sensed, was not only the consciousness of its own freedom on the part of the spirit (in the abstract) but the realization of that freedom in the world (as a concrete reality). Hegel was, however, quite aware that the history of the world had not been a "theatre of happiness" – in fact he implies that history has been a "slaughter bench" on which the happiness of individuals and the wisdom of communities has endlessly been victimized. Nonetheless, like the Buddha, he pleads that "gloomy emotions" lead nowhere and stresses that there is a "reason" unfolding itself in history.

Third, and significantly, Hegel conceived of the idea, or destiny, of the spirit as a potentiality that was abstract: It was a hidden, undeveloped essence. For its realization another element, he felt, was needed, and that element was human activity in its widest sense. The "motive power" that gives spirit or reason its actuality that "puts them in operation, and gives them determinate existence, is the need, instinct, inclination, and passion of man" (22). In a way that is difficult to comprehend, Hegel sees human activity (a blend of reason and passion) as the "middle term" or "medium" whereby the Idea or universal essence (spirit or freedom) is translated into the domain of objectivity (nature or necessity) (27). But this is seen as a kind of historical process in which the "world at large," through spirit (in the form of culture), becomes conscious of itself and realizes, makes concrete, its own freedom in nature.

Finally, as is well known, Hegel appears to suggest that the modern state is the condition through which freedom is realized. As he put it, "The state is the Divine Idea as it exists on Earth" (39). Hegel has therefore been severely criticized both for being an apologist for Prussian absolutism and for glorifying the state; indeed Popper asserts that he is the founder of totalitarian thought. The formula for the fascist brew, wrote Popper, is "Hegel plus a dash of 19th-century materialism" (1945: 61). Bertrand Russell is equally unsympathetic toward Hegel, suggesting

10

that his philosophy implied that the citizen exists solely for the good of the state (1946: 771). Although Hegel undoubtedly idealized the state, and sometimes wrote in terms that seem to justify war, his concept of the rational state embodies the notion of individual freedom and subjectivity. For Hegel, as many commentators have suggested, no state (or community) could be rational unless it reconciled, as Copleston writes, the "conception of the state as an organic totality with the principle of individual freedom" (1963: 260). In Hegel's metaphysics, as Marcuse stressed, reason and freedom presuppose each other, and his philosophy could hardly be used to justify an authoritarian state. Moreover, it is important to note that for Hegel human freedom, if it is to be concrete and genuine, has to be expressed within nature and within a community. For Hegel, Kant's subjective freedom is abstract and empty.

Modern philosophers often stress Kant's claim to having wrought a Copernican revolution in philosophy by combining the rationalism of Descartes and Leibniz with the empiricism of Locke and Hume. In fact, Kant solved very little, for not only did empirical reality become an unknowable "thing in itself" but his critical philosophy, generated, as I have noted earlier, a plethora of antinomies. Kant never went beyond the dualistic thought of the Enlightenment. What is of interest about Hegel is that he attempted not only to forge conceptual categories that went beyond both dualism and mechanism but also to delineate a mode of thought that was radically different from that of the Enlightenment thinkers. He tried to establish a kind of philosophical anthropology that was both rationalist and empiricist. He called it objective idealism. Almost everyone I know has described Hegel's metaphysics as idealism pure and simple. But it is my contention that it is an unusual form of idealism, for the kind of analysis Hegel advocates always begins with empirical data, and he had nothing but praise for the empiricists. "Whatever is true," he wrote, "must be in the actual world and present to sensation" (Weiss 1974: 141). But the kind of knowledge derived from sense impressions – what he calls in *Phenomenology of Mind* (1807) "sense certainty" – is a limited form of understanding and hardly merits the term *consciousness*. He demonstrates that the claim that sense certainty is the basis of knowledge is naive, and this early study is one of the earliest and most important critiques of empiricism. As Marcuse expresses it "To Hegel, the facts in themselves possess no authority" (1941: 27). A higher form of knowledge or reflection is therefore needed, and this Hegel describes as understanding (*Verstand*), which he seems to suggest is characteristic of ordinary mechanistic science in its explication of phenomena by reference to natural laws. But the essence of this kind of understanding is that it is static and dualistic; it sets up, Hegel suggests, a series of un-

11

necessary oppositions: thought and life, reason and reality, mind and nature. So in order to achieve a fuller understanding and the realization of his vision, Hegel searches around for a new mode of understanding. What he required, as Copleston writes, "for the fulfillment of this task is a new form of logic, a logic which is able to follow the movement of life and does not leave opposed concepts in irremediable opposition" (1963: 202). Hegel describes this mode of thought as reason (*Vernunft*) or dialectic. Such thought has been variously described: in terms of the familiar triadic movement – thesis, antithesis, synthesis; in terms of the expression "unity-in-opposition"; or in terms of the concept of "contradiction." The notion of dialectic thought has either been trivialized (see MacIntyre 1970: 35) or treated as some mysterious form of logic that somehow contradicts both common sense and formal logic by denying the validity of the principles of identity and noncontradiction (Stace 1955: 94; Novack 1971). But as Singer writes, there is nothing deep or mysterious about dialectic; it is simply a mode of thought that takes as its starting point the unity of the thinking subject and the processes of the natural world. As Hegel put it "This dialectic is not an activity of subjective thinking applied to some matter externally, but is rather the matter's very soul putting forth its branches and fruit organically... To consider a thing rationally means not to bring reason to bear on the object from the outside and so to tamper with it, but to find that the object is rational on its own account" (1942: 34–5).

In the *Phenomenology* Hegel advocates neither "monochromatic formalism," in which the knowing subject goes around applying forms to whatever it encounters, nor pure description, for "reason is never asleep." Rather, he suggests that the "true is the whole" and that dialectical reason is the realization that spirit (Geist) is immanent and embodied in nature. As Weiss succinctly put it, "Nature produces mind out of itself, and our knowing this Nature is Nature's own coming to know itself" (1974: 10). As with Spinoza, it is hard to judge whether Hegel is an idealist or a materialist, a theist or an atheist (see Kojeve 1980). When Singer suggests that for Hegel the ultimate reality is "mental" or when Harris notes that he "believed that things are expressions of ideas" (1980: 142), they seriously misjudge Hegel's philosophy, though Hegel admitted that his primary interest was in spirit, not in nature, and his whole style of expression is theological. But as the Christian philosopher Frederick Copleston stresses (and Copleston would hardly be one to misjudge or negate the spiritual element), for Hegel spirit is not a transcendental being existing independently of nature, nor can the latter be ontologically derived from spirit. Copleston writes,

The Absolute is the totality, the Universe . . . thus totality is a teleological process. But [the idea or spirit] does not exist as a subsistent reality which is logically prior to Nature and which is the efficient cause of nature. The idea reflects the goal or result of the process rather than a subsistent reality which stands at the beginning . . . Nature is a necessary precondition for the realization of the goal of the total process of reality, the Universe's knowledge of itself in and through the human spirit. (1963: 238)

In an important sense, then, Hegel's outlook is life-affirming, and in the *Phenomenology* he writes critically of Stoic mysticism, which he describes as "unhappy consciousness." In aspiring to be independent of the material world and in asserting the freedom of self-consciousness, the Stoics steadfastly withdrew from the "bustle of existence" (1977: 121). They sought union with god, and to be eternal and purely spiritual, thus existing apart from the empirical world and the finite self. This form of consciousness, Hegel argued, was divided, alienated, and "unhappy." Like Aristotle, and as reflected in many tribal cosmologies (see Schofeleers 1971, on the Ceŵa), Hegel saw spirit and nature as coexisting but interpreted the former not as some transcendental state or being but as the Idea or reason, or in medieval terms, the "plan of providence" imminent in nature (see Stace 1955: 18–29). For Hegel, therefore, it was misleading to equate the human essence with spirit or some transcendental realm, as both historical religions and Cartesian philosophy implied. Instead, human activity (which was both practical and intellectual) was the medium or agency whereby the world spirit came to both know and realize itself in nature, the totality being a cosmic organism (White 1955: 14). In this way the various antinomies aforementioned would be resolved.

Hegel's philosophy of religion

Like Spinoza, Hegel could well be described as a "god-intoxicated" philosopher. All his writings have a decidedly religious tone, for he was centrally concerned with spirit. Yet, although he was a practicing Lutheran Christian, his conception of God was unorthodox. For Hegel had an image of god as a totality that manifested itself in thought (logic), in history (spirit, subjectivity), and in nature (necessity, objectivity). But the ultimate reality for Hegel was nondualistic and was neither spirit (culture) or nature but both: the cosmic process itself. This vision is neither idealist nor materialist: it could well be described as either objective idealism or dialectical materialism. It is also difficult to categorize Hegel in theological categories, for he was not a theist, pantheist, or atheist. In a sense he was all three. In philosophical terms he moves beyond the idealist–materialist dichotomy, giving ontological priority neither to nature or spirit, as both Kojeve and Copleston have insisted. As later existentialists and phenomenologists realized, Hegel's essential focus is on the interaction between the subject and the objective world, "being-in-the world," as Heidegger was later to describe the human mode of existence (see Blackham 1952). Yet whereas existentialists put a central emphasis on the individual subject, Hegel's vision and emphasis is always on the logic of the total cosmos.

With a fundamental faith in human reason, it is hardly surprising that Hegel came to consider his own kind of philosophy as a higher form of consciousness than that of religion. He certainly saw both art and religion as valid ways of apprehending the absolute; indeed he saw them merely as expressions of the cosmic consciousness. Yet for Hegel the religious mode of thought was figurative and one of imagery, and thus limited and inadequate. During his own lifetime, however, Hegel published little on religion, although, as I have implied, his whole philosophy might be described as religious or theological. His main writings on the subject fall into two distinct categories: his early theological essays, written during the period 1795–9, when Hegel was in his late twenties and working as a private tutor; and his three-volume *Lectures on the Philosophy of Religion*, collected by his students and published the year after his death in 1831.

The theological essays, first published in 1907 (Hegel 1948) present Hegel's views on Christianity and Judaism. They are, in their general tenor, anti-Christian or at least antiecclesiastical. In his essay "The Life of Jesus" Hegel offers an interpretation of the founder of Christianity that is in Copleston's view, "thoroughly humanized." There is no mention of miracles, and the supernatural elements of Jesus' life are played down. Copleston suggests that Hegel depicts Jesus as being exclusively a moral teacher, and almost an expounder of Kant's moral philosophy (Copleston 1963: 199; Kaufmann 1965: 35). In 1835 one of Hegel's students, David F. Strauss, published his *Life of Jesus*, a work that created a sensation and fully established a genre that has since seen numerous studies.

In that same year (1795) Hegel wrote "The Positivity of the Christian Religion," an essay that, as Richard Kroner wrote in his introduction to the *Early Theological Writings*, is permeated with a hostility toward Christian institutions. Hegel compares Christianity unfavorably both with Greek religion and with Kant's ethical doctrine. The folk religion of the Greeks (*Volksreligion*), Hegel suggests, was an integral part of their community, reflecting in a natural way its harmony and equilibrium. With the Greeks, spirit is part of a living reality, for the cosmological views

14

of the pagans implied that the gods "had haunted nature only" and were intimately connected with the passions and needs of humans. Hegel even implies that the relationship between humans and the gods who "held sway in the realm of nature" was a reciprocal one and did not involve any divine commands or a lack of freedom on the part of the individual. With the supplanting of paganism by Christianity all this changed, and a transcendental deity emerged that was beyond the reach of human powers and will. It could only be approached in a servile manner, in prayer and through sacraments and supplications. "The despotism of the Roman emperors," Hegel wrote, "had chased the human spirit from the earth and spread misery which compelled men to seek and expect happiness in heaven; robbed of freedom, their spirit, their eternal and absolute element, was forced to take flight to the deity" (1948: 162). God's objectivity is a counterpart to the corruption and enslavement of humans, and such a transcendental, otherworldly conception reflects only the spirit of the age. Thus the result of the transformation to Christianity was, Hegel suggests, essentially negative: The liberty of thought that had been lost, and reason, had given way to faith and revelation; morality became equated with the imposition of divine commands, and humans became alienated from their true selves and from god. Hegel describes Christianity in highly negative terms, although he appears to separate his assessment of Christianity (which he associates with murder and infamy, 163) as an institution from the moral teachings of Jesus.

In the essay "Spirit of Christianity and Its Fate" Hegel is more sympathetic to Christianity, and, as Copleston remarks, Judaism, with its transcendental deity and legalistic morality, "becomes the villain of the piece" (1963: 199). The god of Abraham, Hegel wrote, was utterly separate from the world:

> Nothing in nature was supposed to have any part in God; everything was simply under God's mastery. Abraham, as the opposite of the whole world, could have had no higher mode of being than that of the other term in the opposition, and thus he likewise was supported by God. Moreover it was through God alone that Abraham came into a mediate relation with the world, the only kind of link with the world possible for him. His Ideal subjugated the world to him, gave him as much of the world as he needed. (1948: 187)

The god of Abraham implied a relationship of opposition and mastery toward the natural world. God's divinity, Hegel suggests, was "rooted in his contempt for the whole world," and Abraham remained the deity's "only favourite." As in mechanistic and Kantian philosophy, spirit and

15

nature are alienated from each other, and the relationship between god and humans and between god and nature is one of opposition and mastery. In ways that anticipate the writings of later ecological philosophers, Hegel is critical of the Baconian ethic that is implicit in the Judeo-Christian tradition (see L. White 1975, Glacken 1970) and advocates a "pantheism of love" that unites the moral freedom and subjectivity articulated in Kant's philosophy with Greek pantheism. Even in this early essay, as both Copleston (1963) and Masterson (1973) recall, Hegel is centrally concerned with the theme of alienation and the recovery of a lost unity. In his *Lectures on the Philosophy of Religion* Hegel postulates that Christianity itself achieves this unity between the infinite spirit and the finite world.

Unlike world history, which Hegel saw as passing through a number of stages, religious consciousness, according to Hegel, comprises three essential phases, forming a triadic movement. The first phase, or kind of religion, Hegel calls the religion of nature (*Die Naturreligion*). In this kind of religion spirit is not seen as distinct from nature, and Hegel suggests that magic is the most "immediate" form of this phase of religion. Chinese religion, Hinduism, and Buddhism are seen as more developed forms of this phase and are described as religions of substance, a term essentially denoting what Hegel believed to be their pantheistic or cosmological aspect. Hegel is generally apathetic or critical with respect to the mystical orientations of these religions. The religious systems of the Syrians, Persians (Zoroastrianism), and Egyptians, Hegel felt, indicated in a fragmentary way the conception of spirit developing independently of nature. In this final stage of natural religion, Hegel writes, "the emergence of the spiritual element of subjectivity out of nature . . . appears at first merely as a conflict between the two sides, which are still entangled with one another in that conflict" (Hegel 1970: 203), an opposition reflected in the dualism of early Persian religion.

This conception of deity moves historically to a second stage, the religions of *Spiritual individuality*. At this stage the spirit is conceived as a subject, as a personal deity independent of the natural world. The inevitable triad – for Hegel's whole philosophy is presented in the form of triadic patterns – comprises the Jewish, Greek, and Roman religions, described respectively as the religions of sublimity, beauty, and utility. In these religions, Hegel suggested, God is exalted as a transcendental being above the finite world of humans and nature. God is the ultimate reality, and the finite world receives no recognition.

In the final phase of religion this separation is both annulled and preserved – *Aufgehoben*, in Hegel's famous term. In Hegel's dialectic all truths are both negated and maintained in a higher synthesis, and in

16

terms of the development of religious consciousness this higher synthesis is the absolute religion, namely Christianity. For in Christianity, as a revealed religion, god is conceived as both transcendental and imminent. Hegel saw Christianity as the final stage in which the living spirit comes to be conscious of itself. But, significantly, for Hegel Christianity expressed the absolute truth only as a sensuous and pictorial mode of thought (*Vorstellung*); it was left to philosophy to express this same truth in the form of conceptual thought. Absolute knowledge or perfection, for Hegel, is the concept of the cosmic spirit; the totality is a cosmic organism coming to know itself through human consciousness. Whether Hegel's philosophy can be described as "esoteric Christianity" (Stace 1955: 509) is questionable but it is certainly a theology. The universe for Hegel, as Morton White writes, "is spiritual; it has direction, and the explanation of ordinary facts, human actions, historical changes, and institutions may be grasped once we recognize how they are embedded in this cosmic organism" (1955: 13). Christianity is seen in these terms as a rational form of knowledge that reconciles theism – "the empty elevation of the spiritual to the Eternal" – and mechanistic science, which, although it has knowledge of the finite and the "manifold connections of things," distrusts totality. Whether Christianity deserves to be credited with such a reconciliation is debatable and it is quite misleading and ethnocentric for Hegel to posit Christianity as the "perfected, absolute religion." (For further discussions of Hegel's philosophy of religion, see Fackenheim 1967 and Reardon 1977.)

Hegel's philosophical theology makes an audacious attempt to outline the nature and logic of a cosmic organism in the process of its development. Such a lofty conception and endeavor gives us little help in understanding specific religious systems, for these are, in Hegel's terms, but "moments" in the development of religion or spirit in general. Nonetheless a number of important themes emerge from Hegel's writings on religion.

First, Hegel argues that we must not superficially reject any religious belief and rite as "superstition, error, and deceit" or "value them as merely representing some sort of religious feeling." Instead we must get to know their meaning or truth, "get to know what is *rational* in them" (Hegel 1970: 200).

Second, this truth is seen historically as part of a cosmic process. This means that Hegel saw religion as a general phenomenon that exhibited an evolutionary pattern. Although his evolutionary schema is untenable, given contemporary knowledge, Hegel's discussion of the various world religions is substantive and penetrating, particularly in view of the paucity of reliable information on Eastern religions that was then available to him. But Hegel's understanding of specific religions is both sociological and historical, and even the broad evolutionary schema that he postulates is far more enlightening and credible than the evolutionary schemes of Spencer and Frazer. Indeed, as I have suggested elsewhere, Hegel's philosophy anticipates the kind of holistic philosophy and ecological perspective that emerged at the end of the nineteenth century, in an attempt to go beyond the mechanistic paradigm (see Whitehead 1926, Collingwood 1945, Morris 1981a).

And finally, although Hegel's thoughts are expressed in spiritual terms, by giving human subjective consciousness and human activity a central place in his metaphysics Hegel pioneered a naturalistic interpretation of culture and religion. As Masterson puts it, "The various forms of contemporary atheism such as Marxism, Positivism and existentialism are not simply reactions against Hegel's philosophy of spirit but also and more profoundly progressive refinements of an atheism already laid down if not explicitly recognized in this philosophy" (1973: 66).

The essence of religion

There are many scholars who, though not particularly original thinkers themselves, may nonetheless, as Isaiah Berlin writes, have a profound influence on the history of thought (1963: 76). They provide writers of genius with the spark that "sets on fire the long-accumulated fuel." Ludwig Feuerbach was such a scholar for, along with Hegel, he provided Marx and Engels with many seminal ideas.

Feuerbach was a Bavarian philosopher who began his academic career as a student of Protestant theology, but on entering the University of Berlin he became an enthusiastic disciple of Hegel, whose lectures he regularly attended. Eventually, however, he came to reject both Christian theology and Hegel's philosophy, explicitly advocating a strident atheistic materialism. Feuerbach is often described as one of the left, or "young" Hegelians, for after Hegel's death his followers split into two camps. On the one hand there were the right Hegelians, represented by Karl Goshel and to some extent by Hegel's biographer Karl Rosenkranz, who interpreted Hegel's philosophy in a theistic manner. Thus Hegelianism became compatible with Christianity, and they adjusted Hegel's famous dictum "All that is real is rational" to imply the sanctification and rationality of the current social order. They therefore took a positive view of the Prussian state and were essentially conservative.

On the other hand there were a group of scholars with radical leanings, who made a more pantheistic interpretation of Hegel's philosophy. They noted Hegel's undoubted enthusiasm for the French Revolution and stressed that his dialectical philosophy implied that all cultural phenomena were essentially transitory and that the real was not to be equated with the actual but was a rational movement in the process of becoming. The young Hegelians therefore saw Hegel's philosophy as intrinsically revolutionary and critical, as a demand for a better world, in which human freedom would be both concrete and genuine and in which the opposition between the individual and the state would be overcome. Hegel's basic doctrine implied, as Marcuse writes, that what humans rationally think to be good, right, and true ought to be realized (one of Hegel's favorite words) in the actual organization of their communal and individual life. The idea that "as long as reality is not shaped by reason, it remains no reality at all" (Marcuse 1941: 11) was a guiding premise of the young Hegelians. But their criticisms of the existing order, as Engels (1968) remarked, were only indirectly political. Their main criticisms were expressed in a theological guise and directed mainly at Christianity. And as their criticisms developed, they became increasingly more naturalistic, moving beyond pantheism towards atheism.

David Strauss's *Life of Jesus* (1835) provided almost the first impulse of the young Hegelian movement. Strauss attempted to interpret Christianity in terms of Hegelian philosophy and in doing so came to reject any theological view of the biblical tradition. The gospel stories were viewed as myths to be interpreted in naturalistic terms. Strauss's book was seen as radical and subversive by the authorities; even so, it was criticized by another young Hegelian, Bruno Bauer, who came to express an extreme "philosophy of pure criticism." Bauer, a lecturer in theology at the University of Berlin, was one of the leading members of a group calling themselves the "free spirits" (*Die Freien*), a group to which the youthful Karl Marx belonged. In his various writings Bauer denied the historical existence of Jesus and came to explain the Christian Gospels not in terms of Hegel's philosophy, nor in terms of Strauss's communal mythologizing, but as the free, poetic expression of human consciousness.

But it was Feuerbach's study *The Essence of Christianity* (1841) that represented the most fundamental departure from Hegel's phenomenology and the most enduring document to emerge from that period, apart from Marx's own youthful writings. If the early 1840s took the form of an inquest on Hegel's philosophy, as Paterson suggests (1971: 25), then Feuerbach's study caused a decisive swing toward old-fashioned materialism. Judging from Engel's essay on Feuerbach, the book not only reached a wide audience but had an important "liberating effect" on the radicals of that period. Marx, he writes, greeted its publication with enthusiasm, for it "placed materialism on the throne again" (1968: 592).

Feuerbach took his inspiration from Hegel, but it is clear from his early study *Critique of the Hegelian Philosophy* (1839) that he abandoned Hegel's phenomenological approach at a very early stage, for in this study he argued that Hegel's philosophy was merely theology in disguise. Feuerbach accepted the label of idealist, but for him this meant only a belief in the historical future and a refusal to see the limits of the past and present as the limits of humanity. In philosophical terms, however, he argued that his approach was in "direct opposition" to Hegel's philosophy in being fundamentally practical and materialist. Like Hobbes and Diderot in an earlier period, he took the human subject to be a natural being and advocated an empirical approach to reality. As Feuerbach put it succinctly in the preface to his study, his philosophy took as "its principle not the substance of Spinoza, nor the Ego of Kant and Fichte, nor the Absolute of Schelling . . . [and] Hegel, in short, no abstract merely conceptual being, but a real being – *man*; its principle, therefore, is in the highest degree positive and real. It generates thought from the *opposite* of thought, from matter, from existence, from the senses."

"I hate that idealism," he wrote, "that tears man out of nature." And he continues, "I therein call upon the senses themselves to witness to the truth of my analysis and my ideas." Feuerbach's philosophy, therefore, begins with a simple statement: "I am a real, a sensuous, a material being; yes, the body in its totality is my Ego, my being itself." Feuerbach looked upon his philosophy as a "new" approach. That he did so reflects the degree to which German philosophy had become dominated by the idealist perspectives of Schelling and Hegel, for, as Passmore remarked, materialism is almost as old as philosophy (1957: 35).

Feuerbach's study *The Essence of Christianity* is divided into two sections: Part 1 deals positively with the essence of religion; Part 2 has a negative function and consists of a critique of Christian theology.

In the introductory chapter Feuerbach outlines what he considers to be the "essential nature" of man. He stresses the importance of self-consciousness in distinguishing humans from other animals, and this implies for the individual the recognition of his or her natural limitations. But, suggests Feuerbach, a person "can become conscious of his limits, his finiteness, only because the perfection, the infinitude of his species, is perceived by him, whether as an object of feeling, of conscience, or of thinking consciousness" (1957: 7). The consciousness of the infinite is therefore none other than the consciousness of man's own infinite nature and the perfections of the human being. Man exists, he writes, to think, to love, to will – a divine trinity in humans that exists above the individual person. But he continues, "Reason, Will, Love, are not powers which man possesses, for he is nothing without them, he is what he is only by them; they are the constituent elements of his nature" (3).

Each person as an individual human being recognizes his or her limitations and dependence upon the natural world, but there is also the recognition of the infinity of the human species. Humans have a "twofold life," not merely individuality (which Feuerbach appears to link with natural existence), but also species-being. Humans are at once "I and thou," and their "essence" is the most real being. Hegel's Geist (spirit) has been replaced by man's "essence."

This conception of man's essential nature is directly related to Feuerbach's interpretation of religion. His theory can best be expressed, I think, by selecting a number of quotations from his study, many of which are memorable.

> Religion is man's earliest and also indirect form of self-knowledge. Hence, religion everywhere precedes philosophy... Man first of all sees his nature as if *out of* himself, before he finds it in himself. His own nature is in the first instance contemplated by him as that of another being. Religion is the childlike condition of humanity; but the child sees his nature – man – out of himself... The divine being is nothing else than the human being, or rather, the human nature purified, freed from the limits of the individual man, made objective – i.e., contemplated and revered as another, a distinct being. (1957: 13–14)

> The "infinite spirit," in distinction from the finite, is therefore nothing else than the intelligence disengaged from the limits of individuality and corporeality – for individuality and corporeality are inseparable – intelligence posited in and by itself. (35)

> God is the self-consciousness of man freed from all discordant elements; man feels himself free, happy, blessed in his religion... The divine being is the pure subjectivity of man, freed from all else, from everything objective, having relation only to itself, enjoying only itself, reverencing only itself – his most subjective, his inmost self. (98)

A number of interesting points emerge from Feuerbach's study. First, he regards the antithesis between the divine and the human as "altogether illusory" for religion itself is simply a fantasy expression of man's ideal of achieving human existence, through love, freedom, and reason. This distinction reflects only the antithesis between human nature in general and the human individual (14). In Feuerbach's dualistic schema the latter schism can never be bridged.

Second, since religion is to be understood in terms of its psychogenesis from human nature itself, it implies, as Feuerbach explores, an inverse relationship between the attributes accorded to the deity and those accorded to humans and the finite world. What humans deny to themselves they attribute to god, he suggests: "The more empty life is, the fuller, the more concrete is God. The impoverishing of the real world and the enriching of God is one act. Only the poor man has a rich god. God springs out of the feeling of a want; what man is in need of . . . that is God" (73). A stress on the goodness of god implies the radical corruption of the world and human nature, and, conversely, the "disconsolate feeling of void" needs a God of love.

Third, in seeing religion as a "projected image" of man's essential nature, Feuerbach was critical of the illusions, falsehoods, and contradictions of religion and theology. Religion involves the alienation of individuals from their true selves, from their species-being. It is necessary, he feels, for the true essence of religion to be recognized, for theology to be reduced by anthropology. But this does not imply that religion is pure illusion or an absurdity. "Religion," he writes, "is the dream of the human mind. But even in dreams we do not find ourselves in emptiness or in heaven, but on earth, in the realm of reality." I do nothing more to religion, he suggests, than change the object as it is in the imagination into the object as it is in reality, and reality for Feuerbach is the "species-being" as an idealized essence.

Last, although Feuerbach interprets Christian beliefs and sacraments in crude materialistic terms – the rites of baptism and the Eucharist, for example, are seen as celebrating the natural qualities of water, bread, and wine – his philosophy is by no means strictly empiricist. Indeed, although Masterson has stressed Feuerbach's commitment to a "this-worldly" naturalistic humanism (1973: 79), early writers like Stirner and Engels were extremely critical of the idealistic tenor of Feuerbach's work. The individualist anarchist Max Stirner, who was also one of the young Hegelians and an important. though much neglected, precursor of existentialism, wrote a severe critique of the kind of humanism that Feuerbach, along with Bruno Bauer, espoused (1973). Mankind, Stirner polemically asserted, "has no more reality than Hegel's geist or society – These are but ghosts, dogmatic abstractions." "You are more than a human being," Stirner wrote; "that is just an idea, but you are corporeal. Do you suppose, then, that you can ever become a human being as such?" (1973: 126). Many of Stirner's criticisms of "humane liberalism" were taken up by Marx, who in turn severely criticized Stirner's own uncompromising individualism. But Stirner's main criticism of Feuerbach was that his stress on love and charity was merely a secularization of Christian altruism (see Paterson 1971; Reardon 1977: 137). Engels makes similar and poignant criticisms of Feuerbach's humanism. Feuerbach, he suggests, who on every page of *The Essence of Christianity* preaches sensuousness, absorption in the concrete, and actuality, invariably becomes abstract and idealistic whenever he talks about "man" and human relationships. Feuerbach's "man" is an abstraction, a moral conception that issues, as from a chrysalis, from the god of the monotheistic religions. Feuerbach's theory of morals

> is designed to suit all periods, all peoples and all conditions, and precisely for that reason it is never and nowhere applicable... He clings fiercely to nature and man; but nature and man remain mere words for him. He is incapable of telling us anything definite either about real nature or real men... The cult of abstract man, which formed the kernel of Feuerbach's new religion, had to be replaced by the science of real men and of their historical development. (Engels 1968: 607)

Like Comte, Feuerbach hoped to substitute a "religion of humanity" based on love, wisdom, and justice for what he regarded as the illusions and fantasies of religion. He hoped to reconcile the finite and the infinite in terms of a "social, lived reconciliation of individual limited man with the absolute perfection of the human species" (Masterson 1973: 79). Thus, although Feuerbach is critical of Hegel for allegedly "tearing" mankind out of nature, his own "reconciliation" is accomplished with hardly any reference to human history or to nature. Hegel, in contrast, in spite of spiritualizing culture as spirit (Geist), saw human activity itself as the medium that reconciles infinity and reason with the objective world. No wonder Engels thought Feuerbach's philosophy shallow in comparison with that of Hegel.

Despite its limitations, Feuerbach's philosophy was important in two ways. One is that it had a direct influence on Marx. The other is that it has had an indirect influence on a number of writers within the existential tradition who have sought to retain the ethos of the Judeo-Christian tradition without its faith, its humanism without its theism. The writings of socialist humanists like Erich Fromm and Martin Buber are clearly within the Feuerbachian tradition (Fromm 1949, Buber 1947).

Marx: his life and early writings

The most famous of all the young Hegelians, however, was Karl Marx, a scholar and revolutionary who hardly needs any introduction. In historical terms he is indeed something of a colossus. In a recent introductory text, Peter Singer (1980) suggests that his impact on the world has been comparable to that of religious figures like Jesus and Muhammad, for the lives of millions of people have been deeply influenced by

Marx's legacy, and Callinicos notes that he was one of a handful of thinkers who have fundamentally changed the way we see the world. He thus ranks with Aristotle, Copernicus, Newton, Darwin, Freud, and Einstein (1983b: 7). This being so, Marx is a difficult figure to approach in an unprejudiced manner, for, like Weber and Durkheim, he has been the subject of a wealth of exegetical and critical literature. Contemporary sociologists, in fact, seem to regard these three writers as the founding ancestors of the discipline, notwithstanding the fact that not until the mid–1950s, as Josep Llobera has indicated, did Marx come to be recognized by academic sociology (1981: 233), although, as many have noted, his ghost has been around for a long time. Giddens (1971) articulates this notion of a founding triumvirate of social theory rather well. But, like tribal communities, sociology is continually rewriting its history, and by a process of "structural amnesia" the theoretical significance of writers acknowledged in an earlier decade – figures such as Comte, Spencer, Le Play, Simmel, and Pareto – has now largely been forgotten or bypassed.

In discussions of Durkheim, Marx, and Weber, two kinds of interpretations have been offered, and although they appear to be contradictory, both, I think, have some validity. One of them stresses the similarity between the perspectives of these three scholars, in that they all attempted to go beyond the dualisms inherent in early nineteenth-century thought. In a sense they attempted to overcome opposition between positivism and idealism and to articulate a social theory that was both scientific and humanistic, interpretative and explanatory, concerned with meaning and analysis. As R. H. Brown has suggested, "The founders of modern sociology were astride two horses at once, each galloping off in its own direction. The efforts of Marx, Weber and Durkheim to reign their mounts are instructive for us today...One major attempt to create a middle ground between romantic subjectivism and reductive positivism is the work of Karl Marx" (1978b: 16).

But unlike other scholars (e.g., Avineri 1968), Brown holds that Marx never, in fact, instituted a synthesis between his theory of revolutionizing praxis and his sociology of structural causation. A resolution of the humanistic and deterministic aspects of Marx's work, Brown writes, remained an unfinished project. This conclusion is, I think, questionable, but the important points to note are that there is common ground between the perspectives of Marx, Weber, and Durkheim and that the scientific humanist paradigm stems largely from Hegel.

The other kind of interpretation stresses a contrast between positivist or "bourgeois" social thought (Comte, Weber, Durkheim) and Marxism, seeing them as fundamentally distinctive and linking the academic sociologists to the neo-Kantian school (see Marcuse 1941, Shaw 1972). This distinction and contrast has, I think, some substance, for Marx clearly stood firmly within the Hegelian tradition. But as Tom Bottomore has noted (1984: 3), the relationship between Marxism and academic sociology is complex, for neither of these traditions is uniform. Neither Durkheim nor Weber was a positivist in any simple sense (Hirst 1975), and the development of sociology has been a varied one, with several contrasting approaches. Moreover, Marxism itself, as we shall explore, has been divided into two distinct tendencies, and "scientific" Marxism has always had a strong positivist cast.

Karl Marx was born in Trier in the Rhineland of Germany in 1818. It was an area that had been annexed by France during the Napoleonic wars, and so the ideas of the Enlightenment and of the French utopian socialists were pervasive there. Marx came from a Jewish background, many of his family were rabbis, and he was brought up in a comfortable and fairly prosperous middle-class home. At the age of seventeen he went to the University of Bonn to study law but soon became interested in philosophy, moving in 1836 to Berlin. Here he became absorbed in the writings of Hegel, and he appears to have accepted Hegelian philosophy almost as if it were a religious conversion. After completing his doctoral thesis – on the materialist philosophies of Democritus and Epicurus – he was unable to find, as he had hoped, a post as a university teacher and became a journalist. At the end of 1843 he moved to Paris, having recently married a childhood friend, Jenny von Westphalen, the daughter of a local aristocrat who had introduced the young Marx to the progressive ideas of the Enlightenment. While in Paris Marx began associating with the many radicals and socialists who lived in the city, and he formed friendships with several young Hegelians – Feuerbach, Bruno Bauer, and Stirner. He also formed intellectual friendships with Proudhon and Bakunin; he was later to criticize all of them in harsh tones. In August 1844 he met Friedrich Engels, the son of a German industrialist, who was to become a lifelong friend and collaborator. During his stay in Paris Marx wrote a critique of Hegel's political philosophy and began a serious study of Adam Smith, David Ricardo, and other political economists. These studies, together with Marx's initial reflections on Hegel and communism, constitute what has come to be known as the *Economic and Philosophic Manuscripts* (1844), which, as McLellan notes (1973: 105), were the first drafts for a major work on the capitalist system that eventually appeared, much revised and expanded, in 1867 as *Capital*. In February 1845 Marx moved to Brussels, where he stayed for three years, regularly meeting and corresponding with Engels. Together they wrote a long critique of the left Hegelians, *The German Ide-*

ology (1846), for which they were unable to find a publisher, and Marx himself wrote another polemical work (1847) attacking the French anarchist writer Proudhon. The two men also became involved in political activities and in the founding of the Communist League, with Marx as its president. An open revolutionary organization, the league was a development of the League of the Just, a secret conspiratorial sect associated with the socialists Weitling and Blanqui that had been outlawed in France. Marx and Engels were requested to draft the doctrines of the Communist League in simple language, and the outcome was the famous *Communist Manifesto*. Published in 1848, it gives a succinct and classic outline of Marx's theory. With revolutionary movements and struggles occurring throughout Europe, Marx attempted, as editor of the radical paper *Neue Rheinische Zeitung*, to continue his political activities. But eventually reaction prevailed, and Marx was expelled not only from Brussels but also from Germany. In August 1849 he went to London, expecting his exile to be brief, but there he remained for the rest of his life, supported by his journalism and by financial gifts from his friend Engels.

Marx's final years were beset with financial difficulties and personal tragedy. In 1864 he played a leading part in the founding of the International Working Men's Association in London, but on the whole he was not politically active during his long years of exile. Most of his time and energies were devoted to collecting material and to the writing of his magnum opus, *Capital*, the first volume of which was published in 1867. During the years 1857–8 he wrote an initial draft of the study under the title *Critique of Political Economy* (*Grundrisse*), much of which remained unpublished during his lifetime.

The famous preface to the *Critique of Political Economy*, which gives a brief but cogent account of Marx's materialist conception of history, was published in 1859. The first English translation of *Capital* did not appear until 1887, the original publication being in German. In his last years Marx suffered from constant ill health, and when he died in 1883 it was in tragic circumstances, for he had survived both his wife and his daughter Jenny. (For useful accounts of the life and work of Marx, see Berlin 1963 and McLellan 1973).

It is clearly beyond the scope of the present study to offer an account, however brief, of Marx's social and political theory (there are, in any case, several studies that discuss Marx's theories in detail: Lichtheim 1961, Avineri 1968, Lefebvre 1968, and Kolakowski 1981). I shall instead concentrate on a number of key texts and explore both Marx's writings on religion – though he wrote little specifically on religious topics – and his general approach to the understanding of social life.

It has long been said that Marx's essential achievement was that he both criticized and synthesized three currents of European thought. As Lenin wrote, "Marx was the genius who continued and consummated the three main ideological currents of the 19th century, as represented by the three most advanced countries of mankind: classical German philosophy, classical English political economy, and French socialism" (Callinicos 1983b: 40). Marx subjected the main representatives of these three currents of thought – Hegel, Ricardo, Proudhon – to trenchant criticism, but, unlike some Marxists, he was equally alive to their positive aspects and to their influence on his own thought. In a recent discussion of one of the currents that form the "triple origin" of Marxism, French socialism, Hobsbawm comes to the conclusion that none of the French socialists (Saint-Simon, Fourier, Proudhon) exercised any significant influence on the formation of Marxist thought (1982: 15). Marx and Engels thought otherwise and accepted the validity of some of their critiques of capitalism and private property.

The *Economic and Philosophical Manuscripts of 1844* represent not only, as McLellan suggests, a first draft of *Capital* but a loose, initial synthesis of the "three sources" of Marxism. The notes themselves center on a number of key concepts – capital, labor, communism, alienation, and species-being – and reflect the combined influences of Hegel, Feuerbach, and Adam Smith. A number of themes emerge from these manuscript notes, and from Marx's other writings of the same period, that are either developed more fully in or form an underlying premise of his more mature writings.

First, the young Marx accepts the basic premises of Hegelian philosophy. He writes,

> The outstanding thing in Hegel's phenomenology and its final outcome – that is, the dialectic of negativity as the moving and generating principle – is ... first that Hegel conceives the self-genesis of man as a process, conceives objectification as loss of the object, as alienation and as transcendence of this alienation; that he thus grasps the essence of labour and comprehends objective man – true, because real man – as the outcome of man's *own labour*. (1959: 140)

Engels, many years later, stressed the importance of this dialectic outlook that both he and Marx embraced. The great merit of Hegel's philosophy, he wrote, was that "for the first time the totality of the natural, historical and spiritual aspects of the world were conceived and represented as a process of constant transformation and development, and an effort was made to show the organic character of this process" (Marx & Engels 1968: 408). Callinicos likewise notes that Marx took over the characteristic structure of the Hegelian dialectic (1983a: 42).

It is worth stressing that Marx never ceased, like his mentor, to be a dialectical thinker and that he continually paid tribute to the Hegel's greatness as a thinker. That Hegel was a "monkey' hanging around Marx's neck (Harris 1980: 145) and that Marx made an epistemological leap from ideology to science in renouncing the Hegelian dialectic (Althusser 1969) are both misrepresentations of the relationship between Hegel and Marx. The Hegelian dialectic, Marx wrote, in its rational form enables us to recognize that all historical forms are transient, and is of its very nature critical and revolutionary. But Marx thought Hegel's philosophy limited and one-sided, an "occult critique," and thus mystifying. He wrote in the preface of the second edition of *Capital* (1873):

> Although in Hegel's hands dialectic underwent a mystification, this does not obviate the fact that he was the first to expound the general forms of its movement in a comprehensive and fully conscious way. In Hegel's writings dialectic stands on its head, you must turn it right way up again if you want to discover the rational kernel that is hidden away within the wrappings of mystification. (1957)

Now it is highly unsatisfactory and misleading to interpret these words, and Hegel's philosophy in general, in terms of the old opposition between idealism and materialism, which Hegel had attempted to go beyond. When Callinicos writes of Hegel's view of nature as the "self-estrangement of spirit" (1983a: 98) and Singer says that he thought of mind as having primacy over nature in an ontological sense and of "the purpose or goal of history as the liberation of mind from all illusions and fetters" (1980: 41), they seriously misunderstand Hegel. They take Geist to be some creator-spirit in a theistic sense, whereas for Hegel spirit (culture) is immanent in the world. Hegel's notion of an "original unity" of Being makes such an interpretation – which stems from Engels – untenable. What troubled Marx was that Hegel's conception made spirit (Geist), rather than human beings, the subject of history; culture was in a sense personified. Therefore, he put too much emphasis on consciousness, ignoring, or at least downplaying, humans' active relationships with the natural world. Thus Marx felt that for Hegel the opposition between spirit (culture) and nature was "within thought itself " and that the "humanness of nature" therefore appears as the product of an abstract mind. Marx challenged this kind of philosophy for its mystification, and, following Feuerbach's materialistic approach, both suggested that human beings are the subject of history and offered a definition of humans as a species-being. Marx, in fact, regarded Feuerbach as the only philosopher who had taken a serious and critical look at the Hegelian dialectic. Thus in no sense can Marx be thought of as having simply "inverted"

28

Hegel's philosophy (the latter being seen as pure idealism), for this would attribute to Marx a crude materialism. The transition from Hegel to Marx is rather, as Marcuse and Lefebvre have suggested, a move to a different order of truth. Hegel's social and economic categories are all philosophical concepts with religious overtones, whereas all the philosophical concepts of Marxist theory are social and economic categories (Marcuse 1941: 258). (For other interpretations of the relationship between Hegel and Marx, see Hook 1962, Colletti 1973, and Rose 1981.)

Second, and stemming from this, Marx offers in the Paris manuscripts a definition of the human species. In doing so he took over Feuerbach's concept of species-being, but he gave it an entirely new content. Feuerbach's conception of humans essentially implied that they have a passive relationship to the world, and he gave the concept of "man" an ethical dimension. By contrast, Marx defined human beings not in terms of their self-consciousness nor in terms of their passivity or ethical attributes, but rather in terms of their essentially active relationship with the natural world. He looked upon this conception as naturalism or humanism, and significantly distinguished it from both idealism and materialism, suggesting that his approach constituted "at the same time the unifying truth of both." He wrote,

> Man is directly a *natural* being. As a natural being and as a living natural being he is on the one hand furnished with the natural powers of life – he is an *active* natural being. On the other hand, as a natural, corporeal, sensuous, objective being he is a *suffering*, conditioned and limited creature, like animals and plants . . . and because he feels what he suffers, a *passionate* being. But Man is not merely a natural being; he is a *human* natural being. That is to say, he is a being for himself. Therefore he is a *species* being, and has to confirm and manifest himself as such both in his being and in his knowing. Therefore *human* objects are not natural objects as they immediately present themselves, and neither is human sense as it immediately is . . . Neither nature objectively nor nature subjectively is directly given in a form adequate to the *human* being. (1959: 144–6)

Almost one hundred years before cultural anthropology, Marx was suggesting that culture could not be looked upon as something natural or given, nor is the natural world itself directly accessible to human sensibility. For Marx, as for Hegel, the mutual interdependence of man as a historical being and nature was what was essential. Marx thus combines the materialistic emphasis of the Enlightenment thinkers and of Feuerbach with the spiritual (cultural) emphasis of Hegel's idealism. Humans are both natural and social beings, in essence. But Marx, like Hegel, puts a focus on the interactional aspect; thus what is called world history is "nothing but the creation of man by human labour and the development of nature by man" (1959: 106). As Callinicos writes, "This conception of human nature as constituted by an active redirective, transformative relationship to nature through the labour-process is fundamental to Marx's thought" (1983a: 40). It is not surprising that when the manuscripts were published (in 1932) they had an important impact on existentialists and socialist humanists like Erich Fromm.

In putting emphasis on productive relationships there is the implication that Marx is offering a Promethean ethic, the notion that humans create themselves in opposition to, and through the control and domination of, nature. There is thus the suggestion that this theory expresses the "arrogance" of humanism and the Baconian "man-against-nature" perspective. One writer has indeed argued that Marx never disengaged himself from the dialectic and moral philosophy of the Enlightenment (Baudrillard 1975; cf. Adorno & Horkheimer 1973: 3–42; Ehrenfeld 1978: 250). This is, in a sense, true, but such an approach tends to ignore entirely the fact that Marx, following Hegel, attempted to integrate into his theory the perceptions and values articulated by romantics such as Schiller and Goethe. Marx's model of human activity was artistic as well as economic, and the human relationship with nature that he posited was aesthetic as well as instrumental. Callinicos again expressed Marx's orientation well when he suggested that he "relocated this humanist, aesthetic tradition [of European Romantic literature] within a materialist theory of history starting from the labour-process" (1983a: 40). In stressing the need to overcome alienation between spirit (human culture) and nature, both Hegel and Marx anticipated, I think, the main premises of the ecological movement that emerged a century later (see Dubos 1980). There is also the issue of the absence of the concept "species being" in Marx's later writings. This occurred not, I think, because Marx abandoned the humanistic perspective of his early youth for a mature scientific approach evident in his analysis of capital. Rather, in despiritualizing Hegel's dialectic Marx had to conceive of the human subject as an active, productive being, constituted historically by his or her own interaction with nature. He did not, however, use this as an explanatory concept – and so in no sense can Marx be described as a methodological individualist – but nonetheless it remained an underlying premise of all his writings. For Marx, history was not a "process without a subject" (Althusser 1972: 78); but neither did he posit a transhistorical subject. Social life is a creation of human productivity, and it is fundamentally historical.

Third, the Paris manuscripts outline Marx's initial thoughts on, and thus criticisms of, empiricism – the theory, stemming from Locke and Bacon, that knowledge is based on observation and sense experience and that scientific theories are built by some kind of inductive inference (see Chalmers 1978: 113–15). Marx challenges the validity of this kind of theory in the social sciences. It is of interest that although Marx uses Feuerbach to criticize Hegel's idealism, he uses Hegel to criticize the empiricism of Feuerbach as well as that of the English political economists. Callinicos suggests that it was Marx who initiated a process, continued by Nietzsche and Freud, that has drastically undermined the notion of reason as *theoria*, the disinterested contemplation of an objective reality (1983a: 155). But in fact it was Hegel who initiated this process in his critiques of empiricism, and Marx largely followed, and in doing so developed, Hegel's seminal thoughts. Thus in his essay on "estranged labor" Marx questioned the analyses offered by the political economists. He wrote, "Political economy proceeds from the fact of private property, but it does not explain it to us. It expresses in general, abstract formulae the material process through which private property actually passes, and these formulae it then takes for *laws*. It does not comprehend these laws" (1959: 64).

In *Capital* he develops this contrast between the underlying internal structure of the capitalist mode of production and its surface appearance, again following the trend of Hegel's thought. And he criticizes the theories of the political economists who saw the relations of bourgeois production as "natural laws independent of the influence of time."

Marx is equally critical of Feuerbach's materialism, and in his famous "Theses on Feuerbach" (1845) he criticizes Feuerbach's naturalism as static and unhistorical, for the natural world, he suggests, is not simply given in sense experience. In Marx's view,

> The chief defect of all hitherto existing materialism (that of Feuerbach included) is that the things, reality, sensuousness, is conceived only in the form of the object, or of contemplation, but not as sensuous human activity, practice, not subjectively. Hence it happened that the *active* side, in contradistinction to materialism, was developed by idealism – but only abstractly, since, of course idealism does not know real, sensuous activity as such. (Marx & Engels 1968: 28)

Hence Marx's approach, in refusing to take the empirically given on its own terms, transcends not only the opposition between idealism and materialism but also that between empiricism and rationalism. Again following the trend of Hegel's thought, Marx advocates neither pure empirical description (or inductive generalizations based on these, which could only be like building a house on shaky foundations) nor the imposition of preconceived concepts or schemata on existing data, whether to order or to analyze them. To read *Capital*, as do some contemporary

Marxists, in order to find some theoretical template that can then be applied universally is a kind of scholastic and ahistorical enterprise that is quite alien to the tenor of Marx's thought. Marx always starts with empirical data, whether the writings of other scholars or some given social reality, and, as Maurice Bloch has indicated, Marx never expressed any disdain for empirical knowledge (1983: 45). His mode of social inquiry in *Capital* thus begins with interpretive understanding. But, as Callinicos writes, Marx "refused to take intentional activity at its face-value. This was both because of his view that explanation of necessity proceeds by penetrating beneath the observable surface of things to the inner essence . . . and because Marx believed there to be a systematic discrepancy between the way individual agents perceived the capitalist mode of production and its actual working." Callinicos quotes Marx's famous statement, "All science would be superfluous if the outward appearance and the essence of things coincided" (1983a: 105).

Marx thus had a dialectical and realist conception of science, and though he certainly believed in the methodological unity of the sciences, he was critical of the idea that social life was explicable in terms of natural or mechanical laws, as the social Darwinists were inclined to think (see Keat & Urry 1975: 96–118; Callinicos 1983a: 96–113).

Fourth, an underlying theme of the manuscripts is the concept of alienation, which again Marx derives from Hegel, only he gives it historical substance. Feuerbach had employed the Hegelian form to criticize religion, but Marx uses the notion to describe given social conditions – that of the capitalist mode of production. He describes the antagonistic struggle between the capitalist and the worker in negative terms, suggesting that the factory system is not only injurious to the health and well-being of the worker but reduces him or her to the status of a commodity. Thus the labor process, which should involve both the creation of wealth for human enjoyment and the development of human potential, leads only to the degradation of the worker. The individual is dehumanized, and alienated from his or her true species-being. The workers no longer have control over their own destiny, and even the product of their labor is alienated in the act of production. The essays present essentially a moral indictment of capitalism, but there is an embryonic analysis of the basic economic categories of capitalism – capital, labor, wages, money – that Marx was later to expand and develop in his mature works. There is also a description of the kind of society in which private property is abolished and the self-estrangement of the human subject transcended. Citing French socialists such as Proudhon and Saint-Simon, Marx describes such a state as communism. It is the "genuine resolution of the conflict between man and nature and between man and man – the true resolution of the strife between existence and essence, between objectification and self-confirmation, between freedom and necessity, between the individual and the species. Communism is the riddle of history solved, and it knows itself to be this solution" (1959: 95).

Although the proletariat is defined in these essays, it is not seen as the agency of social transformation, an idea that Marx was to develop in his later studies and that formed the basis of his politics. It has been suggested that Marx renounced Hegel's teleological conception of history, and consequently saw history as an open process and contradiction as a constituent of social reality. It is worth quoting, therefore, the conclusion, to his notes on communism. Marx wrote, "Communism is the necessary form and dynamic principle of the immediate future, but communism is not as such the goal of human development, the form of human society" (1959: 106).

The distinction between Marx and Hegel on this issue is not absolute, for both writers, unlike Engels, tended to see the dialectic as the essential property of culture, rather than of all reality. When, referring to Hegel's political philosophy, Singer writes, "We must search for what is rational in the existing world and allow that rational element to have its fullest expression. In this manner we can build on the reason and virtue that already exists in a community" (1983: 36), he is, in general terms, essentially expressing a mode of thinking that Marx also was in accord with. In studying society, as Worsley suggests, it was essential to separate those elements that were positive and contained potential for future growth from those that were in decline (1982: 24). Thus for Marx communism is not so much a social state – otherwise the dialectic would come to an end – but rather a conscious principle of movement.

In the Paris manuscripts Marx has little to say on religion, for he clearly felt that Feuerbach's critique had dealt with it adequately at a theoretical level. Atheism, in its negation of god, had postulated the existence of man, but "real life," true humanity, could only be achieved through the "negation of negation" – through the annulment of private property. Marx thus believed that simply offering a critique of religion was no longer a tenable position to take, since religion, was, in a sense, a secondary phenomenon and depended on socioeconomic circumstances. It could only be overcome, therefore, when the circumstances that gave rise to religion were themselves transformed.

In 1844 Marx also published an introduction to "A Critique of Hegel's *Philosophy of Right.*" The opening paragraphs of this work give the most detailed summary of Marx's views on religion, and they are therefore worth quoting in full.

For Germany the criticism of religion is in the main complete, and the criticism of religion is the premise of all criticism.

The basis of irreligious criticism is: Man makes religion, religion does not make Man. In other words, religion is the self-consciousness and self-feeling of Man, who has either not found himself or has already lost himself again. But Man is no abstract being squatting outside the world. Man is the world of Man, the state, society. This state, this society, produce religion, a reversed world consciousness, because they are a reversed world. Religion is the general theory of that world, its encyclopaedic compendium, its logic in popular form, its enthusiasm, its moral sanction, its universal ground for consolation and justification. It is the fantastic realization of the human essence because the human essence has no true reality. The struggle against religion is therefore mediately the fight against the other world, of which religion is the spiritual aroma.

Religious distress is at the same time the expression of real distress and a protest against real distress. Religion is the sigh of the oppressed creature, the heart of a heartless world, just as it is the spirit of a spiritless situation. It is the opium of the people.

The abolition of religion as the illusory happiness of the people is required for their real happiness. The demand to give up the illusions about its condition is the demand to give up a condition which needs illusions. The criticism of religion is therefore in embryo the criticism of the vale of woe, the halo of which is religion... Thus the criticism of heaven turns into a criticism of the earth. (Marx & Engels 1957: 37–8)

Although there have been several attempts to suggest that Marx was fundamentally a religious thinker, that he possessed the self-assurance of a prophet, and that Marxism is a surrogate faith akin to the Judeo-Christian tradition with its stress on salvation, the passages just quoted and Marx's other writings strongly confirm that Marx was essentially an atheist. And although he expressed positive attitudes toward the German mystic Jacob Boehme, his general attitude to religion was one of hostility, particularly with respect to its alliance with political oppression. For Marx, atheism was inseparable from humanism (on this issue see Tucker 1965, Ling 1980, and Miranda 1980).

But the crucial idea expressed in the these paragraphs is that although religion is an opium giving people an illusory sense of happiness and consolation, its abolition could not, as Feuerbach thought, come from criticism alone but only by changing the socioeconomic order – the heartless, inhuman world – that made such illusions necessary. The crux of the matter, as Worsley noted, was that to abolish religion one had to abolish an irrational and unjust society – and it was contemporary capitalism that Marx always had in mind (Worsley 1982: 27–8).

Marx's subsequent studies and writings were largely devoted to a detailed analysis of capitalism, but in doing this he was also engaged in two subsidiary, related tasks. One was a historical study of the origins of capitalism and of the various forms of precapitalist societies that had emerged historically. This was an important concern of Marx (and Engels), and Marx's interest in anthropology was both political and scholarly, and lifelong (see Krader 1972, Bloch 1983). The other task was to delineate a method of understanding and explaining social life – to construct a sociology that was both materialist and historical. In doing this Marx developed a number of key concepts. With respect to the understanding of cultural representations, the most important of these was the concept of "ideology." And it is to this latter task that we must now turn.

Historical materialism

In the opening paragraphs of Marx's political pamphlet *The Eighteenth Brumaire of Louis Bonaparte* (1852) (in which he analyzes the political reaction in France after the revolutions of 1848), Marx wrote, "Men make their own history, but they do not make it under circumstances chosen by themselves, but under circumstances directly encountered, given and transmitted from the past. The tradition of all the dead generations weighs like a nightmare on the minds of the living" (Marx & Engels 1968: 96).

Marx goes on to say that the revolutions of the nineteenth century cannot draw upon the "poetry of the past" but only from the future, and in an illuminating class analysis of the period he suggests that the future lies with the proletariat, not with the peasants. But in the present context what is important about this paragraph is that Marx suggests that society is in a sense prior to the individual and holds that what human activity can achieve at a particular historical period depends largely upon the prevailing material and social conditions. Before all else Marx sees the individual as essentially a social being and conceives of thinking and being as having an essential unity (1959: 98). It is hardly surprising, therefore, though somewhat extravagant, that Marx, in collaboration with Engels, should have devoted almost four hundred pages of *The German Ideology* (1846) to a critique of Max Stirner, whose anarcho-existentialism was stridently expressed in the study *The Ego and His Own* (1845). Marx criticized this study mainly on the grounds that Stirner's conception of a "unique ego" was asocial and ahistorical and as much a "phantom" as the conceptions he railed against, that Stirner lacked any understanding of "real, profane history" and that his hostility to such "spectres" as "god," "truth," and "mankind" naively mistook these conceptions for reality. Stirner, he suggests, was essentially an idealist, "stuck fast in the world of pure thoughts" (Marx & Engels 1965: 260). But the more enduring parts of this study are devoted to his continuing critique of Feuerbach's theory of religion and to his initial outline of a materialist conception of history. I will discuss these in turn.

Marx's main criticism of Feuerbach, apart from challenging again his naive empiricism (57), was to suggest that although he had indeed shown that religion was an illusion of the earthly world, he had left a vital question unanswered, namely, how was it that people got these illusions "into their heads"? In spite of his materialism, Marx writes, Feuerbach failed to examine the actual conditions of human existence, stopping short at the abstraction "man." Marx summed up Feuerbach's approach cogently when he suggested, "as far as Feuerbach is a materialist he does not deal with history, and as far as he considers history he is not a materialist" (59). For Marx, human life could be understood only if situated in both a historical and a natural context.

It was in criticizing Feuerbach, however, that Marx and Engels initially set out for the first time their fundamental ideas on historical materialism. These ideas are best expressed by quoting some short extracts. They write,

> The premises from which we begin are not arbitrary ones, not dogmas, but real premises from which abstraction can only be made in the imagination. They are the real individuals, their activity and the material conditions under which they live, both those which they find already existing and those produced by their activity. These premises can thus be verified in a purely empirical way . . .

> The fact is, therefore, that definite individuals who are productively active in a definite way enter into these definite social and political relations. Empirical observation must in each separate instance bring out empirically, and without any mystification and speculation, the connection of the social and political structure with production . . .

> We set out from real, active men, and on the basis of their real life process we demonstrate the development of ideological reflexes and echoes of this life-process . . . Morality, religion, metaphysics, all the rest of ideology and their corresponding forms of consciousness, thus no longer retain the semblance of independence. They have no history, no development; but men developing their material production and their material intercourse alter, along with their real existence, their thinking and the products of their thinking. Life is not determined by consciousness, but consciousness by life. (31–8)

In the same study they outline an evolutionary schema indicating the various stages in the development of production (property, division of labor): the tribal, ancient (the Greek and Roman city-states), feudal, and capitalist "epochs." They also make a distinction between the "real basis" of social life (the sum of productive forces, capital funds, and social forms of intercourse) and the ideological or idealistic superstructure (politics, law, religion), which they imply has no history. Significantly, they describe communism as the "real movement which abolishes the present state of things. The conditions of this movement result from the premises now in existence." (48)

A decade or so later Marx published his famous preface to his *Critique of Political Economy* (1859), and again it is worth quoting from this seminal and oft-quoted work. The guiding thread of his studies, Marx suggests, can be briefly formulated as follows:

> In the social production of their life, men enter into definite relations that are indispensable and independent of their will, relations of production which correspond to a definite stage of development of their material productive forces. The sum total of these relations of production constitute the economic structure of society, the real foundation, on which rises a legal and political superstructure and to which correspond definite forms of social consciousness. The mode of production of material life conditions the social, political and intellectual life process in general.

Contradictions between the forces and relations of production engender social transformations, and Marx continues,

> In considering such transformations a distinction should always be made between the material transformation of the economic conditions of production, which can be determined with the precision of natural science, and the legal, political, religious, aesthetic or philosophic – in short, ideological forms in which men become conscious of this conflict and fight it out ... This consciousness must be explained from the contradictions of material life. (Marx & Engels 1968: 181–2)

There is, as McLellan and others have suggested, an essential continuity in the thought and style of the 1844 manuscripts and Marx's later writings. For within the *Grundrisse* the concepts of alienation, objectification, the individual's dialectical relationship with nature, and his or her generic or social nature still recur. In *Capital* Marx essentially applies the mode of analysis he had outlined programmatically in his earlier studies of the capitalist system, demonstrating that its economic categories were simply ideological constructs that served to hide the real basis, the underlying structure of capitalism (see Geras 1972; Nicolaus 1973; Bloch 1983: 41). Within his mature work, which structural Marxists take as a prototypical scientific study, Marx again has little to say on religion, for he essentially looks upon the "market system" itself as a religious system. But in the section appropriately entitled "The Mystery of the Fetishistic Character of Commodities," Marx notes that Christianity, with its "cult of the abstract human being," was the most suitable form of religion for a system of commodity production, and he concludes the discussion with the words,

> Such religious reflections of the real world will not disappear until the relations between human beings in their practical everyday life have assumed the aspect of perfect, intelligible, and reasonable relations as between man and man, and as between man and nature. The life process of society, this meaning the material process of production, will not lose its veil of mystery until it becomes a process carried on by a free association of producers, under their conscious and purposive control. (1957: 53–4)

Two points of interest emerge from the conspectus of historical materialism illustrated in these extracts. First, it is clear that Marx's mode of sociological analysis involves a "double discourse," two modes of interpretation. This relates to the two different processes that Maurice Bloch alludes to when he writes,

> The first process is part of the interaction of men grouped together in a society and engaged in production. This process leads to concepts, ideas, values and institutions which . . . are the indirect product of the process of production undertaken as a social task. The second process is an aspect of the fact that history also involves the development of exploitation. [This] also leads to the formation of ideas, concepts, values and institutions, but these, unlike those produced by the first process, are geared to operating exploitation, and involve giving the appearance of legitimacy to exploitation, as well as hiding its true nature from the exploited. The second process Marx and Engels call "ideology." (1983: 17–18)

With respect to the first process, Marx advocates a method of understanding that is historical-genetic. In *Grundrisse* Marx outlines several evolutionary schemata in the development of property relations; the various modes of production he outlined, however, are clearly not seen as having a necessary historical sequence. Marx was a flexible scholar and always ready to revise his sociohistorical hypotheses in the light of empirical knowledge (see Marx 1973: 471–95; Rodinson 1974: 63–7). Since Marx looked upon history as a dialectical process, concepts such as "contradiction" and "class" are central to his theory, but it is quite misleading, I think, to see Marx either as a historicist or as a conflict theorist in the tradition of Machiavelli, Hobbes, and the social Darwinists (Popper 1945, Martindale 1961). In *Capital* this mode of analysis is presupposed, and Marx's theories on the origins and development of capitalism are presented elsewhere or broached in the chapter on "primary accumulation" (Chapter 24), which Marx sees as the historical foundation of the system. As Schmidt has suggested, the recent, lamentable "loss of historical consciousness" among many contemporary Marxists in favor of an "abstract sociology" has led to the denial or devaluation of this mode of analysis. But, as Schmidt writes, in *Capital* Marx "used a method that was simultaneously structural-analytic as well as historical-genetic" (1983: 108). This implies, of course, that although Marx clearly saw religion as a changing phenomenon, unlike Hegel he did see it as a manifestation of spirit and thus as having an independent evolution.

The second mode of analysis is structural, critical, and materialist, in Marx's specific understanding of this last term. Such an analysis begins, as Mandel (1962) and others have stressed, with the empirical data as immediately given, but rather than engaging in a search for meaning, in a kind of hermeneutic understanding, Marx follows Hegel in attempting to go beyond such understanding. He belongs, and is indeed the founder, of what Ricoeur has called the "school of suspicion" (1970: 32) (the other writers in this school being Nietzsche and Freud), for Marx endeavors to demystify the surface phenomena. And it is in this task that the conceptual dyads appearance–essence, superstructure–base came into play. In a sense Marx offers a phenomenological analysis, but the "essence" of the phenomena relates to an economic base, or rather to productive relationships. Politics, law, religion are seen by Marx as essentially epiphenomena, as ideological constructs that "hide" exploitative structures. The crucial significance of *Capital*, as suggested earlier, is that Marx saw the economic concepts of capitalism – concepts such as value, labor, property – as essentially religious concepts. As Bloch suggests, "Concepts like labour organized life in much the same way as the notions of God had done in the Middle Ages, and it had as little material reference" (1983: 90). Now although Marx speaks of the "production of material life" as "conditioning" or "determining" other aspects of social life, it is clearly misleading to interpret this, as many Marxist critics have, as implying a simple *causal* relationship between the base and superstructure. To do so invokes a mechanistic paradigm that is quite alien to Marx's tenor of thought. As Merleau-Ponty put it, the economic base is not a "cause" but the "historical anchorage" or "carrier" for law, religion, and other cultural phenomena (1964: 108–12; cf. Hindess & Hirst 1975: 16). Moreover, to situate Marx's distinction between ideology and the material conditions of life in the context of the old debate between the primacy of either spirit or matter is highly misleading. For Marx, as Cole long ago suggested in his introduction to *Capital* (1957), "ideas" and "mind" are a part of what Marx conceived of as the "material." The economic base, for Marx, was those social relations that humans had been obliged to establish among themselves in the production of their material life. The notion of human praxis therefore unites the two "discourses" or methods. In an important sense, as many writers have suggested, Marx is a sociologist concerned with "comprehending the human condition" – not, like Hegel, with trying to comprehend the nature of the universe. But more than this, he was concerned also, through revolutionary practice, with changing the world for the better, basing his actions on a theoretical understanding of the present. He conceived of the future, as Larrain indicates, as the "realization" of those progressive elements already present, "immanent," in the existing social order (1983: 221).

Bloch has suggested that Marx's position was always something of a "balancing act" between idealism and "vulgar" materialism, but in fact Marx went beyond this redundant polarity. His approach was both historical and structural and implied a dialectical form of materialism that simply dissolved the old antithesis between consciousness and nature, mind and matter. Marx had learned his lessons well from "good old Hegel." (For a sound and readable survey of these issues, see Cornforth 1980.)

If Marx cannot, without some distortion, be accused of being an economic determinist, there is nevertheless the implication that his structural method is a kind of functionalism. And in a sense Marx's theory of ideology does have functionalist overtones. Hobsbawm, in a lucid discussion of Marx's contribution to historiography, does indeed suggest that Marxism is the first structural-functionalist theory of society. But it differs fundamentally from the kind of theory advocated by Durkheimian sociologists and anthropologists on two important counts. First, it insists on a hierarchy of social phenomena and stresses the priority of the economic base. This, of course, does not imply that analysis necessarily begins at the earthly level, and it certainly does not imply, as Bloch suggests (1983: 23), that one should (or even could) start by ignoring people's beliefs and ideas. Quite the contrary, for, as I have noted, Marx always begins his analysis at the level of empirical data, and the underlying "reality" is disclosed through analysis. As with Hegel, truth for Marx is always at the end of theoretical research, never at the beginning. The "material conditions of life" at a particularly historical juncture are not something given; they have to be discovered through empirical research and analysis. But in giving theoretical priority to the social processes of production, Marx advocates a mode of analysis that, as Bloch suggests, is distinctive. Second, Marxism insists on the existence within any society of internal tensions ("contradictions") that counteract the tendency of the system to maintain itself in equilibrium. Social life, in

Marx's view, as with Hegel's Geist, is a dynamic, ever-changing process. Thus, as Hobsbawm writes, "The immense strength of Marx has always lain in his insistence on both the existence of social structure and its historicity, or in other words its internal dynamic of change" (1972: 274).

A second point of interest relates to Marx's concept of ideology, which is one of his key and most original concepts. In recent years there has been a wealth of literature on this topic. Various interpretations of Marx's use of the term and several alternative definitions and theories have been proposed. Since these discussions have been ably summarized by Jorge Larrain (1979, 1983), who has dealt critically with the many developments within the Marxist tradition, little need be added here. But three general points may be made:

(1) Although Marx spoke of ideology in terms of "illusions," "mystifications," or "inversions," this did not in the least imply that notions like "god" or "labor" were not social realities that affected human behavior. The concept of labor is an "abstraction," the creation of modern capitalism, but although it has a certain objectivity, it is illusory in the sense that it reifies what are essentially social relations concealing the essential feature of capitalist relations – namely, exploitation (Marx 1973: 103; Geras 1972: 291–301).

(2) For Marx, ideology is a critical concept, and it is clearly unhelpful to equate it either with culture or with consciousness. When Ricoeur says that the "whole of consciousness" is to Marx a false consciousness (1970: 33), he seriously misjudges Marx's intent. As Bloch's comment suggests, Marx conceived of ideology as part of the superstructure and recognized that there were forms of consciousness that were nonideological. He never, as Larrain suggests, equated ideology and consciousness (1983: 112). Equally, to define ideology simply in terms of symbolic practices, or cultural ideas or collective representations, serves only to neutralize its critical import.

(3) The distinction between ideology and science cannot be equated with the distinction between falsehood and truth. For as Kolakowski says, they are distinguishable by their social function, not by their veracity (1973: 119). Marx was a dialectic thinker, and such an opposition is abstract and speculative. There is no sharp distinction between truth and falsity, knowledge and illusion, for the "emergent truth is always mixed up with illusion and error" (Lefebvre 1968: 85). Nor is there a simple or direct relationship between truth and a particular social class. When Marx suggests that the "ideas of the ruling class are in every epoch the ruling ideas," this did not imply that such ideas were simply ideological or total. The theories of the political economists involved illusory concepts, but they also had their truth, which Marx attempted to extract.

41

Science itself could have ideological functions. Marx, in fact, never spoke of "false consciousness": The expression is that of Engels. (For further studies of the concept of ideology, see Seliger 1977, Centre for Contemporary Cultural Studies 1978, and McCarney 1980.)

It seems evident that for Marx religion was the most basic form of alienation, and, historically, the first form of ideology. The functions it fulfilled were seen as essentially those that ideology in general fulfils, namely it served as a moral sanction, as an illusion, as a consolation for unjust conditions, as clouding the "true" reality, and as a justification for inequalities. In formulating this theory Marx was greatly influenced, as Zvi Rosen has explored (1977: 180–201), by the writings of Bruno Bauer. But whereas Bauer, like Feuerbach, was specifically concerned only with religious alienation and expressed a subjective viewpoint, Marx situated the concept of ideology in a sociohistorical context and greatly broadened its scope. Thus, in Marx's view, religion was simply one form of ideology, and he even applied this critical conception to Bauer's own writings. This means, of course, that to explicate religion one adopts a similar theoretical strategy to that adopted in explaining other forms of ideology. It implies exploring the interrelationship between religion and what Marx refers to as the material conditions of life. In *Capital*, in discussing technology as humans' dealings with nature, Marx wrote,

> Even the history of religion is uncritical unless this material base is taken into account. Of course it is much easier, from an analysis of the hazy constructions of religion, to discover their earthly core, than conversely, to deduce from a study of the material conditions at any particular time, the celestial forms that these may assume. But the latter is the only materialistic method, and therefore the only scientific one. The abstract materialism of a natural science that excludes the historical process is defective. (Marx 1957: 393)

Marx therefore denied that religion was an autonomous cultural phenomenon that could be understood in its own terms. Nor did he offer a general theory of religion. Religion could be understood only by examining in specific historical circumstances the linkages between religion as a form of ideology and socioeconomic life. Such linkages were complex, and there was clearly no simple mechanistic relationship between what Marx broadly called the "base" and the "superstructure" (for discussions of this loose metaphor, see Hall 1977 and Williams 1980: 31–49).

Within the Marxist tradition there has been an ongoing debate, and at times harsh polemical exchanges, between two distinct interpretations

42

of Marx. On the one hand, there are what are usually described as the "critical" or Hegelian Marxists. They stress the continuity of Marx with Hegel and view Marxism as a critique rather than as a science. Thus they take a more historicist and humanistic view of Marx's writings and situate themselves in the more literary and philosophical tradition of European culture. Scholars such as Lukacs, Gramsci, Sartre, Marcuse, Fromm, and Goldmann exemplify this "critical" tendency of Marxism; they are often highly critical of modern science and technology. There are clearly important differences in their various perspectives, however, and writers like Lukacs, who were much influenced by the hermeneutic tradition of Dilthey and Weber, are therefore less "Hegelian."

On the other hand there are the "scientific" Marxists, who stress that Marxism is a science of history and suggest that Marx made a clean break with Hegelian philosophy. Among the early writers, Engels, Kautsky, and Plekhanov are in this tradition, and they present a more deterministic and positivistic interpretation of Marx's writings. Such writers were more mechanistic than Marx and were often strongly influenced by social Darwinism. Modern writers who eschew "critical theory" include Godelier, Poulantzas, and Althusser, and they stress a "structural" Marxism that rejects a humanistic interpretation of Marx. This tendency is oriented towards modern technology and science and accepts the great value placed upon them. Althusser posits a radical break between the young Marx, still allegedly enthralled by Hegelian ideology, and the mature Marx, the text of *Capital* being seen as an exemplification of true science.

When taken to extremes the first tendency degenerates into naive romanticism and hermeneutics, whereas the second slides into positivism and mechanistic materialism. There is undoubtedly, as Wright Mills suggested (1963: 98), an "unresolved tension" in Marx's works – and in history itself: the tension of humanism and determinism, of human freedom and historical necessity. And Marx clearly expressed an ambiguous attitude toward science, for as the passage from *Capital* quoted earlier suggests, he was trying to go beyond the mechanistic paradigm bequeathed from the Enlightenment (and adopted by the political economists), without in the process renouncing either reason or the empirical methods of science. But the essence of Marx's contribution to philosophy, as George Novack has argued, is that he consistently tried to unify these two tendencies, advocating an approach that was both materialistic and dialectical. In essence, Marx was a scientific humanist (Novack 1978: 230). (For useful discussions of the "two Marxisms," see Gouldner 1973 and 1980, and Sahlins's critique of historical materialism, 1976.)

Religion and class structure

The history of social thought since the nineteenth century, Wright Mills suggests, cannot be understood without an understanding of the ideas of Marx (1963: 36). It is, then, all the more surprising that both the sociological and the anthropological traditions have tended to keep aloof from historical materialism (see Firth 1975, Llobera 1981). Marx essentially thought in terms of epochs and was a critical thinker who stressed the historical specificity of all conceptions and categories. Very little about human society and history, he felt, could be explained in terms of innate or biological capacities of human beings. And though he stressed the priority of material conditions of existence, he certainly saw no mechanistic or direct causal relationships between productive relationships and religion or other ideological forms.

But the structural relationship between ideology and the material base, as the passage that I have quoted from *Capital* indicates, can be interpreted in two ways. Bryan Turner has recently explored these two approaches. On the one hand an analysis can be made of religion as a form of ideology, and efforts can be made to discover their "earthly core." Such an analysis is a kind of philosophical anthropology that is "grounded in timeless concepts – reification, objectification, alienation – which ultimately presupposes some commitment to [discovering] 'the essence of man' " (1983: 69). Religion is thus seen as a means whereby the dominant class mystify and control the peasants, in feudal society, and the workers in capitalism. It tends to see no institutional mediation between productive relationships and the ideological form (see Abercrombie, Hill, & Turner 1980). Such an approach is explicitly stated in *The German Ideology* and is implicit in the discussion of the "fetish of commodities" in *Capital*. As a form of analysis it is somewhat general and abstract.

The other kind of analysis Marx suggested was truly materialistic and scientific, namely, through a class analysis of a particular period to delineate the forms of ideology that the material conditions generate. The emphasis here is less on the dominant ideology or world view of a particular epoch but rather on class divisions and class conflict. (Marx makes the interesting observation that whereas the dominant ideology in classical Greece or Rome was politics, and in the medieval period religion (the Catholic church), only in capitalism did material interests themselves reign ideologically supreme (1957: 56–7)). Such an analysis suggests, however – and this is implied in the famous preface to the *Critique of Political Economy* – that each class possesses a distinctive ideology that directly gives expression to its class interests. Turner sums up the two

44

approaches to religious ideology as follows: "Where the first theory argues that religion forms the basis of social integration as either social cement or social opium, the second theory points to religion as the principle source, especially in feudalism, of *class* solidarity" (1983: 78).

Although the theories appear to be incompatible, Marx and Engels advocated both structural approaches, suggesting, as Turner points out, that

> religion had the double function of compensating the suffering of the poor with promises of spiritual wealth, while simultaneously legitimating the wealth of the dominant class. One solution to the apparent contradiction of class solidarity versus social integration is thus to argue that by legitimating wealth and compensating for poverty, religion unified society while also giving expression to separate class interests. (80)

Although Engels, as Larrain has suggested, always affirmed the critical meaning of the concept of ideology, it was Engels rather than Marx who made some early, and seminal, materialist interpretations of religion. In recent years Engels has had a rather bad press. There have been attempts to suggest that his ideas were essentially different from Marx's dialectical materialism, reflecting a more mechanistic, positivistic, and scientific interpretation of social life. Engels has been portrayed as a mechanical materialist and saddled with Stalinist deviation toward theoretical dogmatism. This, I think, is extremely unfair to Engels, and often criticisms of him are disguised criticisms of scientific rationality itself. Although Engels frequently expressed a more deterministic approach than Marx, this was largely due to his polemical exchanges with idealist writers, for there was a close communion of thought between the two men. As Novack writes, "History has rarely witnessed so close, harmonious and unabated an intellectual and political partnership" (1978: 87). Within this partnership Engels modestly assigned himself the role of junior partner, but there is no doubt that he was an original and substantive thinker in his own right.

His study *The Condition of the Working Class in England* (1845), published when he was only twenty-five years old, is a classic in historical sociology. Like Marx, Engels attempted to delineate a kind of materialism that was neither mechanistic and reductive nor an agnostic "balancing act" – as suggested by Lukacs and Merleau-Ponty – between idealism and materialism, that denied nature itself an independent existence prior to human history. Unlike Hegel and Marx, Engels pervasively argued that there was a dialectics of nature, but the main reason for this contrast, I think, was probably just that neither Hegel nor Marx expressed much interest in natural science at all. There seems, in fact, to have been something of a division of labor between Marx and Engels, the former focusing his energies and attention on an analysis of capitalism and the writings of the political economists, whereas Engels, with his journalistic talents, undertook the role of popularizing the outlook and ideas of what eventually became the Marxist tradition. But it is clear from his study *The Dialectics of Nature*, a fragmentary work that was not published until thirty years after his death, that Engels not only denied that social life could be understood in a mechanistic fashion but suggested that contemporary developments in physics, chemistry, and biology had completely undermined the mechanistic philosophy of the Enlightenment. A "new outlook on nature," he sensed, was in the process of development. Thus Novack rightly stresses that although Engels (like Marx) used terms such as the "laws of motion," he can easily be absolved of having a mechanical approach to social causation, for he did not "even have a mechanistic conception of natural processes. He adopted a consistently dialectical method in respect to both sectors of reality" (1978: 99). Engels specifically criticized Hegel for not conceding to nature "any development in time." Modern developments in science, Engels suggests, had made the "immutable" conceptions of nature held by Newton, Linnaeus, and Hegel redundant (Marx & Engels 1968: 405–9).

It is therefore somewhat misleading to suggest, without qualification, that Engels held a positivistic conception of science. Within the corpus of his writings it is easy to find, as with Marx, statements that suggest technological determinism or imply that natural laws govern both social and natural processes, thus suggesting that human history is simply an extension of natural history. But Engels, like Marx and Hegel, was a dialectical thinker, and, though he stressed the unity of the sciences, he by no means equated them. For example, he wrote approvingly of Darwin and his theory of development but clearly distanced himself from it, and he criticized the notion of interpreting class struggles merely as a form of the "struggle for existence" (see Nova 1968: 15; Carver 1981: 49–51). One of his lapses into naive empiricism however, relevant to the present context, is Engels's suggestion in his essay "Ludwig Feuerbach" (1886) that the ideas of the soul and of immortality emerged from an intellectual attempt to understand dream apparitions and death and that the "first gods arose through the personification of natural forces" (Marx & Engels 1968: 593–4). In *Anti-Duhring* (1878) Engels wrote in a similar vein, drawing on the ideas of Müller, Tylor, and Feuerbach – all naive empiricists. All religion, Engels suggested,

> is nothing but the fantastic reflection in men's minds of those external forces which control their daily life ... In the beginnings of history it was the forces of nature which were first so reflected and which in the course

46

of further evolution underwent the most manifold and varied personifications among the various peoples. But it is not long before, side by side
with the forces of nature, social forces begin to be active – forces which
confront man as equally alien and at first equally inexplicable ... At a still
further stage of evolution, all natural and social attributes of the numerous
gods are transferred to one almighty god, who is but a reflection of the
abstract man. Such was the origin of monotheism. (Marx & Engels 1957:
131)

Such explanations of religion are speculative and essentially ahistorical,
and quite different from the kind of analysis Engels presents in examining specific religions. In his various essays devoted to the latter, Engels
focuses on two topics: the origins of Christianity, and the nature of the
peasant revolts in Germany in the sixteenth century.

Like Hegel, Engels, seems to suggest that the earliest forms of religion
have a natural or spontaneous quality about them and that it is only with
the emergence of states and priests that "deception and falsification"
appear. In tribal societies religion is "merged" with the social and political
conditions. But with the Roman conquest of the tribes, Engels writes,
not only was their national independence shattered but their religious
systems also collapsed, and there therefore arose within the Roman world
empire a class structure, the subjected communities having to pay tribute
and to provide slaves. It was among the latter that Christianity arose;
Christianity was, Engels suggests, "originally a movement of oppressed
people: it first appeared as the religion of slaves and emancipated slaves,
of poor people deprived of all rights, of peoples subjugated or dispersed
by Rome" (Marx & Engels 1957: 281). He pays tribute to the writings
of Bruno Bauer, who had linked the origins of Christianity to the social
conditions of the period, and continues, "Any resistance of isolated small
tribes or towns to the gigantic Roman world power was hopeless. Where
was the way out, salvation, for the enslaved, oppressed and impoverished
... ?" (ibid.).

It was not, Engels suggests, in "this world." Instead Christianity places
salvation from bondage and misery in a "life beyond," in a "spiritual
salvation" that serves as a consolation in the consciousness of the oppressed, saving them from utter despair. Engels notes that "among the
thousands of prophets" of that period only the founders of Christianity
met with success, and that a clear distinction can be made between the
faith of the early Christians, who expected the imminent return of Christ,
and that of the established Christian church. He notes also the notable
similarities between early Christianity, the later peasant revolts of the
Middle Ages, the Mahdi rebellion in the Sudan (all, he suggests, have
their origin in economic causes), and the socialist movement. But the

latter, he argues, preaches salvation from bondage and misery not in the life beyond but in this world, through the transformation of society (281–2).

Karl Kautsky, in his classic study *Foundations of Christianity* (1908), develops Engels's ideas on the origin of Christianity. But though he offers a similar interpretation in terms of class structure, noting that Christianity in its beginnings was undoubtedly a movement among impoverished classes, Kautsky stresses that it was largely an urban phenomenon and that salvation was not, as Engels believed, in heaven but an earthly redemption. But like Engels he suggests that the gods at first served as "explanations for the processes of nature whose causal connections were not yet understood" (1972: 178) and stresses the distinction between early Christianity, with its communistic ethos and the later Christian church, which became, as the state religion, an organization used for domination and exploitation. Drawing on Feuerbach, Kautsky interestingly suggests that "The more impotent an individual feels himself to be, the more timidly he seeks for a firm support in some personality that stands out from the ordinary average; and the more desperate the situation from the ordinary situation becomes, the more a miracle is needed to save him – the more likely will he be to credit the person to whom he attaches himself as a rescuer, as a saviour, with the performance of miracles" (130–1) – a theme later developed by Erich Fromm in his study of the psychology of fascism (1942).

The second topic to which Engels devoted an exemplary class analysis of religion was the peasant wars in Germany. Written as a series of essays in the summer and autumn of 1850, and thus in the context of the revolutionary struggles of 1848, the study is a classical historical work. Drawing on the writings of Zimmerman, Engels attempted to explain the origin of the peasant uprisings in Germany in the early sixteenth century and to demonstrate that the so-called religious wars of this period involved material class interests. He writes, "Although the class struggles of that day were clothed in religious shibboleths, and though the interests, requirements and demands of the various classes were concealed behind a religious screen, this changed nothing and is easily explained by the conditions of the time" (1956: 42).

At this time, Engels suggests, the Catholic church was the dominant ideology, presenting an all-embracing synthesis and the "most general sanction of the existing feudal domination." Thus any opposition to feudalism and the political order was simultaneously interpreted as a theological heresy. Although the class structure of the period was complex and the various estates – princes, nobility, prelates, patricians, burghers, plebians, and peasants – had varied and highly conflicting interests, Engels suggests that in the struggles of the period three "camps" were formed. First, there was the conservative *Catholic* element, attempting to maintain the existing feudal conditions. This camp included the nobility, the ecclesiastical authorities, and the wealthy urban patricians. Second there was the *Lutheran* reformist camp, which included the rising bourgeoisie (burghers), the lesser nobility, and some princes who hoped to enrich themselves by confiscating church estates. Martin Luther was the recognized representative of this faction, and though initially highly critical of the church and the feudal hierarchy, he eventually turned against the peasants and became a spokesman for the burghers. And finally, there was the revolutionary party supported by the peasants and urban plebians, whose demands were articulated through *millenarian* Christianity. Thomas Münzer expressed the hopes, demands, and doctrines of this faction. Engels notes that Münzer, who became an evangelist preacher when he was twenty-two, preached throughout the German countryside with great success. He prophesied the imminent approach of the millennium and the Day of Judgment for the degenerate church and the corrupt world when the Kingdom of God was to be established here on earth (53–5). As in the earlier millennial sects, such as the Waldenses and Albigenses, and the peasant revolt of 1476 led by Hans Boheim (Hans the Piper), Münzer articulated the demands and frustrations of the peasants. He preached a utopian communism, and among the peasant demands of 1525 were the right to elect the clergy, the abolition of tithes and serfdom, the restoration of rights to the communal lands, and the elimination of arbitrary justice. Engels records the fortunes of the peasant rebellion led by Münzer and its eventual defeat. Engels's main conclusion is that Münzer was the representative of a class – the proletariat – that had not yet fully developed and that "the age was not ripe for the ideas" that Münzer expressed. In drawing an analogy between the German peasant rebellion and the revolutions of 1848–9, Engels predicted a successful outcome for the modern revolutionary movement, for the latter had become a European movement.

Engels's study clearly indicates that religion is not a unitary phenomenon but that in given historical circumstances various interpretations and emphases may be stressed by different groups. His study also suggests that although religion may serve the interests of a ruling class as an ideology, class interests themselves are also indirectly expressed through religion. Often religious movements arise that have a political import and may serve to strengthen interests that are aimed at subverting the sociopolitical order. Contemporary studies of Marxists of millennial cults have supported Engels's general thesis (see Worsley 1957, Hobsbawm 1963). The kind of interpretation that Engels suggests in the essay on the origins of Christianity and the peasant revolts is clearly a materialistic one for it relates religious phenomena to a class structure – to socioeconomic relationships. It is thus very different from the materialistic analyses of religion by Bryan Turner, who, although claiming an allegiance to Engels, links religious beliefs and practices to the "corporality" of the body and to human "corporations" and "populations" (1983: 12–13). It is even further from the "cultural materialist" perspective of Marvin Harris (1980), for Harris postulates a direct causal link between cultural institutions and environmental or biological factors. (For a useful critique of Harris's materialism, see Bloch 1983: 130–5.)

Marx and Engels's theory of religion implies, as we have noted, that to attack religion without also attacking the social order within which it grows (Marx was fond of organic metaphors) is to engage in ideological shadowboxing. This was the essence of their critique in both Stirner and Feuerbach. A consequence of this view of religion, however, is the suggestion that religion will disappear when social conditions that give rise to it have ceased to exist – that is, when communism has come into being. The issue is complicated by the fact that when Engels – and also Lenin in his various writings on religion (see Acton 1958) – wrote about religion in precapitalist or at least prefeudal societies, he explained it not in terms of social structure or the "economic base" but rather as a response to fear or as the result of ignorance of the natural causes of the many adversities of life. This explanation, as I have noted, is psychological, and ahistorical, and it gives religion an existential function. But as Bloch has suggested in discussing Marxist theories of historical change, once the notion of a classless society is postulated, Marxist theory has ipso facto no way of theoretically handling this context in terms of class contradictions (1983: 54). The same applies to the Marxist theory of religion, whether the latter is approached in terms of a class analysis or as an ideological form that cloaks structures of exploitation. If the social ideal of a "free association of producers" in harmony with nature expressed by Marx in *Capital*, comes into being, relationships would no longer be clouded in mystery, and religion would become extinct. Marxist analysis itself, therefore, would also become superfluous.

2

Religion as theodicy

Weberian sociology

Toward the end of the nineteenth century, Hegelian philosophy, outside a limited number of academic preserves, fell into disrepute. Except within the Marxist tradition, Hegel's influence declined, and his writings became unfashionable. There arose in its stead three currents of thought that we may initially consider, since all had an important influence on the sociology of Max Weber.

The first is *positivism*, a term derived from the writings of Auguste Comte, who, at the beginning of the nineteenth century, made the first programmatic statements regarding the new discipline of sociology. He saw this subject as the culmination of his "positive" philosophy. Comte saw scientific knowledge as forming a hierarchy and its development as constituting both a historical and a logical order, sociology standing at its apex. Broadly considered, positivism is a current of social thought that has adopted most or all of the following premises.

(1) It expresses a fundamental aversion to metaphysical thinking, the latter being repudiated as either sophistry or illusion. With logical positivism, a mode of thought lucidly expressed by A. J. Ayer (1936), only logical and scientific propositions (that is, statements subject to empirical verification) are considered valid; all other forms of understanding, such as art and religion, are seen as meaningless.

(2) Science is considered to deal with empirical facts that are independent of the human subject, and scientific knowledge to consist of analytical-inductive generalizations based on sense impressions. Science therefore takes the empiricist approach that Hegel criticized in his *Phenomenology*.

(3) Arising from this, positivism stresses a fundamental distinction between fact and value statements. Judgments of value or morality have no empirical content of the sort that renders them accessible to tests of validity. Thus it follows that not only is scientific understanding, includ-

51

ing sociology, seen as a value-free activity, but positivism repudiates any obvious sociopolitical commitment on the part of the researcher. In this context Marxism is seen as having a normative conception of sociology (see Freund 1979). "Positive" sociology, on the other hand, is seen, like the natural sciences, as neutral with respect to values. Scientific knowledge thus comes to have an instrumental value.

(4) Positivism suggests that the natural and social sciences have an essential unity and share a common logical and methodological foundation. The procedures of the natural sciences are therefore applicable to all spheres of life and culture, and positivism holds that science is the only true form of knowledge. Sociological analysis therefore is involved in making causal or lawlike generalizations, in ways that parallel those of the natural sciences. Although there is the suggestion that this involves adopting a mechanistic paradigm, Comte's own theory was functional and organismic (and his outlook, as many have noted, basically conservative). Such a positivistic approach tends to have a behavioristic slant and to exclude meaning and human subjectivity from the analysis. (For useful accounts of positivism from which these points have been extracted, see Giddens 1974, 1979; Bleicher 1982: 37–51.)

Toward the end of the nineteenth century, positivist approaches became dominant in both anthropology and sociology, and at the turn of the century they became dominant even within Marxism itself, as the writings of Kautsky and Plekhanov (1908) indicate. Sociology was conceived as the "natural science of society," and, with qualifications, as materialistic and mechanistic in its essential perspective. This kind of approach, as Stuart Hughes has shown in his admirable survey of European social thought (1958), largely dominated the Anglo-French tradition. And, as he suggests, in both Britain and France utilitarianism and positivism, democracy and natural science became natural partners. In Britain the high priest of positivism was Herbert Spencer, who welded positivism to social Darwinism. An articulate defender and advocate of laissez-faire capitalism, Spencer had an important influence on both anthropology and sociology. I will discuss his theory of religion in the next chapter, along with that of Emile Durkheim. Durkheim, considered by many as a true heir of Comte, was, Giddens suggests, more influential than any other academic social scientist in disseminating a "positivistic sociology" (1979: 245). All the key sociologists at the turn of the century – Durkheim, Pareto, and, as we shall see, Weber – regarded their work as directly challenging historical materialism, largely on the grounds that the latter was empirically invalid (Hughes 1958: 78–9; Llobera 1981). Hence the antithesis between sociology and Marxism to which I have referred.

In contrast, in Germany positivism never took a firm hold, for, as Hughes writes, the predominant philosophical tradition was idealist, and in an important sense this tradition was historical and deeply influenced by the Romantic Movement. Anthropological studies in Germany largely followed the anthropogeographical school, and although Ratzel had an important influence on Franz Boas, the theoretical influence of this school had a minimal effect on the development of anthropology.

Hughes describes the second current of thought as the "recovery of the unconscious." This refers to the writings of a number of scholars — Nietzsche, Bergson, and Freud are important — who stressed the central role of unconscious motivation in human conduct. This was not simply a part of the Romantic reaction against rationalism and science, for both Nietzsche and Freud were critical thinkers who were unwilling, like Marx, to completely repudiate the intellectual insights of the Enlightenment. Although Bergson, like Freud, expressed a humanistic and psychologistic standpoint, his own philosophy was altogether different: He was more mystical and religious than either Freud or Nietzsche. To suggest, however, that the late nineteenth century was the age of the discovery of the irrational is somewhat misleading, for two reasons. First, as Donald MacRae has noted (1974: 47), the issue of unconscious motivation has a long history and was a central concern of earlier literary figures and philosophers. Second, the stress on the unconscious and, with Bergson, intuition, was only one current of thought, and by no means the dominant one, at the end of the nineteenth century. A crucial figure in this second current of thought was Friedrich Nietzsche.

Nietzsche is a strange, paradoxical figure, a literary philosopher who expressed his ideas in aphorisms. His thought was visionary and prophetic, yet at the same time reactionary. Bertrand Russell (1946) described him as an "aristocratic anarchist," and that perhaps best describes his contradictory personality. Many writers have linked him with Marx and Freud as one of the three key thinkers who have influenced twentieth-century thought. All three were German speakers and lovers of classical Greek thought. All were passionate thinkers who deeply sensed the need for radical change and in various ways were profoundly critical of the temper and culture of their own age. All three had a profound distrust of moral discourse and everyday consciousness, and they collectively represented what Ricoeur has called the "school of suspicion." But in the present context, what is important and what united them was a "common opposition to the phenomenology of the sacred" (Ricoeur 1970: 32), for all three scholars were professed atheists and looked upon the belief in God as a historically determined symptom of human weakness and subordination (Stern 1978: 13–17).

However, although Nietzsche is important as a critical thinker and his polemical writings on what he referred to as the malaise and "decadence" of Western culture are important and poignant, his suggestions for spiritual renewal are banal and reactionary. I find it quite strange that contemporary radicals like Foucault should pay homage to a writer like Nietzsche as supposedly the great liberator from the Hegelian (Marxist) dialectic (see Sheridan 1980). Nietzsche was a tortured soul who suffered ill health for most of his life and finally lapsed into complete insanity in 1889, when he was forty-five years old. And, as Lavrin writes, his quest for philosophical truths was to some extent a surrogate quest for physical and mental health by an isolated and much-suffering man. The philosophy of power that Nietzsche came to espouse was largely, as Russell suggests, delivered from the fantasies of an invalid and the outcome of his fears and pain. His paeans to life and his criticisms of Schopenhauer's oriental ethic of escape and renunciation are laudable, but the misogyny that Nietzsche expresses in his classic study *Thus Spoke Zarathustra* (1884) and his doctrine of the superman are hardly worthy of emulation. His theory of the "will to power" seems to combine, as Lavrin suggests (1971: 84), the notion of the philosopher as the aristocratic ruler and lawgiver with the Darwinian principle of the "survival of the fittest," the latter being the cornerstone of his sociology. Nietzsche was a passionate individualist who had little but disdain for ordinary people; unlike Hegel and Marx he entertained no vision of the future beyond this martial, aristocratic ethic. But he is close to these writers as a critical thinker who attempted to remain true to the rationalist tradition. As Walter Kaufmann put it, "He tried to strengthen the heritage of the Enlightenment with a more profound understanding of the irrational – something Hegel had attempted three-quarters of a century earlier, but metaphysically and rather esoterically. Nietzsche was determined to be empirical, and he approached his subject – as it surely should be – with psychology" (1971: 16). It is not surprising, therefore, that Nietzsche's ideas should closely resemble the main tenets of psychoanalysis (see Sulloway 1979: 467–8).

But with respect to the present study what is significant about Nietzsche is that he had an acute historical sense (like Hegel, he much admired Heraclitus) and that he wrote some of the most devastating criticisms of religion ever penned. This too is something of a paradox, for on both sides of his family Nietzsche came from a long line of Lutheran pastors, and Lavrin even suggests (1971: 63) that he was by nature gentle and a potential founder of a religion. Nevertheless Nietzsche, in various writings, particularly in one of his last studies, *The Anti-Christ* (1888), developed a bitter and hostile critique of Christianity. He was in fact violently anti-Christian, arguing that Christianity is a "slave-morality," which, by teaching submission to the will of God, both denigrates human earthly life and restricts human freedom. He is equally critical of the dogmas and hypocrisy of the Christian church. A short extract will illustrate the nature of his rebellion against historical Christianity, in which he is clearly unable to see anything but weakness, mendacity, and utilitarian cant (Lavrin 1971: 67).

> In Christianity the instincts of the subjugated and oppressed came into the foreground; it is the lowest classes which seek their salvation in it... A certain sense of cruelty towards oneself and others is Christian... Hatred of mind, of pride, courage, freedom, *libertinage* of mind is Christian; hatred of the senses, of the joy of the senses, of joy in general is Christian. (Nietzsche 1968: 131)

As Stern remarks, embedded among the vituperation and incongruities there are some profound insights to be gleaned from Nietzsche's writings, but he offers no theoretical understanding of religion. Like Stirner, he is dogmatic and negative, denying any relevance to religious beliefs. Nor does Nietzsche interest himself in the truth content of religion. As Russell put it, "Nietzsche is not interested in the metaphysical truth of either Christianity or any other religion; being convinced that no religion is really true, he judges all religions entirely by their social effects" (1946: 293) – and these he adjudges to be entirely negative.

When one reflects on the contrast between this critique of Christianity and Nietzsche's own religious background, it comes as no surprise to learn that he felt an acute sense of moral crisis in his own life and period. This is well expressed in the oft-quoted prologue to *Thus Spoke Zarathustra*:

> Zarathustra went down the mountain alone...But when he entered the forest, an old man, who had left his holy hut to look for roots in the forest, suddenly stood before him...
> "And what does the saint do in the forest?" asked Zarathustra.
> The saint answered: "I make songs and sing them, and when I make songs, I laugh, weep, and mutter; thus I promise God...But what do you bring us as a gift?"...
> When Zarathustra heard these words, he saluted the saint and said, "What should I have to give you: But let me go quickly, that I may take nothing from you." And thus they parted from one another...
> But when Zarathustra was alone, he spoke thus to his heart: "Could it be possible! This old saint has not yet heard in his forest that *God is dead!*" (Nietzsche 1961: 40–1)

The theme "God is dead" is a recurrent one in Nietzsche's writings, and it expresses his sense of a cultural crisis. Critical of the notions of progress espoused by evolutionary theorists and positivistic thinkers, and – given his heroic individualism – equally critical of both socialism and nationalism, this loss of religious belief left Nietzsche with an "unbearable loneliness." The "death of god" seemed to him to imply a loss of purpose and meaning both for himself and for European culture. He had a feeling that a spiritual and moral vacuum had begun to overtake the world once religion had lost its validity. The most significant event of the modern world, he felt, was the realization that it was chaotic, mean-ingless, and disenchanted. It is hardly surprising, then, that Nietzsche, though combining Dionysian nihilism with an aristocratic warrior ethic, became one of the founders of existentialism (see Blackham 1952: 23– 42; MacQuarrie 1973).

The third current of thought, the German idealist tradition, essentially involved a return to Kant's dualistic metaphysics, a philosophy that Hegel had attempted to go beyond. Kant had made a fundamental distinction between "scientific" reason, which understood the phenomena of the natural world through the categories of understanding (space, time, causality), and "practical" reason, which grasped ethical reality through intuition. Toward the end of the nineteenth century a group of scholars, conventionally known as the Heidelberg or neo-Kantian school, sought to develop Kant's insights in establishing a science of culture. The more important scholars of this school were the philosophers Windelband, Rickert, and Dilthey and the formal sociologist Georg Simmel. All were critical of the kind of positivistic sociology developed by Comte. The basic tenet of this idealist social thought, especially as formulated by Wilhelm Dilthey, was to suggest a radical distinction between the natural sciences (*Naturwissenschaften*) and the cultural sciences (*Geisteswissenschaften*). The distinction is cogently summarized by Don Martindale as follows:

> The physical sciences deal with *facts*; the cultural sciences with *meanings*. In the physical sciences, thought takes the form of *explanation*; in the cultural sciences it takes the form of *understanding*. Explanation establishes causal laws and approaches its object from the outside, or externally; un-derstanding links meaning with meaning and grasps its object immediately in facts of intuition . . . The method of explanation in natural science is experiment; the method of understanding in the cultural sciences consists in interpretation by means of ideal types or configurations of meaning. (1961: 378)

Bergson's recourse to the faculty of intuition therefore had much in common, as Hughes notes, with the German idealist school. But Dilthey, that "lonely and neglected genius," as Collingwood described him (1946: 171), accepted certain elements of positivism in attempting to make the human sciences as precise and as empirical as natural sciences. Indeed Rickman suggests that Dilthey was a committed empiricist, critical of Hegelian metaphysics (1976: 21). In developing a hermeneutical approach to culture, Dilthey essentially accepted as valid a mechanistic paradigm in the explanation of natural phenomena. But with respect to sociocultural phenomena he advocated a philosophy of life stressing the significance of lived experience and the need for the intuitive understanding of specific cultures or world views. Such understanding, he stressed, could not come through introspection alone but only through a detailed study of history. In a discussion, for example, of philosophical world views (*Weltanschauungen*) Dilthey described three basic varieties: naturalism, reflected in the materialist theories of Hobbes and Democritus; transcendental idealism, exemplified by the dualistic philosophies of Plato, Kant, Schiller, and William James; and objective idealism. The third type Dilthey saw reflected in the speculative philosophies of Heraclitus, Spinoza, Bruno, and Hegel. The implication of Dilthey's approach is, of course, to stress the historical specificity of different types of cultures or world views, and, though highlighting their specific value systems or Geist (spirit), it leaves such values unexplained. It does not account for the "life forms," and as John Lewis has argued, implies a "total relativism" (1975: 28–33).

Dilthey has had an important influence on contemporary social thought. The distinction between the natural and cultural sciences still remains important to critical theorists of the Frankfurt school, and existentialist and phenomenological writers – Husserl, Heidegger, and Jaspers – have acknowledged their debt to him. Ruth Benedict's classic introduction to anthropology, *Patterns of Culture* (1934), was written from the standpoint of the German idealist tradition, and Hans Gadamer's *Truth and Method* (1960) is a more recent exposition of this kind of hermeneutics (see Hodges 1974 for a useful exposition of Dilthey's philosophy, and R. H. Brown 1978a for a good, brief assessment of the interpretative method).

The importance of the sociology of Max Weber is that he attempted to combine elements from all three currents of thought. On the one hand he was critical of positivists like Comte who attempted to assimilate the social sciences to the natural sciences. Weber, like Dilthey, stressed the importance of subjective meanings and denied that human culture could be adequately understood without value interpretations. Yet he insisted that valid generalizations could be derived from historical studies. On the other hand he was critical of those like Dilthey who made a radical distinction between the natural and cultural sciences. What Weber attempted, as Talcott Parsons and others have noted, was to bridge the gap between the two approaches to culture represented by positivism and the Geisteswissenschaften approach. As Dennis Wrong put it, "Weber was attempting to bridge a chasm between two extreme viewpoints representing rival intellectual traditions: the positivism of the natural sciences and German idealism and historicism" (1970: 8). American sociologists like Parsons have always stressed the positivist side of Weber's work, as Wrong suggests, and have ignored his historicism and his stress on meaning-structures.

Max Weber was born in Thuringia in 1864 and was of Lutheran background. His father came from a successful merchant family and was a trained lawyer and a member of the Reichstag. He was authoritarian and conventional, and a staunch nationalist. Weber's mother, on the other hand, was religious and high-minded, and devoted to projects of social welfare. Their marriage, as MacRae describes it, was "one of unhappiness, pietism, and complaint" (1974: 20). Weber's wife Marianne, who wrote an important biography of Weber (1975), also came from a leading industrialist family, so that Weber lived all his life in relative comfort, with ample opportunity for travel, leisure, and study. After studying law at the University of Heidelberg and completing a doctoral thesis on medieval trading companies (1889), Weber became a professor of economics at Freiburg in 1895. But his academic career was cut short due to a "nervous breakdown" that followed a serious quarrel with his father in 1898. The quarrel had all the elements of an oedipal situation, and his father's death shortly afterward left Weber with an acute and crippling depression. After some four years of anxiety he eventually recovered his intellectual powers, and in 1903 he became an associate editor, with Werner Sombart, of a social science journal. It was in the pages of this journal – *Archiv für Sozialwissenschaft und Sozialpolitik* – that he published his famous essays entitled *The Protestant Ethic and the Spirit of Capitalism* (1904–5). During the next decade Weber lived as a private scholar, engaged in intense and wide-ranging scientific research. During that period he produced a series of studies on political economy, religious sociology, and legal institutions that, in their scope and documentation, have never been surpassed. Weber was something of a polymath, and his erudition was quite remarkable and forbidding. MacRae described him as a "magus." Most of his studies were published after he died, in June 1920, at the early age of fifty-six. During the last two years of his life Weber had become a professor of sociology at Vienna and Munich and was working on a major study, *Economy and Society*, also published posthumously.

Although, owing to his personal disabilities, he was hardly able to cope even with the duties of an academic career, Weber all his life had a craving to be politically active. A dedicated German nationalist, he had a fascination with power, and John Lewis describes his creed as the "first unambiguous appearance of Social Darwinism as a political philosophy" (1975: 15). Weber and Nietzsche, in fact, had a lot in common; both were "neurotics of genius," obsessed with the pursuit of power yet unable, owing to psychic incapacity, to engage in active political life, although, of course, Weber's militant nationalism and his puritanical personal life would have been anathema to Nietzsche.

Reinhard Bendix described Weber's political position succinctly when he said that Weber was "a lone wolf born into a liberal, middle-class family in late nineteenth-century Germany [who] saw both the decline of liberalism in an emerging power-state and the threat to the individual in the bureaucratization of modern society" (1959: 7).

Weber associated socialism with this increasing bureaucratic tendency, and thus both politically and in his intellectual work his career has been seen as one "long epic campaign" against Marxism (J. Lewis 1975: 13). I will return to the relationship between Marx and Weber later in the study, but it is important to stress here what Weber himself took pains to admit: namely, that his researches reflected the values and aspirations of the German bourgeoisie. (For interesting studies of Weber's life and career, see Gerth & Mills 1948: 3–31; Hughes 1958: 278–335; and Mitzman 1970.)

Weber's conception of sociology is best described by an extract from *Economy and Society.* Sociology, he wrote,

> is a science which attempts the interpretative understanding of social action in order thereby to arrive at a causal explanation of its cause and effects. In "action" is included all human behaviour when and in so far as the acting individual attaches subjective meaning to it … Action is social in so far as, by virtue of the subjective meaning attached to it by the acting individual(s), it takes account of the behavior of others and is thereby oriented in its course. (1947: 88)

A number of points may be made about Weber's conception of social science and the methodology this implied. First, Weber's emphasis is on social action, not on social structure. The fundamental unit of analysis for Weber is always the individual, at least in his programmatic statements, for in his sociological analyses of religion the emphasis tends to be on interest groups. Weber thus took what Cohen (1968: 14) described as an "atomistic" approach to social reality, an approach that is mechanistic rather than functional. Weber continually recommends treating collectivities – states, groups, associations, corporations – as "particular acts of individual persons" and appears to eschew functional analysis (1947:

101–4). This approach is often described as "methodological individualism." Weber regarded the reification of collectivities as organisms or as cultural totalities as illegitimate. His approach therefore is quite dissimilar to Durkheim's "holistic" approach to social reality. Both Parsons and MacRae view Weber's rejection of functionalism, with its concepts of social structure, function, and institution, as having limited the development of his sociological theory. On the other hand, although Weber's stress on causality would imply a mechanistic model, Weber, unlike Durkheim, was fundamentally a historical thinker. As Hughes suggests, although Weber never formally studied or taught history, "his whole intellectual life was suffused with historical thinking," and his type of sociology was "firmly lodged within the framework of history" (1958: 325). In this regard, Weber was much closer to Hegel and Marx than he was to Pareto and Durkheim, although Parsons invariably categorizes Weber with these latter theorists. When Wrong describes Weber's intellectual development as being shaped by a "profound historical consciousness" and links him to such nineteenth-century thinkers as Hegel, Comte, Marx, and Spencer, who were concerned with universal interpretations of human history and with understanding the emergent capitalist system, he is, I think, closer to the essential Weber. Weber was a historical sociologist, not a systems analyst (Wrong 1970: 2–3).

Second, in putting an emphasis on meaning Weber suggested a specific method of inquiry, *Verstehen*, best described as comprehending social action through an empathetic understanding of another person's values or culture. But the understanding of subjective meanings or motives did not merely imply ascertaining a particular person's account of his or her own conduct or beliefs; rather, Weber saw Verstehen as a "method that could be applied to the understanding of historical events, [even] when there was no one left around to interview" (Parkin 1982: 19). Weber clearly saw this need for interpretative understanding as problematic and suggested that the ability to understand certain mystical states or the feelings and thoughts of preliterate people might be limited (1947: 90–104). Yet in his writings on methodology Weber appears to reject the notion of any "objective meaning," and thus, unlike Marx and Freud, would seem to be unaware of any disjuncture between subjective meanings and an "objective" social reality. But as Gerth and Mills suggest (1948: 58), his actual analyses are not consistent with his doctrinal statements on Verstehen, and he paradoxically adopts a view that is close to Marx's theory of ideology (cf. Parkin 1982: 26).

It is important, however, to note that Weber is centrally concerned also with explaining social facts; social life must be understood not only subjectively but objectively. Thus interpretative understanding has to be supplemented by causal analysis. As Weber put it, interpretations that are "meaningfully adequate" must be complemented by a consideration of their "causal adequacy." For Weber this was seen essentially in historical rather than in mechanistic terms and involved determining the role of various antecedent factors underlying a particular social phenomenon or event. Such a causal analysis could only be hypothetical, he felt, involving an imaginative attempt to locate the specific factor that would have a decisive influence in a given sequence of events (Hughes 1958: 306). Weber's mode of analysis is therefore concerned not with function but with meaning and cause, and given his stress on individual motivations he never, as J. Lewis suggests, lapsed into mechanistic materialism (1975: 49).

In order to structure his analyses in a meaningful fashion, Weber devised the concept of "ideal-type." This was merely an analytical construct that refined what social scientists and historians had long been doing in using such terms as *capitalism, feudalism,* and *economic man.* For Weber it implied no evaluation or ethical standard; it simply referred to the construction of certain elements of social reality into a logically precise conception. As such it was a "one-sided" abstraction that served as a device for understanding and analysis.

Third, in his essay entitled "Objectivity in Social Science" (1904), Weber not only made a distinction between empirical knowledge and value judgments but suggested that science could never "provide binding norms and ideals from which directives for immediate practical activity can be derived" (1949: 52). From these and similar statement it has been inferred that Weber advocated a "value-free" sociology, a social science that is ethically and politically neutral. Yet it is clear, as Wrong and others have suggested, that what Weber objected to was the practice of his academic contemporaries of preaching in a partisan way to a "captive audience." He neither thought that value judgments should be withdrawn from scientific discussion, nor believed that in fact they could be, for in the last analysis all scientific analysis rests, he argued, on certain subjective ideals. "An attitude of moral indifference," he wrote, "has no connection with 'scientific objectivity'" (1949: 60).

The Protestant ethic and the spirit of capitalism

Weber's essays on the "Protestant ethic" and its relationship to capitalism are widely known and have been the subject of numerous critical studies. It is not my intention to review this extensive literature here but merely to outline Weber's basic thesis. His study, *The Protestant Ethic and the Spirit of Capitalism,* and its underlying argument fall into three parts. In the first part Weber defines what he means by the spirit of capitalism; in the second he outlines the Protestant ethic and the distinctive character of the ascetic sects; and finally he explores the relationship between the religious ethic and capitalism.

Capitalism, for Weber, was virtually a universal phenomenon found throughout history, or at least since the rise of city-states. Capitalism, in the sense of enterprises or entrepreneurs utilizing capital (money, or goods with a money value) to make a profit, purchasing the means of production and selling the product, have, like trading activities, a long history and have been found throughout the world. Weber recognized several types of capitalism: booty capitalism, the acquisition of wealth by plunder and speculative adventures; the money-lending activities undertaken by marginal communities; and traditional capitalism, characteristic of earlier enterprises with limited aims, which were not, because of its ethos, geared specifically to profit making. And finally, what he described as rational capitalism; Weber clearly saw this as a recent phenomenon. As he wrote in *The Theory of Economic and Social Organization*, "It is only in the modern Western world that rational capitalistic enterprises with fixed capital, free labour, the rational specialization and combination of functions, and the allocations of productive functions on the basis of capitalistic enterprises, bound together in a market economy, are to be found ... This difference [between rational capitalism and the earlier forms] calls for an explanation, and the explanation cannot be given on economic grounds alone" (Weber 1947: 279–80).

For Weber, therefore, capitalism, as an economic system involving the rational organization of legally free wage-laborers by the owners of capital, for the sole purpose of pecuniary profit, was a modern phenomenon. Moreover, since this system was seen to affect all aspects of life, Weber saw modern capitalism not simply as an economic system but as a culture or world view (*Weltanschauung*). He was also conscious of the fact that the rise of capitalism was intrinsically linked with the growing power of the modern state (1930: 72). But it is significant that what is distinctive about modern capitalism for Weber is not simply the rational organization of free labor and the conversion of labor (and land) into commodities, but rather its "ethos" or "spirit." The spirit of capitalism is not the essence of capitalism as an economic system, but rather an attitude of mind, the psychological motivation that he felt made modern capitalism possible. It is "that attitude which seeks profit rationally and systematically," that performs labor "as if it were an absolute end in itself." It is a "social ethic" devoted to "the earning of more and more money, combined with the strict avoidance of all spontaneous enjoyment of life" (53). Such an attitude is by no means restricted to the capitalist: For modern capitalism to function, the workers themselves, Weber felt, must adopt this ethic. He discusses what he describes as "traditionalism," whereby workers respond to higher wages by doing less work, noting that a person does not "by nature" wish to earn more and more money. The necessary "work ethic" has to be induced. Weber considers Benjamin Franklin, in his writings, to exemplify all the "virtues" that constitute the spirit of capitalism: honesty, punctuality, industry, frugality, and restraint. He describes Franklin as a "colourless deist." He was clearly the first Boy Scout. Yet Weber makes the point that there is no one-to-one relationship between this "attitude of mind" and the capitalist enterprise. The latter may be run on purely traditionalist lines, he suggests, and Franklin, though filled with the spirit of capitalism, lived in the Pennsylvania backwoods of the eighteenth century, where capitalism was barely in evidence. Weber also stresses that the impulse to acquisition of goods and pursuit of gain is not in the least identical with the capitalist spirit.

Weber then moves on, in his second essay, to explore the Protestant ethic, for his basic purpose is to investigate "the influence of certain religious ideas on the development of an economic spirit, or the *ethos* of an economic system" (27) – in this instance modern capitalism. Frank Parkin suggests that there is both a weak and strong thesis regarding this relationship within Weber's study. The weak thesis is that there is simply a degree of congruence between the Protestant ethic and the spirit of capitalism, whereas the strong thesis implies a direct causal link between the ethic and the capitalist mentality (1982: 43). The title of the essay – "The Religious Foundations of Worldly Asceticism" – and the general trend of Weber's thought would suggest that the latter thesis was more fundamental.

A concept that Weber suggests was perhaps unique to Protestant communities, being unknown in classical antiquity or among Catholic peoples, was that of "calling" (*Beruf*), the conception of a task for the individual set by god. Weber argues that Luther cannot be linked with the spirit of capitalism, for his own conception of calling was "traditionalistic": He preached "obedience to authority and the acceptance of things as they were" (86). The key notion for Weber therefore was that of predestination, and the starting point of his analysis was not Luther but the works of Calvin, of Calvinism, and of the other Puritan sects. Weber saw Calvinism as the logical culmination of that great historical process in the development of religions, namely the elimination of magic from the world. This process had begun, he suggests, with the old Hebrew prophets, and, in conjunction with Greek scientific thought, the Calvinists had repudiated all magical means to salvation as superstition and sin. Such a doctrine implied the absolute transcendality of god and the inner isolation of the individual (105). For the Calvinist, god alone is free, and with his quite incomprehensible decrees has decided the fate of every individual. Only a few are chosen to receive eternal grace. The consequence of this doctrine, Weber suggests, was "a feeling of unprecedented inner loneliness of the single individual" (104).

The doctrine of predestination could, of course, have led to an attitude of fatalism, of complete resignation to one's worldly situation. But Weber felt that this was not what had happened; rather, the doctrine created a feeling of "religious anxiety." In order to counteract this and to induce a feeling of self-confidence, intense worldly activity was recommended. In practice, Weber writes, "this means that God helps those who help themselves. Thus the Calvinist, as it is sometimes put, himself creates his own salvation, or, as would be more correct, the conviction of it" (115).

This mode of salvation was not mystical or emotional, for the believer was a "tool," not a "vessel," of the deity. Weber suggests also that the Puritan sects gave an ethical interpretation to Cartesian rationalism and that this produced a faith unique in its ascetic tendency. Thus Weber concludes that Calvinism added something positive to the ascetic ideal, "the idea of the necessity of proving one's faith in worldly activity ... By founding its ethic in the doctrine of predestination it substituted for the spiritual aristocracy of monks outside of and above the world the spiritual aristocracy of the predestined saints of God within the world" (121). In their devaluation of sacraments as a means to salvation, in their repudiation of worldly enjoyments, and in their stress on finding salvation through the everyday routines of life, Weber suggests that Methodism, pietism, and the various Baptist sects, in varying degrees, also advocated a "worldly asceticism." As he put it, Christian asceticism slammed the door of the monastery behind it and "strode into the market-place of life" (154).

In the final essay Weber examines the writings of the Puritan divine Richard Baxter and notes that his objection is not to wealth or property per se but rather to the enjoyment of wealth, with the consequences of idleness and the temptations of the flesh. Particularly important was the preaching of the work ethic. "Work hard in your calling" is a recurrent theme, Weber observes, in Baxter's writings. This implied, of course, disapproval of the spontaneous enjoyment of life or of possessions. An inevitable consequence of this limitation on consumption, combined with acquisitive activity, was, Weber argues, the accumulation of capital. Restraints on the consumption of wealth made possible the productive investment of capital. The Puritan outlook therefore favored the development of a rational bourgeois economic life. As a "psychological sanction" it was equally important to sustain the exploitation of the propertyless worker, including a "specific willingness to work." Thus Weber writes, "The treatment of labour as a calling became a characteristic of the modern worker as the corresponding attitude toward acquisition of the business man" (179).

Weber concludes the study by suggesting that the spirit of capitalism was "born," paradoxically, from the spirit of Christian asceticism, but once having established itself, modern capitalism no longer needed the support of religion. It had now become an economic order bound to the conditions of machine production and deeply influencing every aspect of modern life. Material goods had come to have an "inexorable power over the lives of men," and the order had become a kind of "iron cage." Weber viewed the future with some disquiet. If the capitalist system and its development did not come to an end through the rise of new prophetic movements or the depletion of fossilized fuel, then the future was bleak indeed, a "mechanized petrification."

It is important to realize that Weber, in these essays, was not offering an explanation for the rise of capitalism as an economic system or even suggesting that the spirit of capitalism was derived solely from religious sources. As he explicitly stated:

> We have no intention whatever of maintaining such a foolish and doctrinaire thesis as that the spirit of capitalism could only have arisen as the result of certain effects of the Reformation, or even that Capitalism as an economic system is a creation of the Reformation. In itself, the fact that certain forms of capitalist business organization are known to be considerably older than the Reformation is a sufficient refutation of such a claim. (91)

In his *General Economic History* (1923), Weber discussed in some detail the genesis of modern capitalism, and among the necessary preconditions he lists the free market for labor and commodities, rational capital accounting, calculable law, formally free labor, and a rational technology, but the role of religion in the rise of capitalism as an economic institution appears to be seen as minimal. Clearly Weber saw the worldly asceticism of certain Protestant sects as having had an important influence on the development of the capitalist spirit. And he saw the psychological dispositions that this spirit involved – the disciplined, vocational attitude to human activity – as being an important prerequisite for the functioning of modern capitalism. But in no sense is the Protestant ethic the "cause" of capitalism. Yet, as Moore remarks, Protestant religion is important for Weber not only because of its significance at the level of individual motivation but also because it constitutes a "radical cultural break with tradition" (1971: 85). I will return to this issue later in discussing Weber's sociology of religion. (For useful general outlines of Weber's Protestant ethic thesis, see Bendix 1959: 49–69, and Poggi 1983: 40–78.)

Perhaps no work within the social science tradition has generated as much discussion and controversy as Weber's Protestant ethic thesis. Although I cannot review this literature here, some of the main criticisms leveled at Weber's work may be noted.

The most common criticism directed at Weber's thesis is to deny on empirical grounds, any correlation or affinity between Protestantism and capitalism. The suggestion is that capitalism existed prior to and independently of the Protestant ethic in such countries as Italy, France, Spain, and Portugal. Conversely, in countries like Switzerland and Scotland, where ascetic Protestantism flourished, no capitalist development took place. Samuelson concluded his well-known critique by suggesting that "whether we start from the doctrines of Puritanism and 'capitalism' or from the actual concept of a correlation between religion and economic action, we can find no support of Weber's theories. Almost all the evidence contradicts them" (1961: 154). Along similar lines, H. M. Robertson (1933) argued that the development of capitalism in both Holland and England in the sixteenth and seventeenth centuries was due not to its Protestant ethos but to wider economic factors, particularly mercantile trade. More recently both Trevor-Roper (1963) and Luethy (1970) have stressed that in the Reformation period all the bases of the modern world – high technological development, capital, world trade, and global power – were almost exclusively present in countries that were and remained Catholic (Italy, Spain). Thus they emphasize the crucial importance of the Counter/Reformation in the creation of immigrant business communities in the Netherlands.

The problem with all these various critiques by historians of Weber's thesis is that they are in a sense misplaced, for as Tawney (1938) long ago pointed out, in these early essays on the Protestant ethic Weber made no attempt to advance a comprehensive theory of the genesis and development of capitalism. His aim, as I have noted earlier, was more limited. Moreover, Weber's conception of causation is complex and pluralistic, and he specifically disclaimed attempting to provide the "foolish and doctrinaire thesis" that the spirit of capitalism – let alone capitalism itself – was derived from religion. Weber's primary concern in these essays was only with the origins of the modern capitalist mentality. In an important recent discussion of these issues Gordon Marshall concludes,

As Weber is well aware, a huge number of diverse factors are responsible for the precise nature of the modern economic order: it cannot be derived entirely from ascetic Protestantism. In other words, the world view engendered by the Protestant Churches and sects in question can only have the influence on the direction of economic development and change that Weber claims, where the various other preconditions for such change are also present. "The Spirit of Capitalism" will be associated with modern, rational, capitalistic forms of enterprise only where the objective possibility for the development of such enterprises exists. (1982:138)

Thus the fact that Calvinism in Scotland was not associated with any marked capitalistic development of the economy is no refutation of Weber's thesis, for he never claimed that the Protestant ethic was the causal factor in the origin of capitalism (see Eldridge 1972: 40; Marshall 1980).

A second line of criticism focuses on Weber's depiction of the Protestant ethic. Many writers have suggested that Weber did not accurately represent the original teachings of Calvin, that neither Calvin nor Baxter preached a "free for all capitalism" (Samuelson 1961: 31), and that there was no marked difference between Catholic and Calvinist theology with respect to their condemnation of wealth and their stress on the desirability of orderly and disciplined work. Yet as Marshall indicates in defending Weber against these criticisms, these critiques are also in a sense misplaced (1982: 83–8). Weber did not suggest that Calvinist preachers consciously advocated capitalism, but rather that their stress on "calling," coupled with the Puritan ethic (together comprising a worldly asceticism), had the unintentional consequences of capital accumulation. With regard to Robertson's suggestions of a similarity between Catholic and Calvinist doctrines in their tendency to foster a capitalistic spirit by stressing thrift, work, and calling, both Talcott Parsons (1935) and Marshall point out that he does not seriously engage himself in Weber's argument, particularly with respect to the "psychological sanction" that the Calvinist doctrine of predestination entailed.

A final series of criticisms has recently been put forward by Gordon Marshall (1982: 97–131). Although fully recognizing the specific nature of Weber's thesis and suggesting that much of the criticism against it has been "ill-informed," Marshall argues that Weber's thesis is not fully substantiated by empirical evidence and that at times Weber defines Puritanism and the spirit of capitalism almost in terms of each other, thus rendering his argument somewhat tautologous. (For further discussions of the Protestant ethic thesis, see Green 1961, Eisenstadt 1968, and Nelson 1973.)

Weber's sociology of religion

A unifying theme of Weber's sociology is the notion of the progressive rationalization of life as the main directional trend of Western society. Like Marx, Spencer, and Durkheim, Weber was essentially an evolutionary thinker and was preoccupied with the dissolution of "traditional" European culture and society, the rise of modern science and industrial capitalism, and the increasing bureaucratization and political centralization. By "rationalization" Weber implied a process whereby explicit, intellectually calculable rules and procedures are systematized and specified, and increasingly substituted for sentiment and tradition. It also implied a form of normative control, a kind of legitimized power that Weber called "legal-rational authority." Weber defined the latter mode of legitimacy as "resting on a belief in the 'legality' of patterns of normative rules and the right of those elevated to authority under such rules to issue commands" (1947: 328). Weber contrasted this kind of legitimate domination with traditional and charismatic authority. Significantly, however, he saw this form of domination as the result of a gradual process of social development. As Bendix and others have suggested, Weber followed Hegel in having a teleological conception of history. Like Hegel, Weber insisted that nature comprises of cyclical and repetitive events, whereas history is made up of nonrepetitive acts (Bendix 1959: 387). Yet although Weber was preoccupied throughout his career and writings with the development of rationalism in Western culture and indeed saw rationalization as a central historical trend, he was filled with foreboding about its eventual outcome. Rationalization essentially demystified life and implied a purely instrumental relationship toward the natural world and toward people. He therefore, as Bendix notes, saw both reason and freedom as being in jeopardy in the modern world. The modern bureaucracy epitomized this functional rationality. Weber, therefore, like Freud, is, paradoxically, a pessimistic rationalist. The opening words of Herbert Marcuse's *Eros and Civilization* could well be applied to Weber's sociology. Marcuse writes, "The concept of man that emerges from Freudian theory is the most irrefutable indictment of Western civilization – and at the same time the most unshakable defence of this civilization" (1969: 29). Weber was an articulate spokesperson for bourgeois values and interests, and yet at the same time he was a leading critic of industrial capitalism, not blinded, as John Lewis wrote (1975: 88), by either complacency or optimism. Weber nowhere expressed this better than in quoting a phrase of Schiller's. "The fate of our times," Weber remarked, "is characterised by rationalization and intellectualization and, above all, by the 'disenchantment' of the

68

world. Precisely the ultimate and most sublime values have retreated from public life" (Gerth & Mills 1948: 155). Like Nietzsche and Freud, but unlike Durkheim, Weber was, as Hughes cogently expressed it, a "hesitant, self-divided and enormously troubled" individual (1958: 288). "Not summer's bloom lies ahead of us," Weber wrote, "but rather a polar night of icy darkness and hardness" (Gerth & Mills 1948: 128). Not surprisingly, Hughes concluded that although Weber's politics were potentially dangerous, he was, as a diagnostician of contemporary society, "without a peer" (333).

An underlying theme, therefore, of Weber's sociology of religion is the notion of rationalization: the increasing systematization of religious ideas and concepts, the growth of ethical rationalism, and the progressive decline of ritual and "magical" elements in religion.

Weber's writings on the sociology of religion, leaving aside the essays on the Protestant ethic, fall into two categories. First there are the *Collected Essays in the Sociology of Religion* (*Gesammelte Aufsätze zur Religionssoziologie*, 1920–1), which, besides an introductory essay entitled "The Social Psychology of the World Religions" (Gerth & Mills 1948: 268–301), includes Weber's important discussions of the religions of China (Confucianism and Taoism), India (Hinduism and Buddhism), and ancient Palestine (Weber 1951, 1952, 1958). Second, there is an important section, entitled *Religionssoziologie* (*The Sociology of Religion*), of monographic length, that forms a part of Weber's vast systematic treatise *Economy and Society* (*Wirtschaft und Gesellschaft*), which was published posthumously in 1925 (Weber 1965). The two studies cover essentially the same issues. Detailed in scope, and indicating enormous historical erudition, I can outline only some of the more important themes here.

Unlike Durkheim, Weber refused to define religion. Definition of such a complex phenomenon as religion can be attempted, Weber suggests, only at the conclusion of a study. But he implies that a belief in the supernatural is universal and found in all early forms of society. Tribal religion, however, though "relatively rational," Weber considered to be essentially magical and ritualistic and oriented toward this world. "Elementary" forms of religion, he suggests, are focused on mundane, worldly concerns: health, rain making, prosperity. Thus, he writes, "religious or magical behaviour or thinking must not be set apart from the range of everyday purposive conduct, particularly since even the ends of religious and magical acts are predominantly economic" (1965: 1). The distinction, therefore, between natural causation and magic is a modern one that is not applicable to preliterate thought, which implies a different kind of distinction, namely the degree to which objects and persons are endowed with extraordinary powers. Weber used the term *charisma* to refer to such powers. Folk concepts such as "orenda" and "mana" refer to this "natural endowment." Weber suggests, then, that preliterate thought is essentially naturalistic or preanimistic. The oldest of all "vocations," therefore, Weber suggests, is that of the diviner, the magician or shaman who is permanently endowed with "charisma" and who, through the induction of narcotics or other procedures, is able to experience ecstatic states. The concept of the soul, Weber argues, is by no means universal and is denied even by religions of salvation like Buddhism. Rather, ideas such as the soul and spiritual concepts such as gods and demons develop as part of a process whereby "magic is transformed from a direct manipulation of forces into a symbolic activity." Weber therefore saw a "preanimistic naturalism" as being transformed into "mythological thinking," a pattern of thought that is "the basis of the fully developed circle of symbolic concepts." The importance of analogy is stressed in this substantive evolution of culture, which implies a trend toward formalism and toward the conception of the sacred as an unalterable cosmic order. "Analogical thinking originated in the region of magic, which is based completely on analogy, rationalized into symbolism" (1965: 10).

With the development of culture, this implied, as in Roman religion, that each spirit had a specialized function, although Weber did not see any simple relationship between religious concepts and social patterns. It could not be argued, he suggests, that the development of Mother Earth as a goddess simply reflects the development of a matriarchal (matrilineal) clan organization. But he notes that the belief that earth divinities are inferior to celestial personal gods often follows the development of feudalism and that there is a close relationship between ancestral cults and the patriarchal structure of the economy. Like Durkheim, Weber argues that religion acts as a cohesive force unifying members of a household, clan, or tribal confederation. The primary bond of the household or kin group in tribal societies "is the relationship to the spirits of the ancestors" (1965: 10). Likewise the Greek polis (city-state), as well as decentralized patrimonial states and such early theocratic states as Egypt and China were essentially religious or cult associations. In China, for example, the emperor was also the high priest who monopolized the cult of the spirits of nature.

With the development of religion, the primacy of local deities or even of a simple transcendental god becomes crystallized, but this in no way eliminated the ancient magical notions. Instead it produced a dual relationship between humans and the supernatural domain. Thus a dichotomy arises between the shaman/magician and the priest, and between magic and religion. The unity of the primitive image of the world, in which everything was concrete magic, tends to split, Weber writes, "into rational cognition and mastery of nature, on the one hand, and into mystic experiences, on the other" (Gerth & Mills 1948: 282). Whereas magical rites have an essentially manipulative or coercive character, religious development implies an increasing predominance of non-magical motives. Weber uses the terms *magic* and *religion* as ideal types, noting that religion, practically everywhere, contains numerous magical components. Weber considered priests, in contradiction to magicians, to be religious functionaries who have specialized knowledge and vocational qualifications. They are intrinsically linked with a specific cult or association, though Weber acknowledges that a magician may be a member of an organized guild. In contrast to priests, however, the latter are self-employed and exert influence through personal gifts (charisma). But, significantly, Weber sees the priestly function as associated both with the development of religious doctrine as a rational system of religious concepts and with the systematization of a distinctively religious ethic. There is no priesthood without a cult and no cult without metaphysical doctrines and a religious ethic. With respect to this systematization of sacred ordinances, particularly as indicated in the religious systems of India, Egypt, China, and Babylonia, Weber writes,

> The process of rationalization favoured the primacy of universal gods; and every consistent crystallization of a pantheon followed systematic rational principles to some degree, since it was always influenced by professional sacerdotal rationalism or by the rational striving for order on the part of secular individuals. Above all, it is the aforementioned relationship of a rational regularity of the stars in their heavenly courses, as regulated by divine order, to the inviolable sacred social order in terrestrial affairs, that makes the universal gods the responsible guardians of both these phenomena. (1965: 22)

Weber thus saw such rational cosmological systems as intrinsically linked with bureaucratic states and the stability of their social orders. The development of large empires and the need for orderly legislation is seen as parallel to the "increasing scope of a rational comprehension of an eternal, enduring, and orderly cosmos" (1965: 35). Taboos are also seen as the first and the most general instance of harnessing religion to extrareligious purposes – economic and social interests. It is of interest here to note that Weber denied the universality of totemism, suggesting that the derivation of all groups and all religion from totemism was an exaggeration (40).

Weber saw the priesthood as functioning as the "bearer" of the systematization and rationalization of religious culture, particularly of religious ethics. This was in the nature of a developmental process. The prophet is also seen as a key agent in this process, but this rationalization is achieved through a kind of "breakthrough" to a higher, more integrated cultural order. The prophet, for Weber, is the prototypical charismatic leader. The concept of charisma is a fundamental one in Weber's sociology; it is, he writes, a term "applied to a certain quality of an individual personality by virtue of which he is set apart from ordinary men and treated as endowed with supernatural, superhuman, or at least specifically exceptional powers or qualities" (1947: 358). Weber saw charisma exemplified in many different types – the trance dancer, the shaman, heroes, certain intellectuals – as well as the prophet or savior. He linked charisma to a specific form of legitimate domination, noting that it was outside the realm of everyday routine and the profane sphere and "sharply opposed to both rational, and particularly bureaucratic, authority, and to traditional authority, whether in its patriarchial, patrimonial, or any other form" (1947: 361).

The prophet, therefore, was a "purely individual bearer of charisma, who by virtue of his mission proclaims a religious doctrine or divine commandment" (1965: 46). The person may be a reformer or a founder of a new religion. Because the prophet's claim is based on a personal revelation, his or her function, Weber suggests, is quite different from that of a priest, who dispenses salvation by virtue of his office and is a member of a corporate enterprise of salvation. Like the shaman/magician the prophet is endowed with charisma. Unlike the shaman, however, the prophet proclaims a definite revelation and is not remunerated. The distinction between a magician and a prophet, however, Weber felt to be a fluid one, for prophets very often practiced divination as well as magical healing and counseling. Weber suggests that it is likely that all forms of prophecy first arose in connection with the growth of the Asiatic world empires (48) and that prophecy therefore was not characteristic of early tribal societies. He notes also that prophets rarely emerged from the priestly class and that not all ecstatic cults were prophetic movements. He makes the distinction between religious reformers who were not prophets (Sankara, Ramanuja, Luther, Wesley), since they did not offer a substantively new revelation, and true prophets, suggesting that the prophecy of the latter is of two types. The first is the exemplary type of prophecy characteristic of Lao-tzu and the Buddha, in which salvation is a "way" suggested by personal example. This kind of prophecy is associated, Weber implies, with the kind of pantheistic, cosmological religious systems found in China and India. The second is the ethical type of prophecy, exemplified by the prophecy of Zoroaster, Moses, and Muhammad, in which the prophet is perceived as an instrument or messenger of a personal, transcendental, and ethical deity. Weber sees

72

this kind of prophecy as a Near Eastern phenomenon, and he goes on to suggest that the conception of a transcendental creator-spirit may have arisen out of the circumstances of the Near East. The absolute power of the monarchs of Mesopotamia and Egypt, coupled with irrigation agriculture, which did indeed "produce a harvest out of nothing," may have resulted in the notion of a "free-acting, transcendental and personal god" (1965: 57). But, significantly, Weber suggests that the earliest prophecy was "determined decisively" by the pressure put by state systems on less developed neighboring peoples – specifically, of course, the Hebrew peoples of Palestine, caught between these two powerful theocratic states. What is of crucial significance for Weber with regard to prophets, however, is that they provided for their followers a "conception of the world as a cosmos . . . a 'meaningful,' ordered totality" (59). Philosophy therefore emanated, he suggests, from these cosmological schemata of prophets and priests. Weber indeed implies that there is a metaphysical need or "inner compulsion" on the part of the human mind "to understand the world as a meaningful cosmos" (117). But unlike some contemporary anthropologists, Weber is aware of the distinction between these ordered conceptions of the world and our experience of "life in the empirical world," and he recognized the resultant tensions or conflict between them.

Every prophecy, Weber writes, by its very nature devalues the magical elements of the priestly enterprise, and he notes Buddha's scorn for the spirit cults and the attitude of the prophets of Israel toward magicians and soothsayers. He notes, too, the tensions that have everywhere existed between priests and prophets, though the nature of this relationship is variable. Weber expressed the contrast between these two functionaries as follows:

> Prophets systematized religion with a view to simplifying the relationship of man to the world, by reference to an ultimate and integrated value position. On the other hand, priests systematized the content of prophecy or of the sacred traditions by supplying them with a casuistical, rationalistic framework of analysis, and by adopting them to the customs of life and thought of their own class and of the laity which they controlled. (69)

Weber thus saw the personal following of a prophet as inevitably developing, if the cult is to survive, into a religious "community" or congregation. As he put it, "A religious community arises in connection with a prophetic movement as a result of routinization [*Veralltäglichung*], . . . a process whereby either the prophet himself or his disciples secure the permanance of his preaching" (60). Weber therefore saw a complex interrelationship existing not only between priests and prophetic move-

73

ments but also between priests and the laity, whose needs and aspirations, he suggests, have influenced the content of all the world religions.

Weber's underlying concern in his writings on religion is to determine the historical preconditions that have given rise to specific "economic ethics," not only in western Europe but in India, China, and the Near East. Because he did not see an economic ethic as simply a function of the economic organization, in his essay "The Protestant Ethic" he explored, as we have seen, the relationship between ascetic Protestantism and the spirit of capitalism. But Weber felt that Western capitalism was a unique phenomenon, and he was concerned, therefore, to examine the economic ethic implied by the value systems of Confucianism, Hinduism, Buddhism, Islam – to see if, and to what extent, their religious ethics were conducive to capitalist development. In his studies of comparative religion Weber thus sought to indicate the manner in which the belief systems of the oriental religions acted as impediments to the growth of a "rational" economic outlook. As Wrong indicated, Weber was convinced that Christianity contained within itself the latent dynamism of the prophetic tradition of the Hebrews, a dynamism that was lacking in the religions of China and India. It is not surprising, therefore, that Weber's main concern in his sociology of religion is to indicate the social psychology of the world religions, their economic ethic, and to explore the interrelationship between religious culture and the economic interests of specific social groups. The way in which he related religious beliefs to the class or status position of believers has in fact led some writers to describe Weber as a crude materialist (Parkin 1982: 52–3).

As we have seen, Weber considered the religion of tribal communities to be essentially concerned with practical matters, and as primarily magical and this-worldly. The "sacred values" of preliterate people, he suggested, were the "solid goods of this world": health, long life, and wealth. He saw the folk religion of peasants as having a similar orientation. The lot of the peasants, Weber wrote, is so strongly tied to nature, so dependent on organic processes and natural events, that they have always "been inclined towards magic." They have been little oriented to the rational systematization of religion. "Only tremendous transformations of life-orientation have succeeded in tearing them away from this universal and primeval form of religiosity" (Gerth & Mills 1948: 283). Enslavement or proletarization is linked by Weber to the prophetic movements that "break" this traditional order. And he suggests that the more agrarian the cultural pattern, the more likely that the peasant population will follow a "traditional" pattern and lack "ethical rationalism"; they remain involved in animism and ritual magic. Weber ques-

74

tions the popular notion of "peasant piety," suggesting that this idea stems from the romantic pastoral ideas of an urban literati.

On the other hand Weber suggests that the feudal nobility, the land-owning military aristocracy, had a general aversion to ethical or emotional religiosity. He writes, "Concepts like sin, salvation, and religious humility have not only seeemed remote from all elite political classes, particularly the warrior nobles, but have indeed appeared reprehensible to its sense of honour" (1965: 85). Although prophetic religion is not incompatible with a warrior aristocracy, on the whole they have tended to exhibit a "thoroughly negative attitude toward salvation and congregational religion" (88). Thus neither the lords nor the peasants, under stable conditions, have a desire for salvation, and there is little tendency among these groups to develop a systematic theodicy. The distinctive attitude of a bureaucratic class toward religion also indicates a lack of feeling for salvation or for any transcendental anchorage for ethics. Confucianism, the religion of the Chinese literati, is an important example of this attitude. It expressed a hostility to all forms of ecstatic or emotional religion that went "beyond the traditional belief in spirits, and the maintenance of the ancestral cult and of filial piety as the universal basis for social subordination" (90). Merchant nobles of the medieval period also expressed in their religion a this-worldly orientation lacking any inclination for prophetic or ethical religion.

In contrast to these social strata, artisan classes throughout history, Weber suggests, have exhibited a variety of religious attitudes. These include religions of the sacramental and orgiastic types in the ancient cities and in India; animism and Taoist magic in China; orgiastic dervish religion and contemplative Sufism in Islam; and the enthusiastic and congregational religion of early Christianity. Like Kautsky, Weber argued that ancient Christianity was essentially a religion of urban artisans, its savior Jesus being a semirural artisan and its earliest communities centered in urban settings. From this Weber argues that there is no absolute determinism of religion by economic factors among artisans, but he does suggest that the lower middle class has a tendency toward a rational, ethical religion of the congregational type.

Although the modern proletariat, Weber suggests, are indifferent to or even reject religion, he does strongly indicate that the need for salvation has as its main foci the disprivileged classes. The charisma of the prophet is not confined to the membership of any particular class, but the prophet's doctrine derives essentially from the intellectual horizon of the depressed classes. Weber writes, "As a rule . . . , the oppressed, or at least those threatened by distress, were in need of a redeemer and

75

prophet: the fortunate, the propertied, the ruling strata were not in such need. Therefore, in the great majority of cases, a prophetically announced religion of redemption has had its permanent locus among the less-favoured social strata" (Gerth & Mills 1948: 274).

In his well-known study of cargo cults in Melanesia, Peter Worsley makes some important criticisms of Weber's concept of charisma, noting that it is a datum rather than an explanatory concept (1957: 294), but Worsley's central thesis, namely that millennialism is best understood as a social response to deprivation and oppression, largely accords with Weber's own theory. As Weber wrote, "Since every need for salvation is an expression of some distress, social and economic oppression is an effective source of salvation beliefs," adding, in typical Weberian fashion, the qualification "though by no means the exclusive source." But, significantly, Weber continues, "Other things being equal, classes with high social and economic privilege will scarcely be prone to evolve the idea of salvation. Rather they assign to religion the primary function of legitimizing their own life pattern and situation in the world" (1965: 107).

What the privileged classes require of religion, Weber concludes, if anything at all, is this psychological reassurance of legitimacy. Always trying to encompass the complexity of social life, Weber is hesitant to suggest any direct and simple relationship between religion and economic interests. Yet Parsons's suggestion in his introduction to Weber's work (1965) that Weber is mainly concerned to show that prophetic movements are not movements of economic protest on the part of non-privileged classes is somewhat misleading. The tenor of Weber's discussion suggests otherwise. The lower the social class, he wrote, the more radical are the forms assumed by the need for a savior (102).

In his discussion of both prophetic movements and the development of intellectualism by the priesthood, Weber notes two phenomena of interest. One is the "great receptivity of women to all religious prophecy except that which is exclusively military or political in orientation" (104). Weber notes the tendency among ecstatic cults of the disprivileged classes for women to be accorded equal status and to be the primary devotees of such cults. The other is to suggest that beneath the official doctrines of the world religions, with their intellectual conceptions of an "impersonal and ethical cosmic order" or an "absolutely transcendent god," there developed a "religion of the masses." Thus alongside the Confucian class ethic of the bureaucracy and literati, Taoist magic and animism survived; alongside the Buddhist salvation ethic of the monastic groups the magic and spirit cults of the laity continued to function; finally, "Islam and Catholicism were compelled to accept local, functional, and occupational gods as saints, the veneration of which constituted the real religion of the masses in everyday life" (104).

A strong psychologistic tendency pervades Weber's work. He speaks of the psychological "need" of the ruling classes to legitimize their power and economic status, and he likewise postulates a "drive" towards meaning. But any conception of a meaningful cosmic order must, Weber suggested, come to terms with the world's imperfections. Some explanation for the suffering and injustice that are evident in the world is needed, particularly since with increasing rationalization the interpretation of meaning became, Weber implied, more problematic. The problem of theodicy, as Weber called it, had been resolved by the world religions in three distinct ways, he suggests, leaving aside the messianic eschatologies associated with prophetic movements.

The first solution is the notion of *predestination*, or providence, which Weber saw typified in the story of Job and which he considered was a consistent rationalization of divinatory magic. Such a theodicy is linked with a transcendental conception of a god who has unlimited power over his creation and whose motives are in principle inaccessible to human understanding. As we have seen, Calvinism, and to some extent Islam, represent this kind of solution to the problem of meaning.

The second solution is *dualism*, a theodicy that contrasts god's goodness and purity with its antithesis, the powers of darkness and evil, personified as the Demiurge. This theodicy is expressed by Zoroastrianism, Manichaeism, and gnosticism.

The final and the most complete formal solution to the problem of theodicy Weber saw expressed in the Indian doctrine of *karma*. This is the notion of the world as a self-contained cosmos in which the fate of the human soul depends on a system of ethical merit or demerit. It is a "universal mechanism of retribution," Weber writes, which supplants natural causality. The belief in the transmigration of souls also incorporates animistic beliefs and represents a "radical" solution to the theodicy of suffering. The doctrine of karma is central to both Hinduism and Buddhism and is associated with a nondualistic, immanent conception of divinity.

Weber is aware that the paths to salvation are many and various – through ritual, piety, and ecstasy – and he notes too that not all religions are concerned with salvation (tribal cults and Confucianism, for example). Yet his main concern is to stress the distinction between two primary forms of salvation, which he terms "inner-worldly asceticism" and "contemplative mysticism." The distinction is closely related to his earlier contrast between ethical and exemplary prophecy. The wordly ascetic, for Weber, is a "rationalist" whose opposition to the world takes the form of "rejection" rather than of "flight." Although enjoyment of sensual experience and worldly wealth is deplored, for the ascetic this does not imply inactivity or disengagement from the world. To the contrary, it implies "struggle" and "control" over the world, the ascetic being the "instrument" of god's will. As expected, examples of this type of salvation were to be seen, Weber observes, among the various ascetic Protestant sects discussed in *The Protestant Ethic*. On the other hand, the mystic, exemplified again by Lao-tzu and the Buddha, is considered by Weber to be engaged in a contemplative "flight" from the world, stressing inactivity, cessation of thought, and a "mystical union" with the divine, or a psychological state of nonattachment. The mystic desires to be a "vessel" of god, not an "instrument," and to minimize his or her activity within the world. Weber contrasts the two types of salvation in the following passage, though again he stresses that the distinction between asceticism and mysticism is a "fluid" one:

> Neither asceticism nor contemplation affirms the world as such. The ascetic rejects the world's empirical character of creatureliness and ethical temptations to sensual indulgence, to epicurean satisfaction and to reliance upon natural joys and gifts. But at the same time he affirms individual rational activity within the institutional framework of the world . . . On the the other hand, the contemplative mystic living within the world regards action, particularly action performed within the world's institutional framework, as in its very nature a temptation against which he must maintain his state of grace. (1965: 173–4)

Thus the typical mystic is not a person actively involved in any rational transformation of the mundane world, although, as Weber stresses, he or she would be unable to stay alive if the world were not constantly engaged in that very labor that the mystic brands as sinful and as alienating from god or liberation. Weber emphasizes that the concept of a transcendental god, which he believes arose in Asia Minor and was later imposed upon the Occident, was important in undermining the mystical form of salvation and made the mystical union with god impermissible or possibly blasphemous. Not surprisingly, the Catholic church and orthodox Islam (and Confucianism in China), as well as the Hebrew prophets have consistently denounced ecstatic forms of religion. On the other hand Weber remarks on the association between contemplative mysticism and the Asiatic religions and stresses the importance of labor as the distinctive mark of Christian monasticism. Thus only in the European context did inner-worldly asceticism develop. This kind of religion, he argued, demanded not celibacy but the avoidance of erotic pleasure; not poverty but the elimination of all idle enjoyment from worldly income;

not the life of the cloister but a controlled pattern of life. Only in the ascetic Protestant sects did this kind of religious ethic flourish, and its consequences Weber considered crucial in the development of the spirit of capitalism.

Comparative studies

Although MacRae considers Weber's treatise *The Sociology of Religion*, which I have just summarized, a "very barren text" (1974: 90), in my view it is a wide-ranging survey full of seminal ideas. Talcott Parsons's suggestion in his introduction to the work that it is "the most important single segment of [Weber's] work" is not an exaggeration, for it crystallizes many of the themes and issues that Weber had earlier broached in his comparative studies. Weber, as Bendix and others have noted, was centrally concerned in his comparative work with a number of aims: to delineate the economic ethic and secular implications of the world's major religious beliefs; to determine the factors relevant for understanding the distinctive character of Western industrial capitalism; and to explore the relationship between religious ideas and specific interest groups or classes. With regard to the latter concern, Weber, as we have noted, examined the implications of a particular pattern of life (*habitus* is Weber's main term for this) in determining the style of its associated religion. Unlike Durkheim, therefore, Weber conceived of society not as an organic totality but as an arena of conflicting interest groups or strata. Unlike Marx and Engels, however, his emphasis is not on economic class per se but on status groups (*Stand*). He defines the status group, in contradiction to class, as consisting of a group of individuals who share a common culture or "style of life," an occupation or mode of living, and a specific prestige ranking. In his comparative studies of religion the status groups that are of particular interest to Weber are those that he describes as the "primary carriers" or propagators of the world religions. In Confucianism it is the "world-organizing bureaucrat; in Hinduism the world-ordering magician; in Buddhism, the mendicant monk wandering through the world; in Islam, the warrior seeking to conquer the world; in Judaism, the wandering trader; and in Christianity, the itinerant journeyman" (1965: 132). The influence of these various groups Weber did not consider an exclusive one, and he notes that the dominant strata may change through the course of history, but nonetheless it is these specific groups that, as "ideological carriers," have most strongly influenced the practical ethic of their respective religions.

In his study *The Religion of China* (1951) Weber therefore puts a central focus on the Chinese literati, administrative officials who formed a bureaucratic class. Educated and selected by formal examination, proficient in ritualism but in no sense functioning as priests, these officials were the carriers of the Confucian religion. Not themselves engaged in economic activity, they placed an important stress on filial piety, propriety, learning, and a peculiar form of rationalism that sought to "maintain the order of Heaven, the tranquility of the social order and the inner harmony of man through an ethic of human conduct" (Bendix 1959: 123). Weber stresses that the Confucian religious ethic was essentially this-worldly, rational, pacifist in nature, and lacking in any salvation doctrine. Although there was a religious cult focused on the state emperor, who acted both as a political ruler and as the high priest of the realm, Weber stresses that there was neither a powerful priesthood nor any degree of local political autonomy. What was important at the local level were the ancestral cults, and the popular religion centered on Taoist mysticism and various forms of magical rites and beliefs. Taoism, which represented a kind of official heterodoxy, Weber believed, was even more traditionalist than Confucianism, because of its nonliterate and irrational character. Weber concludes his study of Chinese religion by contrasting Confucianism with Puritanism, suggesting that the former, in favoring adjustment to the world and in stressing familial relationships and piety, was a factor hindering the development of a rational capitalistic spirit. Thus, as Bendix lucidly expresses it, Weber indicated a paradox: Confucianism stressed material well-being, but because of its religious ethic it did not generate an appropriate economic ethic that favored capitalist development; Puritanism, though rejecting the pursuit of wealth as an end, unintentionally helped to create the capitalist mentality and thus to jeopardize true religion, as Wesley pointed out (Bendix 1959: 139).

In contrast, Weber's *Religion of India* (1958) puts the focus on a different kind of intellectual, the Brahmin priest. In many ways the Brahmin was similar to the Chinese mandarin or official. Both claimed high rank and stressed the importance of the classical literature, particularly that relating to the sacred rites and the sacred texts. Both were intellectual officials and landowners who stood close to the center of state power, and both, as Weber put it, "rejected all types of orgiasticism" (1958: 139), such as those expressed by the devotional and ecstatic cults associated with the lower classes. But Weber stresses that the Brahmins were a hereditary caste who monopolized the priestly function – no Indian king or ruler ever performed the functions of a priest – and there thus emerged within the Indian context a bifurcation of authority. The Brahmins, who served as family priests for the kings and political rulers and who officiated at communal sacrifices, were considered of higher social rank than the secular authorities. Throughout Indian history, therefore, Weber argues, there had been protracted conflicts between the priestly caste and the secular rulers, who were largely drawn from the Kshatriya caste. The famous epic *Bhagavad Gita*, Weber suggests, largely depicts the ideals and aspirations of the Kshatriya caste and the notion of duty (dharma) to one's caste function.

In a detailed historical study of Indian culture, Weber sets Brahmanic ritualism within the wider context of the Indian caste system and Hinduism. He outlines the social structure of India, noting that the social and ritual demarcation of the castes was largely based on magical beliefs and that the spread of Hinduism not only involved the incorporation of tribal communities into the caste system through conquest, but that changes in rank status were also related to the process of Hinduization, a theme later developed by Srinivas (1952) with his concept of Sanskritization. Weber also explores the implication of the karma theodicy in inhibiting the development of a universal ethical system and in upholding the social inequalities that were intrinsic to the social structure. Later in the study he explores the social implications of the Jain order and early Buddhism, noting that these religions both emerged at a time of urban development and that they both involved the development of a monastic form of religion that implied an apolitical orientation and a detachment from everyday life. After an initial period when, under the sponsorship of Asoka (in the third century B.C.), Buddhism had become the dominant religion in India, the Brahmin caste eventually reasserted its hegemonic position as priests. This inevitably meant, Weber suggests, coming to terms with the religious interests of the laity. In this "accommodation process" and in the restoration of Brahmanical orthodoxy, which Weber discusses in terms of wider sociocultural changes, various forms of religiosity developed in India, reflected in Shaivaism and the lingam cult, in Tantric magic, and in the various bhakti cults that developed during the medieval period. Weber also discusses the ascetic emphasis in Hinduism and the duality between the idea of a personal god (expressed by the devotional cults) and the concept of an impersonal divine being (Brahman) suggested by the writings of the South Indian Brahman philosopher Sankara. In the concluding chapter to the study, Weber suggests that the religious and institutional development of India precluded any development of a rational economic ethic. As with other Asiatic religions – Confucianism and Buddhism – a rational, practical ethic did not emerge from Hinduism, which, Weber suggests, as a closed form of organismic sacred teaching, was essentially traditionalistic. The caste system and the doctrine of karma implied an indifference to the world and a "search for mystic, timeless salvation of the soul." Such salvation was invariably of the exemplary kind. No inner-worldly asceticism emerged within the Asiatic context, no messianic prophecy that would transform the social order. The latter, Weber argues, appeared only in the Near East, and it had profound consequences.

Weber's study *Ancient Judaism* (1952) is devoted to exploring the "highly particular" historical conditions that gave rise to the "ascetic activism" that was unique to occidental religion and that, as we have seen, Weber saw as a decisive factor in the development of the capitalist spirit. The fundamental distinctiveness in the religious orientation of the Occident – worldly asceticism – Weber suggests, originally stemmed from ancient Jewish prophecy. Although the "wandering trader" is suggested by Weber as the "ideological carrier" of Judaism, Weber's central interest in this study is the Hebrew prophets and their messianic visions.

Ancient Judaism originated in the plains and mountains of Syria and Palestine, whose peoples, the Israelite tribes, formed a loose political confederacy. Alternately coming under the political dominance and oppression of the adjoining theocratic states of Egypt and Babylon, the Israelite tribes had no permanent political institutions until their unification as a centralized state under David and Solomon, around 970 B.C. Shortly after this their own theocratic state, allegedly modeled on that of Egypt, fell apart, largely due to a rebellion of the northern tribes. Although the prophet Moses had initially articulated the ancient covenant of the Jewish peoples with god at the time of the tribal confederacy, the main prophetic tradition was established in the four-hundred or so years after the division of the monarchy into the kingdoms of Israel and Judah. During this period these tribal peoples experienced a series of political and military catastrophes, culminating in the Babylonian captivity and their subsequent dispersion. It was during this time that the prophets Elijah, Amos, Isaiah, and Jeremiah emerged and coherently expressed, through their prophecies, a fundamentally new conception of mankind's relationship with deity.

Weber argued that the idea of a transcendental, omnipotent god, who had created the world out of nothing and who was the supramundane ruler of the changing destinies of nations, was fundamentally distinctive: It separated ancient Judaism from the earlier oriental religions, with their conception of an immanent deity. The world, as he wrote, was conceived by the Jewish prophets "as neither eternal nor unchangeable, but rather as having been created. Its present structures were a product of man's activities, above all those of the Jews, and of God's reaction to them. Hence the world was a historical product designed to give way again to the truly God-ordained order" (1952: 3). In this conception, as Bendix writes, mankind is seen merely as an instrument in the hands of god, and human actions as the means by which god accomplishes his designs (1959: 201). One can recognize here the similarity between this conception and that of Hegel's philosophy, which also views humanity as the medium whereby spirit comes to fulfil its own nature. But intrinsic to the prophetic tradition is the notion that god (Yahweh) had made a covenant with the Children of Israel through the prophet Moses. Weber suggests that this conception of deity took primacy during times of stress but that at other times the Israelite tribes were involved in the cult practices of Baal and of the spirits worshiped by neighboring communities. The prophetic visions expressed the values of the earlier tribal confederacy, but they also projected a utopian vision of the future, envisioning the salvation of the Israelites and their restoration to their homeland. Weber stressed that although the prophets were lonely men whose ecstatic experiences were often preceded by pathological states, their prophetic ecstasy had a distinctive character. There was no use of alcohol nor any evidence of fasting or ascetic practices. The prophets did not engage in any cult activities, nor was there any notion of possession by the deity. The transcendental nature of Yahweh precluded any idea of mystical union with the divine, and the prophets therefore looked upon themselves as simply the instruments or messengers of god. Moreover, though they served as oracles, their prophecy was essentially ethical and political. Their visions, Weber argues, gave ethical meaning and religious significance to the various calamities and misfortunes that confronted the Jewish peoples. For such prophets the visionary experiences were not, as with mystics, seen as significant experiences in themselves but rather as signs of god's power and as a form of communication to his people. Within the Hebrew context, therefore, ecstasy took three forms: that associated with the theocratic ruler (Saul and David); that associated with ecstatic cults, which the priests denounced; and that associated with the prophets. For Weber it was this third form of ecstasy that was historically important, for it laid the basis of inner-worldly asceticism, a religious attitude that sought to transform and control the world. As Bendix put it, "Vigilant in the effort to do what was right in the eyes of the Lord in the hope of a better future, the prophets established a religion of faith that subjected man's daily life to the imperatives of a divinely ordained moral law. In this way ancient Judaism helped create the moral rationalism of Western civilization" (1959: 256).

But Weber stresses that Judaism lacked the distinctive hallmark of inner-worldly asceticism, namely an integrated relationship with the world from the point of view of the individual's need for salvation, a relationship that involved the need to control the world (1965: 257). With regard to Islam, a late product of Near Eastern monotheism, Weber suggested that it "accommodated" itself to the world in a unique way, becoming the religion of a warrior class. There was nothing in ancient and orthodox Islam like an individual quest for salvation, nor was there any mysticism. The development later of the dervish mode of religiosity, with its orgiastic and mystical elements, only served to emphasize the traditionalistic ethic and was very different from the "methodical control of life" found among the Puritans.

Thus Weber concludes that for the popular religions of Asia, in contrast to ascetic Protestantism,

> the world remained a great enchanted garden, in which the practical way to orient oneself, or to find security in this world or the next, was to revere or coerce the spirits and seek salvation through ritualistic, idolatrous, or sacramental procedures. No path led from the magical religiosity of the non-intellectual classes of Asia to a rational, methodical control of life. Nor did any path lead to that methodical control from the world accommodation of Confucianism, from the world-rejection of Buddhism, from the world-conquest of Islam, or from the messianic expectations . . . of Judaism. (1965: 270)

(For a lucid summary of Weber's writings on comparative religion, see Bendix 1959: 83–281.)

Weber's comparative studies are rich in empirical detail and full of suggestive insights. They indicate a number of distinct approaches to the understanding of religion, and within the corpus of his work one finds hermeneutic, materialist, functional, and psychologistic interpretations. Although his use of ideal-type analysis implied, as Parsons suggested, a certain "typological rigidity" and "trait atomism," Weber's sense of historical change and his view that social beliefs could be understood only by a consideration of a multiplicity of causal factors prevent his work from being unduly mechanistic or static. Indeed Parsons's own style of functionalism is a good deal more rigid and static, and, as I have mentioned, his attempt to claim Weber as a precursor of structural functionalism is achieved only at the expense of ignoring Weber's historicism. Above all else, Weber was a historical sociologist. Moreover, Weber tended always to qualify the dichotomies that he postulated, suggesting that the distinctions were "fluid" or not absolute. Like Marx's, Weber's specific analyses of social phenomena are also a good deal more complex and subtle than his programmatic statements imply. Parsons's other criticism, namely that Weber's stress on "prophetic breaks" tended to lead him to neglect the possibility of more gradual and cumulative processes of change, is perhaps valid, but it is important to note that the increasing rationalization of social life is seen by Weber as the dominant world-historical trend. Both Parsons and Sorokin (1927) are, I think, substantially correct in suggesting that Weber's *Sociology of Religion* represents one of the most valuable contributions to the understanding of religion that has appeared this century. In terms of scope and erudition, it has hardly been surpassed.

But the accolades that have been accorded Weber's writings have tended all too easily to gloss over the shaky foundations of his general theory, based as this is on three ideal-type descriptive concepts that are vague and intangible. Indeed Weber's whole sociology is largely spun around three concepts: tradition, charisma, and rationality. All Weber's methodological concepts are related, directly or indirectly, to this tripartite conceptual schema: his three modes of legitimate authority, his three types of religious specialist (magician, prophet, priest), his three basic types of social action. They are evidently akin to Tylor's and Malinowski's three modes of thought: magic, religion, and science.

Tradition is a kind of foundational or primal category that Weber identifies, in his discussion of religious evolution, with a magical, preanimistic stage. There is no evidence at all that such a stage ever existed, for all human communities, as Weber himself acknowledged, have developed notions about spirits or deities. And all religions, as Weber again admits, incorporate "magical" elements in their rites, sacraments, myths, and doctrines. To link tradition to the "sanctity of custom" is also unhelpful, given the fact that all human cultures follow such "traditional" practices. The operations of the U.S. Senate or the New York Stock Exchange are every bit as traditional as any magical rite. Weber also tends to view the systematization of culture through cosmological schemata as indicating increasing rationality, but, again, ethnographic evidence suggests that complex cosmologies are to be found in many preliterate communities (see Lévi-Strauss 1966). All of this would indicate, of course, that one of the serious limitations of Weber's work is his limited understanding of anthropological studies.

Weber seems to suggest that tradition is nonrational, but this too conflicts with his suggestion that magic is "relatively" rational and everyday thinking itself purposive. Weber seems to imply that all visionary experiences or ecstatic states are intrinsically rational, in the sense that they give meaning to social experience. But the concept of *charisma* is somewhat vague, and, as Worsley has argued, has little explanatory significance. It is a descriptive concept and is used by Weber to cover a variety of different meanings. Essentially it refers to the "extraordinary power" of an object and person. But a magician has charisma: The term then becomes virtually equivalent to "magical power." Some have suggested that Weber's concept of charisma is similar to the Durkheimian notion of the sacred (e.g., Aron 1967: 229), but it is important to note that

Weber's concept has a dynamic aspect. Charisma signifies a break with the established order (that is, with both tradition and a rational, bureaucratic order), as well as being an ephemeral or unstable transitional stage. "It is the fate of charisma," Weber wrote, "to recede with the development of permanent institutional structures." Charisma therefore is an unwieldy concept, and whatever its meaning – mana, ecstasy, prophecy – it is something to be explained. If, indeed, one follows the line of Weber's argument, magic (as opposed to everyday activities) is charisma. The distinction, therefore, between ecstasy and prophecy, magic and religion, is based largely on Weber's implicit assumption that complex societies are intrinsically more rational than tribal communities.

Finally, Weber's concept of *rationality* is, as many have suggested, complex. It means many different things. Weber himself distinguishes two distinctive meanings. On the one hand he employs the concept in terms of purposive, or means–end rationality. This implies the explicit definition of goals and the precise calculation of the most effective means to achieve them. Such instrumental rationality is characteristic of bureaucratic administrations. On the other hand he employs the concept of rationality to imply the exercise of reason as such, "the kind of rationalization the systematic thinker performs on the image of the world." In his discussion of religious beliefs reviewed earlier in this chapter, it is this second sense that is inferred (Gerth & Mills 1948: 293; Beetham 1974: 68; Roth & Schluchter 1979).

But what did Weber imply in postulating the increasing rationalization of social life? Clearly many things, some of which I have already touched upon. But with respect to religious evolution, Weber's writings seem to suggest a historical development toward increasing structural differentiation, a process in which economic interests and ideas replace religion, thus implying a decline in ritual and magic. But such a perspective leads Weber to make misleading comparisons between the Judeo-Christian tradition (seen as conducive to ethical rationalism) and other world religions. The organization of life in medieval monasteries is seen by Weber as intrinsically rational, whereas both Confucianism and Islam are considered steeped in traditionalism. With respect to the former, Pitirim Sorokin has written, "I do not see why Confucianism with its evident contempt of supernaturalism and mysticism, its openly agnostic attitude toward the existence of supernatural beings, its extraordinary practical character and, finally, with its systematic and rational theory of the education of man, should be declared more superstitious and less inimical toward magic than Christianity or Judaism" (1927: 695). Sorokin notes that "the traditionalist and the magical" religion of the majority of Japan's population evidently did not hinder at all the very successful development of modern capitalism there. Similarly, Maxime Rodinson has questioned Weber's interpretation of Islam, suggesting that the ideology of the Koran was by no means traditionalist. There is nothing to indicate, he writes, that the Muslim religion prevented the Muslim world from developing along the road to modern capitalism, any more than there is anything to indicate that Christianity directed the western European world along that road. And he suggests that the rationalistic ethic was a "correlative" development, evolving along with the capitalist system – not a precursor (Rodinson 1974: 76–117; cf. B. S. Turner 1974 for an important critique of Weber's interpretation of Islam).

The essential difficulty is that Weber gave the ascetic Protestant sects of the sixteenth and seventeenth centuries a central place in his theory, envisaging them as laying the ideological or psychological foundations for the capitalist ethic – the rational control of nature and the pursuit of profit. Thus he tended to highlight those aspects of the Judeo-Christian tradition that were consonant with the development of worldly asceticism and to play down the mystical, ritualistic, and magical elements of that tradition, and, conversely, to overlook the rational and ethical orientation of non-Western religions.

What is of interest, however, is that in his specific analyses of the world religions, the concepts tradition, charisma, and rationalism do not have prominence. Instead, as we have seen, Weber is more concerned to delineate the relationship between religious beliefs and socioeconomic factors, set within a causal-historical perspective. This, finally, brings us to Weber's relationship to historical materialism, a topic that has given rise to a wealth of discussion.

Weber and Marx

Weber, it is said, worked in an intellectual milieu that was dominated by the social perspectives of two towering personalities, Nietzsche and Marx (MacRae 1974: 52). The influence of Nietzsche is implicit and pervasive but somewhat limited. John Lewis suggests that it was from Nietzsche that Weber derived his elitism (1975; 15), although, as has been said, Nietzsche would never have endorsed Weber's nationalism. Moreover, although they both share social Darwinist tendencies, Weber, in spite of his "methodological individualism" and psychologistic bias, is altogether a more sociological thinker. Nietzsche presented some unsurpassed critiques of religion, but unlike Marx and Weber he never seriously tried to understand it as a social phenomenon. But the importance of Nietzsche for Weber was, I think, twofold. First, in ways similar to the relationship of Feuerbach to Marx, Nietzsche's writings made any substantive critique of religion in terms of its truth value redundant. By the end of the nineteenth century, religion, specifically Christianity, had lost its relevance as an interpretative understanding of the world, and Nietzsche's harsh, aphoristic writings made this clear. What became important, therefore, was to understand religion itself as a sociohistorical phenomenon. Although Weber's interests are more specific than those of Durkheim, he was nonetheless concerned essentially with this issue. Second, Weber was influenced by Nietzsche's stress on resentment (*ressentiment*), the idea that the emphasis on mercy, brotherly love, and morality expressed by the Judeo-Christian tradition was essentially a product of the "repressed" desire for vengeance on the part of the oppressed. In this theodicy of the disprivileged, Weber wrote, "the moralistic quest serves as a device for compensating a conscious or unconscious desire for vengeance (1965: 110). Weber doubted whether such a "simple solution" to the problem of religious ethics, whatever its psychological significance, could be generalized or helpful. But, it is important to note, it led Weber to give special attention to theodicy and to the different forms of ethical "rationalization" whereby different religions interpreted the problem of suffering.

Weber's relationship with Marx is more complex, and it has been the subject of numerous interpretative studies (cf. Lowith 1960; Roth 1971; Gordon Marshall 1982: 140–57). Some have seen the relationship between Marx and Weber as essentially antagonistic and have suggested that Weber's Protestant ethic thesis was intended as an empirical refutation of Marxism. Albert Salomon, indeed, suggested that Weber was engaged in a "long and intense dialogue with the ghost of Marx" (1945: 596). Thus Weber's sociology is seen as countering the economic-determinist theories of Marx with a mode of historical analysis that stresses multiple causation. Others have stressed the affinities between the two scholars, both in their social theory and in their analysis of capitalism. Both are seen as attempting a kind of analysis that avoided the extremes of reductionist empiricism, on the one hand, and subjectivist idealism on the other (Brown 1978: 17). In his well-known essay Karl Lowith argued that both Marx and Weber were philosophical sociologists who were primarily concerned with the problems of human existence and who both offered critical analyses of modern capitalism. In reality, he suggests, their sociological approach "expressed the transformation of Hegel's philosophy of objective spirit into an analysis of human society" (1960: 24). The main difference between them, Lowith notes, is that Marx proposed a therapy, whereas Weber only offered a diagnosis. This difference was reflected in their interpretation of capitalism, for whereas Weber saw the market economy and its associated institutions as the very embodiment of rationality, for Marx capitalism was essentially exploitative. In exploring the similarities and differences between the two scholars, Lowith notes Weber's consistent tendency to see Marxism as a dogmatic kind of theory and to interpret the "materialist conception of history" as implying a vulgar, economistic, monocausal form of analysis. In defending Marxism against such charges, some writers have denied that historical materialism is an economic interpretation of history (e.g., Hobsbawm 1965: 17), and so Weberian sociology and Marxism are seen as essentially complementary. As Lichtheim put it, "The whole of Weber's sociology of religion fits without difficulty into the Marxian scheme" (1961: 385). In his useful essay comparing Marx's and Weber's contrasting interpretations of the genesis of capitalism, Norman Birnbaum suggests that although Weber's concern with the effects of religious ideology on social development may have originated in his polemical encounter with Marxism, Weber built on Marx's work. Eschewing the assumption that there was a simple and mechanical relationship between economic position and ideological values, Weber made explicit what had been implicit in Marx, namely the psychological functions of belief systems (1953: 141).

Although Guenther Roth (1971) has questioned whether the analytical affinities between Marx and Weber were quite as close as such interpretations suggest and implies that the influence of Marx on Weber has been greatly overemphasized, nonetheless most commentators stress that the intellectual milieu in which Weber worked was dominated by Marxist theory. At the end of the nineteenth century, as Lewis suggests, the challenge of Marxism was taken seriously by German scholars, and Weber's friend and colleague Werner Sombart had written a scholarly interpretation of Marx's views on capital, *Modern Capitalism* (1902). Weber's writings therefore indicate a critical awareness of Marx's work, and he often went out of his way to praise Marx's scholarly contributions. Weber described *The Communist Manifesto* as a "scientific achievement of the first order." But although many have noted the close affinity between the two scholars, and Weber's theoretical stance vis-à-vis historical materialism, there are nonetheless fundamental philosophical and political differences between them. These differences are essentially a reflection of the Kantian and Hegelian viewpoints that Weber and Marx respectively adopt, which are, as both Lewis and Marshall suggest, ultimately irreconcilable. Marx's evolutionism and his conception of history as a creative process, his emphasis on human praxis and his refusal, like Hegel, to see fact and value as irreducible opposites, and his claim that social life is ultimately based on material conditions – all these postulates would certainly be contested by Weber. Thus, as Marshall writes, "whatever

89

the substantive similarities that may be identified in their respective empirical and historical analyses, there remains an unbridgeable epistemological gap between the Marxian and Weberian frameworks" (1982: 157).

3

The anthropological tradition

The intellectualists: Müller, Spencer, Tylor, Frazer

About one hundred years ago scholars were preoccupied with questions relating to the origins of religion. They discussed with interest such questions as how people could come to believe in gods and whether there existed any tribes so primitive that they had no religion. Indeed, Sir Samuel Baker, the famous explorer, had suggested in 1866, when addressing the Ethnological Society, that the Nilotic peoples (about whom Evans-Pritchard was later to publish his classic monographs) had no religious beliefs of any kind. He wrote, "Without any exception they are without a belief in a supreme being, neither have they any form of worship or idolatry; nor is the darkness of their minds enlightened by even a ray of superstition" (1867: 231). It was in countering such misconceptions as this that the Victorian anthropologists played such a progressive role in the history of social thought.

The high-level questions about the origins of religion that these Victorian scholars posed and the evolutionary framework within which they set their intellectual problems have long ceased to interest or guide anthropologists; nevertheless, the naturalistic and critical stance they took toward religion has continued to bear fruit. What is of interest is that the men who posed these questions – Tylor, Spencer, and Durkheim, in particular – were not only of the highest intellectual caliber but have had a lasting influence on Western culture, the social sciences especially.

In an important review of the writings of these early anthropologists, Evans-Pritchard (1965) noted, almost askance, that with one or two exceptions the persons whose writings on comparative religion have been most influential were either agnostics or atheists. Influenced by eighteenth-century rationalism, such scholars regarded "primitive" religion as being no more valid than other religions – namely, an illusion. And he writes that these early scholars "sought and found in primitive religions, a weapon which could, they thought, be used with deadly effect

91

against Christianity. If primitive religion could be explained away as an intellectual aberration, as a mirage induced by emotional stress, or by its social function, it even implied that the higher religions could be discredited and disposed of in the same way." And he continues: "Religious belief was to these anthropologists absurd, and so it is to most anthropologists of yesterday and today. But some explanation of these absurdities seemed to be required, and it was offered in psychological or sociological terms" (1965: 15).

With regard to such issues Evans-Pritchard was in an awkward dilemma, being both a believing Catholic and an anthropologist. Although it is perhaps unfair to suggest that the studies of Tylor, Durkheim, and Frazer were motivated purely with the negative intent of undermining Christianity, nevertheless Evans-Pritchard was acutely aware that naturalistic interpretations could only serve to render theistic beliefs untenable. Hence his ambivalence toward anthropology and his insistence that it was a humanistic and not a scientific discipline. Yet the methodology he suggests – "the phenomenological one – a comparative study of beliefs and rites, such as god, sacrament and sacrifice, to determine their meaning and social significance" (17) – and that he followed with success in his own important monographs on the Nuer and Azande has precisely the effect he viewed with alarm, namely of "explaining away" religion, but of explaining it not in terms of "intellectual aberration" or "absurdity" but in terms of social meaning or function. Peter Worsley has rightly indicated and applauded the essentially scientific tenor of Evans-Pritchard's own theoretical pronouncements (1957: 273). Some theologians happily combine theistic and scientific explanations; Evans-Pritchard was too good an anthropologist to do so. But his negative assessment of the motives of these earlier scholars leads to an overly critical assessment of their contribution to social thought.

When theistic perspectives on religion were prevalent, interpretations of alien beliefs could be expressed in theological terms. St. Augustine, for instance, like many missionaries until comparatively recently, could interpret such beliefs by asserting that the gods and spirits of other cultures were devils or demons, powers other than the true god. Their reality was accepted, but it was interpreted in negative terms. Such theological interpretations formed an essential component in the theories of Friedrich Max Müller (1823–1900), who has been described as the most serious contender for the title "father of comparative religion" (Sharpe 1975: 35).

Max Müller, a German by birth and greatly influenced by the German romantic tradition associated with Schiller and Goethe, spent most of his life as a professor at Oxford. A brilliant linguist and a leading Sanskrit scholar, he is justly famous for his translations of the Vedic scriptures (1849–62) and for his editing of the invaluable *Sacred Books of the East*, published in fifty volumes. George Woodcock, in his biography of Gandhi (1972: 22), suggests that the greatest gift that the British gave to India was her own past, as reflected in the translations of the old Sanskrit literature, and for this credit goes largely to scholars like Müller (1972: 22). Besides these translations Müller also wrote several general studies of religion and mythology, his *Introduction to the Science of Religion*, published in 1873 and recently reissued (1978), being an influential text. Müller accepted that a belief in divinity was universal among mankind and, along with language, formed the basis of ethnic identity. Unlike St. Augustine he held that "heathen" religion was not the work of the devil but rather undeveloped conceptions of god. Advocating a comparative approach to religion, even though his own focus was on the Aryan and Semitic "races" (as he put it), Müller argued that there was "truth in all religions, even in the lowest." However imperfect, he wrote, "however childish a religion may be, it always places the human soul in the presence of god; and however imperfect or childish the conception of god may be, it always represents the highest ideal of perfection which the human soul can reach and grasp" (1978: 263). Religion, natural religion, was common to all mankind and formed the substratum of all religion, defined as the "perception of the infinite."

Andrew Lang, among others, has questioned whether this concept of the "infinite" was not altogether too abstract, and quite unlike the conceptions of god held by most people. Nevertheless, Müller took his own abstract god as the basis of all religion and argued against the theories of De Brosses, who, in his work *Le Culte des Dieux Fétiches* (1760) had suggested that fetishism was the earliest form of religion.

Müller argued that such beliefs – "the worship of odds and ends of rubbish" – were corrupt and degraded anthropomorphic forms of a previous higher and more abstract religion. Müller's views, in fact, were taken up in a modified form by later Catholic anthropologists of the *Kulturkreis* school, who came to argue that the earliest forms of religion were monotheistic.

Taking the religion of the Vedic scriptures as the earliest form and as the ideal, Müller sought the origins of religion, and his thesis may be summed up in the following extract, taken from his lectures on the Vedanta philosophy (1889). He wrote,

> We see in the Vedic hymns the first revelation of Deity, the first expressions of surprise and suspicion, the first discovery that behind this visible and perishable world there must be something invisible, eternal or divine. No one who has read the hymns of the Rig-Veda can doubt any longer as to

what was the origin of the earliest Aryan religion and mythology...[The deities'] very names tell us that they were all in the beginning names of the great phenomenon of nature, of fire, water, rain and storm, of sun and moon, of heaven and earth.

This is the essence of Müller's psychological theory of religion. The idea of the divine – the infinite – is derived from sensory experience. Thus we do not have to seek its source in revelation or in some religious instinct or faculty; the first religious conceptions were derived from the personification of natural phenomena.

Owing to devastating criticism by the folklorist Andrew Lang and others, Müller's theory became something of an anachronism even within his own lifetime, and he never came to have the influence that his contemporaries Spencer and Tylor were later to wield (but see Chaudhuri 1974).

Herbert Spencer, from the standpoint of his own period, was an intellectual colossus, and even Darwin considered him his superior. More than any other scholar he typifies the Victorian period, and the philosopher Henry Aitken has aptly described him as the "apostle of evolution." The concept of evolution, of course, did not originate with Darwin, though it was Darwin who first gave the theory of organic evolution its scientific basis, and it was his *Origin of Species* (1859) that ultimately carried the day for evolutionary theory. The main ideas of this theory had long been part of the cultural matrix, and it is quite misleading to think of anthropology as "the child of Darwin" or to assume that Spencer applied Darwinian theory to social life. In fact some of Spencer's key ideas on evolution were published several years before the publication of Darwin's classic study.

Spencer's sociology was simply a part of his "synthetic philosophy," which was an attempt to organize all existing scientific knowledge so as to provide, on a materialistic basis, a descriptive understanding of the entire world – inorganic, organic, and social. His entire philosophy was founded on the basic axiom that evolutionary change consists of a process of increasing differentiation, on the one hand, and increasing integration on the other. As Spencer put it in his well-known essay "Progress: Its Law and Cause," published two years before Darwin's work,

> This law of organic progress is the law of all progress. Whether it be in the development of the earth, in the development of Society, of government, of manufactures, of commerce, of language, literature, science, Art, this same evolution of the simple into the complex, through successive differentiations, holds throughout. From the earliest traceable cosmical changes down to the latest results of civilisation we shall find that the transformation of the homogeneous into the heterogeneous, is that which progress essentially consists. (1966: 154)

94

According to Spencer, therefore, the theory of evolution held true whether the formation of the earth, the evolution of species, or the development of human cultures was being considered. The scope of his theoretical interests, in fact, is quite staggering, and more than most scholars Spencer has suffered from the unacknowledged absorption of his ideas. Ronald Fletcher has noted, for instance, how Teilhard de Chardin has simply appropriated all the main propositions of Spencer, clothed them in mystical garb, and offered them as original thoughts (1971: 327). Worse still, with the undue stress that has been placed on the 1890s as the starting point of modern sociology, emphasizing the work of Pareto, Durkheim, and Weber, Spencer's contribution to social science has been all but denied (see Parsons 1937; Hughes 1958).

Born in Derby in 1820, Spencer came from a nonconformist background. An institutional outsider who rejected all the many honors and titles that were offered him, he was also something of an autodidact, never having attended a university. His interests were narrow, focused mainly on the natural and social sciences to the exclusion of history, literature, and the classics. Described as a "dogmatist of genius," Spencer had an "architectonic instinct" that led him to spend most of his life as a lonely recluse working on his "synthetic philosophy," his grand theory of cosmic evolution. In his important study of Spencer, J. D. Y. Peel suggests that he worked like a *bricoleur*, a "cultural handyman on an enormous scale" (1971: 29). Spencer is reputed to have told Beatrice Webb that he had never been in love and that his only conception of life was an existence devoted to working out his ideas. What he produced in the fields of biology, psychology, sociology, ethics, and education is impressive, and Harry Barnes went so far as to suggest that "his system represents one of the most impressive products of a single human mind since Aristotle" (1948: 82). His sociology and his theory of the "super-organic" is built firmly on his theory of evolution, which, as many have noted, is Lamarckian rather than Darwinian in orientation. Peel sums up the difference between Spencer's and Darwin's theory by suggesting that whereas Darwin's theory accounted for the transformation of each species by the mechanism of natural selection, Spencer's theory attempted to explain the total configuration of nature – physical, organic, and social – as well as its necessary process. Thus in countering Marvin Harris's suggestion that Spencer "biologized history," Peel remarks that he also "historicized biology" (1971: 142–3). Spencer's evolutionary theory reconciled Lamarck with Darwin's theory of organic evolution based on the struggle for existence. As is well known, it was Spencer who coined the phrase "the survival of the fittest," but, paradoxically for Spencer the fittest are those adapted to cooperative social life. But then Spencer's writings are full of paradox, as many have affirmed. Essentially Spencer was a scientific rationalist, and though a strong advocate of laissez-faire individualism he had pronounced antimilitarist and antiimperialist sentiments. (For useful discussions of Spencer's social and political thought, see Barnes 1948, Peel 1971, and Wiltshire 1978.)

In his study *Culture and Society*, Raymond Williams notes that "one of the most important facts about English social thinking in the nineteenth century [is] that there grew up, in opposition to a laissez-faire society, [the] organic conception [of society], stressing interrelation and interdependence" (1958: 146). In citing this quotation Peel asks what we are to make of Spencer, who was both an extreme laissez-faire liberal and the most systematic exponent of the organic analogy (1971: 169). For more than any other scholar, Spencer clearly and systematically advocated the conception of society as an organism. As Wiltshire suggests, the analogy "winds a tortuous thread through Spencer's writings from first to last" (1978: 230) – from 1850 right through to *The Principles of Sociology* (1876). In developing the analogy between society and an organism, Spencer was well aware of its limitations and of the differences. Nonetheless, like Aristotle and Comte before him, Spencer took the analogy seriously, and, along with evolutionism, his organismic conception of society was a fundamental tenet of his sociology. Although there are clear affinities between the work of Comte and Spencer, in that both saw the mutual affinity of order and progress, Spencer is not in any simple sense a positivist. Certainly he argued that the natural and social sciences shared a common logical and methodological foundation, and so thus advocated a "natural science of society," but as an arch-individualist he scathingly attacked the utilitarian theories of Bentham and argued for a scientific morality, a naturalistic theory of ethics that collapsed the duality of fact and value. Spencer may have attempted to fuse together positivism and organicism, but as Martindale long ago noted (1961: 53), there is an inherent tension between them. The most serious flaw, however, in Spencer's sociology is that his functionalism, though combined with rationalist and libertarian politics, tended not so much to have static or conservative overtones but rather to obscure the fact that capitalist relations of production were power relationships: Like contemporary anarcho-capitalists such as Hayek and Rothbard, who follow his teachings, Spencer failed to see the intrinsic connection between the state and capital.

Whether Herbert Spencer was the greatest sociologist of the nineteenth century, as MacRae suggests, may be debatable, but few will deny that his basic ideas and concepts came to permeate the writings of later anthropologists and sociologists, as well as those of modernization the-

96

orists. It is all the more surprising, then, that he barely gets a mention in many important histories of the social sciences (e.g., Sorokin 1927; Lowie 1937; Evans-Pritchard 1981). Neglected indeed!

Spencer devoted a large section of his *Principles of Sociology* (1876) – that "masterpiece of vast erudition and boring irrelevances," as Abraham (1973: 194) described it – to a discussion of religion, and specifically to the religious beliefs of preliterate people. The discussion is somewhat marred by Spencer's assumption of the cultural and intellectual inferiority of preliterate people, but his essential argument is that "primitive" people are rational, and, given the inadequate development of scientific knowledge in their cultures, make inferences that are valid and reasonable. He was aware that the distinction between the supernatural and the natural depended on the idea of orderly causation, and so the distinction may not truly reflect the thought of preliterate people. Nonetheless he sought to explain the genesis of supernatural beliefs. Observing the phenomena of nature, especially those relating to death and dream experiences, the people of prehistory came to conceptualize the notion of duality, the distinction between the body and the soul or spirit. This idea of duality was strengthened by other experiences: temporary insensibility, ecstatic states, reflections in the water, and the like. Thus Spencer came to suggest that the belief in ghosts formed the basis of the earliest supernatural ideas. "The first traceable conception of a supernatural being," he wrote, "is the conception of a ghost" (1876: 281), though this conception may be vague and variable among hunter-gatherer communities. The conception is a rational explanation based on inferences from events and phenomena that would otherwise be inexplicable, the notion of natural explanations only developing in more complex societies. The idea of ghosts developed into that of gods, the ghosts of remote or important ancestors becoming divinities and the offerings placed on their shrines becoming the basis of ritual propitiation. So he concluded that "ancestor worship is the root of every religion" (411) and demonstrated, with reference to a wealth of ethnographic material, that a belief in the spirit of the dead, unlike fetishism, was universal. Moreover, he argues that totemic beliefs are an aberrant form of ancestor worship. But Spencer went beyond this and discussed the distinction between magic and religion, the tendencies to move from polytheism to monotheism with the growth of knowledge, the fact that the earliest rulers were conceived of as divine personages, and, in particular, to the emergence and nature of "ecclesiastical hierarchies" and the various social functions they served. This theory of religion is psychologistic and evolutionary, and because of this – and in spite of the fact that Spencer provided a virtual conspectus for a sociology of religion

97

– Spencer's writings on religion have generally been ignored by students of comparative religion. Nevertheless, as both Evans-Pritchard and Radcliffe-Brown acknowledged, it was Spencer who provided some of the more important concepts of anthropological theory.

Both Müller and Spencer were what Evans-Pritchard has called "armchair scholars." Müller never visited India, and Spencer lived most of his life as an independent scholar, so immersed in his academic studies that he had hardly any intimate friends. In striking contrast, Edward Tylor (1832–1917), who has been described as the founder of social anthropology, traveled to Mexico at the age of twenty-four, a journey that was to stimulate his first anthropological study. On his way to Mexico for health reasons, he met, in a bus in Havana, an enthusiastic archaeologist named Henry Christy, who invited him to join his expedition to Mexico. The trip stimulated Tylor's imagination and interest in prehistory, and the travelogue he wrote describing the trip – *Anahuat* (1861), subtitled *Mexico and the Mexicans: Ancient and Modern* – reflected, in spite of its romanticism, his first attempt at a comparative study of human culture. Subsequently his important study *Primitive Culture* (1871), which is devoted mainly to religion, established Tylor as an anthropologist of the first rank. A Quaker by religion, and deeply anti-Catholic, Tylor came to hold the first recognized university position in anthropology in the English-speaking world, as reader in anthropology at Oxford in 1884. Paul Bohannan, in his introductory anthropology text, is firmly of the opinion that Tylor was a scholar of seminal importance and considers his studies to be the only ones of the period to have stood the test of time (1969: 311–15). Mary Douglas is more circumspect, considering Tylor to be mainly a folklorist, interested only in what "quaint relics can tell us of the past" (1970b: 24). Her sentiments are understandable, but there is more to Tylor than simply an interest in folklore.

Tylor's book *Primitive Culture*, the purpose of which, he suggests, is to discuss the "development of culture," was a typical product of the nineteenth century, and, like Spencer's work, is both evolutionist and intellectualist in orientation. The book contains a wealth of ideas, many of them seminal and of permanent value, which is noteworthy considering the inadequacy of much of his ethnographic data. It is perhaps useful to briefly itemize some of Tylor's central ideas.

First, Tylor defined anthropology as the "science of culture," and writes, "Culture or civilization is that complex whole which includes knowledge, beliefs, arts, morals, laws, customs and other capabilities and habits acquired by man as a member of society." Human culture, he thought, was capable of being investigated on general principles and could be regarded as having evolved through general stages. This is an important departure, for it becomes possible to speak of cultures or the "civilization" of peoples who had been commonly thought to possess neither.

Second, Tylor outlined three broad stages of cultural evolution: the savage, or hunter-gatherer stage; the barbaric, characterized by the domestication of animals and plants; and the civilized, beginning with the art of writing. Literacy, he felt, by enabling history and knowledge to be recorded for the benefit of future generations, "binds together the past and the future in an unbroken chain of intellectual and moral progress."

Tylor's scheme of human cultural evolution, which is by no means as systematic as that of Spencer, was not viewed, it seems, as one of necessary or uninterrupted progress but rather as a pattern of development that the evidence, rather than the imagination, suggested. Although Tylor took data from all over the world out of context and arranged it in a sequential scheme according to a preconceived plan, this approach did seem to make sense of the welter of ethnographic information on other cultures that was then being recorded by travelers and missionaries.

Although evolutionary theory came in for a good deal of criticism by later anthropologists, especially those theories that were founded on the evolution of specific institutions, such as religion, the cultural evolutionists like Spencer and Tylor made a theoretical advance. At a time when many scholars were beginning to divide humanity along "racialist" lines (or even in terms of different subspecies) according to innate capacity, the theory of evolution, as Pocock noted, reestablished the fundamental unity of mankind, for one of Tylor's basic postulates was the principle of the "psychic unity of mankind," the idea that human nature is basically uniform. And as Lienhardt remarks, Tylor, in *Primitive Culture* never lapses into the condescension and sensationalism with regard to "savages" that mar the studies of Darwin and Frazer (1969: 85).

Third, an important aspect of Tylor's evolutionism was the notion of "survivals," which are, as he put it, the "processes, customs, opinions and so forth, which have been carried on by force of habit into a new state of society different from that in which they had their original home, and they thus remain as proofs and examples of an older condition of culture out of which the power has been evolved" (1871: 16). Thus existing survivals – elements of doctrine or ritual in religion – throw light on the history of the past; hence Douglas's assertion that Tylor was in essence a folklorist and not an anthropologist.

Fourth, given Tylor's evolutionist stance, he was concerned to provide a theory concerning the origins of religion, and, like his Victorian counterparts, he sought an answer within the domain of human experience.

99

He thus explicitly viewed religious doctrines and practices as natural phenomena, the outcome of human reason and not supernatural intervention. He begins his inquiry with a definition of religion and suggests, as a minimal definition, the notion that religion is the "belief in spiritual beings." This belief, which he terms *animism*, he sees as underlying all religious systems, and he contrasts it with secular materialism. He would have used the concept "spiritualism," but this term already had specific connotations, being applied to a modern sect, so he had to make do with another term. Many writers on comparative religion, in suggesting that the beginnings of religion lie in animism or in describing the religion of preliterate people as animism, seem to misunderstand Tylor's basic postulate. Animism was the "groundwork" of all religions and had, Tylor suggested, two aspects: a belief in souls and a belief in spirits. How did this notion of a spirit or soul existing independently of material things arise? Tylor gives the following answer:

> It seems as though thinking men, as yet in a low level of culture, were deeply impressed by two groups of biological problems. In the first place, what is it that makes the difference between a living body and a dead one; what causes working, sleep, trance, disease, death? In the second place · what are these human shapes which appear in dreams and visions? Looking at these two groups of phenomena, the ancient savage philosophers probably made their first step by the obvious inference that every man has two things belonging to him, namely a life and a phantom. (Lessa & Vogt 1972: 12)

Tylor then went on to demonstrate that the notion of a human soul or spirit was virtually universal among human cultures. He notes too that there is frequently a linguistic connection between certain ideas – for example, shadow, life, wind, breath – and the religious concepts of soul and spirit, and that in preliterate cultures, animals, plants, and inanimate objects are frequently endowed with "souls." This he saw as a development of the initial "soul" concept. Subsequently this belief developed into the idea of spiritual beings who are believed to explain natural events and phenomena, and polytheism ultimately developed into monotheism, in which the power of the many gods were now ascribed to a single deity – the "animism of civilized man."

Tylor's theory thus assumed that primitive man was a rationalist and a scientific philosopher – that the notion of spirits was not the outcome of irrational thinking; preliterate religious beliefs and practices were not "ridiculous" or a "rubbish heap of miscellaneous folly"; they were essentially consistent and logical, based on rational thinking and empirical knowledge. Although like Spencer he linked "animistic" thought to the feelings many of us experience in childhood (something that Freud and Piaget were both later to explore), Tylor never thought that religion was simply an illusion, as Evans-Pritchard implied. Nor did Tylor fail to distinguish the notion of "spirit" or "soul": He suggested that they were the "two great dogmas" of animism – though this distinction, which Evans-Pritchard sought to argue as fundamental to Hebrew thought, is by no means universal, for the individual soul has been thought of by mystics of many cultures as simply an aspect of god or the world spirit.

Evans-Pritchard's main criticism of Tylor's theory of religion is valid, however, since as an intellectualist interpretation it has the quality of a "just-so story." As Evans-Pritchard said, "The ideas of soul and spirit could have arisen in the way Tylor suggested, but there is no evidence to prove that they did" (1965: 25). Nevertheless, as Robert Lowie intimated (1948: 108), there never has been any rival theory to better it, which is one of the reasons why contemporary students of religion no longer engage in intellectual inquiries into the "origins" of religion.

A final important aspect of Tylor's work was his theory concerning the notion of magic. Like many of his contemporaries, Tylor held that there were three basic ways of looking at the world: that of science, that of magic, and that of religion. Magicians, Tylor claimed, classify things by analogy, through the association of ideas – an empiricist theory derived from Hume, who had suggested that there were three ways in which the mind connects ideas (sensations): by resemblance, contiguity in time and space, and by cause and effect. The procedures of magic, therefore, were eminently rational and scientific, but the magician makes a mistake that the scientist does not make: he or she postulates a causal connection between the things classified also by resemblance and contiguity. A favorite example, cited by Tylor, was the Greek belief that a gold ring will cure jaundice. Thus, for Tylor, magic was an activity similar to science: It was based on genuine observation; it involved a belief in impersonal power (whereas religion was a belief in "personalized" spiritual beings); and it rested on a classificatory knowledge, the first steps in human thought. Magic was thus a "pernicious delusion" – science that did not work. The difference between magic and science is that between an association of phenomena in which the link is subjective and symbolic and an association in which the link is objective and experimentally proven as causal. But the important point is that Tylor saw that magical beliefs have an underlying logic, and, as Burrows suggests, he was the first to take the strangeness out of them and make them intelligible, as the beliefs of people whose mental processes were essentially the same as our own (1966: 249).

101

Moreover, in his discussion of fetishism Tylor realized that the sentiments expressed by the famous hymn "All Things Bright and Beautiful" –

The heathen in his blindness
Bows down to wood and stone

was absurd – that no people worshiped material objects simply as material objects; that animals, plants, and inanimate objects were simply symbols. Thus Tylor initiated a symbolic approach, as well as the intellectualist approach to magico-religious phenomena. The former approach, of course, goes back to Spinoza (1951), the great rationalist philosopher who, although a thoroughgoing pantheist and mystic in many respects, was also a freethinker; he had the temerity to suggest that the Bible should not be interpreted in a literal sense but was simply allegorical. This led to his work being proscribed by the Catholic church and to Spinoza himself being persecuted for most of his life.

Tylor also faced the question as to why members of preliterate cultures seemingly continue to believe in magical beliefs when, to the scientific observer, they seem patently false. He gave several reasons. First, magic appears to work empirically: Rain rituals are often followed by rain, even though it might not come immediately. Second, failure can be attributed to errors in the prescription, ritual, or spell, or to inadequate preparation or observance of taboos. Rites are often repeated to ensure that their effectiveness is not impaired. Third, the magical rite may be counteracted by hostile forces, particularly the machinations of other magicians. And finally, what is accepted as evidence is variable, for there is a flexibility about judgments of success or failure. As Bohannan put it, "One success in six is inadequate for science, but may be sufficient to prove a magical point" (1969: 314).

Many of Tylor's basic "facts" were challenged in later years, and Lowie's *Primitive Religion* gives as succinct a summary of these criticisms as any. Andrew Lang, a talented folklorist and writer, who proclaimed that the question of the "origins" of religion was an "inscrutable mystery" and, unlike most of his contemporaries, was by no means enamored of evolutionary theory, stressed that a conception of "high God" was evident in many tribal communities. There was thus the suggestion of "primitive monotheism," a notion taken up by the Catholic anthropologist Father Wilhelm Schmidt, who, in his study *The Origin and Growth of Religion* (1912) postulated that monotheism was evident among the most "archaic" peoples (the Tasmanians and the Andaman Islanders) and that such beliefs had later become overlaid with polytheistic conceptions. This is a complete reversal of Spencer's theory, in whose evolutionary scheme polytheism preceded monotheism.

Another follower of Tylor, Robert Marett, suggested that the notion of animism was not the most basic religious conception but that the origins of religion were to be found in the idea of an impersonal supernatural force. Marett noted that in many cultures a magico-religious conception of sacred power – orenda among the Iroquois, mana in Melanesia – was evident, and this he considered to exemplify the earlier preanimistic stage of religion. Durkheim, with his notion of "totemic principle," had a similar theory.

The anthropological interest of Lang and Marett had developed out of classical studies; the same is true of James Frazer (1854–1951), who won prizes in Greek and Latin at Glasgow University and wrote an early thesis on Plato's idealism. And it was a reading of Tylor's *Primitive Culture* that turned his interest toward anthropology.

Frazer is an anthropologist whose work is difficult to assess. Ioan Lewis (1971) says that his *Golden Bough* is considered a "monumental exercise in futility," and Mary Douglas (1970b) is scathingly critical of his work and of the "undisguised contempt" for "primitive" peoples he is said to express in his writings. How opinions change. In earlier decades anthropologists lauded Frazer, along with Spencer and Tylor, as one of the founders of social anthropology. Malinowski, in particular, described *The Golden Bough* as the "greatest achievement" of anthropology, praised its style and influence, and commended the fundamental humanism and the extraordinary sympathy and insight with which Frazer had treated the thought and action of preliterate people (Malinowski 1963: 268–92).

Clearly, neither condemnation nor glowing praise helps us to understand Frazer's work, and to criticize him for holding theories and attitudes that later scholarship has found wanting is hardly a fruitful exercise. Sir James Frazer was a first-rate scholar: Industrious, intelligent, and extremely erudite, he spent more than twelve hours every day, for more than sixty years, in academic study. He never had a day of rest, for even when he went on holiday he took his books and notes along with him. He had a personal library of over thirty thousand volumes, and he wrote several encyclopedic works on magic and religion: *Folklore in the Old Testament* (three volumes); *Totemism and Exogamy* (four volumes); and the classic text *The Golden Bough*, which runs to twelve volumes. But though he had a profound knowledge in these fields, his biographer, R. Angus Downie, has drawn attention to his utter simplicity and naïveté in worldly matters.

The Golden Bough on which Frazer's reputation rests, is a vast compendium and an encyclopedic study of magic and religion, and although it is crammed with ethnographic data drawn from innumerable sources, ancient and modern, it is written in a literary and very readable style. Its explicit aim is to explain a strange custom of classical antiquity, namely the ritual murder of the priest of Diana at Nemi, near Rome. In the sacred grove at Nemi, so the legend goes, there was a golden bough, and the priesthood went to the person who could break off the bough and kill the incumbent priest. Frazer set out to interpret in rational terms, and by comparative analysis, the meaning and purpose of this strange, and to him barbaric, custom. The book is a veritable series of intellectual trails and detours along which Frazer wanders, indicating as he goes the widespread occurrence of similar religious beliefs and institutions in different cultures. He never seems to answer the problems he sets himself, but the book is full of good scholarship, and it has had an enormous influence on students of comparative religion. But its theoretical value is limited, for it lacks originality, and most of its central themes are simply an elaboration and popularization of Tylor's theories.

Frazer follows Tylor in seeing a clear conceptional division between magic, science, and religion. Magical thought, he writes, "assumes that in nature one event follows another necessarily and invariably without the intervention of any spiritual and personal agency. Thus its fundamental conception is identical with that of modern science; underlying the whole system is a faith, implicit but real and firm, in the order and uniformity of nature" (1976: 64).

Religion, on the other hand, which he defined as a propitiation and conciliation of powers believed to be superior to man, he thus saw as standing in fundamental opposition to both magic and science. Between the magical and scientific conceptions of the world there was an easy distinction; magic was simply the mistaken application of the association of ideas; "All magic is necessarily false and barren; for were it ever to become true and fruitful, it would no longer be magic but science" (65).

Thus magic is described as the "bastard sister of science," though Frazer accepted that associative logic was a necessary aspect of human knowledge. In fact he systematized Tylor's discussion of magic and described the basic principles underlying magic in terms of two "laws." On the one hand there was homeopathic or imitative magic, based on the law of similarity; on the other, contagious magic, based on the law of contact or contagion. He gives many vivid illustrations of both. He mentions the belief of antiquity that the gaze of a stone curlew would cure jaundice, the virtue of the bird lying not in its plumage but in its golden eye, which naturally, it was thought, drew out the yellow jaundice. This is an example of homeopathic magic. The implicit recognition by Frazer (and in this he followed Tylor) of the logical nature of magical thought, even though marred by a rather negative attitude toward it, was an important legacy that Frazer bequeathed to later anthropologists.

Frazer also followed Tylor in his adoption of evolutionary theory, but the schema he adopted bears little resemblance to Tylor's ideas. Tylor, though he distinguished between magic, science, and religion and held that in contemporary European culture science was becoming the dominant mode of thought, nonetheless implied that all three were present in all human cultures. Frazer, however, placed magic, religion, and science in an evolutionary sequence, and he did this, as Bohannan suggests, in a very revealing way. Magic he held to be logically more primitive than religion: "Obviously," he wrote, "the conception of personal agents is more complex than a simple recognition of the similarity or contiguity of ideas" (71). This schema, he thought, was confirmed by the fact that the Australian aboriginal tribes, who, as hunter-gatherers, were deemed to be the "rudest savages," had no religion – only magic. Needless to say, there is no evidence at all to support Frazer's theory; in fact, as many anthropologists have since demonstrated, the Australian tribal communities have complex religious systems (cf. Berndt 1951, Gould 1969, Stanner 1979). Moreover, Frazer believed that in his own time religion was being superceded by science, a point of view that Spencer also endorsed. This idea has more substance, but it is a difficult one to prove – witness the present resurgence of interest in the occult.

It has been suggested, by Evans-Pritchard and others, that Frazer may have taken over Comte's evolutionary schema, for their theories are superficially similar. Comte had suggested that human thought had passed through three stages of development, the theological stage, the metaphysical stage, and the positive stage. During the first, the *theological* stage, explanations took the form of myths concerning spirits and supernatural beings. Comte discussed three levels of this stage: fetishism, polytheism, and monotheism. The second, or transitional, stage Comte termed *metaphysical*. At this stage humans sought an explanation of the world in terms of "essences" or "ideas," in the manner of the Greek idealist philosophers. And finally there is the *positive* stage, when humans rejected explanations in terms of "gods" and "essences" and sought understanding through observation and experiment (see Giddens 1979: 237–43). There are thus substantial differences between the evolutionary schemata of Comte and Frazer, and Evans-Pritchard is probably correct in suggesting that Frazer merely attempted to systematize Tylor's thoughts. The theory is, as Bohannan remarks, "one of the neatest pieces of sophistry ever penned" (1969: 319). But in spite of the harsh criticisms that have been leveled against Frazer, not all his work, as Evans-Pritchard remarked, was chaff. There was some grain, his typology of magic and his reflections on divine rule being especially noteworthy.

The four major theorists whose work I have briefly reviewed – Müller, Spencer, Tylor, and Frazer – though they postulated different origins of religion shared certain basic assumptions. All viewed human culture in an evolutionary perspective and approached religion with a psychological or empiricist bias. They theorized that the idea of religion sprang from rational inferences based on individual human experiences of oneself or the world. In the decades that followed, this theoretical approach was strongly challenged within the anthropological tradition, most strongly by the French sociologist, Emile Durkheim.

Durkheim's sociology

In the early decades of the present century there was a marked reaction against evolutionary theory on the part of social scientists. Boas and Lowie in America, Malinowski and Radcliffe-Brown in Britain, though by no means repudiating cultural evolutionism en bloc, were nonetheless all critical of the early anthropological theories, especially those that purported to outline the evolution of specific institutions like religion. Radcliffe-Brown, for example, provisionally accepted Spencer's evolutionism but rejected what he called the "pseudo-historical speculations" that had been added to it (1952: 8).

By the 1930s there was a general retreat of evolutionary thought in social science, but, as Robert Bellah noted, nowhere did the retreat go further nor the intensity of the opposition go deeper than in the field of religion. Recently there has been a resurgence of interest in evolutionary theory, exemplified in the writings of Julian Steward, and Bellah, in a now classic article (1964), has attempted to formulate a more sophisticated theory of religious evolution, one that remains firmly in the tradition of Tylor and Spencer. The rejection of evolutionism, however, also involved the repudiation of historical analysis itself in favor of an organic functionalism. This latter mode of sociological analysis is closely associated with Durkheim, although, as Kenneth Thompson has argued, it is misleading to view Durkheim as the founder of an ahistorical, conservative theory of society (1982: 17).

Of all the writers who have proposed sociological explanations of religion, Emile Durkheim is the most renowned; indeed Evans-Pritchard suggested that he was the "greatest figure in the history of modern sociology and the most potent influence on anthropological thought (1965: 53). The writings of Douglas, Turner, Leach, and Lévi-Strauss become intelligible only if set within the anthropological tradition that

Durkheim founded. Certainly he has had a profound influence on the social sciences, and stands with Marx and Freud as a seminal influence on twentieth-century thought. Born in 1858, Durkheim was the son of a Jewish rabbi. At school he experienced a brief crisis of mysticism under the influence of a Catholic schoolteacher, but for most of his life he was a confirmed atheist. Evans-Pritchard feels it necessary to stress that Durkheim was not simply an unbeliever but a militant atheist and propagandist who wished to undermine religion and whose "sociological metaphysic" should be seen in this light (1981: 157). Durkheim is usually looked upon as the heir to Comtean positivism, but Durkheim always spoke of himself as a rationalist and was hostile both to Comte's dogmatic positivism and to the mysticism associated with his contemporary, the philosopher Henri Bergson. In essence Durkheim attempted all his life to establish sociology as an independent scientific discipline based on empirical methods. He was therefore much less involved in the political events of his time than Marx, Weber, or Spencer, and thus his writings are less propagandist and polemical in style (Giddens 1971: 65). He was an austere, dedicated, and dogmatic academic, and, as Hughes suggests, in personal terms Durkheim "does not strike one as a particularly troubled individual" (1958: 288). For most of his life he was a professor of education and social science.

It is not my main purpose here to outline Durkheim's approach to sociological theory, or the foundations of his epistemology. On such issues there are a number of important studies and reviews (Parsons 1937, Lukes 1973, Tiryakian 1978, K. Thompson 1982). But a few general comments may be made on his sociology.

First, Durkheim had an evolutionary approach to social life, but it was expressed at a highly abstract level involving an ideal-type dichotomy between what he termed "mechanical" and "organic" forms of social solidarity. It was an etiolated version of Spencer's theory, profoundly nonhistorical, with a focus on the question of the nature of social cohesion. (But see Wallwork 1984, who suggests that underlying this ideal typology is a six-stage theory of sociocultural change.) The question he asked and that he discussed in his study *The Division of Labour in Society* (1964a) was "What are the bonds which unite men one with another?"

In traditional societies with a low division of labor, the social structure, he maintained, consisted of a "system of homogeneous segments," and integration was achieved by a common value system, the conscience collective, individuals in the society showing identical beliefs and sentiments. In such societies collective norms are maintained by repressive sanctions. In societies with a high division of labor, social groups and institutions are heterogeneous, and solidarity is the outcome not of

107

shared beliefs but of mutual interdependence. In this situation, legal sanctions are restitutive rather than repressive.

With respect to his sociology of religion, two points are worth noting about this formulation that forms the basis of the typology opposing the traditional to the modern that is accepted by many contemporary sociologists and economists. The first point is that the collective representations characteristic of mechanical solidarity – that is, the belief systems of preliterate communities – are seen by Durkheim as essentially religious. The following extract succinctly expresses Durkheim's thoughts on this question:

> But if there is one truth that history teaches us beyond doubt, it is that religion tends to embrace a smaller and smaller portion of social life. Originally it pervades everything; everything social is religious; the two worlds are synonymous. Then, little by little, political economic, scientific functions free themselves from the religious function, constitute themselves apart and take on a more and more acknowledged temporal character. God, who was at first present in all human relations, progressively withdraws from them; he abandons the world to men and their disputes. (1964b: 169)

The multiplex nature of social relations in small-scale societies, discussed by Gluckman and others, is an adequate description of such relationships. But Durkheim's idealist bent is clearly conveyed in this extract, for one could with equal justification argue that "originally" everything was economic. A second point is his assertion that societies based on mechanical solidarity are characterized by repressive sanctions. Durkheim has been severely criticized for this suggestion, for generally speaking the legal systems of preliterate communities aim to restore social relationships rather than administer repressive justice. Interestingly, however, Durkheim's discussion of such issues focuses not on tribal communities but on the early theocratic states. The "luxuriant development of repressive legislation" that he wrote about was the product of literate civilizations, expressed in the Bible, in the laws of Manu, and in other sacerdotal writings.

A second important aspect of Durkheim's sociology is his antipathy toward all theories that attempt to explain social facts by reference to individual or psychological factors. Hence his hostility to Spencer's "methodological individualism," the theory that "all social phenomena should always be understood as resulting from the decisions, actions, attitudes, etc. of human individuals," to use a phrase of Karl Popper's (1969: 98). His rejection of this theory leads Durkheim to stress that social facts are external and constraining to the individual: "We speak a language we did not make; we use instruments we did not invent; we invoke rights that we did not found; a treasury of knowledge is transmitted to each generation that it did not gather itself" (1915: 212).

Durkheim thus viewed the individual and society as a rigid dichotomy and maintained that social facts could be understood only in terms of other social facts. In attempting to establish the "autonomy of sociology" as a discipline, Durkheim, as Steven Lukes, in his admirable study of him remarks, badly overstated his case, as well as virtually severing social life from its natural and economic moorings (1973a: 20). This dichotomy between the individual and society is, as Lukes puts it, the "keystone of Durkheim's entire system of thought" (22). Moreover, like social behaviorists and contemporary structural Marxists, Durkheim conceptualized the individual as an organism. Durkheim's famous definition of the nature of the human subject runs as follows: "Man is double. There are two beings in him: an individual being which has its foundation in the organism... and a social being which represents the highest reality in the intellectual and moral order that we can know by observation – I mean society" (1964b: 16). Like Comte, Durkheim gave little scope for a science of psychology. In an important sense Durkheim retained a "neo-Kantian paradigm" (see Rose 1981: 13–18).

Third, although Durkheim puts a primary emphasis on social facts as phenomena sui generis and, like Weber, is hostile to crude economic determinism, his mode of analysis is essentially materialist. Josep Llobera (1981) has drawn attention to the way in which Durkheim came to deny Marxism's claim to scientificity by focusing on the vulgar interpretations of Marx by certain of his followers. Nevertheless Durkheim's own mode of analysis implies a social-structuralist method that was causal and materialist as well as functional. For Durkheim, social reality consisted of several structural levels. In his review of Antonio Labriola's *Essays on the Materialist Conception of History* (1897), Durkheim wrote,

> We regard as fruitful this idea that social life must be explained, not by the conception of it held by those who participate in it, but by profound causes which escape consciousness; and we also think that these causes must be sought chiefly in the way in which the associated individuals are grouped... For in order that collective *representations* should be intelligible, they must come from something and, since they cannot form a circle closed upon itself, the source whence they derive must be found outside them. Either the *conscience collective* floats in the void, or it is connected with the rest of the world through the intermediary of a substratum on which, in consequence, it depends. (Quoted in Lukes 1973a: 231).

Significantly, however, this substratum does not, for Durkheim, consist of productive relations but of the manner in which people are "disposed

109

upon the earth." It has demographic rather than economic connotations. The "multilayered" model of social reality implied by Durkheim – substratum, institutions, and collective representations – is discussed by Kenneth Thompson (1982: 59–69). Also important in this context is the distinction Durkheim makes between collective representations that have been "crystallized" and "social currents" expressed by ecstatic movements (Durkheim 1938: 4).

Fourth, in arguing against the utilitarian and laissez-faire liberals, who suggested a methodological individualism, and also against the conservative and idealist tradition of social philosophy, Durkheim came to suggest as a fundamental methodological postulate that one should "consider social facts as things" (1938: 14). He advocated a scientific approach that is both empirical and comparative. *The Rules of Sociological Method*, in fact, is something of a manifesto, suggesting two basic forms of explanation: causal analysis and functionalist interpretation. When the explanation of a social phenomenon is undertaken, Durkheim wrote, "we must seek separately the efficient cause which produces it and the function it fulfils" (95). Whereas Hughes has stressed the "unhistorical character" of Durkheim's thought and its positivistic tenor, which the text just quoted implies, Thompson has suggested that Durkheim and his colleagues always set this kind of analysis in a comparative-historical framework (1982: 106–7). Moreover, it is important to stress that Durkheim was not a contemplative materialist or an empiricist, for, as the quotation also suggests he postulated the necessity of going beyond people's ideological preconceptions, as these are reflected in their collective representations. But, above all, Durkheim argued for the necessity of engaging in empirical study: "Social reality cannot be grasped by anyone who refuses to plunge into the detailed empirical investigation of social life" (Giddens 1978: 35). Durkheim's study *"Suicide"* (1897) was intended to be a demonstration of his method. Significantly, it was not published in English until 1951.

Finally, it is worth noting Durkheim's relationship to socialism. Durkheim's sociology has long been characterized as being concerned with order and stability and as being essentially conservative, a part of a counterreaction against the implications of the French Revolution. Emile Benoit-Smullyan remarked that it is a "sociology of a static and monistic type, with no adequate explanation for social change" (1948: 224). The general tenor of Durkheim's work appears to justify such an assessment, although it is worth noting that his concept of "anomie" has a critical aspect, implying that contemporary capitalism is, in a sense pathological. The causes of this Durkheim put down to regimented and meaningless work, class conflict, and an unregulated market economy. Even though his answer to the problem seems to be the state control of the economy and an appeal to justice, Durkheim was by no means an apologist for capitalism. At the end of the nineteenth century, when the forces of reaction were urging a return to Catholicism, royalism, and traditionalism, Durkheim sided with the progressive forces in his advocacy of science, secularism, and democracy. He was, as Hughes suggests, a "true child of the Enlightenment." But he was no Marxist socialist or believer in revolution. "Socialism," in fact, he saw as a social movement, a symptom of the malaise rather than its cure. Essentially Durkheim was a reformist liberal or guild socialist, believing in evolutionary change. He argued that a beneficent state regulating the economy on behalf of the people, and occupational corporations on the lines of the medieval guilds, would be the best safeguards for democracy and for the ideals of the French Revolution – equality, freedom, fraternity. This was the very antithesis of Spencer's advocacy of a free market economy with a minimal state. In noting the affinity of his political views with those of the British socialist R. H. Tawney, Lukes suggests that Durkheim was "in many ways a moralistic conservative and a radical social reformer who would qualify, on most definitions, as a socialist of sorts" (1973a: 546; cf. Gouldner 1973: 369–91).

Elementary Forms of the Religious Life

To understand Durkheim's theory of religion it is perhaps best to consider first two writers from whom Durkheim took many of his fundamental ideas: Fustel de Coulanges and W. Robertson-Smith

Social interpretations of religion have a long history. Aristotle remarked that "men create the gods after their own image," and an old Chinese philosopher suggested that "it is through the sacrifices that the unity of the people is strengthened." Likewise the ancient Chinese Book of Rites (circa third century B.C.) has the sentence "Ceremonies are the bond that hold the multitudes together, and if the bond be removed, those multitudes fall into confusion," indicating that the Chinese aristocracy were aware that rituals served a social function. A more recent example, and perhaps the first really comprehensive sociological treatment of religion, is Fustel de Coulanges's *The Ancient City*, published in 1864.

Fustel de Coulanges (1830–89) was a French historian who insisted that history was a "science of social facts." His classic study *The Ancient City* is concerned with the relationship between religion and social life in classical antiquity. "The history of Greece and Rome," he wrote, "is a witness and an example of the intimate relation which always exists between men's ideas and their social state. Examine the institutions of the ancients without thinking of their religious notions, and you find them obscure . . . , inexplicable" (1900:11–12).

Early ancient society, he argued, was organized around the joint family or patrilineage, and what held this group together as a corporation was the ancestral cult in which the head of the family acted as priest. He then demonstrated that these religious ideas determined the character of the ancient family, the laws of marriage and the forms of kinship, property relations, and all the essential characteristics of ancient society. Then, at a later period of history, the religion of antiquity changed, and another form of belief, based on the deification of nature, emerged. As the religion developed, the social and political structure of ancient society changed too, and the ancient city, rather than the family, became the primary social institution. Evans-Pritchard, surprisingly, summarizes Fustel de Coulanges's theory without comment or criticism. The theory, of course, is a completely idealist interpretation, for Fustel de Coulanges contends that ideas – specifically, religious ideas – are the cause of social changes and the primary factor in social phenomena. The reverse is true. Although Durkheim was a student of Fustel de Coulanges and was profoundly influenced by the historian, nonetheless he rightly criticized Fustel as having mistaken the cause for the effect (1964a: 179). In a sense Durkheim's classic study of religion reverses Fustel de Coulanges's mode of interpretation while retaining most of his key ideas on religion.

In 1869, in the journal *Fortnightly Review*, John McLennan, a Scottish lawyer, who introduced the concepts of endogamy and exogamy into anthropology, published a paper entitled "The Worship of Animals and Plants." In this article he advanced the view that totemism, the worship of animals and plants, was the earliest form of religion and that such a religion was closely associated with an exogamic clan structure. Such ideas form the basic elements of the theory advanced by W. Robertson-Smith (1846–1904) in his study *The Religion of the Semites*, published twenty years after McLennan's paper (1889).

Robertson-Smith was a fellow Scot, and a close friend, of both McLennan and Frazer: It was his friendship with McLennan that stimulated Robertson-Smith to take an interest in kinship and totemism. An intensely orthodox member of the Free Church of Scotland and a Semitic scholar of note, Robertson-Smith had visited North Africa in 1879 and was struck by what seemed to him clear evidence of totemism among the Bedouin Arabs of Sinai; hence the orientation of his studies. In his classic work, Robertson-Smith suggested that the Semitic societies of ancient Arabia consisted of matrilineal clans, each of which had a special relationship to a species of animal, their sacred totem. Between the clan and the animal in question a bond of kinship was envisaged.

For Smith this clan totemism was the earliest form of religion, and it involved the idea that the clan was idealized and deified and was materially represented by the totemic animal. He also argued that the act of sacrifice was the key ritual, involving an attempt to establish communion with the deity. "The fundamental idea of sacrifice," he wrote, "is not that of a sacred tribute, but of communication between the god and his worshipers by joint participation in the flesh and blood of a sacred victim" (345). Sacrifice was deemed to be a sacramental meal in which the clan periodically expressed its unity and solidarity, binding its members to each other and their god. In this, in Evans-Pritchard's view, he led both Durkheim and Freud astray.

Although Robertson-Smith's study is a model of scholarship, it is questionable whether his thesis is supported by the ethnographic evidence. His theory is, of course, an evolutionary one in which he utilizes Tylor's doctrine of "survivals" to adduce evidence for an original totemic stage. As Evans-Pritchard has written, "All one can say of the theory as a whole . . . is that whilst eating the totem animals could have been the earliest form of sacrifice and the origin of religion, there is no evidence that it was" (1965:52). Moreover, though Robertson-Smith thought his theory to be true of preliterate people generally, many, particularly hunter-gatherers, lack any sacrificial rites, and others have sacrifices that are in no sense communal meals. And it is even questionable whether the idea of communion was a feature of the early forms of Hebrew sacrifice. An important aspect of Robertson-Smith's theory was his notion that in primitive religion rituals had primacy over beliefs. From the outset he wrote that "ritual and practical usage were the sum total of ancient religions" (20). His emphasis therefore is on religion in terms of the social group rather than, as with Tylor, on religion as a form of speculative thought. And he interpreted such rituals primarily with respect to their social function in binding people together in the community. As he succinctly put it: "Religion did not exist for the saving of souls but for the preservation and welfare of society." (For interesting studies of Robertson-Smith, particularly of his relationship to Durkheim, see Beidelman 1974 and R. J. Jones 1977.) The classic studies of Fustel de Coulanges and Robertson-Smith provide the essential foundations on which Durkheim built his theory of religion.

Durkheim's classic study *The Elementary Forms of the Religious Life* (1915) has given rise to such a plethora of exegesis and critical commentary and has had such an important influence on later students of comparative religion that it is difficult to approach in anything like an unprejudiced manner. Written toward the end of his life, it is undoubtedly his greatest work, and though many of its themes are not original and its main thesis is highly questionable, it is nonetheless an intellectual study of the first magnitude.

The problem Durkheim set himself in *The Elementary Forms of the Religious Life* was to discern the "ever present causes upon which the most essential forms of religious thought and practices depend" (1964b: 18), and to do this he felt it was necessary to study religion in "its most primitive and simple form," to try to account for its nature by examining its genesis. Thus, like Tylor and Frazer he took an evolutionary perspective and was preoccupied with discerning the origins of religion. And he followed McLennan and Robertson-Smith in believing that totemism was the earliest form of religion. Durkheim was not interested in the epistemological status of religion, the question as to whether religious beliefs were true or false, though it is clear that he himself, as an unbeliever, held no brief for religious explanations. But he was unwilling to believe that so widespread a human institution was based on pure illusion. Like William James, he felt that even the most barbaric and fantastic religious rites and myths must be based on some human need, on some aspect of life, either individual or social. As he put it, in an oft-quoted passage,

> In reality – there are no religions which are false. All are true in their own fashion, all answer, though in different ways, to the given conditions of human existence. So when we turn to primitive religions, it is not with the idea of depreciating religion in general, for these religions are no less respectable then others. They respond to the same needs, they play the same role, they depend upon the same causes; they can also well serve to show the nature of the religious life. (3)

Hence he came to focus his analysis on the religion of the Australian aborigines, the important studies of Baldwin Spencer and F. J. Gillin providing him with detailed and ample ethnographic data.

Durkheim begins his discussion with what Aristotle termed the "categories of understanding," the fundamental concepts that form the basis of all thought – the ideas of space, time, class, and causality. This theme, which Durkheim had touched upon earlier when, with Marcel Mauss, he wrote a short essay on "primitive classification," remains throughout the study a secondary interest, though he does mention that the fundamental categories are the product of social factors. But it is worth noting the two main doctrines concerned with the problem of knowledge that he discusses, for in his criticisms of these Durkheim indicates his own theoretical approach both to the sociology of knowledge and to religion.

Durkheim argues that there are two basic doctrines with regard to the problem of knowledge. On the one hand there are those, such as Kant, who view the categories of thought as prior to experience; they are immanent in the human mind itself and part of what it means to be human. He calls this approach *apriorist*. On the other hand there are those like Locke who see the categories as having been derived from experience, made up of "bits and pieces" with the individual being the "artisan of this construction." Durkheim is dissatisfied with both approaches. The first he considered no explanation at all, whereas the second he felt was essentially individualist and subjective, with a tendency to collapse into irrationalism. His own theory, he thought, united these two conceptions; it was a form of rationalism that was midway between classical empiricism and apriorism. And with respect to the categories of understanding, it suggested that they were neither innate nor derived from individual experiences but were socially derived, the product of human groups, and the intellectual capital accumulated through the centuries.

To understand Durkheim is to see that he applies the same mode of reasoning to the study of religious phenomena. But first he faces the task of defining religion. He is unwilling to define it specifically in terms of the supernatural or the extraordinary, nor is he satisfied with Tylor's minimal definition of religion as a "belief in spiritual beings." Buddhism, he felt, was a religion, but the idea of gods and spirits was absent, or at least played a secondary role. Then there were many ceremonies and ritual observances that did not directly involve "spirits."

So Durkheim was led to seek a broader definition. "Religion is more than the idea of gods and spirits," he wrote, "and consequently cannot be defined exclusively in relation to these" (35). So he came to define religion in terms of the sacred:

> All known religious beliefs, whether simple or complex, present one common characteristic; they presuppose a classification of all the things, real or ideal, of which men think into two classes . . . generally designated by two distinct terms which are translated well enough by the words profane and sacred.

Thus he arrived at his classic definition of religion as

> a unified set of beliefs and practices relative to sacred things, that is to say, things set apart and forbidden, – beliefs and practices which unite one single moral community – all those who adhere to them. (37)

Thus for Durkheim religion is essentially a collective thing, and he indeed distinguishes religion from magic by suggesting that whereas magic is primarily an individualistic enterprise, religion is inseparable from the idea of cult or moral community. Steven Lukes has noted with respect to Durkheim's "love of dualism" how the two main dichotomies social–individual, sacred–profane are isomorphic with one another (1973: 26).

Having defined religion, Durkheim then proceeds to criticize the two leading theories of religion – the animistic theories of Spencer and Tylor, and the naturistic theories of Müller and the German school of *Völkerpsychologie*. He sees these two theories as being essentially similar in that both attempt to derive the idea of the sacred out of sensations aroused in us by natural phenomena, either physical or biological. Müller expressed the empiricist position nicely when he said that "religion, if it is to hold its place as a legitimate element of our consciousness, must, like all other knowledge, begin with sensuous experience" (1889: 114).

For the animist, the origin of religion is derived from dream experiences, for the naturists from certain cosmic phenomena. Durkheim is highly critical of such empiricism. This seems to him a veritable creation out of nothing and gives religious notions an illusory status. He also makes what are essentially empirical points, namely that neither ancestral cults nor the deification of natural phenomena play an important role in the religious systems of tribal cultures. And in this he follows McLennan and Robertson-Smith in arguing that the most fundamental and primitive of all religions is totemism. Cults of the dead, he suggests, take a developed form only in more advanced societies like those of China, Egypt, and the Greek and Latin cities, whereas the deification of nature in preliterate cultures is focused not on cosmic powers but on "humble vegetables and animals": rabbits, lizards, kangaroos, and witchetty grubs. Their objective qualities, he argues, surely, were not the origin of the religious sentiment.

But he makes a further observation that is of interest. Taking the thesis of Spencer and Müller to imply that religion, for preliterate cultures, has an explanatory function, that it was a mode of thought that could guide people's relations with the experienced world, Durkheim asks what practical help religion could possibly offer. In instrumental terms, all religions are nonfunctional: "It is certain that they are mistaken in regard to the real nature of things; science has proved it," he writes (83). Moreover, if ideas that provide such practical help are the basis of religion, why haven't scientific conceptions – genes and atoms – been considered sacred? Thus Durkheim suggests that we must look elsewhere for the reality that will explicate religion.

Durkheim has been criticized by many writers for arguing by elimination, in that alternative theories are first disposed of systematically, thus lending authority to the remaining candidate, Durkheim's own theory (Lukes 1973a: 31). But it is well to note that in *The Elementary Forms of the Religious Life* Durkheim does not consider a priori theories of religion; such theological notions he simply regarded as untenable and unscientific.

In rejecting empiricist theories of religion, Durkheim, as Talcott Parsons suggested, opened up an entirely new line of thought by suggesting that it was hopeless to look for the sources of religion at this level. There was nothing intrinsic in the quality of things that could account for the attitude or respect. In fact, as Talcott Parsons says, echoing Durkheim, "Almost everything from the sublime to the ridiculous has in some society been treated as sacred" (1954: 56). Hence the source of the sacred is not intrinsic. The problem is of a different order, Durkheim suggests: Sacred objects and emblems are symbols. The problem then becomes one of identifying the referents of such symbols.

To solve this problem, Durkheim proceeds, for reasons noted earlier, to a detailed analysis of the religion of the Australian aborigines. Their religious system, which Durkheim identified as a form of totemism and which he saw as an "elementary form" of the religious life, is in fact rather complex. The complexity of their religion is in no way in keeping with the simplicity (as it appears to us) of their stone-age mode of subsistence. Durkheim indeed perceived this, nothing that "totemism" is a "much more complex religion than it first appeared to be" and, arguing against Frazer, suggested that since it offered a "conception of the universe" it was a religion comparable to others. It is worth noting in this context that throughout the nineteenth century, missionaries and travelers had been reporting that the aborigines had no religion at all, and even Baldwin Spencer was reluctant to use the term (Stanner 1965). Durkheim adamantly asserted, however, that totemism was not a form of animal or plant worship, as McLennan had understood it in writing of the religions of antiquity; to see totemism in this way, Durkheim maintained, was to completely misunderstand its real nature. The religion of the Australian tribes, though variable throughout the continent, has certain underlying themes.

First, there are specific cult groups, particularly associated with initiated men, that meet to perform rituals at totemic sites that are deemed sacred. These sites are associated with certain ancestral spirits or mythical beings that are supposed to have arisen from these sacred spots in the mythical period at the beginning of time, usually referred to as "dream time" (*altjira*). A full understanding of aboriginal religions requires a careful study of this doctrine of dream time, for in mystical form it laid the foundation for their whole conception of life. The design of the world was, as it were, fixed once and for all, and it was the task of humans, through historical rites, to maintain and renew this design.

Second, each totemic group has a collection of ritual objects that are believed to possess supernatural power. They are made of wood or polished stones and are oval in shape. They symbolize the sky heroes or totemic ancestors, and are normally engraved with a design representing the totem of the group or clan. Usually referred to as *churinga*, certain types, called bull roarers, have a hole at one end and are swung around on a string to make a whirring noise. These sacred objects, which play an important part in initiation rites, may not be seen or touched by women or uninitiated men.

Third, each totemic group is associated with specific totems, which are normally natural species but may also be natural phenomena – rain, forest, wind. Frequently there are dietary restrictions associated with such species and special ceremonies devoted to the increase of the species. Durkheim gives a description of these rituals (*intichiuma*) among the Arunta people. Since the ceremonies involved the ritual eating of the totemic species – witchetty grub or kangaroo – Durkheim followed Robertson-Smith in considering this a form of sacrifice, a communal and sacramental meal in which the members of the group receive, through the meat, spiritual regeneration (see Elkin 1964).

Thus totemism for Durkheim was a whole complex of belief and rituals that involved a ritual attitude toward nature, and a cosmology that expressed the idea that humans and nature form a part of a spiritual totality.

Accepting that the totemic species, and its emblem, and even class members in certain contexts, were considered sacred by the Australian aborigines, Durkheim still faced the question as to how such religious notions as the soul, reincarnation, and ancestral spirits fitted into this picture. And he answered this question by suggesting that underlying totemism there was the notion of an impersonal power or force – the *totemic principle* – that became incarnate in men and in natural phenomena. It was a "quasi-divine principle," immanent in the world, and he identified this conception both with an impersonal god and with various conceptions described elsewhere by various ethnographers: Wakan the "great spirit" among the Sioux and Omaha, and mana among the Melanesians are the main examples he cites. Durkheim viewed the idea of the soul and of spiritual beings (both of which he considered to be universal) merely as individualized manifestations of god or the totemic principle. "The soul," he wrote, "is nothing other than the totemic prin-

118

ciple incarnate in each individual..., the totemic principle individual-ized" (248–59). Spirits, culture heroes, and gods, according to Durkheim, are conceptions based on the idea of the soul, which presupposes the totemic principle: "The tribal god is only an ancestral spirit who finally won a pre-eminent place. The ancestral spirits are only entities forged in the image of the individual souls." Thus for Durkheim the soul, ancestors, high god – all of which he found in evidence as part of the complex unity of Australian religion – were simply different aspects of the totemic principle. The explanation of religion was therefore an explanation of this quasi-divine principle. Some extracts from Durkheim will succinctly outline the essence of his theory.

> Behind these figures [totems]... there is a concrete and living reality. Thus religion acquires a meaning and reasonableness... Its primary object is not to give men a representation of the physical world... It is a system of ideas with which the individuals represent to themselves the society of which they are members. (225)
>
> The totem is before all a symbol, a material expression of something else. But of what? From the analysis... it expresses and symbolizes two different sorts of things. In the first place, it is the outward and visible form of what we have called the totemic principle of god. But is also the symbol of a determined society or clan. It is its flag,... so if it is at once the symbol of god and of the society, is that not because the god and the society are only one?... The totemic principle can therefore be nothing else than the clan itself, personified and represented to the imagination under the visible form of the animal or vegetable which serves as totem. (206)

Or, as he more concisely put it, "God is only a figurative expression of the society" (226).

Few theories have been greeted with such widespread criticism, or, indeed, scorn; even more objective critics like Goldenweiser (1964) and Evans-Pritchard, though considering the thesis brilliant and imaginative, thought it another "just so story" (1965: 64), and many have faulted Durkheim for reducing religion to the status of an epiphenomenon. Yet few texts have had such a profound influence on subsequent studies and research, and its essential themes have permeated intellectual thought. Who nowadays would quibble with Durkheim's contention that "religion is something eminently social" and that conceptions of divinity have a social origin?

In the proceeding paragraphs I have dealt essentially with Durkheim's theory of religion, specifically in terms of the meaning and derivation of the idea of the sacred. Durkheim's main argument was expressed in *symbolist* terms, namely that religion was best understood as "metaphorical and symbolic," and that the concrete and living reality that it expressed was the social group. But there is also both a psychological and a functional aspect to Durkheim's thesis, and these become explicit in his discussion of ritual. Durkheim was concerned to understand how conceptions of the sacred, which he saw as symbolic expressions of social reality, came to have a transcendental or obligatory quality, especially since preliterate societies were not the "huge Leviathans" that overwhelm a person by their tremendous power; that is, state institutions were lacking in such societies. He was also keen to stress that social and religious ideas live only in and through individual consciousness and that such ideas need reaffirmation for social life to continue. He therefore saw religious rituals as the preeminent occasions on which the authority of the social group is asserted. "It is in spiritual ways," he writes, "that social pressure asserts itself" (209). It is able to do this because at ritual events, when there is a large gathering of individuals, a heightened emotional state is generated, which he called "delirium" or "collective effervescence." Moreover, rituals function not only to strengthen the bonds attaching the believer to god, but they strengthen the bonds attaching the individual to the social group of which he or she is a member; through ritual the group becomes conscious of itself. Before all, Durkheim asserts, "Rites are a means by which the social group re-affirms itself periodically. Men who feel themselves united . . . by a community of interest and tradition, assemble and become conscious of their moral unity" (387). In essence, then, religious rituals are seen as a primary mechanism for expressing and reinforcing the sentiments and solidarity of the group.

Although Durkheim's functionalism has readily been accepted – it is an old idea that few would challenge – writers like Evans-Pritchard and Lévi-Strauss suggest that Durkheim's thesis contravenes his own rules of sociological method, for fundamentally it offers a psychological explanation of social facts. As Evans-Pritchard writes, "No amount of juggling with words like intensity and effervescence can hide the fact that he derives totemic religion . . . . from the emotional excitement of individuals brought together in a small crowd, from what is a sort of crowd hysteria" (1965: 68). Evans-Pritchard, indeed, asserts that Durkheim's theory is a biological explanation of religion, an idea that would have shocked Durkheim to the core. There is no doubt that Durkheim was indirectly influenced by studies in crowd psychology like those of Gustave Le Bon (but cf. R. J. Jones 1977: 294) and thus asserted that collective gatherings generated a "certain delirium," and he even remarks that it is "in the midst of these effervescent social environments and out of this effervescent itself that the religious idea seems to be born" (218). But

120

to see the whole theory as a form of psychologoical reductionism seems to me highly misleading. It is clear that Durkheim saw ritual events not as generating ideas of the sacred but as the means whereby social facts – primarily the preexisting idea of the clan and its accompanying symbolism – are reaffirmed and given authority in terms of individual human consciousness. Collective representations, because they are collective and sanctified through symbolism, become immutable.

Durkheim, like Marx, tried to steer a course between idealism and reductionist empiricism and thought that in sociology he had found a way. Earlier thinkers, he suggested, faced a double alternative: either explaining human faculties and sociality by connecting them to "inferior forms of being" – mind to matter, reason to the senses – which is equivalent to denying their uniqueness, or else attaching them to some supernatural reality, making them untenable in terms of science. Thus it is not surprising that Evans-Pritchard, having labeled Durkheim an empiricist of the worse kind – a biological reductionist – should also accuse him of being an idealist. Perhaps in *The Elementary Forms of the Religious Life* Durkheim tried to be what he always said he was – a scientific rationalist.

It may be fruitful at this stage to briefly examine some of the main criticisms that have been leveled at Durkheim's theory. First, like Frazer and Tylor, though for very different reasons, Durkheim rigidly separates magic and religion and associates the latter only with cult activities. But, as Robert Lowie intimated, this distinction is sociologically untenable for a number of reasons, especially because it seems to deny that religion can be a subjective phenomenon. As Goldenweiser states, "The lives of saints are one great argument against Durkheim's theory" (cf. Wach 1944: 30–3).

Second, Durkheim makes a rigid separation between the sacred and the profane and rests his definition of religion on it. This dichotomy has also been criticized as too rigid and as difficult to sustain empirically. Evans-Pritchard, for instance, notes that in many societies illness is believed to be caused by some moral transgression, so that the physical symptoms, the moral state of the sufferer, and spiritual intervention form a unitary experience. The profane and sacred aspects are difficult to differentiate. He speaks too of Azande ancestral shrines being used for profane purposes. But though such criticisms have substance, nonetheless Durkheim's dichotomy seems to have analytical value and has been widely used by such writers as Mircea Eliade.

Third, Durkheim focuses his analysis on the clan system and sees this kinship group as the fundamental one in preliterate communities. But, significantly, among the Australian tribal groups a clear distinction is evident between the residential aggregates and the clan system. The former is the group consistently involved in economic activities, whereas the latter are essentially ritual congregations associated with totemic sites. What is the point, Evans-Pritchard asks, of maintaining through ceremonies the solidarity of social groupings that are not corporate and that do not have any joint action outside the ceremonies?

Fourth, there is a point stressed by Goldenweiser, who asks where the nontotemic peoples have derived their religion from, for many hunter-gatherers, like the Andamanese, lack corporate kin groups and totems. The difficulty is that Durkheim did not offer an explanation of "totemism" as this concept was understood by Goldenweiser (and as it was later defined by Radcliffe-Brown) but rather of the totemic principle, or god. In fact Durkheim came essentially to define religion in terms of an equation between the "sacred" and an abstract conception of divinity, which was deemed universal and symbolic (200). In this sense, totemism was an aspect of all religions, in just the same sense in which Tylor had used the word *animism*. But whereas Durkheim saw divinity as impersonal, the original mana, Tylor saw it in terms of spiritual beings. And although both writers took an evolutionary view of religion, they saw its elementary "form" at the foundation of all religious systems.

Finally, Durkheim seemed to see religion only in its function in establishing and reaffirming group solidarity and as possessing symbolic significance for a "group" or society. Several problems emerge from this. One is the problematic status of his central concept, "society," which he sees as a homogeneous entity but never, in fact, defines. The notion that a society, whether an ethnic group or nation, may be divided into social categories based on sex, class, status, or ethnic affiliation, never seems to have occurred to Durkheim.

Weber, Marx, and Engels, with their stress on the variations of religious expression among social groups, seem much closer to the social reality. Equally significant, as Giddens suggests, is the fact that nowhere does Durkheim confront the possibility that religious beliefs may have an ideological function legitimating the domination of one group or class over another. Conflicts, whether religious or otherwise, are treated by Durkheim only as transitional phenomena in social development (1978: 130). Millennial movements and ecstatic cults seem to fall outside Durkheim's theoretical paradigm.

Religion and society

Durkheim had an immense influence on the orientation of academic sociology and British anthropology, which, in the decades following the

Second World War, shared a similar structural-functionalist perspective. That Durkheim sociology became a dominant intellectual trend can, I think, largely be attributed to the influential writings of Radcliffe-Brown, who, with Malinowksi, is considered one of the founding fathers of British anthropology.

A. R. Radcliffe-Brown (1881–1955), though influenced by Spencer, took his main theoretical bearings from Durkheim in advocating a "natural science of society," although his own outlook was a good deal more empiricist. The focus of his interest, too, was more restrictive, in that he took as his key concept the notion of "social structure," viewed as a network of social relationships. Except for an ethnographic study of the Andaman Islanders (1922), Radcliffe-Brown published few substantive studies and was not an original thinker, but he was a brilliant teacher and produced a number of lectures and articles, some of the more important of which were published (Radcliffe-Brown 1952, Kuper 1977). Radcliffe-Brown's influence was primarily as a theoretician, for although he was one of the first academics to undertake fieldwork, his ethnographic studies lack the vividness and originality of those by Boas or Malinowski, and even his Andamanese text is largely devoted to a theoretical analysis of the islanders religious beliefs and ceremonies.

The Andaman Islanders, of whom a few still remain, were a group of hunter-gatherers who lived in almost settled local communities of about forty or fifty people, although they were nomadic during the dry season from March to May, when they gathered honey. Compared with other Asian hunter-gatherers, they apparently had a rich mythological and cosmological system. They had complex funerary and initiation rites, which involved complex dietary restrictions and body painting. The main supernatural beings they believed in were the spirits of the dead, associated with the sky, forest, and sea, who were believed to cause misfortune, and various nature spirits. The latter, in essence, were personifications of natural phenomenon, the moon, sun, rainbow, thunder, and lightning all being deities. Of special importance were the spiritual beings associated with the prevailing winds: Biliku was associated with the northeastern monsoon that prevails in the cool season, whereas Tarai was connected with the southeastern monsoon (June through September), the main rainy season when animals were plentiful and hunting pursuits predominated. The religion was evidently of a shamanistic nature, the *oko-juma* (dreamer) having the power of communicating with the spirits in dreams or through possession states, although Radcliffe-Brown's ethnograhy lacks detail. By his communication with the spirits, the oko-juma was able to cure illness and prevent bad weather, associated specifically with Biliku or Tarai or the sea spirits. Such, in brief, are the religious conceptions of the Andaman Islanders.

Radcliffe-Brown suggested in *The Andaman Islanders* that it was possible to differentiate between three types of social action: techniques, moral customs or rules of interpersonal behavior, and a residual category of nonutilitarian action that he termed "ceremonial customs." He devoted much attention to the latter. In the last part of the study he sought an interpretation of these ceremonies, as well as of their myths. Edmund Leach suggests that this section has always been regarded as one of the foundation texts of British social anthropology. Radcliffe-Brown shows no interest in attempting to ascertain the historical origins of institutions, suggesting instead that interpretation consists of two types of explanation, either in terms of "meaning" or in terms of "function." With regard to the first approach, he suggests that gestures, ritual actions, prohibitions, symbolic objects, and myths are *expressive* signs and that their meaning lies in what they express. This can be determined by their associations within a system of ideas and sentiments. As he put it, the customs and myths of the Andamanese, which superficially may appear ridiculous and fanciful, are the "means by which the Andamanese express and systematize their fundamental notions of life and nature" (1964: 330).

The notion of function, on the other hand, rests on the conception of culture an an adaptive mechanism whereby human beings are enabled to live a social life as an ordered community. This approach is based on an explicit organic analogy, for Radcliffe-Brown writes that "every custom and belief of a primitive society plays some determinate part in the social life of the community, just as every organ of a living body plays some part in the general life of the organism" (229). Leach (1971) labels these two approaches *structuralist* and *functionalist*.

Radcliffe-Brown's account is largely given over to a demonstration of the latter form of interpretation and echoes Durkheim's functionalist interpretation of ritual. For instance, among the Andaman Islanders weeping is not a spontaneous expression of feeling but a ritual demanded by custom. It reminds one of Durkheim's comment that "mourning is not a natural movement of private feelings ... It is a duty imposed by the group. One weeps, not simply because he is sad, but because he is forced to weep" (397). The Andamanese, however, weep on many occasions; at peacemaking ceremonies, at the meeting of friends, at a marriage, at the end of a period of mourning. Radcliffe-Brown interprets this rite as having a specific function: It serves to mark occasions "in which social relations that have been interrupted are about to be renewed, and the rite serves as a ceremony of aggregation" (243). Weeping is the affirmation of a bond of social solidarity.

The triadic scheme of Andamanese cosmology

	Sea/water	Forest/land	Sky/trees
Spiritual agencies	Sea spirits (*juruwin*)	Jungle spirits	Sky spirits (*morowin*)
Dietary restrictions during initiation rites	Turtle Dugong Fish Flying fox Monitor	Pork Yams Fruits	
Main ceremonies	Turtle-eating ceremony	Pig-eating ceremony	Honey-eating ceremony
Ritual plants	*Hibiscus*	*Tetranthera*	*Alpinia*
Activities	Throwing	Shooting	Burning
Mythical animals	Monitor Prawns	Woodpecker Kingfisher	Dove Hawk

It is usual to think of Radcliffe-Brown as having such a functionalist approach to totemic and other forms of symbolism, and Lévi-Strauss infers that there was a significant development of his thinking, over the years, toward a more structuralist position. But a closer examination of the Andamanese study reveals, as Leach insists, that it contains an implicit, even if unsystematic, structuralist analysis of the Andamanese ceremonials and myths.

"The legends of the Andamanese," writes Radcliffe-Brown, "set out to give an account of how the order of the world came into existence," rather than being crude attempts on the part of these people to understand natural facts. And the underlying order he delineates, even though excusing himself for his lack of insight into Andamanese ways of thought, is a triadic structure, reflecting "a threefold world, the waters below with their inhabitants, the fishes, and turtle, and other marine creatures, the solid earth, and the upper region of the top of the forest where the flowers bloom ... and the birds pass their lives" (347).

Edmund Leach (1971) in an important and interesting paper, attempts to expand these embryonic thoughts and structuralist insights of Radcliffe-Brown. What emerges is that much of Andamanese thought becomes explicable in terms of this triadic scheme, formulated in myth, enacted in ritual, and expressed in many customs through associative logic. The triadic scheme can be outlined as in the accompanying table. Some brief notes will suffice to illustrate the structural pattern.

In the initiation rites, the novitiate goes through a long series of ceremonies that may be spread over several years. There are essentially three stages, with appropriate dietary restrictions, culminating in the ritual eating of the food that typically represents each of the three ecological divisions. The period of abstention begins with turtle, dugong, and other marine creatures, which the novitiate must not eat. This period is brought to an end by the turtle-eating ceremony. A turtle-hunting expedition is arranged, and the best of the catch is chosen for the meal. The turtle is always killed on its back with head facing the sea. The novitiate is seated on *Hibiscus* leaves and also faces the sea, and is provided with a skewer made of *Hibiscus* wood, for he may not touch the turtle meat with his fingers. *Hibiscus* leaves have the power to ward off sea spirits. The youth is now required to abstain from eating pork and a number of vegetables, fruits, and other animal foods. This period is brought to an end by the pig-eating ceremony. In this ceremony *Tetranthera* leaves replace *Hibiscus* but the rite follows the same pattern. The youth must use a skewer of *Tetranthera* wood to eat the pork, and must sit on leaves from the tree, which keep away the jungle spirits. Significantly the *Hibiscus* is a coastal tree whose fiber is used to make nets and for turtle hunting and fishing, whereas *Tetranthera* is a small tree whose wood is used for the making of pig-arrow shafts. The third important ceremony is the honey eating, which takes place after a period of abstention from honey. During the ceremony the youth decorates himself with leaves of the *Alpinia*, a plant with a bitter sap that is used to ward off bees while honey gathering.

The same sequence, reflecting these ecological divisions, is evident in the myths. Besides this triadic symbolism, there is also, Leach suggests, a systematization of the seasonal patterns, the stormy *kimil* season at the end of the rains being equivalent to the marginal state in rituals. Thus Leach shows, in an examination of Radcliffe-Brown's writings on the Andamanese, that within the functionalist tradition of Durkheim that he consciously followed there is an implicit, even if unsystematic, interest in the structure of Andamanese thought. Radcliffe-Brown's more general writings on religion are a development of these earlier theories and are focused largely on two topics that have continued to be of central interest to anthropologists – the issues of totemism and taboo.

Radcliffe-Brown's general approach to religion, expressed in his lecture "Religion and Society" (1952), closely follows Durkheim, in that he agrees that nothing is to be gained by looking at the epistemological status of religions and declaring them to be erroneous and illusory beliefs. Nor is it fruitful to concern ourselves with the origins of religion; instead we should see religious beliefs and observances as a part of a

126

complex system by which human begins live together in an orderly fashion. We should look, he maintains, at the social functions of religion, that is, the contribution that it makes to the formation and maintenance of a social order. And he follows Robertson-Smith in suggesting that we should concentrate our attention on rituals rather than on beliefs, without treating rites as primary, for both are merely parts of a coherent whole. This theory, he admits, is hardly novel; it is implicit in the writings of the early Chinese philosophers like Confucius and Hsün Tzu. Thus he expresses his basic theory in the following terms:

> An orderly social life amongst human beings depends upon the presence in the minds of members of a society of certain sentiments, which control the behaviour of the individual in relation to others. Rites can therefore be shown to have a specific social function when...they have for their effect to regulate, maintain and transmit from one generation to another sentiments on which the constitution of the society depends. (1952: 157)

This led him to suggest that religions must vary in correspondence with the manner in which the society is constituted. Religious institutions, therefore, both symbolize and, through rituals, help to sustain a given system of social relations. The "sentiments" he refers to are essentially social attitudes.

To illustrate his theory, Radcliffe-Brown devotes some discussion to ancestral cults and totemism, suggesting that in both cases there is a close correspondence between the form of religion and that of the social structure. Ancestral cults, he indicates, are often associated with lineage structures, the sacrificial rites serving to reaffirm and strengthen those sentiments on which social solidarity depends. Australian totemic religion, on the other hand, is a cosmological system in which natural categories are incorporated into the kinship system. In such terms Radcliffe-Brown, with lucidity, builds on the work of Fustel de Coulanges, Robertson-Smith, and Durkheim.

It is this lecture, "Religion and Society," which I have summarized, that Evans-Pritchard reacts to with some hostility, suggesting that when Radcliffe-Brown is not stating the obvious his theory can be contradicted by the facts. He cites, for example, the fact that ancestral cults are often evident in communities lacking a lineage system, whereas the most perfect example of a lineage system is that of the Bedouin Arabs, who are Muslims. But of course Radcliffe-Brown was simply suggesting that religion could best be understood not by thinking of it in the abstract and searching for origins but by explaining how it was related to the social life of a specific community. He admitted that although in some societies there was a direct relationship between religion and the social structure, in others the relationship is indirect and not always easy to trace. Needless to say, Evans-Pritchard's study of Nuer religion, when it seeks to be interpretative, is largely concerned with explaining the "impress" of the social structure on Nuer religious thought (1956: 118), something of which Radcliffe-Brown, no doubt, would have heartily approved.

Radcliffe-Brown's discussion of totemism, though it hardly makes non-sense of Durkheim's theory, as Evans-Pritchard suggests, certainly shifts the focus of the analysis. Lévi-Strauss puts it nicely when he suggests that Radcliffe-Brown reverses, and "naturalizes," the thought of Durkheim. Radcliffe-Brown defines totemism rather narrowly as referring to any situation in which a "society is divided into groups and there is a special relation between each group and one or more classes of objects that are usually natural species of animals and plants but may occasionally be artificial objects or parts of an animal" (1952: 117).

He then goes on to outline the various forms of totemism, identifying the various groups with which totemic phenomena may be associated: sex categories, moieties, sections, and clans. His focus is on the Australian situation, and he notes that the form of totemism found there consisted of a fourfold association between (1) the patrilineal local groups; (2) a certain number of objects, plants, and animals; (3) certain sacred totemic sites; and (4) certain mythical beings who are supposed to have given rise to these sacred spots in the mythical period at the beginning of time. He notes too that there are individual totems and that Australian med-icinemen often derive their ritual power from an association with a specific animal species. Like Durkheim, however, Radcliffe-Brown tended to see totemism as merely an aspect of a complex religious or symbolic system. For primitive man, he wrote, "the universe as a whole is a moral and social order governed not by what we call natural law, but rather by what we must call moral or ritual law." And he continues, "The conception of the universe as a moral order is not confined to primitive peoples, but is an essential part of every system of religion" (130–1). Insofar as natural phenomena are incorporated into this social order (or cosmological system), they become, he writes, either in them-selves or through things or beings that represent them, entwined with ritual value. Radcliffe-Brown's use of the concept of ritual value seems equivalent to Durkheim's use of the term *sacred*, indicating an attitude of respect toward some designated object.

At this point, however, Radcliffe-Brown deviates substantially from Durkheim's analysis. He points out that there are many people – for example, the Eskimo and the Andaman Islanders – who have a ritual attitude toward specific animals and plants but have no totemic system (in terms of his definition) that is a specific association between the animal and some social group. Thus totemism is seen as the outcome of ritual specialization, that is, as a corollary of the differentiation of the society into segmentary groups such as clans. The question for Radcliffe-Brown then becomes, Why do people adopt a ritual attitude toward animals and other natural species? And the answer to this is expressed in the following "law": "Any object or event which has important effects upon the well-being (material or spiritual) of a society, or anything which stands for or *represents* any such object or event, tends to become an object of the ritual attitude" (129, emphasis added). Durkheim's theory was fairly specific, in that the object of ritual value derived its power from incorporating the totemic principle, which in turn symbolized the social group. He was thus largely unconcerned with the question of why particular natural species were selected. Radcliffe-Brown, on the other hand, asks this latter question and provides an answer – that the object has social value or symbolizes something that has social value for the community – but this is so vague as to be virtually no answer at all. But clearly writers like Evans-Pritchard and Lévi-Strauss, who suggest that for Radcliffe-Brown natural phenomena have ritual value because they are useful or "good to eat," seriously misrepresent his intent. This is clearly evident in his discussion of the role of the cicada in Andamanese ritual. He writes, "In the Andaman [Islands] ritual value is attributed to the Cicada, not because it has any social importance itself but because it *symbolically* represents the seasons of the year, which do have importance" (emphasis added). This extends Durkheim's symbolist approach to the natural world and, if not linked firmly to ethnographic data, could become arbitrary in the extreme.

In a later essay, devoted specifically to illustrating comparative method in social anthropology (1951), Radcliffe-Brown made some further theoretical observations on the question of totemism. In this essay he suggested that there were two problems. First, there was the question as to why natural species are endowed with ritual value, and the answer to this, he intimated, he had explored in his earlier studies. It has to do with the source of the ritual attitude, and the quotation just given suggests an answer in terms of social values. The second problem was how "social groups come to be identified by connection with some emblem, symbol or object having symbolic reference" (17). In other words, why are particular birds or animals chosen as totemic species? To answer this question, Radcliffe-Brown specifically examines a totemic system involving exogamous moieties, found among the Australian aborigines. He examines a myth focused on the crow and the eagle-hawk (which are, in one instance, the specific totems involved) and suggests that like so many similar myths this one has a single theme, namely, that the similarities and differences of the animal species are translated into terms such as friendship and conflict, solidarity and opposition. In other words, the world of animal life is represented in terms of social relations similar to those of human society. The relationship of the eagle-hawk and crow expresses, by analogy, a structural relationship – the unity of opposites – that he feels is important in human societies. Joking relationships and the yin–yang philosophy of ancient China are, he argues, similar manifestations of this principle.

Thus totemism, in one of its aspects, expresses symbolically a social-structural relationship that is general in human societies. This provides Radcliffe-Brown with illustrative material to use in arguing that social anthropology is a generalizing science, and quite distinct from historical analysis.

In his essay on taboo Radcliffe-Brown (1952) follows a similar procedure to that in his discussion of the sociology of totemism. He initially defines the concept. The English word *taboo* is derived from the Polynesian term *tapu*, which means "to forbid," "forbidden," and can be applied to many types of prohibition. But in another sense it is equivalent to the term *sacred*, implying a connection with gods or a separation from things profane (*noa*). Icons, temples, chiefs were all said to be tapu, and so were a number of foods. But the term also applied to a corpse, which must not be touched, and implied a contagious element in the prohibition (see Frazer 1903). Thus the original term *tapu* was a highly abstract concept that combined several distinct notions: prohibition, sacredness, uncleanness, contagion. Its multiple meaning led anthropologists like Robertson-Smith and Frazer to infer that one of the hallmarks of primitive religion was that no distinction was made between sacred rites and notions of ritual impurity. This is certainly implied, as Radcliffe-Brown notes, in the original concept, for Polynesians do not think of temples as sacred and corpses as unclean: Both are tapu. Durkheim, it is worth noting, used the term *sacred* as an inclusive term to cover both the holy and the unclean.

Radcliffe-Brown, wishing perhaps to steer clear of terminological problems, uses the term *ritual avoidance* to refer to any "rule of behaviour which is associated with a belief that an infraction will result in an undesirable change in the ritual status of the person" (1952: 135). Such a change usually involves the likelihood of some misfortune. He gives as an example the prohibition in the Book of Leviticus against touching certain animals. In doing so one becomes unclean, and to restore one's ritual status an offering has to be made – a goat or pigeon – and the priest will make a sacrifice as an atonement for the sin. Such customs are widespread throughout the world, and the term *taboo* has come to

130

cover such ritual prohibitions. Radcliffe-Brown faced the problem of separating prohibitions that were of a religious nature – an offence against god or the spirits – and those in which misfortune follows seemingly by a process of hidden causation, which have been referred to as "negative magic." After discussing the distinctions made by Durkheim, Frazer, and Malinowski between religion and magic, Radcliffe-Brown came to the conclusion that this simple dichotomy was unhelpful and that there was a need for a systematic clarification of the meaning and function of rites.

The discussion leads Radcliffe-Brown to propose the concept of "ritual value," which can be both negatively expressed, as in ritual avoidances, or positively manifested through consecration or sacralization. Ritual value is a highly abstract concept that encompasses the concept of taboo, and our attention is directed toward the problem of interpreting the phenomenon. Radcliffe-Brown discounts folk explanation of ritual; these provide important data for the anthropologist, but it is a "grievous error to suppose that they give a valid explanation of the custom." He questions too whether there is any value in attempts to conjecture processes of reasoning that may have led to religious and magical beliefs. Two alternatives, he thinks, remain: either to study ritual in terms of its *symbolic meaning*, as this is indicated in cosmological systems, or in terms of its *social function*. He explicitly expresses his skepticism with regard to the psychological explanation of religion and magic, which suggests that rituals serve as a form of reassurance for the individual, helping the person to cope with situations that he or she cannot control by technical means. He writes, "While one anthropological theory is that magic and religion give men confidence, comfort and a sense of security, it could equally well be argued that they give men fears and anxieties from which they would otherwise be free … the fear of … magic or of the spirits" (1952: 149).

But again, when he offers an interpretation of "food taboos," for example, in symbolist terms, he does not discuss the "structure of ideas" of a specific community (an approach that his methodology suggests) but links such taboos to the notion of social value. Thus he says that the "Andamanese taboos relating to the animals and plants used for food are means of affixing a definite social value of food" (151). This is a truism, and, because of its vagueness, is a rather fatuous interpretation.

Cosmology and social structure

Durkheim's study *The Elementary Forms of the Religious Life* (1915) was concerned not only with offering an explanation of religion but with the sociology of knowledge, with the derivation of the fundamental categories of thought: space, class, time, and causality. Durkheim, as we have noted, offered criticisms of the two main theories directed toward this issue, namely the rationalistic conceptions, which derived knowledge from a priori principles or the structure of the mind, and the empiricist doctrine, in which the individual derives the categories from experience. He rejected both the idealist and empiricist standpoints and offered a theory of knowledge that he considered "to unite the opposing advantages of the two rival theories" (19), namely that the categories of thought have a social origin, they are derived from culture. Thus like many social scientists – as different as Marx and Boas – Durkheim takes up a philosophical position midway between materialism and idealism, avoiding the double alternative of either deriving mind from matter (and denying man's creative and rational faculties) or postulating some supraexperimental reality (which would be beyond science). The way out of this dilemma is achieved by recognizing that the suprareality we experience is not the material world but society itself. In a discussion of this issue, Nye and Ashworth suggest that Durkheim completely failed to solve the problem of synthesizing these oppositions, though in moments of "stylistic glory" he obviously felt he had succeeded. They write, "Other philosophers have avoided this problem by collapsing the dualisms so that one polarity is made more real than the other, indeed the other becomes a fiction. Therefore in refusing to *reduce* one horn of a philosophical polarity to its other horn, Durkheim was driven towards a dialectical synthesis which he was never able to formulate. Instead we are presented with a non-synthesis expressed in the magic word 'social' " (1971: 133).

Lévi-Strauss and others have intimated that he does in fact make a reduction and, as far as religion is concerned, eventually falls back on the vagaries of sentiment and the instinct to be sociable. But Durkheim was struggling with conceptual issues that still remain unresolved, for neither idealism nor a crude empiricism offer viable alternatives to the study of social facts or the derivation of the categories of thought.

It is worth noting here that the doctrines of the later Wittgenstein – a kind of "bluebird" philosophy, as Gellner called it – have a striking resemblance to those of Durkheim, though the latter writer wrote with a clarity and a relevance, and did not for one moment assume that the "social" solution to the problem of category derivation in any way terminated the discussion (Gellner 1964: 183–7).

In accepting that society is the fundamental reality and that the categories of thought are socially derived, Durkheim sought to demonstrate that these categories depend upon the way in which a social group is "founded and organized." As he put it, "It is the rhythm of social life which is at the basis of the category of time; the territory occupied by the society furnished the category of space" (440). He gave a more extended discussion to the derivation of the concept of class and, with Marcel Mauss, compiled a short but influential essay entitled *Primitive Classification* (1963). His essential thesis is contained in the following extract from *The Elementary Forms of the Religious Life*, in which he writes that the first systematic classifications in history were "modelled upon the social organization, or rather . . . they have taken the forms of society as their framework. It is the phratries which have served as classes, and the clans as species. It is because men were organized that they have been able to organize things" (145). Taking as their basic premise the assumption that in the beginning human thought was in a state of indistinction, there being a "more or less complete absence of definite concepts" (1963: 6), Durkheim and Mauss set out to investigate what they considered to be the "most rudimentary classifications made by mankind" (9).

To illustrate, let us examine what they wrote about the "primitive," or what are best described as symbolic or mythological classifications, of one community that they described: the Zuni Indians of New Mexico.

The underlying principle of the Zuni classifactory system is the division of space into seven regions: north, south, west, east, nadir, zenith, and center. Almost everything in the universe, even moral attributes, is assigned to one or another of these seven regions. As an early ethnographer, Frank Cushing, writes, "The sun, moon and stars, the sky, earth and sea, and all their phenomena and elements, and all inanimate objects as well as plants, animals and men" are classified and integrated into this schema (1883: 9). This division is also reflected in the separation of clans within the pueblo, which is divided "in the estimation of the people themselves into seven parts, corresponding . . . to their subdivision of the world" (Cushing 1896:367). The nineteen matrilineal clans of the Zuni were grouped according to this schema. Thus the cosmological schema united diverse aspects of their culture, and, as Cushing wrote, "by this arrangement of the world . . . not only the ceremonial life of the people, but all their governmental arrangements as well, are completely systematized" (ibid., 369). This symbolic classification, as denoted by various Zuni myths, is outlined in the accompanying table. In their essay Durkheim and Mauss also present the symbolic classifications of the Sioux Indians, the Australian tribes, and the Chinese.

Accepting that the idea of class is an instrument of thought and that a model was necessary for its construction, and denying that such categories are given to us a priori, Durkheim and Mauss suggest that the

133

Zuni symbolic classification

	North	West	South	East	Above	Below	Nadir
Hunter-gods of the myths	Mountain lion	Bear Coyote	Badger	Wolf	Eagle	Mole	
Colors associated with regions – mythical mountains or pictographs	Yellow	Blue	Red	White	All colors	Black	Great Mountain Peak
Prey animals	Buffalo Elk	Mountain sheep	Antelope	Albino antelope	Jackrabbit	Rat Cottontail	
Totemic clans	Crane Grouse Yellowwood Evergreen-oak	Bear Coyote Spring-herb	Tobacco Maize Badger	Deer Antelope Turkey	Sun Sky Eagle	Toad Water Rattlesnake	Macaw (considered mother clan of whole tribe)
Associated elements	Wind Air Winter	Water Spring	Fire Summer	Earth End of year			
Activities associated with occult medicines	War Destruction	Hunting Curing	Husbandry Medicine	Magic Religion			

first logical systems reproduce the unity and morphology of the group. Moreover, they intimate that the moiety system was probably the original and most fundamental social organization and that the earliest classificatory systems were dualistic. In short, the first classes of things were modeled on the group structure. Durkheim and Mauss, however, make an important distinction between "primitive" (symbolic) classifications of a religious nature – the first philosophies of nature – and what they term "technological classifications," and they write, "it is probable that man has always classified, more or less clearly, the things on which he lived, according to the means he used to get them; for example, animals living in the water, or in the air, or on the ground. But at first such groups were not connected with each other or systematized. They were divisions, distinctions of ideas, not systems of classification. Moreover, it is evident that these distinctions are closely linked with practical concerns (82). This distinction is significant, though the relationship between the two modes of classification is never explored by Durkheim and Mauss (cf. my essay on Navaho symbolism, Morris 1979).

In an excellent introduction to their essay, Rodney Needham gives a cogent summary of some of the methodological flaws in their theory of primitive classification. Some of these may be denoted briefly.

First, they assume what ought to be proved by subsequent analysis, namely the primacy of the social. Needham, as his polemical work *Structure and Sentiment* (1962) indicated, has an aversion towards causal explanations in social science. In his view, "All that we are permitted to say is that however we may divide the social ideas in question (into "social order" and "symbolic order," for example) they exhibit common principles of order, no sphere of interest being the cause or model of organization of the other" (1963: xxvi). Thus, for Needham, the demonstration of a structural order is all that is required of the anthropologist, and no further explanation can be sought. Lévi-Strauss (1966) adopts an approach similar to Durkheim's except that he reverses the procedure, suggesting that the notion of "species" provides the model for the conceptualization of human groups and relationships. Neither, perhaps, would see the relationship between the two orders as causal; rather it is analogical, a "model."

Second, in many cases presented by Durkheim and Mauss there is a lack of any direct correspondence between social forms and the system of classification. The Arunta, for instance, have an eight-section marriage system but "no complete classification, no integrated system." Moreover, not only do Durkheim and Mauss not subject their theory to concomitant variation, but they tend to explain away any negative cases. They assume, too, Needham suggests, that a society employs only one mode of clas-

135

sification, although in their account of Chinese symbolism, it must be admitted, they are aware that it consists of a "multitude of inter-laced classifications."

Third, Durkheim and Mauss claim in their conclusions that preliterate people conceive of things not simply as objects of knowledge but as infused with certain sentimental attitudes. Such affectivity is considered the "dominant characteristic in classification" (86). And in a manner somewhat reminiscent of Weber's thesis of the increasing in rationalization of social life, Durkheim and Mauss note that scientific conceptions and classifications have shown a progressive weakening of the affective element. Since Durkheim's initial premise holds that social life is in some ways based on sentiments that express themselves in ritual, it is not surprising that cosmological classifications should also be considered to be permeated with emotive qualities. But whereas Lévi-Strauss views affectivity and a lack of differentiation as a protohuman state, thus pushing Durkheim's thesis into prehistory, Durkheim considered both affectivity and the "absence of definite concepts" as characteristic of the least evolved people. Both ideas are misleading. In accepting the Rousseauesque notion of an original formless humanity, Lévi-Strauss ignores, as Hiatt remarked, the intraspecific discriminations (with respect to sex, rank, territory, and incest) evident in vertebrate social life (1969: 91). There seems to be no essential reason why Lévi-Strauss, in postulating that the diversity of species provides the "conceptual support" for social differentiation, needed to have recourse to this "philosophy of an original identification with all other creatures" (1962: 74). In equating culture with intellect and in his hostility to explanations in terms of emotion, Lévi-Strauss was in a sense affirming that the "primitive classifications" that Durkheim and Mauss drew attention to were based on speculative scientific knowledge. In his later study, this was Durkheim's essential thesis.

A final and most significant criticism made by Needham is that Durkheim and Mauss confound collective representations with the faculties of the human mind. Thus if the latter are taken to be a system of cognitive faculties, it is patently absurd to postulate that categories are derived from the morphology of social groups, for the latter itself has to be perceived before it can be utilized in classifying things. Since different cultures conceive of space differently, no comparative study could show how the faculty or concept of classification itself originated. Durkheim and Mauss admit that people have always classified the things on which they live, and, as Needham suggests, even such basic discriminations indicate a formidable array of concepts: space, time quantity, as well as class.

There is, however, a curious paradox evident in Durkheim's writings, for in spite of the fact that sentiment seems to underpin many of his premises and conceptions – and these Lévi-Strauss highlights – he was nonetheless appreciative both of the logic and intellectual nature of religious thought and of the essential continuity between religious and scientific classifications. An extract from *The Elementary Forms of the Religious Life* indicates that both Douglas and Lévi-Strauss took many of their key ideas from Durkheim's classic study.

> If there is one truth which appears to be absolutely certain today, it is that beings . . . such as minerals, plants, animals and men cannot be considered equivalent and interchangeable. Long usage, which scientific culture has still more firmly embedded in our minds, has taught us to establish barriers between the kingdoms . . . But these distinctions, which seem so natural to us, are in no way primitive. In the beginning, all the kingdoms are confounded with each other. This state of confusion is found at the basis of all mythologies . . .
>
> Yet there is nothing in experience which could suggest these connections and confusions. As far as the observations of the senses go, everything is different and disconnected . . .
>
> The essential thing was not to leave the mind enslaved by visible appearances, but to teach it to dominate them and to connect what the senses separated; for from the moment when men have an idea that there are internal connections between things, science and philosophy become possible. Religion opened up the way for them. (1964b: 235–7)

Thus for Durkheim totemism and primitive religious classifications had been of the greatest importance in the evolution of humanity, for in connecting disparate aspects of experience, the first explanations of the world became possible. Between the logic of religious thought and that of scientific thought, he wrote, there is no abyss: "Our logic was born of this logic." Moreover, the realities to which religious speculation is applied are the same as those that later served as the subject of reflection for naturalistic philosophers: nature, man, and society. Religion, like science, serves "to connect things with each other, to establish internal relations between them, to classify and to systematize them . . . The essential ideas of scientific logic are of religious origin." What science does is to bring a spirit of criticism into its proceedings.

I have considered it useful to quote Durkheim at some length because I think Durkheim and Mauss, in their discussion of symbolic classifications, provide an essential key for understanding Lévi-Strauss's seminal study *The Savage Mind*. In fact this work replicates many of Durkheim's ideas on the sociology of knowledge, specifically the logical and scientific nature of religious symbolism.

It has often been said that Durkheim's sociological legacy was handed

137

down to later anthropologists through two divergent trends. On the one hand there was the empiricist tradition of Radcliffe-Brown, which emphasized the concept of social structure, seen as a system of social relationships (see Lévi-Strauss 1963; 302–4). Influenced by Spencer's sociology and Malinowksi's pragmatism, this tradition had a decidedly functionalist and symbolist bias. Function and meaning were the key concepts. Through the writings especially of Talcott Parsons (1937), it became a dominant trend in sociology (P. S. Cohen 1968). The work of Douglas, Leach, and Turner stand in this tradition, although, as we shall note, they were also influenced by other intellectual trends.

On the other hand there was the tradition associated with Marcel Mauss, deriving from the classic essay on symbolic classifications, coauthored with Durkheim, that we have been examining. It was a study that lay dormant, as far as British anthropologists were concerned, for more than fifty years. This tradition focused on cosmological ideas, on the totality of "collective representations," and it had a rationalist and structuralist bias. It is exemplified by the writings of Lévi-Strauss. To conclude this present chapter, I will briefly discuss the writings of Marcel Mauss (1872–1950), who was probably Durkheim's most distinguished pupil. Durkheim described him as "my alter ego."

Known mainly for his classic essay on ceremonial exchange, translated as "The Gift," Mauss was an important Sanskrit scholar who throughout his life expressed an interest in comparative religion. His theoretical approach to religion largely follows that of Durkheim, but his analyses are much more empirical, and he appears to have studiously avoided any criticisms of his uncle (Evans-Pritchard 1981: 190). In cooperation with Henri Hubert he wrote important monographs on sacrifice and magic (Hubert & Mauss 1964, Mauss 1972), and he coauthored with Henri Beuchat an essay on Eskimo cosmology (Mauss & Beauchat 1979). The study sought to demonstrate that Eskimo religion is a product of social concentration and that the pattern of their social life is reflected in and incorporated within their cosmological ideas.

The Eskimo pattern of livelihood, as depicted at the end of the nineteenth century, involved a dualistic pattern of movement. In the summer months they lived in dispersed camps on the tundra, hunting caribou and fishing, and living in small family groups. When the ice formed and they could no longer hunt game animals, they congregated in larger camps in the coastal regions, where they hunted seals. In these communities several family groups lived together, and it was a time when the annual religious ceremonies were performed. The Eskimo believed that the animals they hunted had souls and that when they were killed the souls had to be propitiated or they would cause misfortune. What was believed to invoke such misfortune was the transgression of certain moral taboos, or sins involving either sexual mores or what Ioan Lewis calls their "mystical game laws," for the Eskimo had an elaborate cosmology in which they sought to control and structure their environment. Like the seasonal dichotomy among the Andamanese, the intricate taboo system of the Eskimo embodied the principle that the animals and activities associated with winter must be rigidly separated from those of the summer months. Thus the produce of the sea, specifically seal oil, must not come into direct contact with the produce of the summer, caribou skins and the like. Infringements of these rules or taboos were deemed sins and were thought to result in illness or misfortune. Their taboos served to uphold a structure of cosmological ideas relating to the relationship between humans and the natural world, and this cosmology was bound up with the pattern of their social life. There was a correspondence, as Radcliffe-Brown would have put it, between their religious ideas and the social structure. With his usual skepticism, Evans-Pritchard thought Mauss's theory "ingenious" but no more (1965: 70).

I think it can be said with some justification that the anthropological treatment of religion has largely followed the perspectives of Tylor, Spencer, and Durkheim as the last writer was interpreted by Radcliffe-Brown. Indeed, many of the debates on the rationality of magic and on the interpretation of traditional thought (which I review later) involve a contrast and confrontation between "intellectualist" interpretations of religion (espoused by Jarvie and Horton) and the "symbolist" approach, derived essentially from a specific interpretation of Durkheim's thought (and persuasively argued by Beattie) (cf. B. R. Wilson 1970, Skorupski 1976). Thus the sociological interpretations of religion by Marx, Engels, and Weber have, until comparatively recently, been all but ignored by the majority of anthropologists. Little discussion of these scholars is to be found in Evans-Pritchard's biographical essays (1965, 1981) – though he suggests that Durkheim's theory of religion has affinities with that of Marx in seeing it as a "reflection" of social relations – and both Marx and Weber are conspicuous by their absence in Kardiner and Preble's (1961) survey of the "founders" of anthropology.

In an important sense the anthropological studies of religion have focused on the writings of Durkheim. They have thus incorporated into their texts two major flaws of Durkheimian analysis. One is the stress on "society," conceptualized as a totality of bounded social relationships. Society in this sense is seen as a "structure of social ties informed by moral consensus," not as a nexus of economic, political, and ideological relationships that not only connect with other nexuses (and thus are not bounded) but relate to different levels of social reality. Even in foraging

139

communities, several levels of social organization are evident (Morris 1982: 175–7). It is not simply that societies like the Lele were abstracted from their sociohistorical context, but the community itself tended to be seen as stable and homogeneous and the "social" was divorced from the material substratum. As Eric Wolf has suggested, what was a methodological unit of inquiry for functionalist anthropologists was turned into a theoretical construct (1982: 14). Moreover, in the functionalist interpretations of Durkheim, the mode of analysis shifted decisively toward cultural idealism, in tenor, if not always in substance. A second flaw was to see religion as simply a reflection of social patterns and thus to ignore its ideological functions. In a critique of anthropology, Gunder Frank has noted that the concept of ideology is almost taboo among anthropologists and is rarely mentioned in the anthropological literature (1984: 35). Following Durkheim, many anthropologists have failed to see religious beliefs as in any way sanctioning sectional or class interests or that religion may be a form of alienation. Their attitude toward religion has therefore generally been neutral and apologetic.

4

Religion and psychology

Religion and emotions

Men would never be superstitious, wrote Benedict Spinoza, "if they could govern all their circumstances by set rules, or if they were always fa- voured by fortune: but being frequently driven into straits where rules are useless, and being kept fluctuating pitiably between hope and fear ... they are, for the most part, very prone to credul- ity ... Superstition, then, is engendered, preserved, and fostered by fear" (1951: 3–4). In the next century David Hume expressed similar views. He wrote, "The first ideas of religion arose not from a contemplation of the works of nature, but from a concern with regard to the events of life, and from the incessant hopes and fears which actuate the human mind" (1757: 27).

This in essence gives a naturalistic interpretation of religion quite different from those theories we have examined in the earlier chapters. It is psychological in orientation, but the focus is placed not on the rational interpretation of phenomena but on emotional states. It is func- tional – but for the individual, not for the social group. And it is an interpretation that has a long history. Euripides expressed it in theolog- ical terms when he wrote, "The gods toss all life into confusion: mix every thing with its reverse; that all of us, from our ignorance and uncertainty, may pay them the more worship and reverence." It was, in fact, a long tradition that Spinoza and Hume inherited, and that the latter writer explored in his famous work, *The Natural History of Religion* (1757).

Hume viewed religion in an evolutionary perspective and considered the earliest form of religion to be that of polytheism or idolatry, theism being a later development, although, as Gellner stresses, Hume also suggests a pendulum-swing theory, a cyclic oscillation between polythe- ism and theism (1981: 7–16). But nonetheless it was an extremely psy- chologistic theory. The idea of religion sprang, Hume thought, not from reason but from the natural uncertainties of life and out of fear of the future; it functioned in giving the individual confidence and hope in his or her "anxious concern for happiness." It was a means of overcoming the "disordered scene" of human life (Hume 1956).

Despite Durkheim's unique contribution to comparative studies of religion, the early decades of the present century were characterized by a spate of important studies of religion in which the basic orientation was, like Hume's, psychological.

The theologian Rudolf Otto, two years after Durkheim, published his study *The Idea of the Holy* (1917), a work that achieved a popularity out of all proportion to its substance, and that is still in print. Otto's basic argument is that religion can be understood only through the notion of holiness, an a priori category, a nonrational feeling or intuition of the numinous (Latin *numen*, a supernatural). It is a feeling of awe and mystery, an experience of something "wholly other." This idea manifests itself in the experience of various religious devotees and mystics, and Otto records some interesting experiences of writers like Luther, who was the subject of his doctoral thesis. The book seems to offer, as Sharpe notes, a defense of individualism and immediate religious experience, as opposed to creeds, dogmas, and institutions (1975: 161). In fact, Otto's study is almost a theory of the religious instinct. As such it has little to offer anthropologists and could be left aside as purely of interest to theologians, were it not for the fact that it came to have an implicit influence on two American scholars who have written introductory texts on preliterate religion: Paul Radin and Robert Lowie.

Radin (1957) postulated that at the dawn of civilization men lived in a situation of fear and economic insecurity and that the idea of the supernatural arose out of man's attempt to cope with this uncertain external world. Religion was a means of maintaining life values – the desire for success, happiness, and long life. Out of the sense of helplessness came the feeling of the "wholly other," which crystallized as a belief in the supernatural. Rudolf Otto had conceived of divinity in theological terms as an inborn faculty, though evidently not a universal one. For in *The Idea of the Holy* he asks his readers if they have experienced the feeling of the numinous; if they have not, he suggests they need not bother to read the book. In essence, though Radin cites Otto, his theory of religion is in the tradition of Hume.

Robert Lowie, who, like Radin, was a first-rate ethnographer, also approached religion explicitly from a psychological viewpoint. He defined religion (1948) as a response to abnormal phenomena, a feeling of amazement and awe that "has its source in the Supernatural, Extraordinary, Weird, Sacred, Holy, Divine." Religion was equated with "awe-

142

inspiring, extraordinary manifestations of reality." Durkheim had already dismissed this notion that religion could be defined in terms of the extraordinary, arguing that religious institutions were collective and concerned primarily not with the unusual but with the normal, regular events of life. Lowie's suggestions, of course, imply that there are no religious institutions or behavior, only religious feelings. Evans-Pritchard, with some justification, remarked that for Lowie the belief of the Crow Indians in the existence of ghosts was not a religious belief because the subject was of no emotional interest to them. Lowie may well have been inclined toward this extremely individualistic and emotional approach to religion from his own experiences among the Crow Indians, though it is worth noting that he was skeptical of the thesis that "fear created the gods." For Crow religion, based as it was on the vision quest, was extremely individualistic. Lowie described it as "subjectivism raised to the highest power."

A second writer whose work came to exert an influence on later anthropologists, though again only implicitly, was the American pragmatist William James (1842–1910), whose study *The Varieties of Religious Experience*, published in 1902, has become a classic. James was a strange mixture, for he combined in his writings two divergent trends of thought, a radical form of empiricism known as pragmatism, which derives from Hume, and a form of transcendental philosophy in the tradition of Emerson.

Pragmatism, which has been aptly described as the national philosophy of America, maintains an "operational" theory of knowledge, namely that the truth of an idea lies in its utility. Theoretical ideas are simply hypotheses, tools; if, through experiment, they are found to work, in a practical sense, they are valid. James had his own version of this, based on the notion that "experience" has existential priority and thus evaded the fundamental distinction between the physical and "spiritual" aspects of existence. As George Novack put it, "By making nature depend upon experience, and not experience upon nature, James dissolved the independent objective existence of the real world into the subjective reactions of humankind" (1975: 69).

James also dodged the issue, which had troubled thinkers since the advent of reflective thinking, as to whether god or matter took priority. God was simply a hypothetical idea for James, and since it worked, he thought, for the general good of mankind, it was true. Hence he dismissed materialism, though his own conception of god, it must be noted, was like that of the transcendentalists – a vague conception of divinity. He put his own position on religion clearly when he said, in a post-script to *The Varieties of Religious Experience*, that if one made a division of all thinkers into naturalists and supernaturalists, "I should undoubtedly have to go . . . into the supernaturalist branch" (495). It is not surprising, therefore, that James should define religion in subjective, psychological terms as those "feelings, acts and experiences of individual men in their solitude, so far as they apprehend themselves to stand in relation to whatever they may consider the divine" (1971: 50), divinity being defined rather broadly, covering both Buddhism and Emersonian pantheism as a "primal reality."

James's conception of religion as a subjective experience and as a "solemn, serious and tender attitude" hardly matches the sentiments often expressed in the diverse religious rites found cross-culturally. Indeed this definition allows the subjective feelings of atheists to be described as religious, a point that Evans-Pritchard, as I noted earlier, made about Lowie's definition.

Although James made some interesting reflections on Christian revelation and mysticism and on the psychology of religion, his work is marred by a lack of interest in comparative studies; his classic study, in fact, makes no mention at all of American Indian culture. James essentially was a New Englander who devoted the resources of his psychological theory to defending a theological viewpoint.

The writings of Bronislaw Malinowski (1884–1942), whose brilliant fieldwork among the Trobriand Islanders of Melanesia laid the real foundations of British social anthropology, combined in his approach to religion and magic Hume's functionalism with the psychological-utilitarian theory of William James. He was, then, like both these scholars in temperament and intellectually a confirmed empiricist. Edmund Leach, I think, summed up Malinowski nicely when he said that he was a "unique and paradoxical phenomenon – a fanatical theoretical empiriricist" (1970: 120).

Malinowski, a Polish émigré, spent more than a year on the Trobriand Islands, and his various ethnographic reports on the Trobrianders' social life, of which the first, *Argonauts of the Western Pacific* (1922), is the most famous, have become classics of their kind. As an anthropologist Malinowski certainly looked upon himself as something of a prophet and as the founder of a new theoretical approach, an approach that came to be known as *functionalism*. Critical of the earlier theories of diffusionism and evolutionism – though Malinowski cannot be accused of being antihistorical – he advocated a synchronic approach, suggesting that a society be conceptualized as a whole and an effort made to ascertain how its institutions are interrelated. But his functionalism differed radically from the structural functionalism of Radcliffe-Brown, for it has a decidedly psychological bias. As he put it, "Any theory of culture has to

144

start from the organic needs of man" (1944: 72). Thus, unlike Radcliffe-Brown, Malinowski had little interest in comparative studies of human culture, and, as Nadel demonstrates (1970: 190), he moves on two quite distinct levels. The first is at the level of a particular society, that of the Trobriand Islands, where he is concerned to detail not simply ethnographic facts but a "constructive drafting" of Trobriand institutions and the "manner in which they integrate." He specifically recognizes the divergence between what people say they do and what they actually do, though it is worth noting that each of Malinowski's monographs is focused on a specific institution or activity and that he never produced a simple, coherent statement of Trobriand culture.

The second level on which Malinowski moves is that of human culture in general, and, as Nadel relates, his "generalizations jump straight from the Trobrianders to Humanity" (1970: 190). It is at this more theoretical level that Malinowski explicitly links, using the Trobriand ethnography as illustrative material, social institutions to human biological needs. His general theory of culture, therefore, though hardly contentious – few would deny that human institutions are not geared to sustaining human needs – is nonetheless a form of reductionism that is anathema to most social scientists. Not surprisingly, Evans-Pritchard, though saluting his pioneer efforts as an ethnographer, thought Malinowski's theoretical writings displayed little originality or distinction of thought (1965: 39). Leach put the distinction more bluntly: As an ethnographer, Malinowski, he thought, was a genius; as a theoretician he was a platitudinous bore.

Given the influence of William James, which both Evans-Pritchard and Leach stress, it is not surprising that Malinowksi conceptualized the individual in preliterate communities as essentially practical and down-to-earth. Malinowski was therefore extremely skeptical of both the rationalist emphasis of Tylor and Spencer (the idea that men in tribal communities were "ratiocinating" philosophers he considered little more than a myth) and the irrationalist stress of Lévy-Bruhl. He admitted, and stressed, that the Trobriand Islanders were as rational as any European and possessed a considerable body of empirical knowledge about the world they lived in, but a person was rational only in specific contexts. Malinowski (1974) thus came to make a clear conceptual division, based on the Trobriand ethnography, between magic, science, and religion. In this he followed Tylor and Frazer and, indeed, on his own admission, it was a reading of the latter's *Golden Bough* that prompted him to take up anthropology.

The Trobriand Islanders, in the early part of the century, were a matrilineal people living in small village communities, each village consisting of a group of matrilineally related men and their wives and children. The villages were linked through marriage, and throughout the island the people were united by a complex structure of reciprocal gift exchange. Horticulture, and fishing in the lagoons, were the principal sources of livelihood.

Trobriand conceptual ideas were dominated by a belief in magic and witchcraft. The witches, *mulukuausi*, were women who fed on carrion and knew how to make themselves invisible. They flew around in disembodied form and were associated with the sea, being particularly prone to wreck men's canoes. All important aspects of Trobriand life had their associated magical rites, the Kula and garden magic being the most involved and important. Most deaths were believed to be due to magic, and though the Trobrianders admitted that illness might be due to natural causes, the final touches, as it were, were always put down to sorcery.

After death, a person survived in one of two ways. The person might become a *kosi*, or ghost, a spirit that had a transitory life, hanging around for a while near the haunts of the deceased and playing various pranks on the living. The more important form of survival was as a *baloma*, or soul, which left the body at death and went to the island of Tuma, about ten miles from the Trobriands. In this underworld on Tuma the baloma spirits lived a life very much the same as that on earth, though it was said to be more pleasant and satisfying. As the spirit grew old in the spirit world, its skin became loose and wrinkled. It was eventually shed like that of a snake, and the spirit became an embryo, to be carried by a baloma woman in a basket back to the Trobriands or to get washed there by sea. Eventually it entered the vagina of a woman, and she became pregnant. Such were the Trobriand beliefs. Besides involving the notion of reincarnation, there is the implication here that the Trobriand Islanders were ignorant of the physiological facts of paternity, and since many Australian aboriginal communities hold similar beliefs, an involved debate about "virgin birth" has been engaged in by anthropologists. It is clear from Malinowski's discussion, however, that the Trobriand Islanders held contradictory views about the nature of conception and were fully aware of the fact that a women who had never had sexual intercourse could not have children. Actually, the virtual denial in myth of the father's role in procreation reflects the matrilineal kinship pattern of the society.

The relationship between the baloma spirits and the living had a number of levels. Formulas uttered in magical rites, especially in relation to canoe building and yam production, contained invocations to the spirits. The spirits were also communicated with in dreams and visions. Finally, at the harvest festival, Milamala, when the yams were gathered, all the baloma spirits were believed to return from Tuma to their own matrilineal relatives and villages. Platforms were built for them, ceremonial valuables were put on display, and gifts were offered to the spirits. The harvest festival lasted several weeks, and there was much gift exchange, feasting, dancing, and sexual license. At the end of the festival the baloma spirits returned to the spirit world.

It can be seen that although the spirits of the dead were important to the Trobriand Islanders, this society did not have a developed ancestral cult, nor were these spirits usually invoked as agents of misfortune. Moreover, although certain mythical beings and nature spirits were important, these too tended to be of secondary significance compared with Trobriand magical beliefs; it was magic, according to Malinowski, that plays a crucial role in the tribal life of the Trobriand Islanders.

Given the important influence of William James and Frazer and the nature of Trobriand magico-religious beliefs, it is hardly surprising that Malinowski should have maintained a distinction between magic, science, and religion and offered theoretical explanations in psychological utilitarian terms. He thus began his important essay *Magic, Science and Religion* (1925) with the words "There are no peoples however primitive without religion and magic. Nor are there, it must be added at once, any savage races lacking either in the scientific attitude or in science" (1974: 1).

As I have said, Malinowski was skeptical about Tylor's theory of religion because it tended to make "early man" too contemplative and rational, but he was equally concerned to stress that "primitive" man had his science, a body of traditional knowledge that gave him a working understanding of the natural world. A moment's reflection, Malinowski suggested, is sufficient to show that no productive activities could be carried out in any society without the careful observation of natural processes and a firm belief in their regularity and without careful reasoning – that is, without the rudiments of science. As Nadel (1970) remarked, this is a rather ambitious use of the term *science* which Malinowski, given his pragmatism, largely equated with technology. However, Malinowski was equally critical of, or even hostile to the theories of Lévy-Bruhl, which, according to Malinowski, claimed that preliterate people are "hopelessly and completely immersed in a mystical frame of mind." Malinowski refused to believe that preliterate people were "incurably superstitious" or were immersed in a prelogical mentality. Such theories, he stressed, may make us feel civilized and superior, but they are completely contrary to the facts. You must discard the notion, he wrote, that the "savage is a child or a fool, a mystic or a nincompoop." Preliterate people have a body of rational scientific knowledge that is put to practical purposes. Thus, for Malinowski, religion and science

147

had existed since the beginning of human society; they simply had a different place in human affairs. "Each has its own task and province," he wrote.

Although Malinowski recognized that religion was a "tribal affair" involving the community rather than the individual, he was critical of Durkheim's theory of religion, for a number of reasons. First, and in this he echoes James, he argued that the most deeply religious moments come in solitude, in detachment from the world: "Religion arises to a great extent from purely individual sources" (1974: 59). Second, he noted that many strongly "effervescent" gatherings in tribal communities do not, as Durkheim held, necessarily generate religious feelings but are often of a purely secular character – for example, a tribal gathering for trading purposes. Third, he was highly critical of the notion of "group mind," which he felt was at the basis of Durkheim's theory, regarding it as a highly metaphysical notion. The idea, he wrote, that society is the origin of the divine "reminds one somewhat of Hegel's absolute 'thinking itself' " (1963: 287).

Religion, for Malinowski, has its sources in individual experiences. He accepted, however, that public rituals had a social function, for they were the "very cement of the social fabric," religion being "indispensable for the maintenance of morals." Funerary rites, in particular, served to re-assert the unity of the group. But unlike magic, where the underlying idea and aim is always clear, religious rites had no ulterior purpose or end other than the rite itself. They derived their meaning only in terms of mythology or tradition. Malinowski discussed several aspects of religious phenomena. Sacrifice he considered a form of gift giving, a sharing of food with the spirits or divinities, a ritual rooted in the "psychology of the gift." Totemism he considered both a mode of group organization and a system of religious beliefs and practices, and the ritual attitude, to use Radcliffe-Brown's concept, he saw as being derived essentially from the rites' utility. Nothing could be more pragmatic than this. "As a rule," he writes, "species of animals or plants used for staple food, or at any rate edible or useful . . . are held in a special form of totemic reverence and are tabooed to members of the clan which is associated with the species" (1974: 20). It is this sentence that led Lévi-Strauss, in discussing and criticizing functionalist interpretations, to suggest that totemic species were considered sacred because they were good to eat. Malinowski put his own approach and attitude even more bluntly when he wrote that the "road from the wilderness to the savage's belly and consequently to his mind is very short" (1974: 44).

But essentially Malinowski links religion to life-cycle rituals, particularly those rites concerned with death. Indeed he sees the existential condition of death as being intimately connected with the emergence of religion. Human beings, he felt, are intensely afraid of death, probably as a result of deep-seated instincts. They cannot face the idea of complete cessation, of annihilation. And it is here that religion steps in, providing psychological safeguards. The funerary ritual, he suggested, was the religious act par excellence; it is here that "religion arises out of an individual crisis, the death" of the individual person. According to most religious theories, he continued, a great deal, if not all, of religious inspiration has been derived from the "final crisis of life."

Thus the idea of the spirit and the belief in immortality form the essence of religion, and both have a psychological origin. "Religion," he wrote, "saves man from a surrender to death and destruction" and, in the final analysis, is derived from our instincts. "The saving belief in spiritual continuity after death is already contained in the individual mind; it is not created by society. The sum total of innate tendencies, known usually as the instinct of self-preservation, is at the root of this belief."

Although an agnostic himself, Malinowski gave religion a positive psychological function and implied that it was universal and necessary. Religious inspiration had two sources: the desire for immortality, and a craving for communion with god. It was based on these "twin needs" and gave people a sense of purpose and a feeling of peace and well-being. It gave man the "mastery of his fate," whereas science was only narrowly concerned with control over the natural world. Many have defined religion in these terms, particularly recent theologians. The sociologist Milton Yinger is also an example, for he defines religion as a "system of beliefs and practices by means of which a group of people struggles with the ultimate problems of human life. It is a refusal to capitulate to death, to give up in the face of frustration." (1957: 9). Explaining religion in psychological and emotional terms and giving it a cathartic function is a form of justification and defense of religion. So Malinowski could freely write that religion, even at its worst, is never completely useless or wholly evil.

Malinowski explains magic in similar terms, stressing that it has both psychological and social functions. He was eager to argue that magical beliefs should not be equated with primitive science nor with abstract concepts of "power" such as mana or orenda; the latter, he thought, were crude metaphysical concepts. But magic is a system of beliefs and practices that derive essentially from emotional responses to situations of frustration. Magical rites and spells, though standardized and associated with an elaborate taboo system and mythology, are the outcome of emotional experiences, of natural responses to those "impasses" in

149

practical life when technical knowledge or control is inadequate. When forsaken by his knowledge or coming to a "gap" in his practical activities, the individual's "nervous system and his whole organism drive him to some substitute activity." Thus magic serves to "bridge over the dangerous gaps in every important pursuit or critical situation"; it gives the individual a feeling of confidence and poise. As Malinowski writes, "Magic flourishes wherever man cannot control hazard by means of science. It flourishes in hunting and fishing, in times of war and in seasons of love, in the control of wind, rain and sun, in regulating all dangerous enterprises, above all, in disease and in the shadow of death" (1963: 261).

He cites the fact that for lagoon fishing in the Trobriands, where man could rely completely upon his knowledge and skill, no magic was required, whereas for open-sea fishing, full of danger and uncertainty, there were extensive magical rites to ensure safety and good results. Magic therefore is not utilized when the ends can be achieved by ordinary means. "The savage never digs the soil by magic . . . or sail[s] his canoes by spell." Malinowski therefore saw an intricate and complementary relationship between science and magic, evident in all human communities but especially clear in the Trobriand ethnography where the two activities existed side by side, each, however, having a different functional role. This is indicated in the following succinct statement of the Trobriand horticultural activities and its associated magic, a topic that was very fully explored in his book *Coral Gardens and Their Magic* (1935). Malinowski writes,

> The soil was first blessed for fertility in general; then the plots were cleared by perfectly rational and practical procedures. A second magical ceremony followed to fumigate the cleared ground and thus prevent blights, pests and insects. Then, again, came planting, done skillfully, practically and scientifically. But when the plants sprouted and there was nothing better to do but hope for good luck, magic again was enacted in ceremony after ceremony, designed to make the crops strong and good. And so, throughout the whole series, the rites alternated with the activities, each aspect, the rational and the magical, kept absolutely distinct from the other. (1935: 61–8)

Whereas technical arts had a practical function, the magic had a psychological function, giving the individual confidence and hope, and ritualizing, as Malinowski put it, his or her optimism – although he also stressed that magic had a further function in bringing order, rhythm, and control into the purely technical activities like gardening or the building of a sea-going canoe. Malinowski thus followed Tylor and Frazer in seeing magic and science as quite distinct activities. But whereas these earlier writers, like Radcliffe-Brown, thought that magical rites and beliefs contained their own symbolic logic and had meaning in their own terms, Malinowski saw magic as essentially an emotional response, viewing it, like the logical positivists, as virtually meaningless. It had value and meaning only in terms of its psychological function, and in this, religion was akin to magic: Both "arise and function in situations of emotional stress." Equally, and unlike Durkheim, he did not explore the continuity between magico-religious phenomena and science, for his emotionalist approach denied that magic and religion had an intellectual content. His psychologism also led Malinowski to see religion and magic almost as a part of the human condition, for, he wrote, the rationalist must recognize that religious beliefs are "indispensable pragmatic figments without which civilization cannot exist" (1963: 336).

Many have commented on the contrasting theories of ritual offered by Radcliffe-Brown and Malinowski. George C. Homans perhaps expressed their divergent theories most lucidly when he wrote "Malinowski is looking at the individual; Radcliffe-Brown at society. Malinowski is saying that the individual tends to feel anxiety on certain occasions; Radcliffe-Brown is saying that society expects the individual to feel anxiety on certain occasions. But there is every reason to believe that both statements are true. They are not mutually exclusive" (1941: 86).

Like William James, Malinowski was an apologist for religion, but his psychological approach has closer affinities to that of Hume rather than to that of Sigmund Freud, whose theory of religion is seemingly reflected in the quotation from Homans just cited.

Freud's biological theory of meaning

It is rather ironic that the two men whose ideas have profoundly influenced twentieth-century thought and institutions – Marx and Freud – should, until comparatively recently, have been largely ignored or by-passed by academics. Academic sociology and anthropology to a large extent developed independently of or in covert opposition to Marxist thought, and, strange as it may seem, one can still obtain a degree in psychology without having to read the work of Freud. Some of the central themes of psychoanalysis, reflecting psychological issues lying at the very heart of the human condition – anxiety, repression, sexuality, sadism – hardly get a mention in many psychological texts. The reason for this seems to me self-evident. Although the ideas of both Freud and Marx have permeated the social milieus, the writings of both scholars, if considered seriously, have rather alarming and disturbing consequences, for they both offer radical critiques of Western civilization.

151

Sigmund Freud (1856–1939) stood at the watershed in the development of social theory. Entering the University of Vienna at the age of seventeen – and he was to live in Vienna most of his life – Freud initially concentrated on biology, and, after undertaking some neurological research, eventually qualified as a medical doctor in 1881. Specializing in the treatment of nervous disorders, Freud took as his scientific idol the German scientist Helmholtz, whose "school of medicine" was based on experimental methods. It was a school hostile to any form of vitalism within biology.

Given this background, it is hardly surprising that Freud inherited a positivistic conception of science. He aimed, as Rycroft notes (1966: 12), to establish a scientific psychology (psychoanalysis being the science of unconscious mental processes) by applying the same principles of causality as were then current in the natural sciences. He imbibed from his earlier training a belief in natural law, accepted a theory of psychic determinism, and, as Hughes suggested, even to the end of his life tended to use a mechanistic vocabulary drawn from nineteenth-century physics (1958: 134–5). But in essence Freud's guiding thoughts were biological rather than mechanistic, and a recent biographer has rightly argued that his "fundamental conceptions were biological by inspiration as well as by implication" (Sulloway 1979: 5). Lomas has implied that Freud was unable to emancipate himself from the physical frame of reference" (1966: 116). But what is significant, I think, about Freud is that he shifted his theoretical perspective, avoiding any kind of simple biological reductionism, without losing sight of the fact that the human being is a psychobiological entity and without abandoning causal analysis. As Engels had compared Marx with Darwin as the founder of historical science, so Freud's own biographer, Ernest Jones, was right to bestow upon Freud the title of the "Darwin of the mind," for both Marx and Freud saw the human species as rooted in society and nature. But the theoretical shift that Freud made is important.

Because of this shift psychoanalysis, as it developed, did not remain entrenched in a mechanistic framework. Beginning as a study by Freud of neurosis and as a theory that aimed to explain the origin and development of neurosis, psychoanalytic thought shifted the focus away from organicism and the general nineteenth-century notion that mental illnesses were physical in origin. For around 1900 Freud invoked in his studies a totally new principle of explanation that ran counter to the tenor of thought prevalent at that period. Expressed simply, Freud's theory was that neurotic symptoms have a meaning, and, as Home wrote, this opened up a new way of understanding functional illness: "In discovering that the symptom had meaning and basing his treatment on this hypothesis, Freud took the psychoanalytic study of neurosis out of the world of science into the world of humanities, because a meaning is not the product of causes but the creation of a subject" (Home 1966: 42). Accepting that there is a radical difference in logic and method between the humanities and science, Home thus felt that Freud had made a radical break with past interpretations of neurosis. He had abandoned the earlier attempts at biological reductionism for a "psychological" mode of understanding based on the interpretation of meaning. My feeling is that this disjuncture is false, for what Freud, like Marx, essentially tried to do was to create a humanistic science. In doing so he employed, as many have noted, two methodological approaches (see Bocock 1976: 23–9). In attempting to understand human life Freud therefore adopted both a natural-scientific position, with its causal analyses and a rather mechanistic model of energy flows, and an interpretative account based on meaning. In essence he did not confuse, but rather fused, the two approaches. As Ricoeur put it, Freud's theory reflects a "mixed discourse" (1970: 363).

But it is important to realize that the mode of interpretative understanding that Freud advocated is quite different from the kind of hermeneutics that stems from German idealism. To say that "Freud's psychology belongs to the kind which seeks to understand human behaviour rather than to explain it on a scientific basis; that is, it is Verstehende psychology" (Bocock 1976: 21) is to accept the kind of dichotomy that Freud (as well as Marx and Weber) were attempting to go beyond. Freud did not simply propound a theory of meaning in the understanding of neurosis (or culture) but linked that understanding to a biological reality. To use Ricoeur's words, he did not aim at the "restoration of cultural meanings" nor link such meanings to a "sacred" reality (as with phenomenological analyses) but rather belonged to the "school of suspicion" which advocated a "science of meaning." This latter approach viewed interpretation as a "process of demystification" (Ricoeur 1970: 32–6). As Rycroft rightly indicated, to accept psychoanalysis simply as a theory of meaning is incomplete and misleading without realizing that it is also a "biological theory of meaning" (1966: 20).

In attempting to bridge the gulf between the sciences and the humanities, or, to put it another way, in attempting to go beyond the positivistic conception of science – to broaden, that is, its scope – Freud never lost his commitment to the scientific Weltanschauung (or world view). Although in his personal life he seems to have surrounded himself with uncritical disciples and a sectlike organization (Fromm 1970: 17–24), his writings convey an openmindedness and a strong commitment to science, defining the latter as radical inquiry into human life, based on empirical knowledge. He did not aim, he wrote, at "producing con-viction – my aim is to stimulate enquiry and to destroy prejudices" (1953: 256). But inevitably he has been subjected to criticism from both sides of the intellectual divide. Those who in the positivist tradition have narrowly interpreted all science on the model of the physical sciences – that is, as involving causal theory and experimental methods – have naturally pronounced psychoanalysis to be unscientific and "mentalist." On the other hand, existential psychologists like Sartre have denounced Freudian theory as deterministic and as presenting a dehumanization of the human personality (1943: 50–4). Some have gone even further and described Freud's theory as a "philosophy of helplessness" that de-picts freedom as an illusion (C. Wilson 1981: 62), a viewpoint that not only completetly misunderstands Freud's theoretical intentions but side-steps the cultural problems such as neurosis, that he attempted to un-derstand and grapple with.

Freud's psychoanalytic theory emphasized two interrelated concepts – the unconscious and the libido. Unlike the anthropologist Wilhelm Wundt, who was also engaged in establishing psychology as an inde-pendent discipline, Freud was not particularly interested in psychological functions such as perception, memory, or cognition. These, he thought, were ego functions related to the individual's adaptation to reality. More important for Freud were the unconscious mental processes expressed in dreams, fantasies, and neuroses. The psyche, he felt, could not be equated with consciousness. Moreover to Freud the unconscious was not a descriptive notion but rather a dynamic conception, consisting of those impulses and instinctual strivings that supply the motive power for psy-chological experience. In his early work he suggested that human beings were motivated by two primary drives: an "instinct" toward self-preservation and adaptation to the external world (the *reality principle*), and the libido, or sexual drive, seen as a kind of psychosexual energy (the *pleasure principle*). "Impulses," he wrote, "which can only be described as sexual in both the narrower and the wider sense, play a peculiarly large part... in the causation of nervous and mental disorders. Nay more, ... these sexual impulses have contributed invaluably to the high-est cultural, artistic and social achievements of the human mind" (1953: 26–7). Central to Freud's libido theory was his notion of infantile sex-uality and his suggestion that at around the age of four a child, specif-ically the boy, passes through the oedipal stage. The concept derives from the Greek legend about Oedipus, who unknowingly killed his father and married his mother, thus bringing the plague to Thebes. The resolution of the Oedipus complex is seen of great importance in the psychoanalytic explanation of neurosis.

If Freud's theory of psychoanalysis can be reduced to a single sentence, it is contained in his original formula that neurosis "is the result of a conflict between instinctual demands and opposing official demands." His approach, therefore, is biosocial, though many have seen his concepts of id, ego, and superego as primarily having a metaphorical significance. The id, or instinctual aspects of the human personality, was as I have said, largely conceptualized in sexual terms, the libido being a kind of life energy. But Freud's notion of sexuality was rather broad: It did not focus on the genitals (hence the notion of infantile sexuality), and the function of sexual energy was for the purpose of pleasure, not procreation. Freud saw this sexual energy as essentially unstructured and, along with our aggressive instincts, as part of our biological makeup, always striving for discharge or for self-expression in consciousness. Given these unconscious drives, the ego has divided loyalties, wishing, on the one hand, to experience "instinctual" satisfaction, and, on the other, seeking to accommodate itself to the demands and pressures of the external world. Moreover, Freud held that undischarged sexual energy was converted into anxiety; thus, in essence, neurosis and unhappiness were a result of repressed sexuality.

Clearly there is a dilemma in Freud's basic postulates. He cannot be viewed simply as a reactionary thinker, although he certainly held a Hobbesian view of the nature of human beings. The dilemma is this: On the one hand, the repression of sexual instincts is deemed necessary, and in *Civilization and Its Discontents* Freud even argues that human civilization itself is largely built upon the renunciation of instinctual gratification. But on the other hand he sees the frustration of the libido as a key factor in neurosis; sublimation, therefore, can be achieved only at the expense of human happiness. It is no wonder that Freud thought of the human condition as essentially tragic. The importance of his radical followers like Marcuse and Reich is that they tried to retain the critical elements of Freud's writings, for as Marcuse put it, his basic theory contains within it a "most irrefutable indictment of Western civilization" (1969: 29). To do this they argued that repression was not inherent in the human condition, as Freud held, but characteristic of given historical circumstances (specifically, Western industrial capitalism). (For important and interesting studies of Freud's psychoanalytic theory and his life, see Marcuse 1969, Jones 1964, Ricoeur 1970, Wollheim 1971, and Mitchell 1975.)

Totem and taboo

In 1913, Freud published *Totem and Taboo*, a remarkable, speculative work that Hughes has described as an "anthropological fantasy" (Hughes

1958: 145). I have the impression that no anthropologist who has read the work has failed to be impressed by it; it is a book that "no ethnologist can afford to neglect," Kroeber remarked (1920: 24), yet all have either dismissed it, ignored it, or have, like Kroeber, examined the ethnographic evidence that might support it and thereby "torn it to shreds." Evans-Pritchard outlines the thesis of the book and then dismisses it as simply a "just so story" (1965: 41–3). But then, for Evans-Pritchard any theory that purports to explain religion is suspect, and Freud's study suggests that religion is an illusion. *Totem and Taboo* is thus a difficult book to approach: It is an intuitive study and has a "gossamer texture," like a butterfly, as Kroeber interestingly put it (1939: 25).

For many anthropologists, the opening page of the book gives an immediate jolt to the system, for the work is subtitled "Resemblances between the Psychic Lives of Savages and Neurotics." The impression thus gained is that Freud (and psychoanalysts generally) believe that preliterate people think and behave as neurotics. Ioan Lewis clearly has this feeling about the writings of another psychoanalytic anthropologist, Weston La Barre. This view of preliterate people is not what Freud is implying at all. What he suggests is that there are parallels between the individual and asocial forms of neurosis and the "creations of culture" like taboos, animism, and totemic beliefs, and that psychoanalytic theory offers a way of understanding the latter. Both stem from the "world of phantasy," from "ambivalent feelings" or impulses; in short, from the unconscious primary processes. Freud continually warns us not to take the analogy too seriously and neglect the obvious differences between the psychic expressions of neurotics and preliterate people, and he stresses that the culture (religion and art) of literate civilizations is open to the same kind of interpretation. Rather interestingly, Freud's own assertion that neurotic symptoms are subjective states whereas magical beliefs are social "creations" is used by Evans-Pritchard as evidence against Freud's theory (1965: 46). And it is important to note, too, as Freud put it, that if we "get behind these structures . . . [of superstition] we realize that the psychic life and the cultural level of savages [i.e., preliterate people) have hitherto been inadequately appreciated" (1938b: 154). As Roheim argued, the primary processes (reflected in the fantasies of schizophrenia, in dreams, and in the myths, taboos, and religious concepts of all cultures) are universal. But this does not imply that mythological thought was the only way in which our primordial ancestors (and preliterate people) could think: "If this were true, mankind would have become extinct right at the beginning. We know that for the most part, primitives act within their own sphere just as rationally, or even more rationally than we do" (Roheim 1950: 3).

Another important point is that Freud suggests that a complex social phenomenon like religion can be adequately explained only by employing a variety of research strategies. The psychoanalytic interpretation that he was outlining was, he felt, only one approach among many and could not even claim priority (1938b: 158).

The introductory essay of *Totem and Taboo* deals with incest prohibitions and associated avoidance customs. Freud stressed that these are strongly emphasized in many preliterate communities. Later in the study he expresses his dissatisfaction with the various theories that had been proposed to explain the incest taboo. He finds Westermark's suggestion that there is an innate aversion to sexual intercourse with close kin living together inadequate, and he quotes Frazer's excellent criticisms: "It is not easy to see why any deep human instinct should need reinforcement through law. There is no law commanding men to eat and drink . . . The law only forbids men to do what their instincts incline them to do." But Freud is equally unwilling to accept the explanation that the incest taboo developed to prevent the harmful consequences of inbreeding, suggesting that these facts only became evident when mankind began breeding domesticated animals. Nor could Freud accept Frazer's conclusion that the origin of the "incest dread" was an unsolved mystery. So the incest prohibition is the first phenomenon he sets out to explain.

In the essay "Taboo and the Ambivalence of Emotions," Freud draws parallels between various taboos – especially those restrictions associated with conflicts, the sacred character of rulers, and death – and the various phobias and obsessions he had observed among his neurotic patients. Noting that *taboo* itself is an ambivalent term often associated with things that are forbidden and unclean as well as sacred, he suggests that a taboo is a "forbidden action for which there exists a strong inclination in the unconscious" (1938b: 61). And he goes on to argue that both taboos and phobias are derived from ambivalent impulses and tendencies; they are the result of an "emotional ambivalence," which, like conscience, comes from unconscious sources. Freud then turns to the question of animism and magical beliefs, and in this essay he adopts uncritically the evolutionary perspective suggested by Frazer. This implied the acceptance of the highly questionable "theory of recapitulation," which was widely accepted by scholars of that period. The theory, stemming largely from the influential writings of Ernest Haeckel, suggested that ontogeny, the development of the individual organism, recapitulated phylogeny, the evolution of the species, or more specifically, the cultural evolution of mankind. The theory was not only embraced by Frazer but accepted by the influential psychologist G. Stanley Hall, who was instrumental in introducing Freud's work to the United States and whose book *Adoles-*

157

cence (1904) had a decisive influence in promoting studies of child development.

Freud thus came to suggest that cultural evolution, "man's conception of the universe," had passed successively through three evolutionary phases – animism, religion, and science – and that these corresponded to the stages of object finding (characterized by dependence on the parents) and maturity, when the individual has renounced the pleasure principle and "adapted himself to reality" (1938b: 144). The animistic or mythological stage, the first of the three "great world systems," Freud conceptualized not in terms of Tylor's definition but largely in accordance with Frazer's views. It was a nature philosophy that made it possible to comprehend the totality of the world, a system of thought based largely upon contagious and homeopathic (analogic) magic. But the underlying premise of this system was not a rational explanation of the world; animism, Freud felt, did not stem, as Tylor and Frazer implied, from a "purely speculative thirst for knowledge" (126) but rather, like certain neuroses, from emotional impulses. Animism, for Freud, suggested the "over-estimation of psychic processes." Adopting a term used by one of his neurotic patients, he called this the "omnipotence of thought." Psychic life imposes itself on the reality of things, and this kind of thinking is evident in phobias, delusions, dreams, and religion, as well as in animistic thought.

Freud then turns his attention to totemism, again relying heavily on the writings of Frazer, drawing on data from his monumental study *Totemism and Exogamy* (1910). Writers like Wundt and Robertson-Smith had tried to show that the earliest forms of culture were totemic. Early human societies, it was suggested – and the ethnographic material on the Australian tribes was thought to illustrate this – were divided into a number of exogamous clans. Each clan had a totem, an animal or plant that was treated with special reverence. There were prohibitions about killing or eating the totem, and the animal was considered sacred or thought to embody spirit entities. Often there were special ceremonies, as in the Intichiuma ritual of the Arunta people, which were designed to increase the numbers of the totem animal. Such rituals were seen by Robertson-Smith as the origin of sacrifice, the clan, in eating the sacrificed animal, thus partaking of the spirit as well as expressing the solidarity of the group. Often it was believed that the totemic clan was descended from the totem animal.

Freud expressed his dissatisfaction with existing theories regarding the origin of totemism. He offered criticisms of both the nominalistic and rationalistic theories, as well as of Durkheim's sociological interpretation, which suggested that the totem was a symbolic representation of

158

the community. How, then, does one explain totemism and exogamy? What was the meaning of sacrifice? To answer these questions Freud returns to the Oedipus complex and offers a theory that he suggests is both historical and psychological. It is one of the most amazing, tantalizing, and speculative theories ever propounded by a social scientist. Freud himself described it as "fantastic" (1938b: 217). Taking his cue from Darwin's writing on the "primal horde" and the idea that people "originally lived in small communities, each [man] with a single wife, or if powerful with several, whom he jealously defended against all other men . . . , the younger males being driven out," Freud suggested that human beings had originally lived in this kind of patriarchal family. "There is only a violent, jealous father who keeps all the females for himself and drives away the growing sons"; then "one day the expelled brothers joined forces, slew and ate the father, and thus put an end to the father-horde" (218).

But, filled with guilt and remorse about this "crime of parricide," for they had also loved and admired their father, the sons attempted to assuage their burning sense of guilt. They did this by instituting various rites and moral edicts. In order to live together peacefully they erected the incest prohibition, all equally renouncing the women desired. They instituted rites to repeat and commemorate the criminal act: The totem animal is the substitute father. Animal sacrifices and the Christian Eucharist are sacraments that simply repeat the crime that must be expiated. God, the totemic spirit, is "at bottom nothing but an exalted father" (225). Miller has suggested that Freud's theory is simply a modern version of the ancient doctrine of original sin (1964: 265). Freud, in fact, argues that this primal crime *is* the original sin. The latter, for Freud, was not the appropriation of knowledge, with Eve as the culprit, leading to a loss of innocence, but rather murder and subsequent guilt. "In the Christian myth," he writes, "man's original sin is undoubtedly an offence against God the father, and if Christ redeems mankind from the weight of original sin by sacrificing his own life, he forces us to the conclusion that this sin was murder" (235).

In this single theory, then, of the dissolution of the primal horde by a "mythical tragedy," Freud offered an explanation for taboos, sacrifice, totemism, exogamy and incest prohibitions, religion, and the beginning of social life. In closing his study he expressed this concisely, stating that the "beginnings of religion, ethics, society, and art meet in the Oedipus complex" (239). It presents an origin myth not only accounting for the origin of humanity – the breakthrough from nature to culture – but also suggesting the origin of matrilineal systems.

Hirst and Wooley's suggestion that Freud's theory was simply an explanation of the origin of the incest taboo and "not [of] society" (1982: 152) is, I think, misleading. Freud explicitly stated that human social organization began with the criminal act, although he was to suggest that "patriarchy" was later restored, replacing the original matrilineal "brother clan." Moreover, Hirst and Wooley's suggestion that Freud's totemic contract has echoes of the early social contract theories is hardly surprising, for Freud described it as such, and Fromm had earlier pointed to the similarity between Freud and the classical economists and the fact that his totemic theory was based on a supposed "covenant" (1962: 32).

Freud was aware that this "primal state" of society had nowhere been observed, and he suggested that the ethnographic evidence seemed to indicate that most preliterate communities were based not on the patriarchal family but on "fraternal associations" of men, a democratic system of matrilineal clans. Nevertheless, in spite of presenting his theory as a kind of allegory, Freud seems to insist that the "primal sin" was a historical event. But it was an event that was reenacted within the family in each generation, for Freud considered the Oedipus complex to be a psychic reality or process within the human personality. The "sense of guilt" had psychic continuity through the generations (1938b: 241; 1930: 78–9). (Many writers have felt that Jung's concept of the collective unconscious was a development of this idea of a collective mind.)

Both of these basic assumptions have been questioned, over the years, by any number of critics. The Darwinian theory of a primal horde must now be classed, as Freeman suggests, as a projected fantasy, for there is no evidence that this was an early form of social organization either for humans or for the higher primates (1969: 56). The phylogenetic assumption – namely, that guilt is transmitted through genetic inheritance – is also untenable, since it depends on the rather Lamarckian notion of the inheritance of acquired characteristics. Freeman's reappraisal of *Totem and Taboo*, therefore, though accepting that it contains many brilliant insights, is, on the whole, like that of Kroeber, a negative one, though Freeman agrees in substance with the underlying thesis of the book, namely that myths and rituals of preliterate people have "risen from the impulses and fantasies of the resulting Oedipus situations" (66). This implies that the Oedipus complex is universal in human societies and has explanatory significance in the understanding of cultural phenomena. (For a discussion of the debate on whether the Oedipus complex is a universal phenomenon, see A. Parsons 1969.)

In his later years Freud developed the seminal ideas expressed in *Totem and Taboo* further, extending his analysis to a critique of civilization and religion. His basic concern was the promotion of human happiness and well-being, and this permeates all his writings. For Freud, morality and science are not separate or distinct concerns, although he attempts to keep a sense of detachment. He assumes that "two great powers" are reflected in the human condition, that the communal life of mankind is based on a twofold foundation: the "power of love," and the "compulsion to work." Thus, like Marx and Engels, Freud starts from materialist premises, and he also implies that patriarchy is at the center of human life.

But the crucial difference is that Freud played down the significance of human labor and, like many conservative thinkers, viewed work as a painful necessity, seemingly unrelated to pleasure and creativity. On the other hand, unlike Engels, Freud did not view sex as tied to procreation. Rather Freud thought of sexual love, as we have seen, as a kind of energy that was intrinsically linked to pleasure but that could, through sublimation, be channeled into the development of culture. Put rather crudely, Marx thought of human culture as the product of labor, the creative interaction of the human subject with nature within a given social context. Humans were instinctively social, and labor was both the expression and the realization – or potential realization – of the essence of the human species. For Freud, culture was the product not of human praxis but of the renunciation of the libido, of the repression and sublimation of sexual energy. There was therefore a fundamental antithesis between civilization and sexuality.

This antithesis is explored in his profound and interesting essay *Civilization and Its Discontents* (193). Life as we find it, Freud suggests, is full of pain, suffering, and disappointments, and present social conditions leave little room for the simple, natural love of two human beings. He explores the many palliatives that help us to cope with our miseries and concludes that our instinctual energies are displaced in such activities as art and religion, both involving, like neurosis, satisfactions through fantasy. Freud takes a favorable attitude toward art, regarding it, along with science, as the two highest achievements of mankind. Both represent the antithesis to religion, which Freud regards as intellectually untenable and an unsatisfactory mode of coping with the difficulties of life. Religion restricts choice and adaptation and is a kind of mass delusion, unrecognized as such by those who believe in it. "Its technique consists in depressing the value of life and distorting the picture of the real world in a delusional manner – which presupposes an intimidation of the intelligence. At this price ... religion succeeds in sparing many people an individual neurosis. But hardly anything more" (1930: 31–2).

Such criticisms of religion echo Freud's negative assessment of religion suggested in *The Future of an Illusion*, where he wrote that religion is the "universal obsessional neurosis of humanity; like the obsessional neurosis of children, it arose out of the Oedipus complex, out of the relation to the father" (1978: 39).

In essence the religious attitude – even the simple mystic feeling of "oneness" with the universe – derives, Freud suggests, from infantile feelings of helplessness (1930: 19). But again he warns us that this is only an analogy to help us to understand a social phenomenon and by no means exhausts the essential nature of religion.

Freud argues that there are "three sources" from which suffering comes: nature, our own bodies, and the inadequacy of social life. But, like Schopenhauer, he felt that most of our suffering and unhappiness – war, intercommunal conflict, neurosis – comes not from nature but from social relationships. What we call civilization, he writes, "is largely responsible for our misery." Toward culture, as it was expressed in western Europe, there was, Freud felt, a pervasive feeling of hostility and discontent. But unlike his followers Reich and Marcuse, Freud could see no way out of this dilemma, though offering a radical critique of civilization.

Human beings, Freud argues, instinctively seek pleasure through sexual love, and this is fundamental to their well-being, but culture represses these natural feelings, to the detriment of the individual. Neurosis is the outcome of the ensuing frustrations, and Freud even poses the question of whether specific cultures, or even the whole of mankind, may have become "neurotic" (1930: 91). Thus a further question may be posed, and Freud himself raises it – namely, whether a "re-ordering of human relations" is possible that would remove the discontents that have been expressed, "by renouncing coercion and the suppression of the instincts" (1978: 3). But Freud did not think such a communal life was possible, and he offers some critical observations on socialist theory. The abolition of private property and economic inequalities (and Freud is clearly unhappy about such inequalities) would not make any difference. Private property, he felt, was one of the instruments of aggression, not the cause of it. Every civilization, he felt, "must be built up on coercion and renunciation of instinct" (3), essentially because of the original nature of mankind. And here Freud took a very Hobbesian view, suggesting that human beings by nature were not "gentle creatures who want to be loved" (1930: 58) but, on the contrary, destructive, aggressive, antisocial, and anticultural. Like other bourgeois thinkers, Freud saw the individual as an isolated, self-sufficient entity, in opposition to culture (Fromm 1970: 47). Evidence for this aggressiveness Freud considered to be apparent in the historical record and the atrocities and horrors committed in the acts of genocide and war (1930: 59). It was in relation to such thoughts that Freud (1920) came to revise his instinct theory and to posit aggression as an original, self-subsisting instinctual disposition in mankind. This aggressive instinct, the "hostility of each against all and of all against each" (69), echoing Hobbes's famous phrase, makes "civilization" necessarily coercive and demanding of instinctual renunciation – and thus detrimental to individual happiness. Hence the discontents. The history of mankind becomes, therefore, for Freud a continuing struggle between Eros and Thanatos, between the instinct of life and the instinct of destruction, and, with the possibility that humans could, as Freud notes, with no difficulty exterminate "one another to the last man" (1930: 92), the future can only be uncertain. It is an extremely pessimistic vision. Marcuse presented the essence of Freud's social theory when he wrote, "The concept of man that emerges from Freudian theory is the most irrefutable indictment of western civilization – and at the same time the most unshakeable defense of this civilization" (1969: 29).

By insisting on the importance of unconscious motivations, Freud undermined any blind trust in consciousness or rational thought. Some writers have implied that Freud, in consequence, was an antirationalist. But in spite of his pessimism and his stress on the unconscious, Freud never lost his faith in rational thought, and one can do no better than to conclude this section with an extract from his writings. He wrote:

> We may insist as often as we like that man's intellect is powerless in comparison with his instinctual life, and we may be right in this. Nevertheless, there is something peculiar about this weakness. The voice of the intellect is a soft one, but it does not rest until it has gained a hearing. Finally, after a countless succession of rebuffs, it succeeds. This is one of the few points on which one may be optimistic about the future of mankind. (1978: 49)

But it is well to note, as Fromm suggests (1950: 12), that Freud's indictment of religion goes beyond the attempt to prove that religion is an illusion. He also argues that religion is a danger, in that it tends to sanctify bad human institutions; that by prohibiting critical thinking it leads to the impoverishment of intelligence; and that in linking ethical norms to religious doctrine it puts morality on very shaky grounds. Human happiness, freedom, and truth are all threatened, Freud felt, by religion. He clearly saw himself in the tradition of the Enlightenment thinkers, as a humanistic scientist setting forth to dispel outworn superstitions and to discredit humanity's "naive self-love."

Jung: biographical notes

Freud's attitude to religion was essentially negative, hostile, and critical. Although in the history of the psychoanalytic movement and in terms of his intellectual development Freud's own life was closely linked with that of Carl Jung, it would be hard to find two scholars whose views on religion were so opposed. Religion for Jung was something positive and wholesome, an existential psychic necessity. Freud, like Marx and Durkheim, was a rationalist; Jung was a theologian with a strong bent for empirical studies. God and religious beliefs were thus, for Jung, not something to be explained: They were a given psychic reality and virtually equated with the unconscious.

Carl Gustav Jung (1875–1961) was a "scholar in the grand style," a scholar who has, in recent years, become something of a legend. This is rather paradoxical, for his influence on academic psychology has been limited and muted, even though many of his concepts – "complex," "extrovert," "introvert," "self-actualization" – have entered the vocabulary. He has been endlessly rebuked for his mysticism, though surprisingly, given his deep interest in religion and his own visionary experiences, this phenomenon is rarely mentioned in his writings. Marcuse thought Jung's psychology was obscurantist and reactionary, a kind of pseudomythology that cut away the instinctual and social roots of Freud's psychoanalytic theory (1969: 191). Yet unexpectedly Jung has had an important influence on a number of radical scholars, such as Lewis Mumford and Herbert Read, as well as on anthropologists like Radin. And recently Jung's insights on the nature of the psyche have been widely used by feminist writers in their critiques of patriarchal culture (see J. Singer 1977, Colegrave 1979).

Jung was born at Kesswil on Lake Constance, in Switzerland, the son of a pastor in the Swiss Reformed Church. After obtaining a medical degree at the University of Basel, he became, at the age of twenty-five, an assistant at Burgholzli Mental Hospital in Zurich. He worked there for some nine years, studying during the period under Bleuler and Janet, both eminent psychiatrists. Unlike Freud, Jung therefore had firsthand experience of working with mentally disturbed patients. In 1909 he gave up his post at the Burgholzli Hospital and devoted the rest of his life to his private medical practice and to travel, research, and writing. He is said to have led an outwardly uneventful life, showing little interest in politics. For most of his life he lived near Zurich. In spite of his travels he was, like Frazer, something of a Victorian scholar living in the twentieth century, observing the culture of tribal peoples as if they were simply a reflection of the "archaic man." He writes perceptively of his African travels and of the "spiritual peril" that his encounter with African culture entailed; Jung indicated, like his racist, colonial contemporaries, his psychological fear of "going native," interpreted as a "violent assault of the unconscious psyche" on his European consciousness. Sexual contact in particular was seen by Jung as undermining European hegemony in Africa (1963: 273–91).

Early in his career as a psychiatrist, Jung read Freud's important study *The Interpretation of Dreams* (1900). It made, on its second reading, an important impact on Jung's thought, for it indicated not only that dreams could be understood by the interpretation of their meaning but that repressive mechanisms were operant in them. This corroborated Jung's own experiments in word association, and in 1906 Jung sent Freud a copy of his articles *"Studies in Word Association."* The following year the two men met in Vienna. They clearly had a lot of admiration for each other, and on their first encounter they are said to have talked nonstop for thirteen hours. But their friendship was not simply an intellectual one, for Jung and Freud had a psychological need for each other, and their relationship had all the elements of a surrogate father–son relationship. Although Jung became president of the first International Psychoanalytic Association, over the years increasing personal and intellectual disagreements between the two men surfaced, and the final schism came at the end of 1913. Freud and Jung never saw one another again. Each, as Brome says, "subsequently claimed malicious damage from the other" (1978: 154), but it is clear that the break was inevitable, given the contrasting theoretical perspectives of the two men.

Their dispute was concerned with two issues. One was the emphasis that Freud put on sexual factors in the interpretation of neurosis and dreams. Jung thought that Freud put undue emphasis on sexuality; sexuality, he suggested, played only a subordinate role in most cases of neurosis. Although Jung thought Freud an extremely intelligent and shrewd scholar, he found this stress on sexuality unacceptable and put it down to the morbid consequence of Freud's own repressed sexuality. There is no mistaking the fact, he wrote, that Freud was "emotionally involved in his sexual theory to an extraordinary degree" (1963: 173). The other source of conflict was Freud's attitude to religion and occult phenomena. This, Jung wrote, "struck at the heart of our friendship... What Freud seemed to mean by 'occultism' was virtually everything that philosophy and religion had learned about the psyche" (173). Toward such phenomena, as we have seen, Freud's attitude was consistently negative and critical. Anthony Storr summed up the essential difference in the fundamental values of the two men in this way:

> Freud undoubtedly attributed supreme value to the orgastic release of sex, whereas Jung found supreme value in the unifying experience of religion. Hence Freud tended to interpret all numinous and emotionally significant experience as derived from, or substitutes for, sex: whereas Jung tended

to interpret even sexuality itself as symbolic; possessing "numinous" significance, in that it represented an irrational union of opposites, and was thus a symbol of wholeness. (1973: 19)

The perspectives of the two men were thus based on contrasting and incompatible materialist and idealist premises.

It is common to see Jung as a neo-Freudian scholar, who, by rejecting Freud's pansexualism, forged his own theory of psychoanalysis and his own method of psychotherapy, which together became known as *analytical psychology*. Jung is thus seen as one of the "early schismatics" (J. A. C. Brown 1961), a deviant member of the psychoanalytic school. But this is somewhat misleading, for Jung had already had six years of psychiatric experience before he met Freud and had published an important study of schizophrenia, *The Psychology of Dementia Praecox*, in 1906, a book that he had sent to Freud and that prompted the invitation to Vienna. Jung was an original thinker, not a renegade Freudian. (On the relationship between Freud and Jung, see Freud 1938a; Jung 1963: 169–93; E. Jones 1964; McGuire 1974; and Brome 1978.)

Both in his personal life and in terms of his basic intellectual premises, Jung is an individualist, and his whole style of thought is psychologistic. Jung always claimed that external events were relatively unimportant to him, and all have commented on the lack of detail about his personal relationships in his autobiography *Memories, Dreams, Reflections*. His wife and lifelong collaborator Emma barely gets a mention. Jung was a solitary thinker. But more than this, his conception of psychological science is extremely circumscribed. Storr expresses this well, as follows: "This predilection for the solitary accounts for the fact that Jungian psychology is principally concerned, not with interpersonal relationships, but with processes of growth and development of personality seen as taking place within the charmed circle of the individual psyche" (1973: 10). Jung's theoretical outlook is, therefore, fundamentally ahistorical and asocial, and contrasts again markedly with that of Freud. For Freud, maturity or normality is intrinsically linked with satisfactory personal relationships. For Jung, "The individual is the only reality" (1964: 45).

In Jung's psychology the psyche is virtually seen as a closed system, though it derives its energy from the metabolic processes of the body. This life force or *libido* is seen as nonsexual. The psyche itself is described by Jung as having three essential levels: the ego or conscious mind; the personal unconscious, which consists of those experiences that have been forgotten or repressed from consciousness; and the collective unconscious. The notion of a transpersonal unconscious, prefigured in the writings of Freud, is the most original and controversial part of Jung's personality theory. Indeed it is the key concept around which Jung's whole theory and philosophy revolves.

Jung saw the psyche as a kind of self-regulating mechanism in which the conscious and unconscious parts reciprocally influence each other. He also saw the total personality as made up of different attitudes (extrovert and introvert) and psychological functions (feeling, thinking, sensing, and intuiting), thus giving rise to different personality types. On this subject he wrote a massive and important study, *Psychological Types*, drawing on material from diverse sources, both philosophical and comparative (1921). But although Jung stresses the oppositions and compensatory mechanisms operating within the psyche, he also posits a transcendental function, the striving for integration and selfhood that he suggests is achieved in the latter part of life. This unity and balance, for Jung, could only be achieved through religion. In an important sense Jung saw his psychology as not only a synthesis of Freud and Adler's contrasting theories but also as a reconciliation of religion and science.

After travels to the Pueblo Indians in New Mexico and to northern and eastern Africa in the 1920s, Jung became more and more interested in comparative religion, mythology, and such phenomena as alchemy and mandala symbolism. On these topics he wrote some important studies that reveal wide learning and erudition. He relates to and attempts to explicate these phenomena in terms of his concept of the collective unconscious. (For an introduction to Jung's work, see Fordham 1953 and Bennett 1966.)

Religion and the collective unconscious

In his study *Psychology and Religion* (1938), Jung suggests that religion is not only a sociological or historical phenomenon but also has a profound psychological significance. He defines religion as a numinous experience that seizes and controls the human subject. It is a definition shared by theologians like Otto, religious experience being submission to a cause or power external and superior to the human subject. The person, Jung writes, is the "victim," not the "creator," of this experience (4). Religious rites and doctrines are seen as simply the codified form of an original religious experience.

Jung suggests that we approach this topic from the point of view of phenomenology. He claims that this is a scientific approach and that he will deal with religion from a "purely empirical point of view" (2). He claims to be dealing with facts and not judgments, and suggests that religious beliefs such as the virgin birth are "psychologically true," since the idea exists in someone's mind. He also suggests that "certain ideas

167

exist almost everywhere and at all times and they can even spontaneously create themselves quite apart from migration and tradition . . . They are not made by the individual" (4).

There are a number of serious problems relating to this formulation. One is that to define religion in terms of experience or feeling is highly problematic and vague, as Evans-Pritchard suggested in discussing the writings of Lowie and Radin (1965: 38–9). In any case, the kind of religious feeling that suggests the experience of an external numinous power hardly seems to match the ecstatic feelings of detachment suggested in Buddhist writings or the sense of oneness with god or the universe described by religious mystics. Indeed, several writers on mysticism have described this phenomenon in terms of the "unitive state," not in terms of power and control (see Underhill 1911).

Second, to imply that religious beliefs are "facts" that do not involve judgments, and that they are "psychologically true" simply because someone believes in them, is a form of cultural relativism that can hardly be sustained. The existence of an idea does not make it true, and, as Fromm suggests, even to speak of "delusions" or "fantasies" implies a judgment on what is considered objectively true by the psychiatrist. Jung seems to imply that the difference between the subjective and objective depends on whether or not a belief or idea is shared. But again, as Fromm writes, "Have we not seen that millions of people, misguided by their irrational passions, can believe in ideas which are not less delusional and irrational than the products of a single individual?" (1950: 16).

Finally, although Jung speaks of his approach as being empirical and phenomenological, his writings go beyond that of description, for he suggests that religion can best be understood by relating it to a "collective unconscious," a psychic reality shared by all humans. To grasp the meaning of this important concept, it is perhaps best to quote some relevant extracts from Jung's writings:

> The collective unconscious contains the whole spiritual heritage of mankind's evolution, born anew in the brain structure of every individual. His conscious mind is an ephemeral phenomenon that accomplishes all provisional adaptations and orientations. The unconscious, on the other hand, is the source of the instinctual forces of the psyche and of the forms or categories that regulate them, namely the archetypes. All the most powerful ideas in history go back to archetypes. This is particularly true of religious ideas, but the central concepts of science, philosophy and ethics are not exceptions to this rule. For it is the function of consciousness not only to recognize and assimilate the external world through the gateway of the senses, but to translate into visible reality the world within us. (Jung 1971: 45–6)

168

Even dreams are made of collective material to a very high degree, just as, in the mythology and folklore of different peoples, certain motives repeat themselves in almost identical forms. I have called those motives archetypes, and by them I understand forms or images of a collective nature which occur practically all over the earth as constituents of myths and at the same time as autochthonous, individual products of unconscious origin ... Even complicated archetypal images can be spontaneously reproduced without any possible direct tradition. (Jung 1938: 63–4)

A number of points may be made about this conception of a universal collective unconscious.

(1)   Jung argues strongly against the idea of equating mind with consciousness but suggests that the transpersonal unconscious "inherited from the past" is no "mere depository" but has a dynamic aspect. It is not, he writes, a "sort of abandoned rubbish heap" but a living system of reactions, the psychic counterpart of biological instincts.

(2)   He notes that this concept of "primordial ideas" is not an original one and had earlier been suggested by Adolf Bastian and Nietzsche. He also links his ideas to the writings of Lévy-Bruhl, who had suggested that the culture of preliterate people was prelogical. Lévy-Bruhl implied that preliterate thought involved the "mystical participation" of events and ideas, a cosmological mode of thought that linked entities that rational thinking would appear to separate. (Lévy-Bruhl's theory is discussed more fully in Chapter 5.) Although Jung rarely engages in the discussion of other scholars' work, it is clear that he was strongly influenced by the writings of Nietzsche, Lévy-Bruhl, Bergson, and William James – all psychologistic theorists.

(3)   Jung postulates that the collective unconscious represents a biological substratum; hence primordial images may spontaneously and of their own "free will" be expressed in consciousness or dreams. The latter are, in a sense, "natural symbols." But such symbols, as opposed to signs, have an emotional import and express "unconscious" aspects of the mind. The meaning of the symbol is therefore far from straightforward, and since the symbols refer to the "unknown" the meaning can only be ascertained by studying both the personal background of the individual and comparative mythology.

(4)   Jung sees the unconscious psyche, expressing itself in archetypal patterns, as being evident in such phenomena as dreams, myths, ecstatic visions, religious symbolism, the cultural beliefs and rites of preliterate people (which he essentially saw as archaic survivals of ancient culture), and in pathological states such as hysteria, compulsive neuroses, phobias, and schizophrenia (which were viewed as "rooted" in, or as "irruptions" of, the collective unconscious), as well as in "active imagination." As with

Freud, such phenomena are seen as analogous and as implying a different mode of thought from that of rational consciousness. But whereas Freud saw fantasies, symbols, dreams, and neurosis as having an infantile, wishful, and an essentially sexual origin, Jung saw them as deriving from a neutral unconscious. Thus for Freud neurosis and fantasy (and religion) were a limited and inadequate mode of adaptation to reality, functioning only in times of stress or crisis. Jung holds a similar view, but he does not see unconscious motivation as in any way inferior to that of rational or conscious thought. As Storr writes, "Jung ... puts the inner world of myth and archetype upon an equal footing with the external. He sees the ego poised, as it were, between inner and outer, between subjective and objective, with an equal need to relate to each world. The idea that the inner world is in any sense infantile or pathological appears to be alien to him" (1973: 74).

As Jung himself put it, "I attribute a positive value to all religions. In their symbolism I recognize those figures which I have met with in the dreams and fantasies of my patients. In their moral teachings I see efforts that are the same or similar to those made by my patients ... They seek the right way of dealing with the forces of the inner life (1933: 137).

(5) Much of Jung's work on the unconscious is devoted to exploring the nature of the various archetypes that he sees manifesting themselves as various symbols or mythical themes. Among the more important of these archetypes are the wise old man; the earth mother; anima and animus (the "feminine" and "masculine" aspects of men and women); the cross; the mandala; the quarternity (or element of "fourness"); the hero; the divine child; the self; god; and the persona. Jung tends not only to personify such archetypes but sees them as having "their own initiative and their own specific energy" (1964: 67). (Such archetypal representations in myths have been explored by many Jungian scholars, e.g., Campbell 1949 and Neumann 1955.)

(6) Jung sees the "collective unconscious" (mythology and religion) as having important functions for the human personality, not only giving meaning to known existence but having a therapeutic role. Jung asks why we should believe in religious illusions and "unknowable" ideas like that of god. And like William James, he answers, "There is a strong empirical reason why we should cultivate thoughts that can never be proved; it is that they are known to be useful. Man positively needs general ideas and convictions that will give a meaning to his life and enable him to find a place for himself in the universe" (1964: 76). And on religion's therapeutic value, he writes, "We regard the personal complexes as compensations for one-sided or faulty attitudes of consciousness; in the same way, myths of a religious nature can be interpreted as

a sort of mental therapy for the sufferings and anxieties of mankind in general – hunger, war, disease, old age, death" (68).

In Jungian therapy, therefore, a prominent place is given to dream interpretation, to the understanding of comparative mythology, and to helping the patient to find a religious viewpoint that will give his or her life meaning. Mental health, for Jung, is achieved by integrating the different aspects of the personality with this transpersonal and transcendental realm of the unconscious.

(7) Jung not only spoke of the collective unconscious but often in his writings referred to a racial or ethnic unconscious and freely spoke about the "oriental mind," "modern man," the "Aryan unconscious," and other such generalizations. During the 1930s Jung was the center of much controversy about his alleged anti-Semitic sentiments and for his support of fascism, though he and his followers have always strenuously denied such charges (see Brome 1978: 217–20). It is often unclear whether Jung is writing about cultural attributes at a conscious level or about the "collective unconscious."

(8) Finally, it is worth noting that like Weber, Jung felt that the "impact of modern civilization" had led to a decline in spiritual values and that there had been a disenchantment of the natural world. We have stripped all things of their mystery and numinosity, he wrote: "Nothing is holy any more" (1964: 84). As scientific rationality has increased, so the world has become dehumanized, and the individual has become "isolated in the cosmos." Human beings have lost their "unconscious identity" with the natural world, which has ceased to have any symbolic meaning. As this intimate contact with nature has been severed with industrialization, so has contact with the unconscious. This "despiritualization of the world" had begun with the Greek philosophers, and Jung looked upon this with regret, the "helpful numina" having fled from the woods, rivers, and mountains. The idea of the domination of reason in contemporary society, he suggests, is "our greatest and most tragic illusion" (1964: 91).

Such, in brief, are the basic tenets associated with Jung's concept of the collective unconscious. It is clear that Jung not only reduces religion to a psychological phenomenon but, as Fromm remarks, elevates the unconscious to a religious phenomenon (1950: 20). Although Freud, and his followers like Marcuse, by no means denied the importance of aesthetics, fantasy and art, Freud tended, as has been said, neither to denigrate reason nor elevate this mode of adaptation to the level of the reality principle. Moreover, he kept a distinction between art and religion, which he thought, though both derived from unconscious motivation, had quite dissimilar social implications. Jung, on the other hand, saw religion as a psychic "reality" that is as real as the natural world. The human subject has to come to terms with both the external world and the "inner world" of the unconscious, which is described in essentially religious terms and as having a "life" of its own. For Jung, religion and mythology are expressions of an "objective reality" as real and as imposing as the natural world. Jung refuses to explain religion and mythology in naturalistic terms, except insofar as he explicates religion in functional and psychologistic terms, as earlier writers had done. Religion thus is a theodicy giving meaning to life; it enables human beings to face the exigencies of life: death, illness, and misfortune. Jung therefore combines the perspectives of both the intellectualists and such writers as Spinoza and Hume. That a meaningful existence may be achieved without religion; that religion itself may be responsible for and related to wars and the dehumanization of the human spirit; that religion may have negative functions, both social and personal, does not seem to occur to Jung. He seems to see religion only in terms of its positive qualities. He writes, "No matter what the world thinks about religious experience, the one who has it possesses the great treasure of a thing that has provided him with a source of life, meaning and beauty and that has given a new splendour to the world and to mankind" (1938: 113).

Jung, rather surprisingly, but significantly, interpreted the rise of fascism as a revival of archaic religious forms but was quite unable to see the social implications of this, given his underlying assumption that god is a psychic phenomenon. Needless to say, he completely bypassed Freud's critique of religion and his suggestion that religion serves to sanctify bad human institutions and hampers critical reason. Jungian therapeutic procedures imply a similar neglect; as Kovel suggests, the positive indifference to the actual details of life in favor of religion is a dangerous way to approach emotional problems (1978: 140). And fantasies and delusions – which, as Storr suggests, are often linked to social isolation – can hardly be deemed healthy or put on a par with mental health, even though they may be viewed as symbolically meaningful and have a creative function in enabling the individual to cope with stressful situations.

Understandably, Jung's philosophy has been criticized as mystical and reactionary, in that it replaces mundane and materialist explanations with transcendent ones. In fact, to explain religion (even in its fascist form) or mental illness simply as "irruptions" of the unconscious explains nothing. As J. A. C. Brown suggests, this simply describes the partly known in terms of the totally unknown (1961: 44). Jung always defended himself against the charge of mysticism, suggesting that he could not be held responsible for the fact that "mankind has everywhere and always

172

spontaneously developed religious forms of expression, and that the human psyche from time immemorial has been shot through with religious feelings and ideas" (1933: 140). True. But Jung took a further crucial step and assumed that such phenomena constituted a psychic reality. The evidence for doing so, he felt, was the universality of certain motifs in the dreams and delusions of children and mental patients, as well as in the myths and religious beliefs of people everywhere. The unconscious and its expression as archetypes have, for Jung, a "reality" akin to that of the natural world. And as religion is intrinsically associated with this unconscious inner reality, it remains essentially something inexplicable. Indeed Jung speaks of myths as being the "word of God" in a literal sense and remarks that god speaks chiefly through dreams and visions (1964: 92). Yet as Roheim and others have argued, human beings of all cultures share certain common experiences: All have parents; are born, and die, and live in an earthly realm in which the sun, earth, self, mother are existential realities; so it is hardly surprising that in their dreams and myths they express common and universal themes. The hypothesis of the collective unconscious is, from this point of view, an unnecessary elaboration to "explain" certain phenomena that can be more simply explained in another way (J. A. C. Brown 1961: 47), though whether the unconscious has any explanatory significance is debatable. Historical change and the variations in human culture, of course, are not explicable within Jungian psychological theory. In addition there is the question of whether or not Jung's archetypal symbols are in fact universal; one student of mythology answers adamantly that they are not (Kirk 1970: 275).

Jung tended to view conscious thought as rational and linear (a dubious assumption) and to imply that the "logic" of dreams and myths was essentially "analogical." In an interesting study (1972) he posits an acausal principle that he terms *synchronicity*, which he defines as "a meaningful coincidence in time," and thus independent of time, space, and causality. He sees this principle as bound up with the archetypes, with intuition, with magical (that is, analogical) thought, with divination and astrology, with the Chinese concept of Tao, with the medieval attitude of mind, with holistic thought, and with extrasensory perception. Thus, by a kind of analogical reasoning of his own, Jung equates quite distinctive phenomena. Rather than helping us to understand such phenomena, his theory merely classifies them under a heading that is meaningful only in terms of modes of consciousness (see Ornstein 1972). As a result, the religious conceptions lose their historical specificity.

Jung was fundamentally an antirationalist thinker, in spite of his constant pleas that he was an empiricist and used a scientific approach to religion and mythology. Thus one can but conclude that he was a "myst-agogue." Hughes's harsh judgment of Jung is, I think, close to the truth: "In trying to deepen Freud's teaching, he did just the opposite. He retreated from all the advanced positions that psychoanalytic theory had staked out. He abandoned or completely watered down the concepts of 'the unconscious, infantile sexuality, repression, conflict and transfer-ence,' that were its minimal principles. His critics are on firm ground in calling him a 'reactionary' " (1958: 160; cf. Glover 1950).

In counterbalancing Freud's "obsession with the body," Jung became more and more preoccupied with religion and the occult and more and more insistent that science could never replace religion and that some kind of religion was necessary for the psychic health of humankind. It was a perspective that contrasted markedly with that of rationalists of many persuasions – Marx, Durkheim, Frazer, and Freud – whatever their other differences.

Religion as archetype

It is somewhat remarkable, as Mircea Eliade noted (1969: 40), that during the nineteenth century, at the very height of materialistic and positivistic interpretations of social reality (exemplified in the work of Comte and Spencer), an interest in comparative religion also emerged. Much of this interest was incorporated into the anthropological tradition (discussed in Chapter 3). But there was a line of thinking about religion that was quite distinct from the rationalist and sociological approaches of Tylor and Durkheim. It is an approach that can be situated within the German idealist tradition, and it is best described as hermeneutic or phenome-nological, although its connection with philosophical phenomenology is tenuous, one of affinity rather than substantive. Müller, Otto, and in some senses Jung stand close to this tradition.

This approach to religion was given its earliest and clearest expression in Friedrich Schleiermacher's *Discourses on Religion*, published in 1799. Schleiermacher was a Protestant preacher and theologian who was greatly distressed at the social and intellectual implications of the En-lightenment, which not only discredited and debased religious thought but threatened to make it redundant. Schleiermacher's study therefore was a conscious attempt, as Otto suggests in an introduction to the study, "to recapture the position religion had lost in the intellectual world, where it was now threatened with total oblivion" (1958: ix). The study is essentially in the romantic tradition, leaning toward fantasy and mys-ticism, and is antirationalist in orientation. Copleston (1963: 188) de-scribed Schleiermacher as a "romanticized Spinoza" for Schleiermacher

174

had a quasi-mystical consciousness of god as the underlying, undifferentiated unity of the world spirit and nature. For Schleiermacher religion was an existential reality on a par with the natural world, and for its understanding there could be no "reduction" of spirit to the world. The understanding of the "essence" of religion therefore could not be achieved through reflection nor conceptual thought but only through "intuition." Indeed, he insists that religion is grounded on the immediate, intuitive feeling of dependence on the infinite. The true nature of religion, Schleiermacher wrote, "is the immediate consciousness of the deity as he is found in ourselves and in the world" (1958: 101). Schleiermacher is, then, a fundamentally religious thinker: Religion can be understood only in its own terms, and its essence can be ascertained only by intuition. Both Rudolph Otto and Jung, as we have seen, are close to this tradition of thought. But the contemporary writer who has expressed the phenomenological approach with cogency in a number of important comparative studies is Mircea Eliade. It is to his work that we turn in this final section.

Eliade was born in Romania in 1907, and, though widely traveled – he studied in India for many years – for most of his life he has been a professor of the history of religion on various theological faculties. His writings on comparative religion are voluminous and indicate, like Frazer's before him, wide erudition. His work has been the subject of a number of critical assessments from within the hermeneutic tradition (see Altizer 1963, Allen 1978). This tradition is, I think, best described in the words of Paul Ricoeur, whose own study *The Symbolism of Evil* (1967) exemplifies it. Ricoeur makes a distinction between two modes of interpretative understanding, ignoring the important tradition of Durkheim, which is both reductive and noncritical. One he describes as the "school of suspicion," represented by Marx, Nietzsche, and Freud. This mode of interpretation is critical and reductive and views understanding as demystification, though neither Freud nor Marx saw the "whole" of consciousness as illusory or "false," as Ricoeur seems to suggest (33). The other mode of interpretation is hermeneutics proper and involves what Ricoeur refers to as the "restoration of meaning." This mode, contrary to "suspicion," is based on "faith." He writes of this mode of understanding,

> Phenomenology is its instrument of hearing, of recollection, of restoration of meaning. "Believe in order to understand, understand in order to believe" – such is its maxim; and its maxim is the "hermeneutic circle" itself of believing and understanding... The first imprint of this faith... is to be seen in the care or concern for the *object*, a characteristic of all phenomenological analysis. That concern, as we know, presents itself as a

175

"neutral" wish to describe and not to reduce. One reduces by explaining through causes (psychological, social, etc.), through genesis (individual, historical, etc.), through function (affective, ideological, etc.). Thus...the task is to understand what is signified, what quality of the sacred is intended. (1979: 28–9)

This approach to the understanding of religion is thus quite different from those we have reviewed so far in this study, all of which, from Spencer and Marx to Weber and Freud, would be deemed "reductive" by Ricoeur. It is an approach consonant with the German idealist tradition (Dilthey) and that of phenomenologists such as Edmund Husserl.

Like Dilthey, Husserl drew a distinction between the methods of the natural and social sciences and suggested that phenomenological understanding is not limited to the senses; in fact, empirical knowledge based on generalizations he felt to be limited. But rather, beginning with concrete experience, the external world must first be "bracketed" or held in suspension (*epoché*), and attention must be switched to the experience itself; then an attempt must be made to describe the structure of consciousness, to discover the underlying "essence" of the phenomena. Husserl refers to these "eidetic" structures as being intuited by insight, not by experience. This stress on consciousness is a form of "radical rationalism," and Husserl was critical both of traditional metaphysics and empirical psychology. Mircea Eliade's mode of understanding is similar to that of Husserl and is cogently outlined in his essay on methodology. (For an account of Husserl's phenomenology, see Pivcevic 1970.)

Eliade, like Jung, insists that the phenomenological approach to religion follows an empirical method; it implies a descriptive and sympathetic understanding of religion as religion. Thus it presupposes a universal religious experience and posits that religion must be understood within "its own frame of reference" as a religious phenomenon. Eliade holds that we must respect the fundamentally *irreducible* character of the religious experience and writes that "to try to grasp the essence of such a [religious] phenomenon by means of physiology, psychology, sociology, economics, linguistics, art or any other study is false; it misses the one unique and irreducible element in it – the element of the sacred" (1958: xiii). In stressing the irreducible character of religious experience, Eliade thus consciously follows the perspectives of Jung, Otto, Joachim Wach, and Gerardus Van Der Leeuw, whose study *Religion in Essence and Manifestation* (1938) is a classic attempt to present a phenomenology of religion that can delinate its "inner structures" or "essence" (Elaide 1969: 12–36). Religion is thus viewed by Eliade as a phenomenon sui generis, which can be understood only in its own terms. Although such a stance may imply a sympathetic attitude towards the subject matter,

176

by denying that religion can be understood from other perspectives Eliade offers a very narrow and limited viewpoint. In any case, in Eliade's view all systematic attempts to understand religion are in some sense "reductive," including his own approach (see Allen 1978: 81–101). To suggest that "it would be useless, because ineffectual, to appeal to some reductionist principle and to demystify the behaviour and ideologies of *homo religiosus* by showing, for example, that it is a matter of projections of the unconscious, or of screens raised for social, economic, political, or other reasons" (1969: 68) is to ignore the contributions to social understanding that have been offered by the materialist scholars that have been reviewed in the preceding pages. Though they may not serve hermenutics, the perspectives of Marx, Weber, Durkheim, and Freud can hardly be dismissed as useless fallacies. To accept religion in its own terms is really to deny that it has any ideological function.

Given this initial phenomenological epoché, Eliade then suggests that the work of a historian of religion, as he describes himself, involves "deciphering the deep meaning of religious phenomena." He seeks to understand religion in terms of both its meaning and its history, and "he applies himself to deciphering in the temporally and historically concrete the destined course of experiences that arise from an irresistible human desire to transcend time and history. All authentic religious experience implies a desperate effort to disclose the foundation of things, the ultimate reality. But all expression or conceptual formulation of such religious experience is embedded in a historical context" (1959a: 88–9).

This indicates that Eliade, like Jung, sees religion as linked to an unconscious striving on the part of humans for cosmic meaning and significance. But to grasp the "essence and the structure of religious phenomena," Eliade suggests that comparative studies are necessary (1969: 35). He argues against the kind of phenomenology that restricts itself to the descriptive understanding of one particular religion or culture and is equally against the construction of simple typologies of religious data. All historical manifestations of a religious phenomenon have to be studied in order to discover what such a phenomenon "has to say." "Structure" and "meaning" are key concepts for Eliade, and he considers himself to be both a historian and a phenomenologist of religion. Given this approach, it necessarily follows that Eliade sees all religious phenomena as having a symbolic character, and indeed, following Cassirer and others, he defines the human being as *homo symbolicus*.

In his definition of religion Eliade follows and combines those of Otto and Durkheim. With Otto, he views religion as an essentially numinous experience of "the other," but he adopts Durkheim's terminology and approach in linking religion to the sacred, the domain that is opposite to profane life. He speaks of the sacred and the profane as "two modes of being in the world" and says that an "abyss" divides these two modalities of experience (1959a: 14). Every religious act and every cult object is therefore, by definition, related to this metaempirical reality, the sacred, and Eliade writes, "When a tree becomes a cult object, it is not as a tree that it is venerated, but as a *hierophany*, that is, a manifestation of the sacred. And every religious act, by the simply fact that it is *religious*, is endowed with a meaning which, in the last instance, is 'symbolic,' since it refers to supernatural values or beings" (1959a: 95).

All studies of religion in this perspective involve, therefore, a study of its symbolism. To understand myth, shamanism, or initiation rites is to "seek to decipher" the "implicit symbolism" that they manifest, the underlying "symbolic structures" that analysis discerns. Eliade insists that the search for such structures is not a work of reduction but of integration and that it is done by comparative analysis. For Eliade the hermeneutic search for meaning implies both the phenomenological suspension of judgment and the delineation of "structures of synchronicity" through comparison.

Eliade has described the general characteristics of religious symbolism in the following terms. In defining the symbols as functioning to "point beyond themselves" (Tillich 1955) to reveal a reality more basic and profound, it follows that an essential feature of religious symbolism is its *multivalence*; a symbol may express simultaneously several meanings. For in essence the symbol reveals the structure of a cosmic structure that is not evident at the level of immediate experience. In unveiling this sacramental dimension, the symbol "reveals the *world as a living totality*, periodically regenerating itself and, because of this regeneration, continually fruitful, rich and inexhaustible" (Eliade 1959a: 98). This is not, Eliade suggests, a question of reflective knowledge but one of "immediate intuition," for the "logic" of symbols indicates its own "autonomous mode of cognition." Linked with this is the notion that symbols have a unifying function; through religious symbolism an "arbitrary assemblage of heterogeneous and divergent realities" is integrated into a system and given a cosmic significance. Even "paradoxical situations" and the "contradictory aspects of reality" are expressed and integrated in this "cosmic unity" or totality." In translating the human situation and existential activities into cosmological terms, *meaning*, Eliade suggests, is given to human existence. Humans do not have a feeling of "isolation" when situated within such a cosmic schema (1959a: 102–3). Eliade assumes that preliterate people "live in a sacralized cosmos" and have an essentially religious attitude to the world, and he even implies that within the religious

178

experience "the cosmos in its entirety can become a hierophany" (1959b:12).

This may be true of the mystic state, but to apply such a notion to preliterate culture is highly misleading. As Malinowski and others have indicated, there is a pragmatic and material dimension to human life, and the "sacred" is never total. In contrast, contemporary human culture is seen by Eliade as implying a completely profane attitude towards the world, "a recent discovery in the history of the human spirit." Modern Europeans live in a "desacralized cosmos." The rise of mechanistic science is thus seen, as with Weber, as implying the disenchantment of the world; their shared viewpoint is understandable in that both Weber and Eliade remained close to German idealism in their essential premises, even though Weber struggled to go beyond this. (For critical assessments of this sacramental view of nature, see my essays of 1978 and 1979.) Many writers have suggested that this has theological implications for Eliade, that he looks upon this process of secularization as something of a "fall" and thus insists on the reality of the prefallen state (Altizer 1963). The same may well be said of Jung.

In Eliade's "comparative phenomenology" an inner tension is said to exist between his hermeneutical interpretation, which relates to universal coherent structures that are nontemporal, and historical understanding. For as Douglas Allen writes, "To assert that all religious phenomena are historical is to acknowlege that all religious phenomena are conditioned" (1978: 174). As with other structuralists, this dilemma is never faced, let alone resolved, for the invariant structures in themselves explain nothing. But Eliade is aware that numerous symbols have salience only because specific sociohistorical conditions obtain. For example, agricultural work could not be viewed as homologous to the sexual act until agriculture itself had been invented (1959a: 104).

Eliade's essential thesis is that religious thought, and preliterate culture generally, are characterized by an underlying structured schema that unites diverse aspects of existence into a cosmological unity through symbolism. "What we may call symbolic thought," he writes, "makes it possible for man to move freely from one level of reality to another ... Symbols identify, assimilate, and unify diverse levels" (1958: 455). In the process, people in precapitalist culture – "archiac man," as he describes them – feel a part of a living cosmos, and their existence is not broken, differentiated, or alienated. Both Lévi-Strauss and Douglas describe preliterate cultures, as we shall see, in a similar fashion. It is by no means a new conception, for Franz Boas likewise described "primitive thought" as being united by symbolic associations (1938: 135). It is,

179

however, somewhat misleading to equate this symbolism with the "thought" of preliterate people, and equally limiting to ignore the degree to which science, technology, and economics provide cognitive and symbolic orientations in contemporary capitalism.

But Eliade suggests more than the fact that religious experience is structured through symbolism. Like Jung, he argues that this symbolism manifests itself around specific archetypal patterns. Distinguishing his own concept of archetype from that of Jung, Eliade defines it as a synonym for "exemplary model" or "paradigm." What he means by this is perhaps best expressed in his own words:

> As the rite always consists in the repetition of an archetypal action performed in *illo temore* [before "history" began] by ancestors or by gods, man is trying, by means of the hierophany, to give "being" to even his most ordinary and insignificant acts. By its repetition, the act coincides with its archetype, and time is abolished. (1958: 32)

> Myths serve as models for ceremonies that periodically reactualize the tremendous events that occurred at the beginning of time. The myths preserve and transmit the paradigms, the exemplary models, for all the responsible activities in which men engage. By virtue of these paradigmatic models revealed to men in mythical times, the Cosmos and society are periodically regenerated. (1974a: xiv)

> Every construction or fabrication has the cosmogony as paradigmatic model. The creation of the world becomes the achetype of every creative human gesture, whatever its plane of reference may be. (1959b: 45)

In a series of interesting comparative studies (1958, 1959a, 1968, 1974b), Eliade sought to demonstrate how all rites and symbols are related to cosmogenic myths about creation and about the structuring of the living cosmos from a primordial reality or chaos. This structuring was achieved at the beginning of time by supernatural agents. Thus the secret initiation rites of Australian tribal communities are interpreted as a reenactment of their cosmogomy (dream time); lunar symbolism is linked to the regeneration of the cosmos and of life itself and with ideas of polarity and resurrection; the symbolism of the cosmic tree is also linked to the periodic regeneration of the universe, to the paradigmatic image of vegetation and to the symbolic links between heaven and earth; the role of water symbolism (baptism, the flood) is associated with the reenactment of the primordial chaos and the dissolution of all forms; the notion of the cosmogenic egg and divine androgyny (earth mother) are noted as symbols of the generative fertility of the cosmos.

In summary: Eliade interprets myths as having a single function, namely to establish a sacred cosmos from the primordial chaos, and he sees all religious rites and symbols as a repetition or manifestation of the paradigmatic events or model suggested by the cosmogenic myths. Such an interpretation goes well beyond that of descriptive analysis in positing archetypal symbolic structures. There is clearly some truth in Eliade's formulations, for what he essentially delineates are the common – but by no means universal – patterns to be found throughout the world in various religious systems. But in giving these patterns a privileged ontological status and in denying that religion can be adequately under- stood in terms of social and psychological factors, Eliade betrays his idealism. There is more to ecstatic cults, witchcraft, and rites of initiation (with respect to their sociopolitical functions) than Eliade's mode of phe- nomenological analysis is able to convey.

5

Religion: meaning and function

Lévy-Bruhl

Within the anthropological tradition outlined in Chapter 3, I noted four distinctive approaches to the study of religious phenomena: the intellectualist approach stemming from Tylor and Frazer, which tended to see magic and religion as essentially explanatory and theoretical; and the functionalist, symbolist, and structuralist approaches. Of these last three, the first two are explicit in the writings of Durkheim and Radcliffe-Brown, whereas the structuralist approach is a kind of hidden thesis within their work. Recent discussions of the structuralism inherent in Durkheim's study have tended to conflate the contrasting functional and symbolist approaches to religious phenomena (Schwartz 1981, Rossi 1983). Here I keep them distinct. In this chapter I will examine the symbolist approach, exemplified in the writings of Douglas and Turner, and will briefly discuss its relationship to functionalism as formulated by Ioan Lewis. In the next chapter I will discuss its relation to the intellectualist tradition.

But initially we must consider the writings of two scholars who have had a tremendous influence on anthropological studies: Lévy-Bruhl and Evans-Pritchard. Although belonging to different generations, they contribute, like Mauss and Radcliffe-Brown, a conceptual link between Durkheim and later scholars. Equally important, they may be regarded as the precursors of the symbolist and structuralist approaches, respectively, though neither scholar is discussed by Ino Rossi (1983) in his recent study of structuralism.

A contemporary of Durkheim, Lévy-Bruhl was a philosopher by training, but late in life he was influenced by the sociologist and turned his attention to anthropological literature and to the sociology of knowledge. His first book on the subject, translated in 1926 as *How Natives Think*, was published in 1910, when he was fifty-three. Several other texts subsequently appeared, developing and amplifying his basic ideas on the nature of "primitive mentality," as one of his many books was titled. Such writings aroused a good deal of criticism from anthropologists, and Lévy-Bruhl became, and remains, a controversial figure; as Evans-Pritchard noted, few contemporary writers fail to "take a swipe at him" (1965: 78). But he remains an important figure, and writers like Needham and Evans-Pritchard have sought to defend his intellectual integrity, if not his theories. Bohannan's introductory text significantly gives Lévy-Bruhl equal treatment to that of Tylor, Frazer, and Durkheim. But let us first outline his essential theory, with Needham (1972: 159–75) and Horton (1973: 250–58) as our guides.

Lévy-Bruhl, having been deeply influenced by Durkheim's writings, takes as his subject "collective representations" – that is, the sociocultural order that is "imposed" upon the individual and that preexists and survives members of the group. He therefore offers a critique of the theories of Tylor and Frazer, who attempted to explain religion in terms of individual psychology. This is an important point, for when Lévy-Bruhl speaks of "primitive mentality," he is not referring to individual mental faculties but to the cultural content of thought. The mental attitude of the individual is derived from the collective representations of his or her society, which are obligatory. Although Evans-Pritchard notes that such representations are the function of social institutions, Douglas (1970b) has rightly suggested that Lévy-Bruhl was not especially interested in contrasting social structures but only in comparing modes of thought.

In studying the mode of thought of preliterate people, Lévi-Bruhl felt that it was so different from European thought that to apply our own canons of scientific logic to it could only lead, as with Frazer, to its being labeled "childlike" or erroneous. This, Lévy-Bruhl sensed, was unhelpful, and so he came to postulate that the "thought" of preliterate people was radically different from that of modern industrial society. The reasons for this he put down to various emotional needs and to the fact that collective representations in small-scale societies allowed little scope for individual reasoning. Rationality, therefore, was not the key to understanding such beliefs. This led him, as Evans-Pritchard notes, to focus on the contrasts, rather than the similarities, between preliterate culture and modern culture. These are in a sense postulated as two contrasting ideal types.

Primitive thought, Lévy-Bruhl argues, is essentially mystical. The world is not perceived in a natural sense but is highly colored by and invested with emotion and with notions about supernatural entities. He admits that like us a nonliterate person perceives the general differences between phenomena such as birds and stones and trees and has an "exact knowledge" of the world that has a practical value. Preliterate people, he says, are never "as ignorant as we may be tempted to imagine" (1965: 19). But he stresses that stones and trees are never just perceived as natural objects, for they may be receptacles of mystical powers or be possessed of sacred characteristics. He cites from the ethnographic record numerous illustrations of this attitude and of the "feeling of unity of life with plants and animals" that many preliterate people express. This notion of a "personalized universe" and of a "mystical awareness of the actual affinity of things which survives amongst us only as a metaphor," to quote one commentator on African religion (J. V. Taylor 1963: 72–9), Lévy-Bruhl argued, typifies the mental attitude of preliterate people. "The reality in which primitives move," he writes, "is itself mystical. Not a being, not an object, not a natural phenomenon in their collective representations is what it appears to us" (1926: 30–1).

But, significantly, he stresses that such representations (as Evans-Pritchard noted) both control perception of the world and are fused with it, and this implies that primitive people see the world differently. Since their thought is infused with mystical ideas, they have a low evaluation of perceptual experience. Thus phenomena like dreams and visions, which are considered subjective in European thought, have a reality for preliterate people that is on the same footing as ordinary, everyday perception. This leads Lévy-Bruhl to suggest that since there is often a kind of identity assumed between a perceptual object and its mystical aspect (as with a totem animal), as well as between two perceptual objects that share the same mystical connotations (the Nuer's referring to a cucumber as an ox in their sacrificial rites is a famous example), then an important characteristic of preliterate thought is what he termed "homogeneity," or "mystical participation." A collective belief in a spiritual essence, whether in the form of gods and spirits or in an impersonal form, as in the notion of mana, indicated for Lévy-Bruhl that preliterate thought implied a mystical reality and "participation." This, in turn, led him suggest that since such mystical thought involved "contradictions," preliterate thought was indifferent to such considerations and was essentially "pre-logical." Again he indicated an awareness that preliterate people were capable of registering and avoiding contradictions, but stressed that their mystical thought took precedence over such conceptions.

Given these leading thoughts, Lévy-Bruhl came to suggest that because preliterate people's perception was invested with emotion and their thought cast in a mystical and personal idiom, they could more accurately be described as communing with the natural world than as perceiving it. In fact, the general tenor of Lévy-Bruhl's thesis on preliterate thought is replicated in an influential book by John V. Taylor, *The Primal Vision* (1963).

In his study, devoted to exploring the nature of African religion and citing anthropological studies, Taylor speaks of a "primal view" that involves a "sense of cosmic oneness" and in which a person's position vis-à-vis the world is "not one of exploitation but of relationship" (72–5). And like Lévy-Bruhl, Taylor equates African religion with African "thought" and sees the latter as essentially mystical. When Taylor writes that in primal religion the "self is thought of as spilling out into the world beyond the confines of the experiencing body" (45) and that man and the natural world are seen as inseparably involved in a "total community," he is echoing the thoughts of Lévy-Bruhl. The very contrast he makes between African and European thought follows Lévy-Bruhl's essential premises, although, as Horton indicated (1973), the latter writer did not explicitly define what he envisaged as "modern" thought. Horton suggests that his writings imply the following characteristics of European thought:

–that it is naturalistic, and, in the sense that perception is controlled largely by the organs of sight and touch, it tends toward objectivity.

–that emotions tend to be discounted, and thus inductive generalizations relating to natural events are made. Thus science and common-sense experience are almost equated.

–that since a mystical orientation is lacking, European thought frees our natural sensitivity to contradiction and allows us to perceive the world as something separate and distinct – something to be mastered and controlled rather than related to.

For Lévy-Bruhl, then, preliterate thought is essentially mystical, whereas modern thought is essentially positivistic. A fair generalization, but nevertheless inadequate.

From the outset Lévy-Bruhl's thesis attracted a good deal of interest, and it was subjected to much criticism. Malinowski stressed the practical and "scientific" aspect of Trobriand social life, whereas Evans-Pritchard's study of the Azande, although not mentioning Lévy-Bruhl, was largely devoted to exploring the complex relationship between what he termed "ritual" and "empirical" behavior (1937: 439). This implied a critique of Lévy-Bruhl. Thus among anthropologists there was a general consensus that Lévy-Bruhl had, in focusing largely on their religious conceptions, made the mental world of preliterate people seem more mystical than it really was. As Horton put it, "He portrayed them as living continuously upon the mystical plane, whereas in fact they spent much of their time at the level of common sense, where the Western ethnographer could meet them without any difficulty (1973: 256).

Likewise, as Evans-Pritchard stresses, Lévy-Bruhl equates "civilized" thought with scientific logic and ignores the diversity of thought to be found in European culture. Evans-Pritchard goes on to discuss the sociologist Vilfredo Pareto, an extreme positivist, who considered almost all religion, art, and morality as essentially nonlogical and reserved the idea of rationality to describe the logico-experimental methods advocated by science. Thus Pareto in a sense extends Lévy-Bruhl's ideas to all human cultures, seeking to explain, in his treatise *The Mind and Society* (1935), the individual and social functions of "non-logical conduct."

Lévy-Bruhl's intellectual integrity and scholarship have never been questioned, although Needham (1972) seems to feel that the criticisms of contemporary anthropologists are designed only to belittle him or present a travesty of his theoretical ideas. But like Douglas, Needham holds that Lévy-Bruhl's importance lies in the value of the intellectual questions he posed rather than in the specific answers he gave, for Needham does not seek to defend Lévy-Bruhl's theory of "primitive mentality." In fact, in his later years Lévy-Bruhl, in response to the criticisms, came to abandon most of the essential tenets of his theory. In his posthumously published notebooks (1949), he concedes that preliterate people spend only some of their time in the world of mystical influence and admits that the term *prelogical* is a misleading one. Evans-Pritchard (1965) suggests that by the end of his life Lévy-Bruhl may have "reversed his position" on the nature of preliterate thought. But as Horton has argued, although Lévy-Bruhl came to admit that there is a good deal of everyday realism to be found alongside the mystical in preliterate cultures and to allow for the presence of mystical thought in European culture, "his characterization of the mystical remains unrepentantly the same...We still find common sense lumped together with science, and both of them radically contrasted with the mystical" (1973: 258). Thus, as Horton stresses, Lévy-Bruhl's approach was essentially similar to that of later "symbolist" anthropologists, as well as Freud.

Anthropology and history

The sharp contrast that Lévy-Bruhl, like Pareto and Malinowski, made between the "empirical" and the "mystical" is taken up by Evans-Pritchard, particularly in his study of the Azande. But Evans-Pritchard interprets the "mystical" domain (religion, witchcraft, magic) quite differently from the functionalist and symbolist anthropologists whose work we shall examine in this chapter (Douglas, Turner, Lewis). Indeed it is difficult to say with any precision what exactly Evans-Pritchard's theoretical approach to religious phenomena entailed, for within the

186

corpus of his work he offered, like Weber, several contrasting approaches. In many ways he was a Weberian sociologist, for his style of theorizing combined interpretative understanding with sociological analysis. It is of interest that in his important surveys of anthropological thought (1951, 1981) he outlines only two theoretical traditions, the French lineage of anthropology stemming from Montesquieu (including such scholars as D'Alembert, Saint-Simon, Comte, Durkheim, and Lévy-Bruhl) and the British tradition stemming from the Scottish moral philosophers like Adam Smith, Ferguson, and Hume. This tradition, with its empiricist bias, is best represented by Herbert Spencer. For Evans-Pritchard, then, anthropology was a "child of the Enlightenment," and he saw both traditions as being fundamentally similar in their conception of social science; they insisted, he wrote, "that the study of societies, which they regarded as natural systems or organisms, must be empirical, and that by the use of the inductive method it would be possible to explain them in terms of general principles or laws in the same way as physical phenomena had been explained by the physicists" (1962: 149).

Thus Evans-Pritchard completely failed to explore in his writings the tradition that was closest to his own style of anthropology, namely the German historical tradition. This oversight is significant; Hegel, Marx, Dilthey, and Weber are conspicuous by their absence in his work. Yet fundamentally Evans-Pritchard was a historical sociologist, struggling, like Weber, to go beyond the positivist tradition that he had inherited. The figure that emerges from his writings, as Ernest Gellner suggests in his characteristically perceptive introduction to Evans-Pritchard's *History of Anthropological Thought* (1981a), is "not that of a prophet, but rather an intellectually restless, ever-questing, skeptical Hamlet, ... wondering, puzzled, quizzical, ironic, sometimes cross, but above all, *troubled.*"

As we have seen, these are precisely the terms in which Hughes described Weber – intellectually troubled. None of this is evident in Mary Douglas's recent biography of Evans-Pritchard (1980), which rather misleadingly tends to suggest that he was simply a precursor of contemporary intellectual fashions. Thus she suggests that in his analyses Evans-Pritchard anticipated cybernetic functionalism; phenomenological and subjectivist analyses, with their focus on accountability and consciousness; ethnomethodology, with its stress on "everyday knowledge"; games theory; and the kind of positivist philosophy that was advocated by Wittgenstein. Such an interpretation seems to me to reflect Douglas's own recent interests rather than the theoretical premises that formed the basis of Evans-Pritchard's work. Such an interpretation, as Gellner suggests, hardly does him justice, for Evans-Pritchard had "far too much sense of political and external reality to be drawn into the cloud-cuckoo-lands where you invent your world by your concepts." There is, as we shall note, a materialist and historical as well as a structuralist dimension to Evans-Pritchard's work that Douglas's study entirely overlooks.

Evans-Pritchard was born in 1902 and studied anthropology under C. G. Seligman at the London School of Economics. After initially conducting ethnological surveys on behalf of Seligman in the Sudan, Evans-Pritchard made, from 1926 until the outbreak of the Second World War, a series of anthropological expeditions to Kenya and the Sudan. He undertook important fieldwork studies among the Azande (1926–30) and the Nuer (1930–6), the latter researches being on behalf of the government of the Anglo-Egyptian Sudan. The political context of this research is important to note, for although Evans-Pritchard briefly describes this context and mentions his difficulties in undertaking research among the Nuer, he indicates no interest in exploring how the Nuer themselves were reacting against the colonial aggression. At the time when Evans-Pritchard was making his studies, large-scale military operations were being conducted against the Nuer, including bombing and the destruction of property (Evans-Pritchard 1940: 134–5; Stauder 1974). Douglas's explanation that an urgent request by the colonial government called Evans-Pritchard to report on the "unruly Nilotic tribe whose insurrection would be put down by force unless someone could interpret their intentions" (1980: 43) tends to obscure the fact that the same government had already machine-gunned the Nuer into submission.

During the Second World War Evans-Pritchard spent two years (1942–4) as a political officer in Cyrenaica. In 1944 he became a Catholic. From 1946 until his retirement in 1970 he was professor of anthropology at Oxford. Evans-Pritchard's reputation rests firmly on his ethnographic studies, particularly those on the Azande (1937) and the Nuer (1940, 1956). Lucidly written, rich in detail, they have deservedly attained the status of anthropological classics. Before we consider these studies, however, something needs to be said about Evans-Pritchard's general approach to anthropology.

In an oft-quoted passage, David Pocock suggested, in contrasting the perspectives of Radcliffe-Brown and Evans-Pritchard, that the latter writer instigated the movement from "function to meaning" (1961: 76). This is to some extent true, but it both ignores the fact that "meaning" was an important aspect of Radcliffe-Brown's understanding of religion and obscures the diversity and complexity of Evans-Pritchard's work. And it is of interest that Evans-Pritchard's important critique of his former tutor, Radcliffe-Brown, rather than advocating a hermeneutic or symbolic approach to anthropology, stressed the need to create a dialogue between anthropology and historical understanding. This critique is significant, for in criticizing functional anthropology Evans-Pritchard clearly expressed, though in programmatic terms, his own conception of anthropology.

Although Evans-Pritchard was somewhat critical of Durkheim's theory of religion, which he described as "an unconvincing piece of sociologistic metaphysics" (1965: 70), his general attitude to "philosophical rationalism" was far from hostile. Indeed he described Durkheim's influence on British anthropology as both profound and beneficial (1962: 18). Nor was Evans-Pritchard particularly hostile to functional analysis per se and recognized that it had heuristic value. But he viewed the kind of functional or organismic theory that stemmed from the conservative thinkers of the early nineteenth century and that was set forth with clarity by both Spencer and Durkheim with extreme skepticism. Yet their conception of societies as natural systems and their search for "social laws" was at least placed, he felt, within an evolutionary framework, problematic and speculative though this might be. But with modern functionalism, such as that advocated by Radcliffe-Brown, this diachronic perspective had been jettisoned and the view expressed that a society could be understood satisfactorily without reference to its past. With the bathwater of speculative history, Evans-Pritchard wrote, "the functionalists have also thrown out the baby of valid history" (21). The notion that one could understand the functioning of institutions at a certain point in time without reference to the past Evans-Pritchard thought an "absurdity," and he suggested that this kind of analysis, taken to extremes, could only lead to absolute relativism.

Evans-Pritchard thus came to suggest an approach that is at once hermeneutic, structural, comparative, and historical. Anthropological analysis, he wrote, consists of three essential phases, or levels of abstraction. First the anthropologist seeks, just like a historian, to understand the significant features of a culture and to translate them into terms used in his or her own culture. The first stage, therefore, is one of interpretative understanding, though Evans-Pritchard was rather skeptical that this could be achieved simply by some sort of empathy. Second, the anthropologist attempts to go a step farther and, through analysis, disclose the underlying forms or structure of a society or culture. Again, good historians, he suggests, do the same. "This structure," he wrote, "cannot be seen. It is a set of abstractions, each of which, though derived, it is true, from analysis of observed behaviour is fundamentally an imaginative construct of the anthropologist himself. By relating these abstractions to one another logically so that they present a pattern he can see the society in its essentials and as a single whole" (1962: 23). Finally, in the third phase, the anthropologist compares the social structures of different societies, something that is done either explicitly or implicitly. Evans-Pritchard thus concludes that the difference between anthropology and history is matter of technique, emphasis, and perspective, not of method and aim. Historians, he suggests, write history, as it were, forward, whereas anthropologists tend to write it backward (60). For Evans-Pritchard, therefore, both history and social anthropology are branches of social science, and the kind of approach he advocates we may well call, as he does, *historical sociology*. Indeed the scholars he applauds for exemplifying the kind of historiography he advocates include the following: Vinogradoff, Pirenne, Bloch, Marx, and Weber. He cites his own book, *The Sanusi of Cyrenaica*, as a good example of an anthropological study written from a historical perspective. Worsley has written appreciatively of Evans-Pritchard's attempt to define anthropology as a comparative and historical science, even though he stressed its links with the humanities (1957: 272–4). It is clear that like Marx, Weber, and Freud before him, Evans-Pritchard was struggling to establish an approach that is both humanistic and consonant with the aims and methods of science.

It is not my purpose here to discuss Evans-Pritchard's work in detail, but rather to briefly outline some of the more interesting aspects of his three studies of religious ideology.

Evans-Pritchard's study of the Azande (1937) was one of the earliest attempts to describe, without prejudice and undue sensationalism, the beliefs and rites relating to magic and witchcraft among a non-European people. His approach is stated clearly in the introduction to the book; it is to show how mystical beliefs and rites form an "ideational system" and how this system is expressed in social action. He does not think it necessary to describe other aspects of Azande social life; the whole emphasis of the book is therefore intellectual, focusing on how witchcraft is related to misfortune as a stereotyped form of explanation. Why did he place such emphasis on witchcraft and sorcery? Did he simply wish to highlight the esoteric and irrational side of the culture of a preliterate people? The answer to this is twofold.

First, Evans-Pritchard indicates throughout the book that the Azande are rational in their essential thinking and that their thoughts and actions are based on sound empirical knowledge. Indeed the distinction between what he terms "empirical" thought and "mystical" thought is a key theme running through his study, and he implies the coexistence of these two thought patterns amongst the Azande. Although, unlike ourselves, the Azande have no conception of a "natural order," they nevertheless, he writes, perceive a difference between the workings of nature, on the one hand, and the workings of magic, ghosts, and witchcraft on the other (81). There is thus an implied criticism of Lévy-Bruhl's notion that the thought of preliterate people is essentially prelogical and mystical. It is worth noting, in this context, that Evans-Pritchard, in attempting to adapt himself to Azande culture by "living the life of my hosts," often came to react to misfortunes in the idiom of witchcraft. "It was often an effort," he wrote, "to check this lapse into unreason" (99). Thus, although the subject of the book is witchcraft and sorcery, he did not conceive of the Azande as either being steeped in mysticism or as lacking empirical knowledge.

Second, there is the important point that the religion or supernatural beliefs of the Azande, unlike those of their neighbors the Nuer and Dinka, are largely permeated with notions about witches and magic. This is mentioned by Seligman in his foreword, where he notes the "paucity" of magic among the Dinka and Shilluk. Evans-Pritchard stresses that witchcraft is ubiquitous and a normal factor in Azande social life, people discussing it as part of everyday conversation. His book therefore reflects what would appear to be a central aspect of Azande religious beliefs.

The Azande are a Sudanic people who in precolonial times were organized into a number of separate kingdoms, each ruled by a member of an aristocratic clan. The belief in a supreme creator-spirit Mbori and in the ancestral ghosts (*atoro*) is important to the Azande, especially in the domestic context, but it is a belief in medicines (magic) and witchcraft that predominates in Azande culture. Witchcraft, in particular, plays its part in almost every activity of social life:

> If blight seizes the ground-nut crop it is witchcraft; if the bush is vainly scoured for game it is witchcraft; if a wife is sulky and unresponsive to her husband it is witchcraft; if a prince is cold and distant with his subjects it is witchcraft; if a magical rite fails to achieve its purpose it is witchcraft; if, in fact, any failure or misfortune falls upon anyone at any time and in relation to any of the manifold activities of his life it may be due to witch-craft. (63–4)

The Azande attribute almost all misfortunes (including death) to witch-craft, unless they are due to scorcery or can be clearly attributed to incompetence or failure to observe a moral rule. Evans-Pritchard suggests that to the Azande witchcraft is a commonplace happening and that hardly a day passes without someone's mentioning the subject. But the Azande recognize a plurality of causes of misfortune: For instance, the breaking of the incest taboo is said to cause leprosy, and the deaths of babies from certain ailments, or diseases that are considered incurable, (smallpox and sleeping sickness, for example) are attributed to the high god Mbori. Moreover, certain social situations demand a common-sense rather than a mystical explanation for a misfortune. Thus, if you tell a lie or commit adultery or a theft, you cannot elude punishment by saying that you are bewitched.

For the Azande, a witch (*boro mangu*) is a person who has the ability to cause other people misfortunes or even to kill them. A witch performs no rituals, utters no spells, and possesses no medicines. The act of witchcraft is "psychic," for the witches have this ability because witchcraft (*mangu*) is considered to be an organic phenomenon that is inherited. For the Azande a witch is a person whose body contains, or is declared by the oracles or by a diviner to contain, the witchcraft substance. The latter is a material substance, an oval black swelling found near the liver. It is transmitted from parent to child, a woman inheriting the substance from her mother, a man from his father, and it can be discovered by autopsy. Witches may also be known by their reddish eyes. Nocturnal birds and animals are associated with witchcraft and are even thought to be servants of the witches. Witches are also believed to join together in feasts and in carrying out their nefarious schemes, as well as possessing a special kind of ointment, which, rubbed into their skins, makes them invisible in their nocturnal expeditions (38). Both men and women may be witches, but usually women are bewitched only by members of their own sex. Members of the aristocratic clans are not accused of witchcraft, whatever feelings may be held privately. Usually a witch attacks a person when motivated by hatred, envy, or greed, and it is social equals who accuse each other.

Thus, like the Trobriand Islanders and African communities such as the Lovedu, the Azande make a clear distinction between witchcraft (*mangu*) and magic (*ngua*), the latter term covering not only magical techniques but also herbal and other medicines. Witchcraft involves psychic powers, and misfortunes may be caused unconsciously, whereas magic involves rites, spells, and the conscious manipulation of medicines, usually plant materials. In a sense magic is a means of combating witchcraft. Medicines are used for both good and immoral ends. Normally, "good" magic is moral because it is used against unknown persons – for example, when one does not know who has committed a crime. If a man knows who has stolen his spear or killed his kinsman, he normally takes the matter to the chief's court. On the other hand, "bad" magic is made against specific persons one suspects, and, because the sorcerer has no legal case, is by definition immoral. Among the Azande, medicines (the term *ngua* also means "plant") are individually owned, and the rites are performed privately. The efficacy of the magic is said to lie in the medicines and the rite, and their power is unconnected with the ghosts.

Although every Azande has a knowledge of medicines, magicians (*boro ngua*) are usually old or middle-aged men who have no great prestige in Azande society. Their knowledge of herbalism (leechcraft) may, however, be extensive, and every illness or ailment has its appropriate medicines.

When Azandes think that they are being bewitched, they consult a witch doctor (*abinza*), who is both a diviner and a magician. As a diviner, he (for women are rarely witch doctors, though they may be herbalists) exposes the witch; as a magician, he thwarts the witch by the use of medicines. The abinza is a member of a professional association into which he has been initiated and thus has a vested interest in the knowledge of medicines and rituals, though there is often keen rivalry among individual witch doctors. Often a witch doctor is under the patronage of a member of the aristocracy. The Azande expressed some skepticism about the motives and veracity of witch doctors, and Evans-Pritchard devotes a chapter to discussing the degree of faith individuals have in these ritual specialists. Nevertheless, the witch doctor plays an important role in Azande culture, though his activities make sense only in relation to the people's belief in witchcraft.

There are four main forms of divination used by the Azande; the rubbing-board oracle, the termite oracle, the seance, and the *benge* or poison oracle. Only the benge oracle is used in court cases, since it is considered the most reliable. A chicken is administerd a dose of red powder from the benge creeper (a form of strychnine), and then its behavior is observed. From the fowl's response to the poison – death or recovery – the Azande receive an answer to the questions put before the oracle. In many other parts of Africa the suspected witches themselves went through the poison ordeal.

By subtle questioning on the part of the witch doctor and by the use of such oracles, the identity of the witch is revealed. Evans-Pritchard puts it nicely when he wrote that "a witch-doctor divines successfully because he says what his listener wishes him to say, and because he uses tact" (170).

The victim or one of his relatives then approaches the suspected witch and asks him or her to withdraw the witchcraft. In the past, suspected witches might be killed, but usually magic is employed against the witch responsible, even though the exact identify of the witch might be unclear. Generally, though, witches protest their innocence of intention and ignorance of the harm they are doing to their neighbor. The witch may do a water-blowing ritual and, addressing his or her stomach, plead with his or her mangu to become inactive (95–6).

After his detailed descriptive account of Azande witchcraft, which has

193

been summarized here, Evans-Pritchard offers an interpretation of these beliefs, suggesting that they provide a theory of causation that supplements the theory of natural causation. He gives an instance of an old granary's collapsing after being weakened by termites, injuring people sitting beneath it. The collapse of the granary may be explained by the Azande in empirical terms: They might say that the supports of the granary were eaten away by termites. To us the collapse of the granary, and the fact that people were sitting beneath it, are two independent facts that simply coincide in time and space. We have no theory that links these two events. Zande philosophy, Evans-Pritchard suggests, supplies a "missing link" (70), for witchcraft theory provides an explanation as to why these particular people were sitting under this particular granary at the particular moment when it collapsed. Thus Azande belief in witchcraft in no way contradicted empirical knowledge of cause and effect. The Azande say that "death has always a cause, and no man dies without a reason (111). Witchcraft provides reasons with respect to the "particularity," as Gluckman termed it, of misfortunes.

The complex relationship between common-sense (empirical) and mystical thought is an issue that, as Evans-Pritchard admits, is confronted on almost every page of the book. It is not surprising, therefore, that he should approach magic and witchcraft in intellectual terms and ask why the Azande do not perceive the "futility of their magic" (475). He gives a number of possible reasons. First, witchcraft and magic form an intellectually coherent system. The main purpose of magic is to combat other mystical powers rather than to change the objective world; since its action therefore transcends experience, it cannot easily be contradicted by experience. Second, skepticism is recognized and inculcated, and the Azande often observe that medicines are unsuccessful. But this skepticism extends only to certain medicines and certain magicians, and by contrast the magical system is affirmed. Third, the failure of a rite is accounted for in advance by a variety of mystical notions: witchcraft, countermagic, or breach of taboos. Fourth, magic is utilized only to produce events that are likely to happen in any case, and it is seldom asked to produce a result by itself: It is always accompanied by an empirical action. A man makes beer by proven methods, and uses medicine (magic) only to hasten the brew. He would not dream of trying to make beer by "medicines" alone (475).

This discussion follows that of Edward Tylor and indicates the "intellectualist" orientation of this classic text on Azande witchcraft. But the main thrust of Evans-Pritchard's argument in this text is a contextual one, an attempt, as he himself clearly said, to make intelligible a number of beliefs, exotic and strange to Europeans, by showing how they form

194

a comprehensive system of thought and how this system of thought is related to social activities, social structure, and the life of the individual (1951: 98). To suggest that Evans-Pritchard is simply engaged in interpreting witchcraft as a "system of accountability" or in making a "translation" of Azande concepts is to severely misjudge and narrow his intentions and his achievement.

Evans-Pritchard's account of the Sanusi of Cyrenaica is a very different kind of study from that on the Azande. It is a superb study in the genre of historical sociology, and Douglas's suggestion that it is an example of a "voluntarist" analysis, and a kind of polemic against reductionist theorizing and sociological determinism, is highly misleading. Like Marx and Weber, Evans-Pritchard is against reductionist analyses, but equally, and again like his forebears, he is against the kind of phenomenological reasoning that severs ideas from their moorings. For Evans-Pritchard, religious concepts are anchored – firmly anchored – to a social and material reality. If sympathy with the oppressed and a stress on human agency makes an analysis "voluntarist," then Engels's study of the peasant wars in Germany is a fine example of such an approach.

The Sanusiya order was a militant and austere form of Sufism that, toward the end of the nineteenth century, had a dominant influence over a wide area of North Africa, focused on Cyrenaica. It was a highly orthodox Islamic fraternity and, unlike other Sufi orders, was nonecstatic, its members strongly disapproving of processions, flagellation, trance states, and music. It was founded by an Algerian scholar al-Sanusi, who traveled extensively and first established the order near Mecca in 1837. Unable to return to his homeland because of the French invasion, he settled for some years in Cyrenaica. In 1856, when he was nearing seventy, he moved the seat of his order to Jaghbub, then a remote desert oasis, where he died some three years later. Under his elder son Sayyid al-Mahdi the order expanded rapidly, and by the end of the nineteenth century almost all the Bedouin of Cyrenaica and the surrounding area had become followers of the order, which had established a theocratic empire controlling trade and having administration over a wide region. Evans-Pritchard argues that although the Sanusiya originally began as a reform movement among the Bedouin Arabs of Cyrenaica, it developed into a theocratic state, largely in response to external political pressures. The order, based on the tribes and not on the towns – for the lodges of the order were founded as tribal institutions – gave the Bedouin a national symbol and provided an administrative structure for what had hitherto been a segmentary political structure. Moreover, the austere and orthodox nature of the order harmonized well with the lifestyle of the pastoral nomads. The order had established a kind of stable rapport with the Ottoman Empire through the local Turkish officials, for the officials allowed the Sanusiya to perform many of the functions of government in the interior – those concerned with education, justice, the maintenance of security, and even, to some extent, the collection of taxes. Evans-Pritchard sums up the situation at the end of the nineteenth century by suggesting that "the Sanusiya...used the Turks to buttress its position in its dealings with the tribes, and combined with the tribes to resist any encroachments on its prerogatives by the Turkish Government" (1949: 99).

This situation drastically changed with the decline of the Ottoman Empire and with the Italian invasion of the country in 1911. Apart from a period of accord at the end of the First World War, for more than twenty years the Bedouin tribes, under the leadership of the Sanusiya order, resisted Italian aggression. During this guerrilla war, which Evans-Pritchard describes in detail, the Sanusiya gave leadership and served as a common symbol in the long and bitter struggle. In doing so, the term *Sanusi* ceased to have a religious content and became more and more a purely political symbol, whereas the order itself became a national as well as a religious movement. Evans-Pritchard, like the Bedouin themselves, saw the issue of Italian aggression in terms of their right to live by their own laws in their own land, but he notes that "in fighting for their lands and herds the Bedouin were fortified by the knowledge that they fought also for their faith. Without due appreciation of the religious feelings involved in the resistance it would, I think, be impossible to understand how it went on for so long against such overwhelming odds" (1949: 166). The conflict is thus interpreted by Evans-Pritchard in materialist terms, yet it can, he intimates, be fully understood only if the religious dimension is also taken into account.

By 1932, their herds having been indiscriminately slaughtered, their country desolated, and having suffered thousands of casualties, the Bedouin were eventually defeated and the Sanusiya destroyed. Resistance finally came to an end with the capture and hanging of Umar al-Mukhtar, a simple and courageous man who was already over sixty when he joined the struggle. He was, Evans-Pritchard suggests, the "soul" of the resistance movement. The book may well, as Douglas suggests, affirm the "power of personal interventions" in historical events, but al-Mukhtar's intervention has little affinity to the bourgeois "individual" that Douglas depicts in her other writings.

Turning now to Evans-Pritchard's other classic study, *Nuer Religion* (1956), we move again onto an altogether different theoretical terrain, but one equally stimulating and seminal.

Evans-Pritchard published a trilogy of books on the Nuer, a group of seminomadic cattle-herding people living in the marsh and savanna country of the southern Sudan. *The Nuer* (1940) is, as its subtitle suggests, a "description of the modes of livelihood and political institutions" of these people. It is deservedly an anthropological classic and is invariably looked upon as a functionalist study. But as Dumont and others have suggested, there is very little in the book about "social integration," and the study has a strong materialist and structuralist orientation. Dumont speaks of the "radical ambiguity" inherent in the work (1975: 342). Evans-Pritchard outlined his intentions in the following words:

> I tried to show that some features of their mode of livelihood can be understood only if we take their environment into account; and also that some features of their political structure can be understood only if we take their modes of livelihood into account. I did not, however, try to explain their modes of livelihood as a function of their environment or their political structure as a function of their economy. (1956: 320)

Thus Evans-Pritchard sees social life firmly anchored in the material world, and, like Marx and Weber, does not treat politics (or religion) as autonomous realms, nor does he propose a reductive analysis or suggest that the different levels of social reality are simply reflective. It is therefore important to stress that although *Nuer Religion* specifically focuses on the religious beliefs and practices of the Nuer, its underlying orientation is similar to that of the earlier study and is neither idealist nor phenomenological.

It is, I think, important to note that although *Nuer Religion* is an exemplary study, rich in ethnographic detail, Evans-Pritchard's field research was limited both by time and circumstances: He admits that he met only one prophet and attended only one possession rite during his stay in Nuerland, which makes his account even the more remarkable.

The first part of the study is devoted to an analysis of the Nuer concept of spirit (*kwoth*) and its various manifestations. The term also has a plural form (*kuth*), and the spirits consist of two main categories, the spirits of the above (associated with the air, rivers, or lightning) and the spirits of the below. The latter are mainly totemic spirits, associated with such animals as the monitor lizard, the lion, the crocodile, and the python, as well as with various plants. Evans-Pritchard notes that these are low-status supernaturals and that there is no marked utilitarian element in their selection. The animals, plants, and artifacts most used by the Nuer in their daily life are absent from their list of totems. He thus suggests that the data on Nuer totems does not support Malinowski's contention that totemism is a "ritualization of empirical interests" (1956: 80). Nor are the totemic species necessarily those that are prominent in their

197

folktales. Evans-Pritchard therefore suggests that the interpretation of the totemic relationship must not be sought in the nature of the totem itself but in "an association that it brings to mind . . . It is not in their intrinsic nature but in their character as symbols through which spirit manifests itself to human intelligence" (82). The Nuer therefore respect the creatures not for themselves but because they are symbols. But the spirits of the air and the totemic spirits are intimately related to the social structure. He writes,

> We find the same refraction of spirit by the social order in the totemic spirits, which are spirit in a more immanent and material form . . . Each of the totemic spirits is spirit in a particular relationship to a lineage, which expresses its relation as an exclusive social group to God in the totemic refraction by respecting the creature which stands as a material symbol of the refraction. The imprint of the social order on the conception of spirit is very evident in the totemic beliefs and observances of the Nuer. (91)

Evans-Pritchard goes on to suggest that in all societies religious thought bears the impress of the social order. With the Nuer this impress is evident at all levels of social reality. As the creator, spirit is patron of all people; figured in spirits of the air (such as Deng), he is the patron of lineages and families; figured in nature spirits and fetishes, he is the patron of specific individuals (118). This "structural configuration," Evans-Pritchard contends, is evident through sociological analysis, but he warns that a "structural interpretation explains only certain characteristics of the refractions and not the idea of spirit in itself." But as spirit is manifested only in its relationship to nature, culture, and historical experience, it can never "in itself" be known. It has the same status as Kant's noumenon, the "thing-in-itself" – experienced but unknowable.

In an interesting chapter entitled "The Problem of Symbols," Evans-Pritchard sought to interpret the meaning of certain symbolic equations that the Nuer made, namely that "twins were birds" and that in their sacrificial rites a cucumber was an ox. He argues against Lévy-Bruhl's idea that this was evidence of "mystical participation" and that the Nuer somehow mistook an ideal relationship for a real one. These equations are not, he suggests, statements of identity but involve a "symbolic nexus" and imply experience on an imaginative level of thought where the mind moves in figures, symbols, analogies, and poetic metaphors. Evans-Pritchard thus interpreted such beliefs in terms of symbolic associations, with reference to the Nuer structured cosmology. (On the issue of the nature of Nuer "religious thought," see Firth 1966 and Hayley 1968.)

Evans-Pritchard stresses that Nuer religion is fundamentally a this-worldly religion, "a religion of abundant life and the fullness of days"

(154), and that the Nuer neither pretend to know nor do they care what happens to them after death. This would seem to confirm Weber's suggestions about the nature of tribal religion. He also points out that the Nuer have little interest in ghosts, or spirits of the dead, and, in marked contrast to the Azande, make little use of medicines. Divination and herbalism are practiced, but they appear, according to Evans-Pritchard, to be of minor importance to the Nuer. They regard medicines, he suggests, as something foreign and strange. The orientation of Nuer thought is "always towards spirit" (104). "Sin, with the suffering it brings about," writes Evans-Pritchard, "is central to the study of Nuer religion." Thus Douglas feels it necessary to stress that Evans-Pritchard's essential "method" involved the tracing of notions of "acountability" through institutional forms and that his analysis start with the moral subject. This comment, however, simply expresses a truism, for, as Weber long ago indicated, all religions are intrinsically connected with morality and human suffering and therefore imply a system of ethics and theodicy. All descriptive studies of religion have therefore a focus on "accountability": Evans-Pritchard's study is simply one of the best in this genre.

All serious sickness or misfortune among the Nuer was invariably attributed to an infraction of a moral interdiction, referred to as *nueer*. Adultery, incest, and homicide, in particular were viewed as grave faults that implied not so much the breaking of a social regulation as the breaking of a taboo and the confounding of a spiritual order. A person, or even the community, thus became ritually polluted, and only ritual activity could put matters right again. As such transgressions were seen as offences against spirit, the Nuer thought that it was the spirit(s) who punished them. The Nuer virtually identified disease with sin, so that the term *rual* refers to both incest and syphilis. Evans-Pritchard sums up the matter in the following words:

> Since sickness is the action of spirit, therapeutic action is sacramental. The sickness is only a symptom of the spiritual condition of the person, which is the underlying cause of the crisis, and it can only be cured by expiation – sacrifice – for the sin which has brought it about. This, then, is a further characteristic of sin. It causes physical misfortune, usually sickness, which is identified with it, so that the healing of the sickness is felt to be also the wiping out of the sin. (192)

Evans-Pritchard emphasizes that the Nuer do not get morally indignant about sin, because nueer infringements are not fundamentally concerned with people's morals. Such interdictions have a spiritual rather than an ethical significance and are quite different from breaches of custom or conventions, or the failure to fulfill social obligations. It is therefore somewhat misleading to interpret Nuer religion purely in terms of "games theory" (with spirit the dealer in a poker game) or in terms of the "bookkeeping" accounts of a petty shopkeeper, as Douglas appears to do (1980: 100–2). Such metaphors are misplaced. Rather, it would seem that religious activities are closely linked with their cosmological ideas and with the dissolution and redefinition of their symbolic categories (Beidelman 1971: 379). Evans-Pritchard himself suggests that these ritual prohibitions make sense only when viewed in the total context of Nuer social life.

Evans-Pritchard describes Nuer cosmology as fundamentally dualistic, there being a rigid separation of spirit (kwoth) and the earth, which is the domain of humans. This dichotomy is bridged on two important occasions; in possession rites (when spirit comes to earth and enters a human being), and in sacrifice. The latter ritual essentially involves the symbolic separation of spirit (life) and the earth, made necessary because of spirit's intervention in the world in sending sickness and misfortune. The latter, in turn, is a response to the neglect on the part of humans of certain ritual obligations.

Sacrifices are performed by the Nuer on many occasions, but they fall roughly into two classes. Some are performed mainly for individuals at times of misfortune – sickness, infertility, or disease. They are then essentially rites of affliction and are done to appease the spirit. Others are performed on behalf of a collective, mainly as part of a rite of passage such as initiation, marriage, and death. Essentially sacrifices are concerned with moral and spiritual crises rather than with natural events, except insofar as these interfere with human well-being. Sacrificial rites are mainly performed during the rains and consist of four acts: the presentation of the animal, ideally an ox, to the spirit; the consecration of the animal; the invocation performed by the priest, who, holding a spear, states the intention of the sacrifice and matters relating to it; and, finally, the killing and immolation of the sacrificial victim. Evans-Pritchard writes that the life and blood of the victim are believed by the Nuer to belong to the spirit, whereas the meat of the animal is taken by the participants. This is eaten afterward in a communal feast that has no sacramental significance. Evans-Pritchard therefore questions Robertson-Smith's communion theory of sacrifice, suggesting that the Nuer rite is essentially concerned not with fellowship with the spirit but rather with separation. Paradoxically, "God is separated from man by an act which brings them togther" (275). In a discussion of an alternative theory, namely, the idea of Tylor and Spencer that sacrifice is a gift exchange, Evans-Pritchard's essential point is that such notions as redemption, oblation, atonement, expiation, and purification are central to the Nuer conception of sacrifice. He suggests that the animal is essentially a substitute for a person and has the role of a scapegoat, and that the Nuer kill cattle only for sacrificial purposes or in times of dire necessity. The sacrifice is usually made either by an agnatic kinsman or by a priest of the earth (*kuaar muon*). Often referred to as "leopard-skin chiefs," the priests have no direct political or admininistrative role in the Nuer, but they have an important mediating role in the settlement of disputes (see 1940: 172–6). The priest's mystical relationship to the earth, Evans-Pritchard writes, "accords with the general idea of man being identified with the Earth and God with the sky, the priest being essentially a person who sacrifices on behalf of man below to God above" (292).

Possession rites are also important among the Nuer, and, like the priest, the prophet also mediates between the conceptual opposition of spirit and earth (humans). Possession is generally known by sickness, usually of a severe and sudden kind, and it is diagnosed as being due to a particular spirit. The seizure may be temporary or permanent, and as in ecstatic cults described elsewhere (see I. Lewis 1971), the possessed person, on recovering from the misfortune, may form a specific relationship with the spirit. When the possession is permanent, the person becomes known as a prophet. The Nuer call such a charismatic person *gwan kwoth*: owner or possessor of spirit. This gives him or her powers of healing, divination, and foresight. In the past, the main function of the leading prophets, Evans-Pritchard suggests, was to direct cattle raids against the Dinka and fighting against foreign intruders. He implies, however, that the recognition of prophets is a recent development that can be interpreted as a reaction or response to colonial rule. But he adds that this is a development of potentialities in their traditional religion and thus has a religious form. Many women became minor prophets, but only men made sacrifices or had a "hermeneutic role in warfare" (308). The British colonial administration dealt harshly with the prophetic movement among the Nuer. Evans-Pritchard stresses the contrast between the priest and the prophet, one a traditional functionary whose virtue resides in his office and who has no cult, the other deriving personal power through charismatic inspiration and having certain cultic features (304). Beidelman (1971) doubts whether the boundaries between the priests and the prophets can be so rigidly drawn, noting that the former often sought to augment their power through charisma and political manipulation, whereas prophets sought to routinize their charisma in establishing a more stable authority. Beidelman notes that Evans-Pritchard makes no mention at all of the classic study of priest and prophets, Weber's *Ancient Judaism*, which I have discussed earlier, though he employs Weberian concepts.

201

In his discussion of "spear symbolism," Evans-Pritchard notes that the spear is always held in the right hand and that Nuer youths often go to some lengths to incapacitate the left arm, in the same way as they often mutilate the left horn of their favourite cow, forcing it to grow downward. Such observations lead Evans-Pritchard to suggest that there is an underlying structural pattern – a "deeper symbolism" – in Nuer social life (1956: 231–8). This dualistic classification can be expressed as follows:

Spirit	*Earth*
Above	Below
Spirit	Humans
Light	Darkness
Right	Left
Strength	Weakness
Good	Evil
East	West
Prophet	Priest
Masculinity	Femininity

(We shall examine such dualistic classifications more fully in the next chapter, but for a "supplementary view" of Nuer religious classifications, see Pocock 1974).

The final chapter of *Nuer Religion* is devoted to his reflections on the study. He stresses that Nuer religion is a highly complex historical phenomenon and questions whether it can be understood in psychological or psychoanalytic terms. Most of these theories (that is, those of Tylor, Spencer, Malinowski and Freud), Evans-Pritchard suggests, "have long ago been discredited as naive, introspective guesses" (312). Thus he implies that religion can only be understood by sociological analysis, by relating religious phenomena to the social structure. This is true of Nuer religion, he writes. "I do not think... that the configuration of spirit, the faults which are regarded as sins, and the roles of the master of ceremonies, priest, and prophet in sacrifice can be fully understood without a knowledge of the social order" (313). Earlier he had stressed that human thought and expression are inevitably constructed out of man's experience of the world around him, indicating an essentially materialist perspective. It is surprising, then, that in the last pages of the book, after devoting the entire text to a sociological analysis of Nuer religion that is exemplary (augmenting this analysis where necessary with hermeneutic, contextual, structural, and symbolic interpretations of specific religious elements), Evans-Pritchard suggests that religion is ultimately an "interior state." "Spirit" in itself is a "mystery," and "intuitive apprehension," a "spiritual experience" (314–15). As a definition of religion this is inadequate and hardly enlightening: as an interpretation or explanation of religion it is simply a nonstarter. When the purely social and cultural aspects of Nuer religion have been abstracted, Evans-Pritchard writes, we are left with only a relationship between man and "something which lies right outside his society": spirit. Of this "experience" the Nuer could tell him only that it was like the wind or air. It is hardly surprising, then, that Evans-Pritchard devotes over three hundred pages to sociological analysis and only a page to this experiential state. At that point, he handed over the analysis to the theologian.

In the final chapter he speaks of need for a comparative study of African philosophies, noting that the "dominant motif" varies among the different African cultures, according to whether they attribute misfortune to ancestral cults, witchcraft, or, like the Nuer, to spirit (315). It is this suggestion that is taken up by Mary Douglas in *Natural Symbols*, and it is to her writings that I now turn.

Animals, anomalies, and abominations

More than a decade ago two important books were published in anthropology. It would be wrong to think that they created an entirely new way of looking at things, for both were in the tradition of Durkheimian social science, but both books in their way caused something of a stir. I have to admit that when I first read them as a novitiate anthropologist I found them virtually incomprehensible. Wide-ranging and comparative in approach, and replete with metaphorical asides and scholastic diversions, they seemed to belong to a different intellectual genre than the other writings I was then prompted to savor. But although I found difficulty at times in following the arguments and though I chafed at the polemics, the obscurities, even the disguised truisms, nevertheless I found both books tremendously exciting. One of them, Lévi-Strauss's *The Savage Mind*, has become a classic: it is discussed at some length in the next chapter. The other is Mary Douglas's *Purity and Danger* (1970b). Yet in spite of stimulating a good deal of research into such topics as animal and body symbolism, Douglas has been a neglected figure, and has not, unlike Lévi-Strauss, been the focus of debate and exegesis (but cf. Wuthnow et al. 1984).

Yet the striking similarities between these two writers in their structural approach to religious symbolism is evident to anyone reading the two books. For the central thesis of both works is the argument that "primitive" cultures are integrated at the conceptual level. Douglas speaks of an "undifferentiated" world view, suggesting that whereas we moderns operate in many separate fields of symbolic action, for many "primitive" cultures "the fields of symbolic action are one." Lévi-Strauss, as we shall see, stresses the same idea, noting that many preliterate cultures do not have any sharp division between their various levels of "classification" – the way they order the biotic and social world. Moreover, both writers are not so much concerned, like Frazer, with separating so-called primitive thought from science as with suggesting that for many preliterate people their rituals and symbols create a symbolically meaningful and consistent universe. The general perspectives of the two writers are indeed remarkably similar.

But whereas Lévi-Strauss is mainly concerned to desacralize the concept of totemism, Douglas is concerned in *Purity and Danger* to interpret pollution rules and food taboos by reference to a society's total structure of thought, and in doing so she deviates less from Durkheim's position. With Lévi-Strauss one is never too sure as to what "level" of reality or experience the symbolic systems are based upon or whether any reduction is possible or advocated, other than a reduction to formal structures. With Douglas, however, the message is straightforward (even if implicit in specific cultures), for she follows Durkheim closely in seeing the structure of social regulations as the underlying basis of symbolic and religious phenomena. Stemming from this is another major difference. Douglas is concerned with meaning-semantics, Lévi-Strauss with the "grammar" of culture-syntactics. The former has some substance about it, the latter has not, leading many, including Douglas herself, to criticize the dry formalism of the Lévi-Straussian approach. This is why Lévi-Straussian structuralism has been linked to a delibinized version of psychoanalysis and why the major concerns of *Purity and Danger* – experience, sex, and morality – are singularly absent from the writings of Lévi-Strauss.

Mary Douglas was educated in a Catholic convent, and after obtaining a degree in politics and economics at Oxford, she worked for a while at the Colonial Office. Developing an interest in anthropology, she returned to Oxford to study and then undertook fieldwork studies among the Lele of Zaire. *Purity and Danger*, published in 1966, is devoted to an analysis of the concepts of pollution and taboo. Although wide-ranging in scope, drawing on material from several ethnographic monographs, her analysis is focused primarily on a discussion of the culture of two peoples, the early Hebrews and the Lele, though she draws extensively on the writings of her tutor, Evans-Pritchard.

Douglas begins her discussion with a survey of the writings of some of the early anthropologists, specifically Robertson-Smith, Frazer, and Durkheim. She is anxious to counter the notion that there is a wide gulf separating our own culture from that of preliterate people, especially the theory that "primitive" people do not make any distinction between ideas of holiness and defilement. Our approach to religion and magic, she suggests, should not be narrowly concerned with "spiritual" entities nor with rigidly demarcating the boundaries between religion and magic; instead we should try to compare people's views about human destiny and man's place in nature. And our approach should be sociological.

To understand pollution ideas and taboos, therefore, it is necessary and useful, she suggests, to examine our own ideas of dirt. For although dirt avoidance may be more a matter of hygiene and aesthetics than religion to us, nevertheless in our culture it plays a role similar to that of ritual taboos in primitive culture, for dirt is the "by-product of a systematic ordering and classification of matter" (48). Thus she suggests that taboos – "ideas about separating, purifying, demarcating, and punishing transgressions" – have as their primary function to impose system on an inherently untidy experience (15). She notes Sartre's discussion of viscosity in his *Being and Nothingness* (1943) and the work of Festinger on cognitive dissonance, and she discusses the various ways in which cultures handle ambiguity and anomalous events. Twins or deformed infants, for instance, are frequently killed at birth.

With respect to food taboos, the following extract (referring to the Lele) succinctly expresses her general theory.

> Certain animals ... are appropriate for men to eat, others for women, others for children, others for pregnant women. Others are regarded as totally inedible. One way or another the animals which they reject as unsuitable for human or female consumption turn out to be ambiguous according to their scheme of classification. Their animal taxonomy separates night from day animals; animals of the above (birds, squirrels and monkeys) from animals of the below; water animals and land animals. Those whose behaviour is ambiguous are treated as anomalies of one kind or another and are struck off someone's diet sheet. (1970b: 196).

She thus proposes a theory very similar to that of Leach (1964). To illustrate her thesis she reexamines that "hoary old puzzle" of biblical scholarship, namely the dietary rules set forth in the early chapters of the Bible.

In the creation of Genesis, a rough sketch is outlined of three earthly domains, namely (1) "the dry land," which god called earth, (2) the gathering together of the waters, which the creator called the "seas," and (3) a region "above the earth in the open firmament of heaven," which is henceforth designated air. This schema is very reminiscent of the cosmological system of the Andaman Islanders in that it consists of a tripartite schema of sky, earth, and waters. Significantly, each of these domains is linked with a particular category of "moving creatures," that

205

are brought forth by the creator in chronological order. The living creatures of the earth are subdivided into "beasts" and "creeping things."

In the list of dietary prohibitions (the unclean animals) tabulated in Leviticus and Deuteronomy, there is conformity with this classificatory schema, for the restrictions are broadly grouped under four headings. Within each category, both clean and unclean animals are stipulated. This is succinctly stated in the following passage: "This is the law of the beasts, and the fowl, and of every creature that moveth in the waters, and of every creature that creepeth upon the earth, to make a difference between the unclean and the clean" (Lev. 11:46–7). We may take each of these categories in turn.

(1) *"All that are in the waters."* The identification of prohibited species in this category is fairly straightfordward; only typical fish are considered edible by the Hebrews. As Leviticus (11:9–10) puts it, "These shall ye eat of all that are in the waters: whatever hath fins and scales ... and all that have not fins and scales shall be abomination unto you."

(2) *"The fowls."* In *Purity and Danger*, Douglas ignores this category, because she suggests that they are only named, and not described, and that their names are open to doubt. This is certainly true, since there is a wide discrepancy between the names as given in the authorized and revised versions of the Bible. The translators were certainly no ornithologists. But following Cansdale (1970) we can arrive at a rough estimate of the species prohibited by the Mosaic scriptures. They include the following:

peres	Bearded vulture
racham	Egyptian vulture
ʾayyah	Kite, or honey buzzard
qaʾath	Usually translated as "pelican," but more like an owl
shachaph	Probably seabird, gull
tinshemeth	Sacred ibis?
anaphaa	Heron
chasidah	Stork
nesher	Imperial eagle
dukiphat	Hoopoe
ʿoreb	Raven

It will be seen that all of these birds are either birds of prey or possible scavengers, although two of the species – ibis and hoopoe – were considered sacred by the Egyptians. Even these might be considered to have scavenger habits; the hoopoe's nest, in fact, is extremely evil-smelling.

It is worth noting here that birds, particularly turtledoves and young pigeons, were used as sacrificial animals, especially in rites of atonement for sin or in rites of purification for the cleansing of a leper or a menstruating woman (Lev. 14–15).

(3) *"Beasts."* The Bible says, "These are the beasts which ye shall eat among all the beasts that are on the earth: whatsoever porteth the hoof, and is cloven footed, and cheweth the cud, among the beasts, that shall ye eat" (Lev. 11:2–7). And it goes on to stipulate that the camel, the hyrax, the hare, and the pig are unclean and prohibited because they do not conform to this classificatory scheme.

Deuteronomy (14:4–5) lists the edible species, and, following Cansdale, the suggested identifications may be noted:

Hebrew	Authorized version	Identification
shor	Ox	Ox
keseb	Sheep	Sheep
ʿez	Goat	Goat
ʾayyal	Hart	Deer sp.
tsebi	Roebuck	Gazelle sp.
yachmur	Fallow deer	Bubale
ʾaqqo	Wild goat	Nubian ibex
dishon	Pygang	Addax
teʾo	Wild ox	Oryx
zemer	Chamois	Mountain sheep

It is worth noting that many of these species are now rather rare desert species and protected. Although Douglas suggests that the Hebrews, as pastoralists, may not have relished wild game (68), this is not evident from the Scriptures, for there are frequent references to the trapping of wild animals.

Leviticus also mentions that "whatsoever goeth upon his paws" among the beasts is a prohibited category, but the passage gives no details.

(4) *"Creeping things."* The relevant passage suggests, "These all shall be unclean to you among the creeping things that creep upon the earth; the weasel and the mouse, the tortoise after his kind; and the ferret, and the chameleon, and the lizard, and the snail and the mole. These are unclean to you among all that creep" (Lev. 11:29–31).

This listing evidently refers to most of the lizard family and to small rodents. Douglas suggests that this category consists of creatures "endowed with hands instead of front feet, which perversely use their hands for walking" (70), but the creatures considered are "creeping things," and they are itemized separately from the group of animals (unspecified in the Scriptures) to which her quotation refers (Lev. 11:27). One could hardly consider lizards to have paws, and the "mole," whose forefeet, Douglas comments, "are uncannily hand-like" (70), is certainly a mistranslation, for the animal is not found in Palestine. The passage may,

207

of course, as many biblical commentators have speculated, refer simply to typical mammals.

Returning to Douglas's analysis, it is worth noting initially that she is dissatisfied both with piecemeal explanations of the Levitican dietary prohibitions – attempts to explain the restrictions by a number of factors – and with what she terms "medical materialism," the reduction of religion and symbolism to questions of hygiene and material benefits. An example of the latter is Marvin Harris's interpretation of the taboo on the eating of the sacred cow in India (1977: 14–30). In his discussion of the "riddle of the pig," Harris explicitly defends the materialist approach of Moses Maimonides, whose theories, Douglas suggests, are typical of the medical materialist approach. Moreover, Douglas is unwilling to follow Robertson-Smith and many biblical scholars in considering the prohibitions irrational, and thus aribtrary. Her own interpretation, advanced in *Purity and Danger* and developed in later essays (1975), is contained in the following extracts. She suggests that the Hebrews had

> a very rigid classification. It assigns living creatures to one of three spheres, on a behavioural basis, and selects certain morphological criteria that are found most commonly in the animals inhabiting each sphere. It rejects creatures which are anomalous, whether living between two spheres, or having defining features of members of another sphere, or lacking defining features. Any living being which falls outside this classification is not touched or eaten. (1975: 266)

> In the firmament two legged fowls fly with wings. In the waters scaly fish swim with fins. On the earth four-legged animals hop, jump or walk. Any class of creatures which is not equipped for the right kind of locomotion in its element is contrary to holiness. (1970b: 70)

But it is evident from a critical examination of her theory that in fact few of the mammals and birds named are anomalous according to the classification she outlines. Most of the birds listed in Leviticus conform to the morphological criteria required and thus must be anomalous on other grounds. The fact that they are largely scavengers or birds of prey may be interpreted to mean that they are anomalous not in terms of ecological domains but in terms of invading the human sphere. They transgress the nature–culture dichotomy. The "beasts" are equally difficult to match with her ecological schema. According to Douglas, anything that moves along on four legs and does not creep or crawl conforms to the earthly mode of life; it has the "mode of propulsion proper" to its element. Since of all the quadrupeds known to them only the ten listed in Deuteronomy are considered edible by the Hebrews, Douglas therefore either has to admit that the numerous "abominations"

Land creatures of the earthly domain

	Beasts		Creeping things	
Specified in scripture as edible	Abominations (implied)	Abominations (specified)	Abominations (specified)	Abominations (implied)
Ox	Dog	Pig	Weasel	Snake
Sheep	Hyena	Hare	Mouse	Scorpion,
Goat	Lion	Hyrax	Lizard	etc.
Deer	Jackal	Camel	Gecko	
Gazelle	Wolf		Monitor	
Bubale	Fox		Skunk	
Addax	Hedgehog			
Mt. sheep	Porcupine			
Oryx				
Ibex				

indicated by the Mosaic rules are not anomalies – and thus her thesis remains unproved – or that they are anomalous, in which case she has yet to tell us exactly in what way the wolf, jackal, pig, hare, hyrax, badger, and so on (through all the animal life of Palestine) are classificatory anomalies. It is clearly unhelpful to suggest that they are anomalous because they do not "chew the cud and have the hoof cloven" and thus assign the edible category (of ten species) to the earthly element, everything else being an anomaly. With regard to the pig, she does in fact suggest this, remarking that "the sole reason for its being counted as unclean is its failure to get into the antelope class" (69). Presumably, if the jackal had cloven hooves and ruminated, it too would have been considered edible. (For another interesting discussion of Douglas's Leviticus thesis, cf. Hunn 1979.) The accompanying table outlines the animals associated with the "earthly" domain.

We must conclude, therefore, that Douglas's analysis of the abominations of Leviticus provides inconclusive evidence to support her thesis that classificatory anomalies are tabooed categories. In responding to criticism of *Purity and Danger*, which intimated that she had ignored the social activities of the Hebrews, Douglas remarked that such an approach was against the whole spirit of the book. This is true, for Douglas follows Durkheim closely in giving social institutions primary importance in interpreting cosmological beliefs, even though her analysis of the prohibitions in Leviticus was focused purely on the Hebrews' system of ideas. In later essays on the Hebrews she has attempted to redress these short-

Hebrew classification of animals

	Birds	Beasts	Creeping things	Water creatures
Edible				
Fit for the altar	Turtle dove	Ox		
	Pigeon	Sheep		
		Goat		
Fit for the table	Sparrow	Deer	Grasshopper	Typical fish
	Quail	Oryx	Locust	
		Ibex		
		Gazelle		
Inedible: unclean	Owl	Camel	Snake	Shrimp
animals	Hawk	Hyrax	Weasel	Dugong
	Vulture	Pig	Lizard	
	Hoopoe	Hare		

comings, and, like Leach and Tambiah, has offered some interesting thoughts on the analogies between animal categories and social relationships evident in the Scriptures.

In her essay "Deciphering a Meal," Douglas (1975) suggests that the Hebrews roughly classed animals into three categories: those considered edible and fit for the altar (as sacrifices); those considered edible in a profane context; and those considered unclean and inedible. This categorization can be illustrated as shown in the accompanying table.

The important part that sacrifice played in early Hebrew religion, as one commentator put it, cannot be exaggerated, for it formed the main ritual element. Robertson-Smith, as we have seen, suggested that the leading idea behind such sacrifices was not that of a gift to god but rather that it was an act of communion, in which god and his worshipers united by partaking together of the flesh and blood of the sacred victim. Yet it is worth noting that the most characteristic phrase used in connection with sacrifice is "to make atonement" – to recover for the person, as it were, free access to Yahweh. Animals played a crucial role in such rituals, and the following features are significant:

(1) The animals offered for sacrifice had to be "without blemish" and, for the burnt offering (in which the whole animal was consumed at the altar), of the male sex (Lev. 22:19–20). Thus no injured or diseased animal was fit for sacrifice.

(2)   The "firstborn" (*bekor*) was always consecrated for divine sacrifice, "Both of man and beast: it is mine" (Ex. 13:12).

(3)   Only livestock should be offered for sacrifice, or possibly a turtledove or young pigeon. Robertson-Smith noted that "deer, gazelles and other kinds of game were eaten by the Hebrews, but not sacrificed" (1889: 218).

(4)   Both the fat and the blood of sacrificial animals were considered to belong to Yahweh, and a significant passage reads, "The life of the flesh is in the blood; and I have given it to you upon the altar to make an atonement for your souls:...therefore I say unto the children of Israel no soul of you shall eat blood" (Lev. 17:10–12). Furthermore, any clean animal or bird secured through hunting must have its blood poured onto the ground and covered with dust.

(5)   There is reason to believe that meat from a sacrificial animal was considered holy or sacred and could be eaten only by persons who were ceremonially clean.

(6)   All livestock had to be killed sacrificially and brought to the "tabernacle of the congregation" (*mishkan*) as an offering to Yahweh. In making the sacrifice, the priest sprinkled the "blood upon the altar of the lord," and such places were considered sacred or holy (Lev. 6:26–27).

At the opposite ends of the spectrum in terms of ritual value – Douglas uses the phrase "degrees of holiness" – are the unclean animals. Anyone touching such animals was considered unclean until the evening. The contagious quality of the unclean (*tame*) animals is borne out by the fact that any dead animal falling on a vessel of wood, or on skins, or on clothing rendered such articles unclean. Notions of impurity were associated with other aspects of Hebrew social life. A woman was considered unclean for seven days after the birth of a child and was not allowed to touch any "hallowed things" nor come into the sanctuary. Menstrual discharge and leprosy were the focus of similar beliefs and restrictions.

The Israelites considered themselves to be descended from Abraham and to have a covenant with Yahweh, and, as Y. Kaufman remarks, their folk religion distinguished two realms, the land of Yahweh (holy land) and impure, foreign lands (1961: 26). Amos's warning to Amaziah that he may die in a "polluted land" (Amos 8:17) reflected not only stringent rules of exogamy but the popular view that the lands of other cultures were impure.

In addition, there were various rules relating to priests and to the holy sanctuaries. First, the Levites are taken as representing the "firstborn" of Israel (Num. 3:12) and consecrated to the service of Yahweh, and from this tribe the priests, restricted to the sons of Aaron, are drawn. Only Levites without "any blemish" or physical deformity could become priests, and they had to observe strict rules in order not to profane their function, such as to marry virgins, not to touch dead flesh, and so forth.

Second, the place of sacrifice was considered sacred, and, as Douglas writes, no person in an unclean state or who had sinned morally, could enter the temple (1975: 267).

This biblical data serves as background material to illustrate the various analogies that Douglas has cogently described. An analogy between animal and social categories is, of course, evident. Among animals only livestock come under the covenant, and only those "without blemish" are fit for sacrifice; in addition, the "firstborn" are given to divine sacrifice. Likewise, only Levites without bodily blemish can become priests, and they too are held to represent the firstborn of Israel. The relationship can be expressed as follows:

	Increasing purity →	
	Under covenant	Without blemish or firstborn
Human	Israelites	Levites (priests)
Animals	Livestock	Sacrificial animals

Further analogies are expressed in the next table, but for an equally succinct summary of the various homologies evident in the Scriptures we can do no better than to quote Douglas:

> Between the temple and the body we are in a maze of religious thought. What is its social counterpart? Turning back to my original analysis [in *Purity and Danger*] of the forbidden meats we are now in a much better position to assess intensity and social relevance... At every moment they are in chorus with a message about the value of purity and the rejection of impurity. At the level of a general taxonomy of living beings the purity in question is the purity of the categories... At the level of the individual living being impurity is the imperfect, broken, bleeding specimen. The sanctity of cognitive boundaries is made known by valuing the integrity of the physical forms. The perfect physical specimens point to the perfectly bounded temple, altar and sanctuary. And these in their turn point to the hardwon and hard-to-defend territorial boundaries of the Promised Land." (1975: 269)

Douglas denies that this is a reductionist analysis, reducing dietary rules to political concerns; nevertheless she tends to view social relationships as the underlying foundations of symbolic systems, especially in her two major works, *Purity and Danger* and *Natural Symbols*. The homologies that she analyzes are expressed in the accompanying table.

The form of symbolic interpretation that I have just outlined moves

Homologies among animal, human, and ecological categories

	Unclean (tame)	Profane (chol)	Sacred (qadush)
Animal categories	Abominations	Edible categories	Sacrificial animals
Human categories	Foreigners	Israelites	Levites (priests)
Ecological categories	Other lands	Land of the Israelites	Temple or sanctuary

the discussion away from the specific focus on dietary prohibitions, but it is a development of ideas contained in *Purity and Danger*, where Douglas sought to show that ideas about the body have a symbolic dimension. Pollutions, she writes, are used as analogies for expressing a general view of the social order, for the structure of "living organisms is better able to reflect complex social forms than door posts and lintels." In arguing against the psychoanalytic theories of Bruno Bettelheim and Norman Brown, she examines the pollution ideas of the Hebrews, suggesting that preoccupations with the boundaries of the body "express danger to community boundaries." Likewise, in a discussion of the caste system she argues that it is a "symbolic system, based on the image of the body, whose primary concern is the ordering of a social hierarchy" (149). Thus we can understand pollution rules, she suggests, if we are prepared to see in the body a symbol of society. In the final chapter of *Purity and Danger* she even asserts that "the body . . . provides a basic scheme for all symbolism. There is hardly any pollution which does not have some primary physiological reference" (193).

In relating pollution rules and dietary restrictions to the way in which people conceptually and symbolically structure their environment, Douglas struck a rich theoretical vein and has offered suggestions that antedated, in many respects, the perspectives of Lévi-Strauss. Certainly her analyses take us beyond Firth's notion that taboos relate to objects and actions that are significant for the social order and "belong to the general system of social control." I will therefore conclude this discussion by briefly outlining Douglas's analysis of the main symbolic categories of the Lele and the notion of their "mediation." These primary categories can be schematically noted as in the diagram.

The primary contrasts depicted in these schemas are the following: human–animal, male–female, and forest–village. But what is of interest is the existence of spheres and categories that are, in a sense, mediating

213

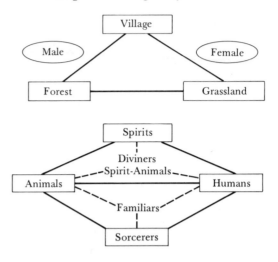

elements between the contrasting domains. Spirits mediate between man and the animal world, for only if ritual is correctly performed and human relations peaceful are men successful in the hunt and women fecund like animals. Similarly, the grassland gardens form an intermediary zone between the village and the forest, whereas diviners mediate between humans and the spirit world. In addition to these, Douglas suggests, there are two kinds of "mediating bridges" between humans and the "wild," one for evil, the other for good. With respect to the former she writes, "The dangerous bridge is made by a wicked transfer of allegiance by humans who become sorcerers. They turn their back on their own kind and run with the hunted, fight against the hunters, work against the diviners to achieve death instead of healing. They have moved across to the animal sphere and they have caused some animals to move in from the animal to the human sphere" (1966: 198).

Significantly, of course, the latter animals, who become familiars (*mikadi*) are often carnivorous animals who invade the village sphere in search of prey. It is noteworthy that in traditional literature on witchcraft the witch is often portrayed either in ambiguous terms or in terms that symbolize the inverse of the moral order. Douglas goes on to suggest that sorcerers, twin-diviners (members of a specific cult), and the pangolin are mediators between the human and wild (forest) spheres because they are anomalous with regard to these categories. It seems possible, however, that these categories become mediating elements between two spheres, because they already straddle two other domains. Thus twins, who "break the normal limitations," as Douglas puts it, and are "anom-

214

alous" because they exhibit what the Lele think of as an essentially animal characteristic – fecundity – are able to mediate between the spirits and the human world (as diviners).

There is therefore, as Douglas stresses, a subtle interplay in Lele symbolism between the three primary categories – animals, humans, and spirits – in terms of the ritual hunt, in terms of the various prohibitions, as well as in terms of the mediating elements – diviners and spirit-animals. The animal that can be seen to play an essential part in this symbolic "system" is of course the pangolin, which, for a number of reasons, occupies a key position in their symbolism. On the one hand, it is a spirit-animal, on account of its fishlike scales and burrowing habits and its association, as a ritual animal, with one of the main cult groups. On the other hand, it is not easily categorized by the Lele, who think the pangolin almost humanlike in that it bears its young in a human fashion – simply – and does not fear humans. Thus the ritual significance of the pangolin seems to me to be consonant with its positioning in the Lele system of symbolic classification, rather than to its anomalous status as a "scaly, fishlike monster." (In an interesting analysis of Lele symbolism, Evan Zuesse, 1979: 63–71, attempts to interpret Douglas's material in terms of transcendental structures of meaning, a mode of analysis that largely follows that of Eliade.)

Although her mode of interpreting religious symbolism implies a tendency to emphasize structural patterns, Douglas was aware that every society is built on contradictions (1966: 166) and that all social categories and demarcations are transgressed by choice (innovation), by default (hence social sanctions), or by necessity. But given her Durkheimian stance, she rarely interprets religious symbolism as ideology, and in her most recent essays (in contrast to *Purity and Danger*) the "implicit" meanings of symbolism are not directly identified with political power or with systems of social control.

Yet *Purity and Danger* expresses the two streams of Durkheim's thought concerning the interpretation of symbolism: (1) the structuralist stream, which is exemplified by Douglas's attempt to understand dietary prohibitions by reference to a "system of classification"; and (2) the social-structural stream, which assumes that "society" is the entity expressed in ritual symbolism and that the relationship between ritual categories and the social order is simply metaphorical. This latter approach Douglas develops in her study *Natural Symbols*, which I will discuss in the next section. To conclude this section, let us briefly examine some of the limitations of the general thesis expressed in *Purity and Danger*.

In her discussion of "primitive worlds" Mary Douglas suggests that we have to face the question as to why some preliterate cultures are "pollution-prone" whereas our own culture is relatively free of pollution beliefs. Some attempt must be made, she writes, to make a viable distinction between "primitive and modern" culture. As I shall explore later, such a dichotomous categorization is rather misleading, but Douglas is alive to the dangers of making preliterate people seem more mystical than in fact they are and "civilized thought more rational than it is" (1970b: 93). In this she echoes Evans-Pritchard's criticisms of Lévy-Bruhl. Indeed she commends Evans-Pritchard's study of the Azande as a first attempt to relate collective representations to social institutions, a type of analysis that Evans-Pritchard rebuked Radcliffe-Brown for suggesting. To understand preliterate cultures, Douglas argues, we must follow a Durkheimian analysis and realize that just as there has been a differentiation of social institutions – the mechanical-organic solidarity – so there has been a "comparable movement in the realm of ideas" (95). The difference between Western culture and that of preliterate people, therefore, is not that we are more scientific or lack symbolism but that our conceptual ideas are not unified by an all-embracing cosmology. "Our experience is fragmented," she writes. "We moderns operate in many different fields of symbolic action." In contrast, the cultural ideas of preliterate people are unified: "All their contexts of experience overlap and interpenetrate, nearly all their experience is religious." Their rituals "create one single, symbolically consistent universe." Or, as she puts it succinctly in her article on pollution, "The different elements in the primitive world view are closely integrated; the categories of social structure embrace the universe in a single, symbolic whole" (1975: 57). She describes this as an "undifferentiated" world view. This leads her to suggest that Christianity, like other world religions, cannot be classed as "primitive," for it has, with the increasing complexity of society, taken on a more "specialized" role.

This formulation has affinities with the writings of Bellah and Lévi-Strauss, as well as of earlier writers like Boas (1938) and Laura Thompson (1945). For Bellah (1964) speaks of religious evolution in terms of an evolution from a compact to a differentiated symbol system, and Lévi-Strauss suggests that preliterate people do not have any conception of a sharp division between the various levels of classification. Such a formulation, although indicating important guidelines for research, is problematic for a number of reasons.

First, it suggests that only the religious systems of preliterate people have a unifying or cosmological effect, and this is untenable. Although Radcliffe-Brown had suggested that all religions have a conception of the universe as a moral order, and Berger (1973) indeed defined religion as a human enterprise by which a sacred cosmos is established, the truth probably lies between these two extremes. In some cultures, religion indeed attempts to conceive of the entire universe as being humanly significant, building on a conception of an "all-embracing sacred order" (Berger 1973: 59). But in other cultures, religious ideas certainly have a more limited scope. There may be a marked absence of religious classifications. The "scope" of the religious symbolism, to use a term of Clifford Geertz's (1968: 111), may be much narrower. In this sense Buddhism and the religion of the Dogon are similar, whereas some tribal cultures, as I have discussed with specific reference to the Hill Pandaram of South India, are lacking in complex religious symbolism (cf. Morris 1976). Geertz, in fact, makes an interesting contrast between the religious systems of Morocco and Indonesia – both Islamic communities – in this respect. In Indonesia, he suggests, almost everything is "tinged with metaphysical meaning, the whole of ordinary life has a faintly transcendental quality about it," whereas in Morocco religion is operative, as in Western culture, only in a "few fairly well demarcated regions of behaviour" (112).

In a later essay, in which she questioned the notion that preliterate people are universally of a religious disposition – the myth of the "pious primitive" – Douglas suggests that there may be some variation in the degree to which symbol systems are structured and unified. The question is, she writes, "whether tribal societies sustain their social reality by creating all-embracing universes of meaning, or whether there are not some which get along with partial systems of explanation" (1975: 76). This essay is an important corrective to the general tenor of *Purity and Danger*.

Second, there is no clear correlation, as Douglas suggests, between institutional differentiation and the fragmentation of a unified symbol system. Indeed, a society with a high division of labor (organic solidarity) – Indian society – provides Douglas (1970b) with some of her best illustrations of pollution behavior. Again, as I have noted elsewhere, symbolic classifications reach their most ornate and complex elaboration not in tribal cultures but in early theocratic states. It is with the rise of literacy and state institutions in early agrarian civilizations – the Egyptian, Aztec, Chinese, and Indian civilizations are examples – that structured symbolism reaches its apotheosis.

To some extent, in tribal communities, it is the kinship system rather than religion that provides the "dominant locus of symbolic production," whereas in theocratic states the symbolism is largely provided by religion. Moreover, as Sahlins has suggested, we must not lose sight of the fact that in Western society the economy, to a large extent, has symbolic and cultural significance as an ideological system (1976: 210–17). Cultural integration is provided by the market mechanism. Thus, in broadest terms, religion and classificatory symbolism are utilized as ideological systems and developed most fully in theocratic states rather than in tribal communities.

Third, Douglas's suggestion that in preliterate communities "nearly all their experiences are religious" is questionable in that, as both Geertz and Maurice Bloch (1977) have indicated, the religious attitude is only sporadically adopted by people, and for the most part they live in a cognitive world of "matter-of-fact" realism. Thus, as Geertz writes, the "actual employment of sacred symbols . . . takes place in specialized settings and in particular rituals" (1975: 108). To equate cosmological systems of thought with consciousness, or with preliterate thought generally, is misleading. Bloch, indeed, has suggested that there are two aspects of culture, two forms of communication, the one related to practical activities and based on universal notions of time and cognition, the other being a ritual form of cognition that is culturally specified and that postulates a variant of a "timeless" static order (1977; 287).

The interpretation of symbols

In recent decades there has been a wealth of studies devoted to symbolism, both ethnographic and theoretical. The works of Jung and Eliade have been reissued, and several important anthropological texts have been published. It will my purpose in this present section to briefly outline some of the approaches that have been suggested for the interpretation of symbolism. But first I must define what is meant by *symbol*. This is no easy task, for as Edmund Leach remarked, the technical literature on this topic is voluminous and goes back several centuries. We can perhaps begin with Ernst Cassirer and his interesting study *An Essay on Man* (1944).

Cassirer, like Lévi-Strauss, saw language and symbolism as the essential characteristics of human culture and was thus moved to define the human species as *animal symbolicum* (28). With the acquisition of symbolic communication, Cassirer suggested, the whole of human life was radically transformed; compared with other animals, human beings now live not simply in a broader reality, but rather "in a new *dimension* of reality" (26). Cassirer therefore argued that symbolic representation was a central function of human consciousness and basic to our understanding of all human life: language, history, science, art, myth, and religion. Symbolism, he said, because of its universality, is the "open sesame" to an understanding of human culture. Interestingly, although like Lévi-Strauss he stressed that the thought of preliterate people did not divide life into different spheres or domains, for Cassirer this unity was synthetic and

218

one of feeling, rather than analytical and cognitive. Mythical thought he held to be symbolic but essentially nontheoretical.

In this study Cassirer offers reflections on various aspects of human culture: language, art, history, religion, and science. All are seen as facets of a "symbolic universe," and all hinge on his distinction between sign and symbol, which are seen as belonging to two different universes of discourse. A *sign* belongs to the physical world of being, it is an "operator," there being an "intrinsic" or "natural" connection between the sign and the thing it signifies. A *symbol* on the other hand, is "artificial," a "designator," and belongs to the human world of meaning. Thus human knowledge by its very nature is symbolic. The difference between religion and science, for Cassirer, is that whereas religion and myth "merge" the symbol and the signified, science (like ordinary language and common sense) differentiates them and from this differentiation produces "systems of relations."

Two recent studies of symbolism offer refinements of this basic distinction, which derives from earlier writers, although the terminology used is variable and often confusing. Raymond Firth (1973), largely following Pierce, makes a distinction between four different signs. An *index* is a sign that is directly related in fact to what is signified – part to whole, particular to general. An example is the footprint of a lion or the smoke from a fire. A *signal* is considered the dynamic aspect of an index. An *icon* is a sign used when a sensory-likeness relationship is intended or interpreted: For example, the statue of a lion is iconic. And finally, a *symbol* is a sign that has a complex series of associations, but there is no direct relationship or resemblance between the sign and the object signified. The relationship is based on convention and may seem arbitrary: For example, the lion is the symbol of bravery.

Edmund Leach makes a series of similar distinctions but views symbol and sign as subsets of index. Leach, however, uses the term *sign* to refer to "symbols" in which the relationship between the sign and the thing signified is contiguous (part to whole) and thus mainly metonymic, rather than simply an arbitrary association based on metaphor. For Leach an example of a sign is a crown, representing sovereignty. Leach makes these analytical distinctions in order to provide conceptual tools for the structural analysis of symbolic systems, the latter including myth, magic, and religion. Unlike Firth, he makes a distinction between two types of symbols. A sign expresses a relationship that is intrinsic, in the sense that the sign and the thing symbolized belong to the same cultural context, the relationship being metonymic. He notes that natural indexes entail the same sort of relationship. A symbol, on the other hand, represents an entity belonging to a different cultural context, and the relationship

219

is metaphorical. Leach suggests that melody and harmony express the same contrast as metonymy and metaphor.

Leach is an interesting writer with whom to begin this survey of the various approaches to the study of symbolism, for not only has his eclecticism led him to produce many seminal essays on the subject, but he combines in his writings the two main streams, or at least emphases, of the Durkheimian tradition, the *social-structural* and the *structuralist* approaches. To what extent they correspond to the empiricist (Radcliffe-Brown) and a rationalist (Lévi-Strauss) interpretation of Durkheim it is difficult to say, but clearly Leach sees himself as combining these two approaches. However, Leach tends to see the distinction between rationalism and empiricism as based not upon epistemology but on the aspect of social life that is studied. Rationalists allegedly study systems of ideas and "thought," whereas empiricists focus upon "objective facts" – economics and social action. By such criteria, Marx is an empiricist. Leach's study *Culture and Communication* (1976), from which these definitions are taken, is an introduction to the "structuralist" approach, and is, significantly, subtitled "The Logic by Which Symbols Are Connected."

Leach's earlier study of the political systems of highland Burma, however, interprets symbolism in a more strictly Durkheimian fashion, although he is critical of the "integrative" bias of Durkheim's sociology. He is critical, too, of Durkheim's dichotomy between the sacred and the profane and the suggestion that ritual refers specifically to social action that occurs in the sacred context. Leach suggests, rather, that social actions fall on a continuum. At one extreme are actions that are entirely profane, entirely functional, technique pure and simple; at the other extreme are actions that are sacred and technically nonfunctional. Viewed this way, Leach suggests, technique and ritual, profane and sacred, do not indicate types of social action but aspects of almost any kind of behavior. Ritual, in this sense, is a symbolic statement that "says" something about the individual or event; thus Leach conjoins, under the heading of ritual, behavior that is considered simply communicative – such as shaking hands – and magico-religious behavior. Ritual is symbolic action, and myth is simply its counterpart in the realm of ideas. "Myth and ritual are essentially one and the same," he writes (1954: 264). But what does ritual action symbolize? On this Leach is fairly explicit; it "represents" the social structure. He writes, "My view is that ritual action and belief are alike to be understood as forms of symbolic statement about the social order." And he continues, "Ritual makes explicit the social structure... The structure which is symbolized in ritual is the system of socially approved 'proper' relations between individuals and groups" (14–15).

220

But, significantly, although Leach suggests that social structure in practical situations "consists of a set of ideas about the distribution of power between persons and groups" (4), he was aware that social structure is an ideal model, and in his book on the Kachin Leach describes the oscillation between two structural patterns, one based on a feudal hierarchy (*gumsa*), the other on a segmentary tribal system (*gumlao*). "Real" Kachin society, however, which is seen as flexible and changing, is never grasped theoretically, and changes in social structure are seen by Leach as the outcome of "abstract" individuals actively seeking their own interests.

An example of this mode of approach to symbolism, which posits a concordance between ritual symbolism and social structure is implied in Leach's classic article "Magical Hair" (1958). This essay was largely a response to the suggestion put forward by a psychoanalyst that the cutting of hair was a symbolic form of castration, in that the genitals are universally, though unconsciously, associated with hair (Berg 1951). Although admitting that hair rituals and sexuality are frequently associated cross-culturally, Leach stresses that such conceptions are patterned social responses, related to "ideal social categories." He notes the following pattern, which is widespread in the ethnographic record:

Long hair	Unrestrained sexuality
Short, tightly bound hair	Restricted sexuality
Closely shaved hair	Celibacy

Leach shows that this pattern is related to social status. For example, among many Burmese hill tribes unmarried girls wear their hair short, whereas married women wear their hair long. He notes, too, the important role that hair rituals play in rites of passage, reflecting the progression of the individual through set stages in the social system. A more recent essay by C. R. Hallpike has developed these ideas and suggests that hair rituals cannot be reduced to sexual symbolism. He suggests instead that long hair is frequently associated with being "outside society," wholly or in part, and the cutting of the hair symbolizes reentering society or living under a strict code of rules: "Cutting the hair equals social control," Hallpike writes (1969: 260–1). Leach himself had remarked on the contrasting hair styles of the two religious specialists of South Asia, Sannyasin and Brahmin.

221

This social-structural approach to symbolism, which relates symbols to social categories, was reflected, of course, in Leach's essay "Animal Categories and Verbal Abuse" (1964), in which he sought to uncover underlying correspondences, expressed in metaphor, between animal and social categories. I must now turn to the other mode of interpretation utilized by Leach, namely that of structuralist analysis. This approach too was incorporated in this essay: Leach's basic thesis was that taboo is an expression of ambiguity between category divisions – specifically, binary classifications. Leach's introductory study *Culture and Communication* (1976) is a development of these thoughts and clearly shows the influence of Lévi-Strauss in its structuralist bias. No longer is there an explicit distinction between the "structure of ideas" (ritual) and the "structure of society" (social structure), for the two levels are now seen as aspects of a "single interacting whole." And the emphasis is now on the *"logic* by which symbols are connected" not on the *basis* of the symbolism. But even in his earlier studies the two approaches are not easily differentiated: Although Leach saw ritual symbolism as a reflection or metaphor of the social structure, the latter itself is conceived as a "thought-of" order, an aspect of an ideological system. This is an important insight, but it treats conceptual ideas and ritual behavior as somehow autonomous of economic realities: or, to use Leach's terms, the relationship between the "communicative" and "pragmatic" aspects of culture is never explained.

Leach, therefore, like Lévi-Strauss, treats culture (or at least those aspects of culture that are essentially symbolic) as a system of communication and suggests that the task of the anthropologist is to "decode the messages" embedded in the symbolism, to study the "semantics of cultural forms." Because, he suggests, symbols convey meaning in combination, he is critical of Firth's approach to symbolism, which is to discuss symbols with respect to specific empirical categories – hair, food, gift giving – and to denote the meanings that have cross-cultural relevance. Leach maintains that such "codes" are potentially a "transformation," in any given culture, of any other code – that is, they indicate the same message. To decode cultural forms, to "decide what customs can be said to 'mean' " (6), Leach advocates two basic analytical tools.

The first arises from Leach's distinction between sign and symbol. This is the suggestion that the relation between symbols is either intrinsic and prior, and thus metonymic (*syntagmatic*), or "arbitrarily" related and metaphorical (*paradigmatic*). This distinction, which is an elaboration of Frazer's distinction between homeopathic and contagious magic, suggests homologies between different levels of experience (codes or classifications). It also suggests that there can be, as has been mentioned, a transformation (translation) of the "message" between different codes.

The second places an emphasis on binary codes and on a third (ambiguous) category that mediates the opposition. Van Gennep's tripartite schema, which is postulated as a universal form of transition rites, and Leach's own discussion of taboo typify this mode of analysis.

Taken together, the suggestion is that they form a "logic," structural principles that constitute the underlying structure of myth, magic, and symbolism. Since social categories are held to have the same status as other codes or classifications, in the symbolic system, the problem of this sort of analysis is that the "meaning" seems to be purely formal, for the "message" has no substance. For example, Leach notes the ambiguous status of every married woman in a society with exogamous patrilineal descent groups. On the other hand, with respect to the local lineage group, she is an alien; she is "intrinsically evil, a foreign object, a sexual object, dirty." But on the other hand, the continuity of the descent group depends upon her, and she is therefore intrinsically good, and the antithesis of a sexual object. Leach notes the congruency of the oppositions:

Wife	:	Mother
Sexual	:	Asexual
Dirty	:	Clean
Sinful	:	Sinless

He remarks that this is reminiscent of the contrast between the Virgin Mary and Mary Magdalene (Eve) in Christian mythology. But clearly such myths have meaning only in terms of concrete, living relationships. The message surely is the ambiguous status of women in such societies and the myths and pollution beliefs simply express, or attempt to resolve in thought, real contradictions.

A further limitation of this type of analysis is that the stress on binary oppositions obscures the fact that many symbols not only reflect a complex hierarchy but often express the ultimate unity – as in Dogon symbolism and the yin–yang division – of all divisions.

Equally unsatisfactory is Leach's handling of the concept of the sacred. On the one hand, the term is equated with the symbolic aspect of all social relationships: on the other, it is seen as a mediating category in binary classifications.

But what is important about Leach's suggestions is the idea that symbols cannot be understood in isolation and that there is no universal symbolism, even though there may be some common symbolic themes.

Symbols are always potentially polysemic, and they derive meaning only when contrasted with other symbols as part of a set. Thus to understand symbolism is to explore in detail a specific ethnographic context – and Leach himself has made several interesting analyses of early Hebrew culture (1969, 1983).

In discussing Leach's writings, I have tried to describe two contrasting approaches to the study of symbolism, both derived from the "symbolist" aspect of Durkheim's thought. The first is a structuralist approach, which attempts to delineate the underlying formal structures or patterns within a given symbol system. Such an analysis may have an empiricist bias, as in the studies of Beidelman (1973), or their focus may be more rationalistic and formal, as with Leach and Lévi-Strauss.

The second is the social-structural approach, which gives one aspect or facet of the symbol system theoretical priority, for it takes the social structure as the basis of the various symbolic codes. Again, such an approach may have an empiricist bias, as in the writings of Douglas (which I discuss again later in this section), or may be more rationalistic, in sensing that the social structure itself is of an ideal order. Or, as Lévi-Strauss's well-known phrase puts it, "Social structure has nothing to do with empirical reality but with models which are built up after it" (1963: 279). Leach's study of the Kachin exemplifies this approach.

Both approaches are illustrated in recent studies of symbolism. An example of the structuralist approach, though of a rather restricted kind, is the study of animal symbolism by Roy Willis, *Man and Beast*. Willis is a self-proclaimed structuralist, and in this study he makes a comparative analysis of three African communities, the Nuer, the Lele, and the Fipa. His basic premise is that because human beings have a biological heritage, animals almost universally have a profound symbolic significance for human culture. As he put it, "Animals would seem to be especially apt to this ultimate symbolic role because . . . they lend themselves to the expression of two primary and polar modes of human thought, the metonymic and the metaphoric" (1974: 128). That is, they are singularly apt symbols both in representing certain aspects of human life – the existential and the normative – and in expressing what he terms the ultimate value, the "meaning of life." Although Willis employs structuralist terminology, this sort of analysis would seem to be a far cry from the formal analyses of Lévi-Strauss and Leach. Willis has a cryptological rather than a structural approach to symbolism, and, moreover, sees the "meaning" of the symbols as relating to what Beidelman has suggested are but "glib generalities" (1975: 329) – the "meaning of life." Not surprisingly, in his analysis of the symbolism of each of the three cultures Willis centers his discussion entirely on a single theriomorphic theme:

224

the Nuer and their cattle, the Lele and the pangolin, and the Fipa and the sacred python. As Beidelman remarked in his critical review of the book (1975), such an approach is extremely narrow and does not do justice to the rich and complex symbolism that each of these cultures exhibits. Willis's study can be described as structuralist only in the sense that it attempts to understand symbolism within the parameters of the ritual system, for its method is profoundly antistructuralist.

Several of the essays from a symposium collection edited by Willis, *The Interpretation of Symbolism* (1975), offer more commendable examples of the structuralist approach, although they all tend to view symbolism as a system of meaning and anchor the analysis to social structure. Two examples are worth briefly outlining. A structuralist perspective is suggested by Sherry B. Ortner's contribution, "God's Bodies, God's Food: A Symbolic Analysis of Sherpa Ritual" (1975), in that she explicitly denies that any form of reductionism is useful in the analysis of symbolism. She writes, "We cannot, if we understand ritual fully, emerge with a clearcut assertion of the primacy of the social or cultural or psychological dimension of meaning" (167). Since she defines religion as a metasystem that solves "problems of meaning" by grounding the "social order" within a theoretical ultimate reality (expressed through symbols), her analysis can only replicate the system of religious symbolism. Such an analysis is of interest, and clearly necessary for a descriptive understanding of Sherpa ritual – but it is not an interpretation. Although taking her bearings from the writings of Clifford Geertz (1975), she does what he repudiates, namely, treats culture "purely as a symbolic system."

A second essay from the same collection, though again offering an analysis of a dualistic system in structuralist terms, implies that there is a social-structural basis to the symbolism. This is Rosaldo and Atkinson's essay "Man the Hunter and Women" (1975), which explores the symbolism associated with the sexual division among the Ilongot people of northern Luzan. In an analysis of the magical spells associated with hunting and swidden cultivation, the two primary economic activities, they suggest that there is a sex-linked symbolic opposition, which expresses asymmetry but complementarity. This "symbolic parallelism" can be roughly outlined as follows:

Forest	Garden
Men	Women
Game	Rice
Warfare	Motherhood
Hunting	Cultivation
Life Taking	Life Giving

This dualism is similar in many respects to that found in many other

225

tribal cultures, examples of which will be discussed in the next chapter, and Rosaldo and Atkinson note its occurrence among many peoples in Southeast Asia. But unlike many writers who have offered analyses of symbolic dualisms (the binary opposition, for such writers, is the structure), Rosaldo and Atkinson indicate that the "symbolism of the sexes is a likely ground for discovering abstract and universal symbolic themes" (43). Willis interprets this as implying that the sexual division everywhere provides a metaphorical basis for the elaboration of cosmological systems. This runs counter to Fox's suggestions, in his essay in the same collection, "On Binary Categories and Primary Symbols," in which he interprets Needham as asserting that only certain societies – those with prescriptive marriage alliance – are characterized by a pervasive concordance of complementary oppositions (1975: 118). This is not my reading of Needham, who wants, indeed, to argue the contrary (cf. 1972 : 156). And as Goody remarked, many of the analyses of conceptual systems in binary terms have related to African communities that lack prescriptive systems (1977 : 62). But the important point is that the suggestions of Rosaldo and Atkinson and of Fox suggest a social-structural approach to symbolism. Although the former writers indicate that the relationship between the sexual division, production, and symbolism is by no means straightforward, they imply that the symbolism can be understood as symbolic statements about the relations between men and women. Their discussion is therefore cast largely in the idiom of a social-structural approach.

We can examine the latter approach in more detail by returning to the writings of Mary Douglas, for her study *Natural Symbols* is a clear, unambiguous statement of the social-structural approach to symbolism. Whereas both Leach and Douglas combined the social-structural and the structuralist approaches in their earlier work, Leach, under the influence of Lévi-Strauss, has moved closer to structuralism, whereas Douglas has repudiated Lévi-Strauss and thus retained a continuity with Durkheim's symbolist formulations. Her criticism of Lévi-Strauss is that although he has provided an invaluable technique for the analysis of symbolism, his form of analysis only indicates underlying universal structures and thus tells us little about cultural variations. For Douglas, what is important is to indicate the "structures underlying symbolic behaviour." As she writes, "The structural analysis of symbols has somehow to be related to a hypothesis about role structure" (1970a: 95).

Natural Symbols is both a critique and a development of her earlier study. But whereas *Purity and Danger* was concerned to interpret pollution ideas by reference to a structure of ideas, in the later work this mode of structuralist analysis is left behind, and her primary focus is on

226

delineating structural correlations or a concordance between symbolic patterns and social experiences. "We must look," she writes, "for tendencies and correlations between the character of the symbolic system and that of the social system" (12). Such an approach suggests several important things.

First, since social life is variable there can be no universal patterns of symbols. The quest for "natural symbols," therefore, she writes can only be unrewarding, if not ridiculous (11).

Second, the general theme of *Purity and Danger*, namely that the symbolic codes of preliterate communities are unified, is here abandoned as empirically invalid, and Douglas attempts to explain variations in cosmological ideas.

Third, Douglas assumes that in all human cultures there is a "drive to achieve consonance in all levels of experience," and that the relationship between body symbolism and cosmology and the social structure is unproblematic and simply "reflective."

Fourth, in discussing the basis of the symbolism, Douglas equates social structure, which may be of an "ideal" order and a part of the "model" or symbolic system, and power relations. She therefore takes an empiricist view of the social structure, which is problematic.

Douglas begins her study by considering the general antiritualist tendency of much of Christianity, which is expressed in several ways: in its contempt for external ritual forms, which are assumed to be empty symbols of conformity; in its internalization of the religious experience; and in the move towards a more "secular" orientation. Such an individualistic and nonritualist approach to religion, she suggests, must not be seen as somehow superior to other forms of worship but rather as an expression of a specific type of social structure. Conversely, the idea that the religion of preliterate people is magical and taboo-ridden and that human history simply reveals a progressive decline of magic is equally misleading. There are preliterate communities like the Mbuti, who lack elaborate ritual or cosmic categories, and others like the Basseri nomads, whom one might describe as secular and irreligious. The degree of elaboration of ritual and the type of cosmology, she suggests, are the product of a specific form of social experience and may have nothing to do with urban life or modern science.

Developing the theories of the sociologist Basil Bernstein, who had suggested an association between linguistic codes and types of family authority, Douglas postulates a variable scale of social constraints on the individual, contrasting "an entirely personal form of relationships, unstructured by fixed principles," with a system of social control equivalent to the structured "positional" family. Douglas, like Bernstein, uses the

227

term *personal* to describe a situation that is eminently social, for a person who is a "prisoner of a system of feelings and abstract principles," to quote Douglas, is no more free of social constraints than is one who is controlled by status imperatives. Nevertheless Douglas goes on to establish two scales of increasing social control, two variable social dimensions, which she terms "grid" and "group."

Grid refers to "order, classification, the symbolic system" and reflects the degree to which a culture's symbolic system is ordered and codified, so as to constitute a coherent world view.

Group, on the other hand, refers to the degree to which the individual is controlled by social relationships; a tightly-knit group would constitute a strong group (83).

Initially Douglas keeps these variables separate and attempts to plot specific cultures in terms of a quadrant schema. In different editions of her study the orientation of these quadrants varies, and so does the meaning of the term *grid*, but essentially Douglas is attempting to relate specific cosmological ideas with varying types of social constraints. The basic patterns and correlations are as follows.

(1)   In situations where there is a lack of public classification and where social groupings are fluid and flexible, so that there are few social constraints on the individual, there emerges a cosmology that is benign and unritualistic. The Mbuti typify this mode, for their religion is one of internal feeling, not of external sign.

(2)   In the opposite situation, where there is "high classification" coupled with strong social controls over the individual, the cosmology tends to be regulative; there is a routinized piety toward authority and its symbols, and a belief that misfortunes are just punishments for moral transgressions. The Tallensi are an example of this type.

(3)   In situations where the "group is strong but the grid weak," namely those societies that have small-bounded communities but where authority is ill-defined and there is a general lack of coherent classification, one finds, according to Douglas, "witch-dominated" cosmologies. Here the belief system is dualistic, and there is a sharp distinction between inside and outside, good and bad. The Ceŵa and the Yao exemplify this type. Douglas's chapter "The Problem of Evil" discusses this type in detail, and she notes how sects like the Exclusive Brethren express in their beliefs and ethos a similar pattern. There is a strong sense of group identity – all within the fellowship, united by the spirit, are saints – but internal structures are lacking, and there is a corresponding dualistic cosmology. As she writes, "The cosmic implications of God and the devil; inside and outside; purity within, corruption without; here is the

complex of ideas that is associated with small groups with clearly marked membership and confusion of internal roles" (144).

And finally (4) there is a social situation Douglas describes as "strong grid," which is characterized by the "big-man" situation of New Guinea and a competitive social ethos. Here the cosmology is essentially secular and pragmatic.

But Douglas suggests that not only are cosmological ideas related systematically to patterns of social life, but there is a "concordance between social and bodily expressions of control." The physical body, she writes, is a microcosm of society. There are thus "two bodies," and there can therefore – and Douglas seems to follow Mauss in this – be no such thing as natural behavior, for "the social body constrains the way the physical body is perceived. The physical experience of the body, always modified by the social categories through which it is known, sustains a particular view of society" (93). She continues – and this sentence contains the crux of her thesis – "The less highly structured, the more the value on informality, the more the tendency to abandon reason and to follow panics or crazes, and the more the permitted scope for bodily expressions of abandonment" (103). This leads her to refine the social variables discussed earlier and to postulate a single scale of increasing social control, together with its corresponding symbolism.

Such a schema leads Douglas to postulate two forms of religion, one of control and the other of ecstasy, and to suggest that the latter – exemplified in spirit-possession cults, Pentecostalist sects, and millenarian movements – are a reflection of social situations that are in a sense anomic or unstructured. The characteristics of the two forms are shown in the accompanying table. The writings of Lorna Marshall (1969) on the !Kung and of Calley (1965) on West Indian Pentecostalists provide Douglas with some illustrative material to use in arguing that "trance... will be more approved and welcomed the weaker the structuring of society... It is the lack of strong social articulation, the slackening of group and grid which leads people to seek, in the slackening of bodily control, appropriate forms of expression" (114).

This leads her to argue against all theories of spirit possession or millenarianism that seek to understand such phenomena in terms of deprivation and oppression. For example, she describes the "extreme ritualism" of traditional Navaho culture as a function of their tightly knit community life and asserts that the rise of the Peyote cult was the outcome not so much of their impoverishment and inadequate involvement in a market economy – which she recognizes – as a reflection of the breakdown of the community and the "atomism" of personal life that

229

Two forms of religion postulated by Douglas

	Conditions for effervescence (ecstasy)	Conditions for ritualism (control)
Social dimension	Weak control by grid and group: Self and society not differentiated	Strong control and high classification: Society differentiated and exalted above self
Symbolic order	Diffuse symbols: No interest in magic or ritual differentiation; control of consciousness not exalted	Condensed symbolic system: Magical efficacy attributed to symbolic acts; symbols express high value on control of consciousness

occurred. Here, she writes, is a fascinating small-scale model of the Protestant Reformation. To support this thesis, she discusses the religion of Irish immigrant workers in London – the Bog Irish – suggesting that although experiencing insecurity, they nonetheless cling to a ritualistic form of Catholicism. In a discussion of spirit-possession cults I will return to this issue.

The remainder of Douglas's study is a development of her thesis that bodily symbolism and cosmological patterns are a reflection of social structure. Of particular interest is the contrast she makes between two hunter-gatherer communities, the Mbuti and the Hadza. Whereas the Mbuti have no conception of pollution, the Hadza men fear contact with menstrual blood and this contrast, Douglas suggests, is reflected in the two cultures' social organization. The Mbuti have a very fluid social life, in terms of both social categories and groups, whereas the Hadza have a strongly marked sexual division. Again Douglas stresses the concordance between the symbolism, expressed as pollution beliefs, and the social structure.

Although Douglas's general thesis postulates a correspondence between social structure and symbolism, her discussion of millenarian movements suggests that these occur as a reaction against structure, for she intimates that the "very structure of social grid predisposes the rank and file to millenarial movements," or again, "The destruction of categories of any kind is a symbolic act which replicates social life over-structured by grid, the experience which has always driven people to value unstructured personal experiences and to place their faith in a catastrophic event which will sweep away all existing forms of structure" (169). Such an interpretation seems to run counter to her general hypothesis.

Inevitably, Douglas's symbolist approach to spirit-possession cults has given rise to much debate, particularly when contrasted with the functionalist approach strongly advocated by Ioan Lewis. We may briefly examine this debate here.

Ioan Lewis's important study *Ecstatic Religion* is a sustained attempt, in the functionalist tradition, to offer a sociological interpretation of shamanism and spirit possession. His aim, as he puts it, is to try to isolate the "particular social and other conditions which encourage the development of an ecstatic emphasis in religion" (1971: 28). This leads Lewis to make some critical and sometimes disparaging remarks about theorists who have offered alternative approaches to the study of religion. The debate as to whether religion is analogous to science, discussed later in the next chapter, is thought by Lewis to indicate the "poverty" of the present sociological initiative, and Lévi-Straussian structuralism and cognitive anthropology are criticized for ignoring the social context. Such analyses, in treating religion as a thing in itself "with a life of its own" are, Lewis feels, consonant with a theological perspective and the contemporary interest in the occult. Lewis argues strongly for a Durkheimian approach that retains and explores the links between religious culture and the "social environment" in which it is grounded.

In his comparative study Lewis suggests that spirit-possession cults can be divided into two broad types, although the distinction between them is not absolute, and historically one type can develop into the other.

On the one hand there are what Lewis terms "peripheral" possession cults. These are spirit-possession cults that coexist with a more dominant moralistic religion, such as Christianity, Islam, or Buddhism. On the other hand, "central" possession cults occur in situations where the main form of religious expression is focused on spirit-possession rites. Such cults, as among the Tungus, have been specifically referred to as *shamanism*, and they are widespread among tribal communities.

As we have noted, Mary Douglas views ritual as essentially a symbolic replication of the social order. Thus in her terms, trance states and spirit possession are to be seen as expressing a social situation in which relationships are loosely structured and fluid. The !Kung and the West Indian Pentecostalist sects are taken as examples of her thesis. This leads her to offer a sustained polemic against those theories, including Lewis's, that attempt to explain spirit possession and similar cult movements in terms of deprivation. On the other hand, Lewis, in presenting an alternative theory of spirit possession expresses dissatisfaction with the concept of "anomie" as a theoretical catchall, and in a more recent contribution he has made some strident criticisms of Douglas's theory, concluding that the "ecstatic style of religiosity is typically a response not to lack of structure, but to an oppressive excess of it" (1977: 12). There is some validity and cogency in Lewis's criticism of Douglas's theory, especially her assumption of a *direct coincidence* between religious experience and social structure, but given the fact that there is some consistency, in all cultures, among different levels of experience (as Lewis admits), it is unhelpful to dismiss her hypothesis as gross oversimplification. It is misleading, too, to equate her approach with that of Eliade, whose theoretical orientation, involving the delineation of archetypal patterns, is quite different from Douglas's symbolist approach.

Lewis's own approach is essentially to see shamanism and spirit-possession cults as "religions of the oppressed." The peripheral possession cults are, in his view, "protest cults" that enable individuals who lack political influence – especially women – to "advance their interests and improve their lot, even if only temporarily, from the confining bonds of their allotted stations in society" (1971: 127). In his discussion of the central possession cults, Lewis offers a similar interpretation, relating the ecstatic tendency to external pressure. Factors that explain why people like the Akawaio Indians or the Tungus of Siberia have possession cults, Lewis suggests, include "the existence of overwhelming physical and social pressures, where social groups are small and fluctuating, and general instability prevails." Thus both central and peripheral ecstatic cults "are forms of religious expression which imply the existence of acute pressures. In peripheral cults these pressures arise from the oppression to which subordinate members of the community are subject ... In central ecstatic religions, the constraints are external to the society as a whole" (175–6). Thus ecstasy, as Lewis writes, ultimately asserts that "man is master of his fate."

But Lewis implies a close relationship between pressure and instability, and indicates that "social stability seems to favour an emphasis on ritual rather than on ecstatic expression" (175), so perhaps there is not such a wide gulf between Douglas's theory and Lewis's own functionalist approach. But as a general theory, Lewis's interpretative stress on "deprivation, frustration and discontent" leaves us with many loose ends. Douglas's suggestion that there may be deprived social groups whose mode of religious expression is ritualistic rather than ecstatic must be explored rather than dismissed. And the suggestion that environmental pressure is the primary factor in the interpretation of central possession cults, which Lewis advances, must also be tested. Should not the Somali, given the harsh environmental conditions Lewis describes, have central shamanistic cults? If the !Kung, the Mbuti, and the Andamanese live under rather benign conditions, easily obtaining their basic livelihood, as ethnographic accounts of these communities suggest (Katz 1982; Turnbull 1965; Radcliffe-Brown 1964), should not their religious patterns be nonecstatic? Although not involving spirit possession, !Kung trance performances are clearly shamanistic. Where do such hunter-gatherer communities fit into Lewis's analysis? Central possession cults – shamanism – seem to occur under a wide variety of environmental conditions, not all of which involve the existence of "acute pressures" like those experienced by the Eskimo and the Siberian herders. (For further discussions of these issues, cf. Morris 1981b and Rayner 1982.)

In more recent essays (1982b), Douglas has developed the general ideas expressed in *Natural Symbols*, and though her essential focus is still on the relationship between social experience (viewed in terms of grid and group) and cosmology and she sees this relationship as one of correspondence, she has stressed more an ethnomethodological approach. There is need, she suggests, to situate the human subject within the analysis, but the individual seems to be viewed essentially in bourgeois terms – competitive, choosing, autonomous, controlling, manipulating, negotiating – all in a social environment of low grid (*individualism*). She sits, as Dumont would put it, in the "metaphysical armchair" of her own culture (1975: 339). I must admit being somewhat out of sympathy with the typological approach she suggests, for the kind of analysis she offers and the ethnographic illustrations she presents seem to me to be highly problematic. She interprets the relationship between the individual and society in terms similar to that expressed by early social contract theorists; offers generalizations that are either so gross as to be unhelpful or else simply invalid (the Mbuti may have a benign attitude toward the natural world, but the capitalist entrepreneur and the frontier individualist certainly have not); mistakes the ideology of free-market capitalism for its reality; and tends to conflate a social context analytically defined (in terms of grid and group) with specific social formations. The "impressionistic" nature of "natural symbols" that she admits to is equally evident in her later essays, though other scholars have taken up her suggestions with reference to grid-and-group analysis (see the collection of essays edited by Douglas in 1982).

A final example of the social-structural approach to symbolism is that recently offered by Barry Schwartz, who, in an analysis of "vertical classifications" suggests that they are based on the parent–child relationship; such dichotomies (of high versus low) are rooted, he writes, "in mutual relationships of love and nurturance, power and conflict," implying that they are almost organically generated (1981: 174).

I have discussed the social-structural approach to symbolism at some length because it seems to me to be the dominant trend within anthropology, although the writings of Turner (which I shall discuss in the next section) complements this "symbolist" perspective with an empiricist or orectic bias.

A third, and important, approach to symbolism seeks an interpretation of its meaning in terms of archetypal forms, either, as with Jung, of an unconscious nature or, as with Mircea Eliade, by reference to a pan-human mythical paradigm. (Since these approaches were discussed fully in Chapter 4, little needs to be added here.)

A fourth approach to symbolism has been advanced recently by Dan Sperber (1975), who has argued that symbolism is best understood not in semiological terms but as a cognitive mechanism, which "alongside perceptual and conceptual mechanisms, participates in the construction of knowledge." He thus argues against the idea that symbolism can be understood by reference to underlying tacit knowledge; that is, he questions whether a valid interpretation can be ascertained by relating the symbol to a tacit meaning, as in the model of the relationship between sound and meaning in ordinary language. To give myths and symbols an explanation in terms of meaning, he suggests, propositions must either relate to the world of experience – the social or natural world – or to the categories of thought. He offers criticisms of both these modes of symbolic interpretation.

Sperber discusses the first reexperience in the chapter appropriately entitled "Hidden Meanings," and he offers criticisms of the approaches of both Turner and Freud. Turner's is an example of a cryptological approach, whereas Freud's is psychoanalytical. Sperber's argument is that if one examines a symbolic system in its entirety, rather than isolating ad hoc aspects found here and there, then it is clear that symbolic associations are multiplex and that the associations may be explicit or implicit, conscious or unconscious. Thus to say that some element or aspect of experience is the meaning of the symbol is not an interpretation but rather indicates simply another aspect of the symbolic system. And this is the case whether the meaning is conscious or unconscious. As Sperber puts it, "Exegesis, like unconscious representation, does not constitute the interpretation of the symbol, but one of its extensions, and must itself be symbolically interpreted" (1975: 48). Social structure therefore cannot be the basis of the symbolism, for, as Lévi-Strauss implied, it is itself part of the symbolic order. This leads Sperber to assert that all keys to symbols are part of symbolism itself.

Sperber links the second semiological approach to symbolism, which refers meaning to "categories of thought," with Lévi-Strauss, whose structuralist approach he examines in the the chapter entitled "Absent Meaning." Sperber argues that structural analysis is more a heuristic device than a viable theory, in that it seems to organize symbolic data rather than to explain or interpret symbolism. And he concludes by suggesting that Lévi-Strauss came to demonstrate the opposite to what he continually asserts, namely that symbolism and myths constitute a language. Sperber feels that Western culture is bedeviled with the notion of meaning, semiology being a part of our basic ideology, and he thus applauds Lévi-Strauss, who, though he expressed himself in the language of semiology – "decoding the message" – was one of the first to propose a form of analysis of symbolism that did not concern itself with the "absurd idea that symbols mean" (184).

Having dismissed semiological approaches to symbolism – the search for meaning – and questioned the adequacy of structural analyses as modes of interpretation, Sperber suggests that symbolism can be more clearly understood if viewed as a form of knowledge. He draws a distinction between semantic (analytical) and encyclopedic (synthetic) knowledge and then indicates that symbolic knowledge is derived largely from the latter. However, the precise delineation of what constitutes symbolic knowledge is not clearly specified, and, as Maurice Bloch has commented, we left with an "unsubstantiated statement of the psychological origins of we are not quite sure what" (1976: 129).

But, interestingly, in discussing Malinowski's functionalist theory of myth, Sperber asks why, if myth was simply semiotic, there was a need to invoke a "long, complicated and obscure discourse" (6). Sperber himself, in suggesting that symbolism is a cognitive mechanism, never gets round to answering this question; indeed, it is doubtful whether it can be answered in terms of his own theory that symbolism is a form of knowledge. But such a question introduces the final approach to symbolism discussed here, namely that which attempts to interpret symbols in terms of their relationship to political structures.

I have elsewhere (1979) offered some thoughts on this issue, noting that one of the few writers who have explicitly acknowledged the intimate connection between symbolism and power (Cohen 1974) tended to focus on power struggles and on the manipulation of symbols by specific groups, rather than on the symbols' ideological significance. (For a critique of Sperber's theory of cognition, though not dealing with the issue of symbolism per se, see Toren 1983.)

Ritual symbolism and social structure

Over the past two decades a series of monographs and ethnographic studies of the Ndembu people of Zambia have been published. Written by Victor Turner, who spent about two and one-half years among the Ndembu during the early 1950s, they constitute an impressive and seminal contribution to anthropological knowledge.

Turner's first study of the Ndembu, *Schism and Continuity in an African Society* (1957), is devoted to a study of their village life and of how political stability is maintained in a society without a "strong centre of authority." An Ndembu village of about thirty or forty people is built around a core of male matrilineal kin, of whom the oldest male member of the senior generation is usually headman. Marriage, however, is virilocal, a woman going to live in the husband's village. There is thus a "contradiction" between the principles governing village structure – matrilineal descent – and virilocality, and this is accentuated by the fact that ambitious headmen try to build up their communities by keeping both their own and their sisters' children within the village. Understandably, village sites are often changed, and village organization is unstable. There is a high frequency of divorce and residential mobility. In such a situation the only stable unit is the matricentric family, consisting of a mother and her children.

The Ndembu village economy is based on shifting cultivation, the staple crop being cassava, with millet important for making beer. Hunting, which is exclusively a male occupation, is extremely important, and Turner suggests the Ndembu social system is almost "pivoted" on the importance of hunting (1957: 25). Hunting is ritualized, as with the Lele, and is associated with virility and masculinity and with the bond between father and son, thus running counter to the matrilineal ties within the village, which govern rights to property, status, and residence. This opposition is paralleled by a structural opposition between the sexes; indeed, though hunting and cassava cultivation are complementary activities, they are seen by the Ndembu as opposed and competitive. But though agriculture is of paramount importance in the village economy, it is undervalued and is not ritualized like hunting. Turner speaks of the sexual division as the basic opposition in Ndembu society, one expressed by the Ndembu saying "For the man hunting, for the woman procreation" (27).

Thus Turner suggests that Ndembu society, especially with respect to the village structure, is "inherently unstable" and is "torn with perennial disputes"; "there is little harmony and much conflict between its dominant principles of social organization, and in secular life there is little to bind together more than a small number of people in habitual co-operation" (301).

Turner therefore saw his book as a study of social conflict and of "the social mechanisms brought into play to reduce, exclude or resolve that conflict" (89). There is no doubt that Turner's analysis was influenced by Max Gluckman's studies of ritual (which I will discuss later), but Turner's studies were altogether more detailed, and he introduced the concept of "social drama" to elucidate the processes through which conflicts within a village community were resolved.

In this study Turner made a detailed analysis of five consecutive "social dramas" in one long-established Ndembu village and concluded that the structural patterns underlying Ndembu social organization remained intact despite these conflicts and schisms. Turner thus came to view ritual as having a politically integrative function, and his analysis echoes the views of Gluckman, who saw ritual "not simply as expressing cohesion and impressing the values of society and its social sentiments on people, as in Durkheim's and Radcliffe-Brown's theories, but as exaggerating real conflicts of social rules and affirming that there was unity despite these conflicts" (1963: 18).

Turner was therefore led to write, in his monograph on Ndembu village life, that ritual was an expression of the failure of secular mechanisms to redress conflicts within and between communities. But though local groups were inherently unstable, such rituals served, through cult associations, which operated independently of kinship ties, to establish links between different village communities. As he put it "The function of maintaining the widest social unit, the Ndembu people, devolves mainly upon the ritual system" (292). The unity of the Ndembu was thus a moral rather than a political unity. "Conflict," Turner wrote, "is endemic in the social structure, but a set of mechanisms exists whereby conflict itself is pressed into the service of affirming group unity" (129). The ritual patterns of the Ndembu are the primary mechanism, according to Turner, of achieving this solidarity.

Before we examine the relationship between ritual and social structure in more detail, a brief outline may be given of the main features of Ndembu religious life. One thing must be said immediately about the Ndembu: ritual plays an important part in their social life. Turner notes how the constant beating of ritual drums forced him to take an interest in ritual and says that one of his great difficulties was to decide, on a given day, which ritual performance he would attend.

At the level of belief, Ndembu religion has four main components. First, there is a belief in the existence of a high god, Nzambi, who is said to have created the world and then left it to its own devices. He is never worshiped in prayer or ritual, though he is vaguely connected with the weather and fertility.

Second, there is a belief in ancestral spirits (*mukishi*), the spirits of deceased relatives. Turner uses the term *shades* to describe these super-

237

naturals, who have the power (*ng'ovu*) to bestow the good things of life on their living kinfolk or to withhold them. Two reasons are given as to why the spirits inflict misfortune on the living. One is that offerings of beer and food have not been placed at the village shrines and the spirits are angry at having been neglected; the other is that the kin group have quarreled or have acted in ways disapproved of by the spirits. Significantly, female reproductive troubles, including menstrual disorders and frequent miscarriage, and, for the men, lack of success in hunting are always thought to have been inflicted by ancestral spirits.

Third, Ndembu believe in the intrinsic efficacy of certain animal and vegetable substances (*yitumbu*), which can work either good or harm, provided that they are prepared and used by a qualified practitioner in a ritual setting.

Fourth, there is a belief in the antisocial, destructive power of witches and sorcerers (both called *aloji*). Both witches and sorcerers possess familiars, who take the form of stunted men with feet pointing backward or appear as jackals, owls, or rats. Witches are women, usually old women without male kin, and are believed to inherit their familiars from deceased kinswomen. Sorcerers, on the other hand, are men. They do not inherit their familiars but generate them from evil medicines. Significantly, masculinity is associated with control and autonomy, femininity with necessity.

These religious beliefs have a certain simplicity when compared with the various ritual practices of the Ndembu, which are extremely complex. Turner uses the term *ritual* when referring to "prescribed formal behaviour for occasions not given over to technological routine, having reference to beliefs in mystical (or non-empirical) beings or power." Ndembu rituals fall into two main categories. There are, first, the life-crisis rituals associated specifically with death and puberty. The two important initiation ceremonies are the *mukanda*, or boys' circumcision rite, and the *nkang'a*, or girls' puberty ritual.

The other group of rites Turner refers to as *rituals of affliction*, and these are associated with various misfortunes, primarily thought to result from the action of mukishi spirits. There are three main types of afflictions, and these correspond to the various cult associations.

First, there are the cult associations that deal specifically with misfortunes associated with hunting. The spirit of a dead hunter may cause a kinsman to miss his aim or may drive the game animals from a particular area. For the Ndembu, hunting is exclusively a male activity and is highly ritualized. The ritual specialists (*chimbuki*) who organize these hunting rites tend to be men who are not headmen of stable villages; rather they are individuals who have preferred to be residentially mobile, thus representing a wider field of interest than the local village community. Because of their ambiguous status in relation to the village, such men are often referred to as "flying squirrels," a piece of lore that supports Douglas's theory.

The second group of rites of affliction Turner describes as *reproductive cults.* A woman who has had a miscarriage, or an excessive menstrual discharge, or who is sterile is thought to have offended an ancestral spirit, who comes out of the grave and "catches" the woman. Usually the offending spirit is a matrilineal relative, the woman's mothers' mother, but it may be her mother or sister. "Forgetting" the ancestral spirit is invariably the cause of the misfortune. Significantly, because of virilocal residence, a woman may have actually forgotten her deceased female relatives, whose souls are expected to return to their matrilineal villages. Thus it would seem, as Turner remarks, that being "caught" by a matrilineal spirit serves as a sharp reminder that a woman's first loyalty is to her own matrilineal village (13).

There are three main rituals associated with reproductive troubles. The Nkula rite, associated with menstrual disorders, is perhaps the most important of these. The term, as with the other cult associations, is both the name of the affliction and the name of the cult group. In fact the patient is at the same time a candidate for initiation into the cult, and the doctor or ritual specialist treating the disorder is an initiate of the cult. The women, who are the practitioners of the cult, thus must at one time have been patients themselves and may not become practising doctors unless they are generally considered to have been cured by the treatment. Men may become cult members if they have acted as ritual assistants to a patient. As with the hunting cults, a woman's ritual status becomes higher the more she participates in rituals of this type and the more she learns about medicines and ritual techniques. (For a descriptive analysis of the Nkula rituals and of the Wubang'u and Isoma rites, see Turner 1968: 52–88; 1974b: 11–79.)

Although these three cult associations focus on women's reproductive problems, the principal doctor (*chimbuki*) at each ritual is a man. He is usually a close relative of the woman undergoing the ritual and tends to specialize in a specific rite. Usually he has a leading woman doctor as assistant, and many women initiates participate in the cult activities.

The third and final category of rituals of affliction are the *curative rites.* Various types of cults are associated with these rites, many of them of foreign origin, but the two main types described by Turner are *chihamba* and *kayong'u.* The first type is associated with many types of misfortune,

239

crop failure, bad hunting, and a variety of illnesses, as well as with reproductive disorders, whereas the kayong'u cult helps patients with breathing difficulties and is also associated with divination.

Turner's anthropology stands firmly in the Durkheimian tradition, as developed by Radcliffe-Brown. Turner's approach to religion, indeed, echoes the latter's formulations, for Turner writes that social action must be considered "both in respect to its meaning for those who carry it out, and in terms of its contribution to the functioning of some social system" (1968: 26).

He interprets the social function of ritual in terms of an analysis of conflict resolution, ritual being a mechanism of redress. In his earlier work he stressed that what was important about the cult associations was that their membership operated independently of kinship and local ties. They were intervillage congregations and were thus able to express Ndembu social values. What generally happened was that an individual's misfortune tended to bring to light some specific conflict in interpersonal or intergroup relations. Ritual was then invoked, under the pretext of curing the patient but in reality to settle the conflict. "The affliction of each," Turner wrote, "is the concern of all." He analyzed the social processes involved in a chihamba ritual performed for a woman named Nyamukola, who was suffering from leprosy (1957: 303–17). Divination had suggested that she had been "caught" by an ancestral spirit, a deceased matrilineal relative. About seventy people, from about twenty villages, attended the ritual, either as adepts or candidates for membership in the chihamba cult, and at one of the night dances Turner estimated that about 400 people were present. Turner suggests that this cult ritual had a number of social functions, namely,

(1)   It reduced hostility felt by many villagers against Nyamukola, whom some had accused of being a witch, for it made her the object of sympathy at a public ritual.

(2)   It tended to close a breach opening between different factions within the village, since the organization of the rite demanded cooperation among leading members of each faction.

(3)   It gave prestige to the host village and reestablished friendly relations with neighboring villages.

(4)   It made a dramatic restatement through ritual of the values of Ndembu society.

In other words, Turner came to see ritual as having a politically integrative role and as being part of a social mechanism that restores the equilibrium and solidarity of the group. He writes, "The typical development of a ritual sequence is from the public expression of a wish to cure a patient and redress breaches in the social structure, through exposure of hidden animosities, to the renewal of social bonds in the course of a protracted ritual full of symbolism (1968: 272).

But as he stressed in *The Drums of Affliction*, ritual did not express consensus in Durkheim's sense; rather, the very norms of Ndembu social structure, in their contradictions, produced conflict and disputes among individuals. Moreover, Turner stressed a lack of corporate groupings or structural integration in Ndembu society. This led him to suggest that the Ndembu had a "repetitive" social system, conflict and change being contained within the society through periodic rituals. The conflicts did not generate structural change. In this, his analysis is similar to Middleton's study (1960) of the Lugbara.

Complementing this functional approach to ritual, Turner also studied the ritual system of the Ndembu in terms of meaning and has produced several detailed analyses of their ritual symbolism. Turner follows the general definition of symbol as a thing regarded by general consent as naturally typifying or representing something else by possession of analogous qualities or by association in thought or fact. Elsewhere he defines a symbol as a "storage unit," the basic unit or "molecule" of ritual behavior, or, as he puts it, "The symbol is the smallest unit of specific structure in Ndembu ritual" (1967: 48).

The Ndembu term for symbol is *chinjikijilu*, from *kujikijila*, "to blaze a trail." Thus it means, in the vernacular, a blaze or landmark. In attempting to understand the meaning of ritual symbols, Turner notes that this has its problems. Some anthropologists, like Nadel and Wilson, have suggested that anthropologists should not go beyond the ethnographic data and assign "meanings" to ritual symbols that are not evident or articulated by the people themselves. This, Turner feels, is rather restrictive, and he accepts Jung's distinction between *sign*, as an analogous representation of a known entity, and *symbol*, as the expression of a relatively unknown fact. The task of the anthropologist is to uncover these hidden meanings. As an aid to interpretation, Turner suggests some interesting analytical distinctions.

First, ritual symbols have the property of "condensation." Discussing Edward Sapir's article on symbolism, Turner noted his distinction between two classes of symbols. The first, *referential* symbols, which include ordinary speech and writing, flags, and signaling, and which are predominantly cognitive, refer to known facts and are equivalent to Jung's definition of sign. The second, *condensation* symbols, Sapir defines as "highly condensed forms of substitutive behaviour for direct expression, allowing for the ready release of emotional tension in conscious or unconscious form." Sapir stressed the emotional quality of this class of symbols and their condensation of many meanings in a single form.

241

Turner finds this illuminating and a pointer to the definition of a ritual symbol. Thus symbols are *multivocal* and may stand for many things. This is especially the case with dominant or focal symbols, which may have a "fan" or "spectrum" of referents (50).

Second, each symbol has a *polarization of meaning*. At one pole cluster a set of referents of a natural or physiological character, relating to general human experiences of an emotional kind. They thus arouse desires or feelings. At the other pole cluster a set of referents that refer to principles of social organization, to kinds of corporate groupings, and to the norms and values inherent in the social structure. Turner refers to these as the sensory, or *orectic*, and the ideological, or *normative*, poles of meaning.

Third, in ascertaining the meaning of a ritual symbol it is important, he suggests, to distinguish three levels:

(1) the level of indigenous interpretation, whether by layman or ritual specialist (he calls this the *exegetical* meaning);

(2) its *operational* meaning – how the symbol is utilized within the ritual context; and

(3) the *positional* meaning; that is, the meaning of the symbol as determined by its relationship with other symbols "in a totality, a Gestalt, whose elements acquire their significance from the system as a whole" (51).

Turner's approach to symbolism is on the whole sociological, for he argues that Ndembu symbols refer essentially to the basic needs of social existence (hunting, cultivation, fertility) and to the shared values on which communal life depends. Anthropological studies inevitably focus on the ideological pole of symbols. As I have noted, he is critical of those anthropological approaches that refuse to go beyond the ethnographic data and that take the indigenous meaning of the symbolism as the only interpretation sociologically relevant. This, he felt, was too limiting, especially since much ritual symbolism has no manifest meaning. But he was equally critical of psychoanalytical approaches to ritual, which regard preliterate religious customs as virtually identical with the symptoms of neurotics and psychotics, and indigenous interpretations as simply rationalizations. Psychoanalysts, Turner wrote, in treating the latter interpretations as irrelevant, "are guilty of a naive and one-sided approach. For those interpretations that show how a dominant symbol expresses important components of the social and moral orders are by no means equivalent to the 'rationalizations' and the 'secondary elaborations' of material deriving from endopsychic conflicts (36). These were, he stressed, social facts and must be treated as such. The "social aspect" of ritual symbolism was of equal importance to the biophysical drives as factors in our understanding of symbolism. But he did not deny the orectic quality of symbols; on the contrary, he stressed its importance, for the emotions generated by a symbol's association with human physiology – blood or milk, for example – served to "energize" the social order, thus making the Durkheimian "obligatory" desirable (1969: 49). Indeed, like both Freud and Durkheim – who, incidentally, share many basic theoretical assumptions about the human condition – Turner sees a basic conflict between society and the individual, between the need for social control and certain innate and universal human drives whose complete gratification would result in a breakdown of that control (1967: 37). "To make a human being obey social norms," Turner writes, "violence must be done to his natural impulses. These must be repressed or re-directed" (1968: 236). Both Freud and Durkheim would have understood this viewpoint.

Turner has offered many detailed and interesting analyses of Ndembu rituals, using as guidelines the analytical framework just described. We may take as an example his semantic analysis of the nkang'a, the girls' puberty ceremony (1968: 198–268).

During this ceremony, which is performed when the young girl's breasts begin to develop rather than after her first menstruation, the initiate is wrapped in a blanket and placed at the foot of a mudyi sapling. The mudyi tree (*Diplorrhynchus condylocarpon*) is conspicuous for the white latex it exudes. In Ndembu ritual idiom, the nkang'a is considered a "white" ritual, for the mudyi tree is described by Ndembu women as the "senior" tree of the ritual or the dominant symbol. The women say that the mudyi tree stands for human milk and represents the social tie between a mother and child. Discussions with a ritual specialist convinced Turner that the tree was also a symbol of matrilineal kinship and of the unity and continuity of Ndembu society. As one Ndembu put it, "The mudyi tree is the place of all mothers; it is the ancestress of men and women. The tree is the place where our ancestors slept, to be initiated there means to become ritually pure and white."

By examining the way in which the mudyi tree was involved in the social dynamics of a ritual event. Turner suggested that such a contextual analysis revealed that the symbol had other values and meanings. For example, in the nkang'a ceremony the women as a group dance around the "milk-tree," and they initiate the novice by making her the hub of a whirling circle of women. The tree is a symbol of the women as a group, in opposition to men, who are excluded from the ceremony. During the time of the ritual, the women as a group go around the village taunting and abusing men, especially the village elders. But in other contexts, the milk-tree represents the novice herself and symbolizes

243

her new social personality. The site of the mudyi sapling is known as *ifwilu*, the place of dying or suffering. In yet other contexts it represents the novice's own matrilineage or even life and learning itself. As a symbol, therefore, the mudyi tree is said by Turner to have a multiplicity of meanings and to have a polarity of reference, expressing both social and organic phenomena.

All Ndembu rituals are organized around certain key symbols. These are referred to by the Ndembu either as *ishikenu*, or "first medicines," or as *mukulumpi*, the "elder" symbol. Turner refers to them as the dominant symbols of the ritual. These are always certain species of trees, and each is associated with a specific color. According to Ndembu principles of classification, the mudyi tree is a white symbol. The dominant symbol of the nkula ceremony is the *mukula* tree (*Pterocarpus angolensis*), which exudes red latex, and other rituals also have specific tree species as key symbols and incorporate an elaborate color symbolism. Indeed, Turner writes that "at the apex of the total symbolic system of the Ndembu is the colour triad, white-red-black" (57), and he has devoted a paper specifically to Ndembu color classification.

During their initiation rites, Ndembu are taught the "mystery of the three rivers" that are said to flow from Nzambi, the high god. There is the river of the red water (Kachinana), of the white water (Katooka), and of the black water (Keyica). These three "primary" colors, therefore, are conceived by the Ndembu as being in the nature of eternal powers that permeate reality. "Color" therefore has "power" (ng'ovu) and a mystical quality for the Ndembu. One Ndembu told Turner that the main or "elder" river is the "river of whiteness," the "river of red water" being junior, and this is followed by the river of the black water. Ndembu symbolism therefore expresses a hierarchy and largely revolves around a triadic structure based on color, not, as with the Andamanese and Zuni, on spatial categories. But as in these cultures, it is through myth that the symbolic structure is established.

The colors red, white, and black are the only colors for which the Ndembu have primary terms. Other colors are either derivative – gray is *chitookocoka* – or consist of a descriptive or metaphorical phrase. Colors that we would distinguish from these primary colors are linguistically identified with them by the Ndembu. Blue, for example, is described as black, and yellow and orange objects are lumped together as red. Certain features of this color symbolism are worth noting.

First, although a dualistic patterning is often evident in Ndembu ritual, there is no fixed correlation between colors and sexual categories. Color symbolism is not consistently sex-linked, even though red and white may be situationally specified to represent the opposition of the sexes. There is no underlying symbolic dualism among the Ndembu such as we find in many other African cultures; what dualism is evident is subsumed and contained within the triadic schema.

Second, of the three colors, white seems to be dominant and unitary; red is ambivalent, for it is both fecund and "dangerous"; and black, Turner suggests, is a silent partner, the "shadowy third" color, in a sense opposed to both red and white.

Third, each of the three primary colors has certain basic meanings. Among the many senses of whiteness are health, life, prosperity, purity, authority, and to make visible. White clay and the mudyi tree are basic white symbols. Black contrasts with white, especially in therapeutic procedures, and is associated with badness and evil, misfortune, disease, witchcraft and sorcery, sexual passion, darkness, and what is "hidden." Charcoal and the black fruits of the *muneka* tree are black substances. Redness has an equivocal meaning and is associated with power, strength, menstrual blood, murder, and hunting. As the Ndembu say, "Redness acts both for good and ill."

In terms of the body, blood denotes redness and is identified with power; white is associated with the life fluids, semen and milk, and black stands for body dirt and the fluids of putrification.

A good deal of Ndembu ritual and magic (a term that, significantly, Turner avoids using), as well as their herbal medicine and therapeutic procedures, can be understood in terms of this color symbolism. For example, a sterile man takes medicine made from the *mucheki* plant, which is believed to make his semen white. The root of this plant epitomizes the purest whiteness. Treatment is offered to a woman with lactation troubles in a similar fashion, her "red" breast milk being "whitened" by the medicines.

In a cross-cultural analysis of color classification, Turner indicates that the primary colors, black, red, and white frequently have ritual significance and that there is wide agreement about their symbolic connotations. Black is associated with inferior, evil, pollution, suspicion; red with power, might, and wealth; and white with purity, light, and joy. Turner quotes at length from the Upanishads and from other Hindu texts citing passages that suggest a tripartite color schema, the individual colors being considered as deities, and each color being associated with specific aspects of existence. In the Sankya scheme of salvation, for example, three strands (or *gunas*) of existence are posited: *sattva*, which is virtue or purity; *rajas*, the active principle, associated with passion; and *tamas*, or dullness. To what degree the classification is consonant with other symbolic classifications evident in Hindu culture Turner does not explore, but it is interesting to note that the four *varnas* (a term that means color) of the Rg Veda, the fourfold division of Indian society, were each associated with a color and with parts of the body.

Brahman	White	Head
Kshatriya	Red	Arms
Vaisya	Yellow	Belly
Sudra	Black	Feet

This leads Turner to suggest that the triadic color schema, based as it is on psychobiological experiences – the emissions of the human body, namely milk, blood, and excreta (or bodily dissolution) – represents a "kind of primordial classification of reality" that provides the basis of other classifications. "It is only by subsequent abstraction," he writes, "from these configurations that the other modes of social classification employed by mankind arose" (1967: 90–1).

Turner thus completely reverses the formulations of Durkheim and Mauss, who gave social categories logical priority in religious classifications, and his theory differs, too, from that of Lévi-Strauss, who in his writings on totemism suggested that natural species provide the model for symbolic classifications. For Turner, it was the human organism and its crucial experiences that was the *fons et origo* of such classifications.

One may question whether the various semantic themes associated with color symbols have the universality that Turner implies, for in many cultures white is associated with mourning and black may have auspicious connotations. His stress on the triadic nature of the color symbolism, moreover, obscures the hierarchic and hence ideological nature of symbolism. Nonetheless his discussion of the meaning of symbolism reflects the dualism of his thought, for Turner links Ndembu symbolism to both social structure and to human organism – the normative and the oretic poles. In his book *The Ritual Process* he explores the relationship between these two aspects of the human condition, the individual and society, in more detail, and in doing so virtually abandons his Durkheimian approach by ignoring the links that bind religion to the social structure.

The ritual process

"The life of an individual in any society," wrote Van Gennep, "is a series of passages from one age to another" (1908: 3). In the majority of human communities the primary transitions, or what have been termed the *life crises* – birth, puberty, marriage, and death – are the focus of elaborate rites. In preliterate communities such rites constitute an important aspect of cultural life. Many earlier writers (Frazer, for example) had noted similarities between different life-crisis rituals – between puberty rites and funerals, for example – but it was Arnold Van Gennep who, in his classic study *The Rites of Passage*, first indicated the underlying pattern common to all transition rituals.

Van Gennep, a contemporary of Durkheim, argued that the universe itself was governed by a periodicity that had repercussions for human life. "Man's life," he wrote, "resembles nature, from which neither the individual nor the society stands independent" (3). This premise led him to suggest that there was a considerable similarity among all rituals that involved a transition and that such rites constituted a specific class of rituals. Unlike Durkheim he did not conceive of religion and magic as separate categories but looked upon religion as the theoretical, and magic as the practical, aspect of the magico-religious. Religion as an ideational system, he thought, veered between what he termed dynamism, which designated an impersonal, monistic conception of the sacred, and animism, which implied a dualism and a personal, spiritualistic notion of deity or spirits. But Van Gennep's introductory chapter and his classification of various rites is of secondary interest; what is important is the "underlying arrangement" he perceived that was evident in all transition rites. Although his discussion focuses on life-crisis rituals, Van Gennep indicated that fertility and calendrical rites; rituals associated with territorial movements and thresholds; consecration rites; and rites of initiation into fraternities, cult groups, or high status were also examples of transition rites. He even indicated that when taken to extremes transition rites could have a cyclic or cosmic form, as in Buddhism or in the theory of the eternal return.

Van Gennep suggested that all these transition rituals exemplified a typical form, consisting of three essential ritual phases. First, there were rites of separation, a preliminal phase indicated by such ceremonies as purification rites, the removal of hair, and scarification or cutting. Next there was a liminal period, the rite of transition, in which the person undergoing the rite is symbolically placed "outside society" and frequently has to observe certain taboos or restrictions. During this period, he noted, the normal rules of the community may be suspended, or the rite may be seen as a symbolic death, leading to a new rebirth. And finally, there is a postliminal phase, rites of incorporation that complete the transit to a new status. The lifting of restrictions, the wearing of new insignia, and the sharing of a meal signify this phase of the rite of passage.

Van Gennep's formulations, expressed in a short monograph, have had an enormous theoretical infuence on social anthropologists. We have already discussed the work of Leach, who adopted Van Gennep's schema in advocating a structuralist approach to symbolism – but not without some modifications.

247

First, Van Gennep took the Durkheimian distinction between the sacred and the profane as being, along with sexual division, a fundamental categorization in all human societies. He saw transition rituals as being necessary in making a passage between these two domains. The liminal period itself was not seen as specifically sacred. Leach, although he eschewed the sacred–profane categorization as a "scholastic illusion" (1968), in his essay on the symbolic representation of time (1961) adopts Van Gennep's scheme entirely and equates the liminal or marginal phase of rituals with the sacred.

Second, in developing a structuralist method Leach has applied the scheme not only to the ritual process but to all binary classifications and again has equated the sacred with the ambiguous sector, as in his theory of taboo.

Douglas, too, has been influenced by Van Gennep's study. But the writer who has developed Van Gennep's theories most interestingly has been Victor Turner, who, in his writings on the ritual process, has sought to establish a veritable general theory of society and history, based on Van Gennep's insights. But a more immediate influence on Turner were the writings of Max Gluckman, who, throughout his long career, was a consistent advocate of a functionalist approach to culture.

Gluckman, born in South Africa of Russian-Jewish parentage, undertook his major fieldwork studies among the Zulu of Natal in the late 1930s, later making ethnographic studies in Barotseland. Although standing in the sociological tradition of Durkheim, Gluckman saw social equilibrium as problematic and sensed that in preliterate societies there was no neat integration of norms and values. Often there were conflicting values and principles, as well as conflicting interest groups. Thus ritual was not seen as expressing the cohesion and solidarity of the group in Durkheim's sense, but rather as tending to exaggerate the "real conflicts" and thereby affirming that there was "unity despite the conflicts" (1963: 18). He had derived these notions, he said, from Bateson's study *Naven* and from Fortes's writings on ritual (1959, 1966).

The essence of Gluckman's approach to ritual is contained in his classic essay "Rituals of Rebellion in South East Africa" (1963). Gluckman begins this essay by citing the famous passage in Frazer's *Golden Bough* describing the ritual of the priest of Nemi, who had gained rule of the sanctuary only through "murder." Gluckman noted that throughout this study Frazer had described similar "rituals of rebellion" and that in many societies "mock kings" were elected, only to be later banished or sacrificed. And he noted, too, Frazer's interest in the relationship between these priest-kings and a number of agricultural rites, widespread throughout the world, in which people conserved the "spirit of the corn"

248

(grain) in the last sheaf or in animals, human beings, or effigies. Though paying tribute to Frazer's scholarship and though not denying the importance of his "intellectualist" interpretation, Gluckman felt that a more sociological analysis of such rites was necessary. For what struck Gluckman about the ritual ceremonies among the Bantu peoples of southeastern Africa, many of which were analogous to those described by Frazer, was that whatever the rituals' ostensible purpose they invariably expressed social tensions. For example, in certain rites women assert their dominance over men, or princes behave toward the king as if they coveted the throne, or the subjects of a state openly express their resentment of authority. Gluckman termed these "rituals of rebellion" and discussed two examples.

The first were the agricultural rites traditionally performed by Zulu women at the beginning of the planting season. These rites were done in honor of the female spirit Nomkubulwana, who was associated with the rains and fertility, and, according to Gluckman, was a goddess of the same kind as the corn goddess of the ancient world. These agricultural rites were performed locally by women and involved songs and festivities, and they contrasted with the national fertility rites held annually by the king. The significance of the agricultural rites among the Zulu was that they "required obscene behaviour by women and girls. The girls donned men's garments, and herded and milked the cattle, which were normally taboo to them. Their mothers planted a garden for the goddess far out in the veld, and poured a libation of beer to her. Thereafter this garden was neglected. At various stages of the ceremonies women and girls went naked, and sang lewd songs. Men and boys hid and might not go near" (1963: 113).

Gluckman noted that this temporary dominant role of women, which was publicly instituted, contrasted markedly with the norms of these patriarchical people. The ceremonial actions of the women, marked by dominance and lewdness, were quite different from their usual modesty and subordination. Gluckman stresses that legally women were always minors, and socially always considered subordinate to men, for they married out of their kin group and could not in general become politically powerful. Ritually, their role was highly ambivalent, and women were generally considered evil, though they could attain ritual status through divination, for most of the diviners were women.

The dropping of normal restraints and the inverted and transvestite behavior, in which women assumed dominance, were believed by the Zulu to be conducive to social well-being. Although accepting that the psychological and social mechanisms involved in such rites were complex, Gluckman suggests that they essentially involve an act of rebellion.

249

Since the national ceremonials associated with the Zulu kingship fell into disuse when the Zulus were defeated by the British in 1879, Gluckman chose as his second example the Incwala ceremony of the Swazi. This ceremony had been described in great detail in Hilda Kuper's study of the Swazi, *An African Aristocracy* (1947). The Incwala was an elaborate royal ritual, extending over many days, performed annually on the occasion of the first fruits. No one was supposed to touch certain crops until the rites had been performed, and of the royal clan, only the king could stage them. What interested Gluckman about these rites was that many of the sacred songs that are sung during the ceremonies expressed and dramatized the idea that the king was hated and rejected by his subjects. During the ritual the king also walked naked in front of his people, while the women wept. Gluckman suggests, therefore, that this ceremony was not a simple assertion of national unity but a "stressing of conflict, a statement of rebellion and rivalry against the King, with periodic affirmations of unity" (1963: 125). The political structure was thereby made sacred through the person of the king. This symbolic dramatization of social relations in their ambivalence, Gluckman writes, was believed to achieve unity and prosperity: "This acting of conflict achieves a blessing – social unity" (126). This leads Gluckman to suggest that the Swazi state was an example of a "repetitive" social system, in which there were rebels but not revolutionaries. Political conflicts involved rival claimants who sought the kingship, and thus a rebellion, paradoxically, supported the kingship rather than leading to revolutionary change. In this situation rituals of rebellion functioned as a mechanism of social unity, and Gluckman indeed indicates that such rituals were probably a correlate of loosely integrated state systems or perhaps were confined to societies where strong tensions are aroused by conflict among different structural principles that are not controlled in distinct secular institutions (136).

These two examples of rituals of rebellion, Gluckman suggested, may have a cathartic significance, but on the whole he eschewed psychological explanations, stressing that his own interests and competence were sociological.

Gluckman's thesis has been criticized by a number of writers. Edward Norbeck, in his critique "African Rituals of Conflict" (1963), interprets Gluckman as suggesting that the ritual enactment of conflicts of interest has a cathartic function and eliminates the threat of disunity. In the Zulu agricultural rites this is done by women's behaving in ways contrasting sharply with their normal behavior – acting lewdly, wearing men's clothing, and assuming other male prerogatives. But Norbeck notes that Gluckman makes no mention of rites that are the male counterparts of

these rites of rebellion. And he indicates, with examples, that transvestism, sexual license, and obscene behavior are characteristic of many
types of ritual and are particularly widespread in boys' circumcision rites.
He asks, "If transvestism, lewdness and obscenity on the part of females
in a given society constitute rebellion, what do the same acts on the part
of males represent?" (201). He questions, too, whether among the Zulu
the women expressed dissatisfaction over their roles as women; the ethnographic record, at least, gives no indication that this was the situation.
Norbeck does admit, though, that sexual antagonism probably existed
among the Zulu.

With respect to the Incwala ceremony of the Swazi, Norbeck argues
that there is inadequate data to support Gluckman's thesis that the rites
involve a rebellion against the king by his subjects. Instead, he writes,
"the expression of conflict seems to take the form of a ritual drama
portraying the many dangers the King must face in pursuit of his duties
of office, especially the hatred and hostility of his rivals in the royal clan"
(207). The Incwala songs refer to the hatred of the king by his rivals
rather than by those singing the songs, his subjects. But the important
point, Norbeck stresses, is that although antagonism and hostility may
be stressed in these and similar rites, they are not rituals of rebellion.

This leads Norbeck to conclude that although Gluckman is to be commended for suggesting that ritualized conflicts may have a positive functional value, they do not express rebellion. They should be seen, rather,
as part of a larger category of ritual events that provide for the controlled
and periodic relaxation of social rules. Institutionalized license and obscenity, role reversals, the expression of sexual and other social antag-
onisms (which may involve the deriding and ridiculing or even the
physical assaulting of people in certain social categories) are seen by
Norbeck as serving a common function in "making memorable and en-
hancing the importance of the social occasions upon which they are
observed" (218), whatever may be their other functions.

A writer who has also expressed misgivings about Gluckman's thesis
is T. O. Beidelman, who, in a reanalysis of the Swazi rites (*Swazi Royal
Ritual*, 1966), suggested that Gluckman, by limiting his interest to the
ceremonies' latent function, had provided an inadequate interpretation
of them. Beidelman makes a number of suggestions:

(1)   The main theme of the Incwala is not the expression of conflict
or rebellion but the separation of the king from the other groupings in
the nation, so that he is free to assume the mystical powers associated
with the kingship.

(2)   To understand this ritual, Beidelman suggests that it is important
to delineate the cosmological ideas of the Swazi and stresses that the

251

significance of symbols depends upon the meanings and values assigned to them by a particular culture. He felt that Gluckman's analysis, by ignoring the cosmology, had placed too much emphasis on conflict, which was certainly not a dominant theme of these elaborate rites.

(3) And finally, Beidelman noted that Gluckman's reliance on the notion of catharsis implied an "hydraulic model of personality," and he goes on to argue that an understanding of the efficacy of ritual symbols necessarily involves psychological variables.

In his response to Norbeck's criticisms, Gluckman said that his thesis had been misunderstood, in that it was assumed to be a psychological analysis. This, Gluckman argued, was precisely what he did not seek to make. He wrote, "I do not assert that when Zulu women don men's clothing and behave obscenely they are rebels against their lot. Indeed I clearly state the opposite: they are performing prescribed, socially approved actions, for communal good. The conflicts enacted are conflicts in social principles" (1963: 260). The feelings and desires of individual women, whether conscious or unconscious, are not the issue, for these, Gluckman felt, might be variable. Only a psychological study could indicate their feelings. The difficulty is that Gluckman's use of the term *catharsis* implies a psychological dimension to his analysis, as Beidelman noted, and it is therefore problematic, as Ioan Lewis has pointed out, to insist (as Gluckman does) on a rigid separation of social and psychological variables (1977: 9).

I have already noted the important influence that Gluckman had on the theoretical writings of Victor Turner. Both the use of extended case-study material as a mode of ethnographic illustration (see Kuper 1973: 183–4) and the analysis of rituals as a mechanism that highlights structural conflicts and thereby affirms group unity were theoretical strategies derived from Gluckman. But whereas Gluckman remained throughout his life a confirmed functionalist, Turner, in his later writings on religion, has attempted to go beyond the structural-functionalist framework, which has become, he remarks, a fetter and a fetish. This has led him to offer a theory of ritual somewhat at variance with the perspectives of his earlier writings, especially the theoretical slant of *The Drums of Affliction*. In this study a functional relationship is perceived between ritual symbolism and social structure, which Turner documents with detailed case-study material, the concept of social drama having a significant theoretical role. In contrast to these detailed ethnographic studies, Turner's later writings are more comparative, and this has led him to develop an alternative theory of ritual.

Turner takes as his starting point the work of Van Gennep – the "father of formal processual analysis," as he calls him – and, accepting

Van Gennep's tripartite analysis of transactional rituals, explores the nature of the liminal phase, the "interstructural situation." An earlier paper, "Betwixt and Between" (1967: 93–111), is devoted to a discussion of the nature of this limited period in ritual. Turner argues that the rite of passage involves a transition between two fixed "states," defining "state" as a "relatively fixed and stable condition." This has important consequences, as we shall see, for it leads him to conceive of social structure as static and unchanging and of ritual as a fluid creative process. He makes some interesting observations on the symbolism of the liminal period:

(1) that it is seen as an ambiguous condition, and here his ideas are consonant with the theories of Leach and Douglas. Thus neophytes may be seen as sexless or bisexual, or considered unclean or polluting.

(2) that we find in ritual a dissolution of all categories and classifications: The initiate may symbolically be treated as an embryo or a newborn infant, or thought of as "dead." The metaphor of dissolution is often expressed by the fact that the neophytes go naked, or dress in filthy rags, or are identified with the earth. They may have nothing "to demarcate them structurally from their fellows" (99).

(3) that there are role reversals, or a suspension of normative obligations: Individuals dress and behave as members of the opposite sex, a chief or king may be reviled or beaten, behavior may be allowed that is normally thought immoral or indecent.

(4) that there is often a period of seclusion when the initiate is separated from normal life. This too may be symbolized in various ways: A person may undergo a period of seclusion, or enter a sanctuary, or may observe certain taboos or restrictions.

And finally (5) that there is a stress on the absolute authority of the ritual elders. Such authority is moral and ritual rather than secular and is seen as expressing the "common interest," the elders reflecting the axiomatic values of the community. This is linked to the importance of secret, esoteric knowledge – the *sacra* – which Turner thinks constitutes the "crux of liminality."

Turner's study *The Ritual Process* (1974b) develops these ideas and attempts to explore the social rather than the symbolic properties of the liminal phase of ritual. The first part of the book is devoted to a semantic analysis of two Ndembu rituals, the Isoma and Wubwang'u rites, a form of analysis we have already discussed. But the remainder of the study develops Turner's ideas on liminality and outlines a theoretical paradigm that not only constitutes a seminal approach to religion but a veritable theory of society.

Summarizing his earlier discussion, in which he asserted that "liminality is frequently likened to death, to being in the womb, to invisibility, to darkness, to bisexuality, to wilderness, and to an eclipse" (1974b: 81), and that neophytes are liminal beings who have no status, property, or secular clothing to indicate their rank or role, that they are passive and submissive to authority and tend to develop among themselves intense comradeship and egalitarianism. Turner argues that such liminality is an expression of what he calls *communitas*. He thus presents a dualistic model of social life that consists of two aspects, *social structure* and communitas. Before discussing the various modalities of communitas, it seems important to define these two crucial concepts.

By *social structure* Turner means a system of social relationships and statuses, "an arrangement of positions . . . which involves the institution-alization and perdurance of groups and relationships. He thus has a functionalist and empiricist conception of social structure, quite differ-ent, as he acknowledges, from that of Lévi-Strauss, and he intimates that this is a limiting concept as used by anthropologists, for it excludes dimensions of social life usually of interest to those in the arts and humanities. Thus for Turner social structure is the notion of society as a differential system of structural positions that implies hierarchy and exploitation (1974a: 272). Structure is essentially conceived of as a closed and static system "rooted in the past and extending into the future"; it is cognitive, classificationary, pragmatic, and instrumental, and, for the individual, a world that is "arid and mechanical."

In contrast, *communitas* is defined as "a relationship between concrete, historical, idiosyncratic individuals," but Turner admits that this concept is difficult to define. It is, he writes, "elusive" and "hard to pin down," and therefore, he suggests, recourse has inevitably to be made to met-aphor and analogy. Thus his thesis is sprinkled with imagery drawn from diverse sources; communitas emerges where social structure is not (1974b: 113), it is the emptiness between the spokes of a wheel, "a mo-ment in and out of time," or, in Blake's phrase, "the winged moment as it flies." Thus whereas social structure is narrowly and clearly defined, communitas is a metaphorical concept that is identified with a mode of relationship, a group, or a belief or ideology, as well as with existential or spontaneous events and experiences. One extract will suffice, I think, to succinctly summarize the social dichotomy Turner is endeavoring to make and sustain:

> All human societies implicitly or explicitly refer to two contrasting social models. One . . . is of society as a structure of jural, political and economic positions, offices, statuses and roles, in which the individual is only am-biguously grasped behind the social persona. The other is of society as a communitas of concrete, idiosyncratic individuals who, though differing

254

in physical and mental endowment, are nevertheless regarded as equal in terms of shared humanity. (166)

Turner succumbs to the temptation to present this distinction as a series of binary oppositions, and we may note some of these.

Structure	Communitas
State	Transition
Heterogeneity	Homogeneity
Inequality	Equality
Property	Propertyless
Secular	Sacred
Pride	Humility
Complexity	Simplicity
Classification	Anonymity

Turner sees the communitas aspect of social life as being manifested in various social events and movements, and these may be discuss separately. First, as I have already noted in discussing the genesis of his theoretical ideas, Turner links communitas with the liminal period of transition rituals. In *The Ritual Process* he gives the outline of the installation of the Ndembu chief Kanongesha, and he describes how the chief is clad in nothing but a ragged waist-cloth and is harangued and manhandled by the headmen and made to perform various menial tasks. He notes the various themes associated with the liminal period – sexual continence, submissiveness and silence, and anonymity – and the close relationship between these rituals and the characteristics of other transition rituals. What is interesting about this liminal period, he writes, is the blend it offers of "lowliness and sacredness, of homogeneity and comradeship" (82).

Although Turner evidently recognizes that initiation and other rites reduce the neophyte to a tabula rasa, a blank slate, on which is inscribed the knowledge and wisdom of the group (90), he avoids the theoretical implications of this stress on the painful humiliations and on the initiate's harsh subjection to authority by emphasizing instead the "essential and generic bond" of humanity allegedly evident in such rites. In the structural perspective that Turner offers, liminality is seen as indicating individuals or principles that fall between the "interstices of social structure."

Second, communitas is linked with the notion of marginal states and outsiders, which include the following: shamans, diviners, mystics, mediums, priests, those in monastic seclusion, hippies, and gypsies (233). It seems somewhat problematic that these categories are not deemed part of the social structure, but such marginal categories are thought to manifest the attributes of communitas and to be linked with a third characteristic of communitas, that of "structural inferiority."

Turner provides a stimulating and interesting discussion of the various institutions, movements, individuals, and social categories that are alleged to express communitas or liminality, for the latter concept becomes detached from transition rites and is applied even to such phenomena as pilgrimages. Indeed, he suggests that liminality has given rise not only to religion and mysticism but also to philosophy and pure science (242).

Let me discuss two of these manifestations of communitas – hippies and mystics – in summary fashion.

Hippies. The values of communitas are strikingly expressed, according to Turner, by what is often referred to as the counterculture. In our society urbanized hippies, he writes, generalize and perpetuate the liminal and outsider condition, for they stress personal relationships rather than social obligations, and in their dress and life-style opt out of the social-structural order. He notes their frequent interest in Zen Buddhism and tribal cults. "The Hippie emphasis on spontaneity, immediacy, and 'existence' throws into relief one of the senses in which communitas contrasts with structure," Turner writes (1974b: 100).

Mystics. Turner also holds that many mystics and founders of religious orders exemplified communitas. St. Francis of Assisi and other medieval religious mendicants, with their advocacy of poverty and their renouncement of worldly property, are cited as examples, the Franciscan order, in its original conception, being a kind of "permanent liminality." Allied to these are the various bhakti (devotional) religious movements in India, and Turner discusses the Vaishnavas of Bengal (Dimock 1966) and the Virasaiva Saints of South India. Both movements stressed devotion as a form of salvation, rather than the scrupulous observance of caste duties and rituals. Turner also discusses other religious leaders besides St. Francis, who, though "structurally" well-placed, have espoused humility and communitas: Gautama the Buddha, Gandhi, and Tolstoy. He notes, in fact, that the holy man who makes himself to all appearances poorer than the meanest beggar may, and in fact often does, come from a wealthy and aristocratic background (1974a: 265). Mystics and saints of all the major world religions thus exemplify "ritual liminality" in that they are placed outside the structural system and espouse various symbols that express their marginal status or structural inferiority.

A third aspect of Turner's concept of communitas is his suggestion that communitas, though it may be expressed as a spontaneous or existential "happening" – which he tends to equate with charisma or a mystical experience (see 1974b: 125) – very frequently becomes a normative or ideological structure or institution. He has in mind various religious sects or utopian societies.

Fourth, pilgrimages are seen as social institutions that typically exemplify communitas; as Turner explicitly writes, they are "liminal phenomena." And in a seminal essay on pilgrimages, which form an important aspect of all the major historical religions, Turner notes certain characteristics that suggest liminal attributes:

(1)   The pilgrim shrines are often to be found in localities away from normal settlements, in the hills, caves, or forests, often at some distance from urban areas.

(2)   The pilgrimage itself is often seen as a "retirement from the world," and in contrast to the stable, structured system of everyday life.

(3)   While people are on a pilgrimage there is a stress on equality and on the social bond among pilgrims, caste and status distinctions being played down.

(4)   Though undertaken as a matter of free choice, the pilgrimage is often seen as a religious obligation and as a penance.

(5)   The catchment area from which a particular shrine draws its pilgrims expresses a wider community than that of the localized religious congregations, as well as frequently stretching across political and national boundaries.

Turner notes that with improved transportation and communication and with the advent of the mass media, pilgrimages have become increasingly important in many parts of the world, with many thousands of people visiting some of the better-known shrines. The famous shrine of the Virgin of Guadalupe in Mexico is visited each year by Catholics from all over the world, and Turner gives an interesting discussion of the nature and significance of the Mexican pilgrim shrines (1974a: 208–28; Turner & Turner 1978: 40–103). Turner concludes that pilgrimages are equivalent to initiation rites in tribal cultures; they are, he writes, "the ordered anti-structure of patrimonial feudal systems" (1974a: 182).

Fifth, Turner suggests that one of the more striking manifestations of communitas is to be found in millenarian movements, and he notes the similarity of many of their attributes to that of the liminal period. He mentions the absence of property, the reduction of all to the same status, the wearing of uniform apparel, the minimization of sexual distinctions, abolition of rank, maximization of religious as opposed to secular attributes, and the total obedience to the prophet or cult leader.

Finally – and significantly, because it gives communitas an essentially positive character – Turner links communitas with Martin Buber's discussion of I–thou relationships and community. Thus communitas comes to be defined as an egalitarian, existential relationship. As Turner writes

"Communitas is spontaneous, immediate, concrete – it is not shaped by norms, it is not institutionalized . . . It is that 'sentiment for humanity' of which Hume speaks, representing the desire for a total, unmediated relationship between person and person" (1974a: 274). Thus the concept of communitas embraces an "ill-assorted bunch of social phenomena," and it is identified with communalism, certain social movements and categories, and interpersonal relationships.

Reading Turner's thought-provoking discussion of communitas, I was reminded of the writings of a contemporary mystic who has had a wide appeal among adherents of the counterculture, Meyer Baba. For this holy man there are only two possible ways for a human being to relate to the world. Either he or she affirms his "separateness," so that his or her relationship to others becomes one of opposition and exploitation, or, through love, individuals become united in a spiritual consciousness in which there is no sense of separateness. Thus the choice is between normative relationships that are mechanical and unsatisfying, and relationships that involve a mystical union. There seem to be no alternatives. Such a perspective, oblivious to the concepts of reciprocity and mutual aid, prevents us from exploring the possibilities of establishing a real human community. In postulating a stark dichotomy between structure and communitas, Turner's theory not only serves as an apology for religion but seems to me to imply a similar vista.

Let us, then, examine some of the limitations of Turner's theory. Clearly, what is labeled "social" is a matter of definition, but surely few contemporary anthropologists would equate "social" with social structure – that is, include only institutionalized roles or jural relationships in their definition of what constitutes social life. For several decades now, writers have been aware that social action can be placed on a continuum that runs from highly formalized normative action to behavior that is spontaneous, transient, and highly idiosyncratic. The distinctions made between formal and informal groups, the external and internal system of formal organizations, the jural and moral aspects of kinship, and Firth's distinction between social structure and social organization all relate to what I am suggesting. In addition, those analyses employing case-study material, or network or transactional analysis, also reflect an approach that assumes that there is more to social life than "social structure." Moreover, Turner treats such structural relationships as being entirely pragmatic and as lacking any symbolic dimension, whereas reprocity and patterns of mutual cooperation, and social relationships that do not involve hierarchy, are left entirely out of account. The informal, egalitarian, and interpersonal relationships that are a part of everyday life – and that embody the notion of community – Turner chooses to ignore.

All structured relationships are assumed by Turner to be unequal, and though essential in that they constitute the key productive activities, to be impersonal and alienating. Outside the ritual context, Turner would appear to suggest, there are no "human" personal relationships, except among utopian sects. This leads Turner to challenge the premises of writers like Marx and Lewis Morgan, who implied that kinship-based societies were essentially egalitarian, and to argue that structure (inequality) and communitas (religion, equated with fraternity) are aspects of all societies. Some crucial differences between social structures thereby get obliterated, and kinship patterns of tribal societies are veritably equated – as structure – with the worst despotisms.

Equally problematic and misleading is Turner's concept of communitas. Turner's thesis essentially suggests that religion and ritual are liberating aspects of human culture, associated with equality and fraternity, creativity,and human well-being. Thus, having defined structure in terms of inequality, exploitation, and formal secular roles, Turner conceptually demarcates such productive relationships from religion and symbolism (communitas). But just as he ignores the informal and communal aspects of secular social life, so he leaves out of his analysis not only any explanation of the intimate relationship between religion and political authority but the hierarchical nature, in thought and structure, of religious institutions themselves. In short, Turner fails to recognize the ideological nature of religious symbolism. But before discussing this issue, let me recount some of my own experiences of liminality, for this may take the mystical edge off communitas and cast doubt on whether this modality of interrelatedness (as manifested in initiation rites) is quite the spontaneous, existential "sentiment for humanity" that Turner seems to think it is.

A decade or so ago I was forcibly removed from my usual surroundings and separated from the community. My hair was cropped, and I was put into a uniform without any symbols of personal identity. I was referred to by a number and housed, along with my fellow neophytes, in almost Spartan conditions, and underwent certain physical and mental hardships. Needless to say, I faced much personal abuse and was generally humiliated. The similarities between my own ordeals, if I may so describe them in retrospect, and the experiences of neophytes in many initiation rites is, of course, obvious. And the self-inflicted hardships of members of monastic orders and ascetics certainly fall into the same general category; as Turner notes, there are striking parallels between the neophytes of the Ndembu circumcision rites and the monks of St. Benedict.

But having said this, where does the analysis move? For Turner it moves towards the personalist philosopher Martin Buber and his concept

of community as a "spontaneous, immediate and concrete experience."
Buber, like the mystical existentialist Berdyaev, whom he closely resembles, viewed modern industrial capitalism as threatening the individual
personality, and he therefore laid great emphasis on the importance
of personal relationships. Like other socialist anarchists he makes a
distinction between state institutions and communal life and views the
former as essentially enslaving mechanisms. But other than the "cama-
raderie" expressed by neophytes undergoing the ritual, the connection
between Buber's concept of community and initiation rites is rather
slender. Indeed what is curious about Turner's account is that he mentions Erving Goffman's study *Asylums* (1962) and seems to imply that
Goffman's suggestions support his own thesis. Goffman had written of
the "stripping" and "levelling" processes of total institutions, and Turner
felt that this paralleled the liminal experience. In fact Goffman's important exposition, had Turner followed it through, leads to a very
different perspective. Goffman in fact is suggesting that neophytes of
total institutions are subjected to what he called "mortification," that is,
a process in which elements of their personalities – and not specifically
status attributes – are systematically stripped off. Thus the process is
essentially one of depersonalization for, as many educationalists have
suggested, total institutions are agencies of attempted resocialization
rather than of personal development. This is suggestive of something
quite different from Turner's perspective, and it is of interest to note
that in his own work he completely disregards the institutions mentioned
by Goffman – asylums, military establishments, and prisons. In these,
liminality is clearly evident, as it is in concentration camps (cf. Zuesse
1979: 144–6, for an analysis along the same lines).

Turner seems to overlook the fact that the symbolism of initiation
expresses precisely this mortification; the circumcision rite among the
Ndembu is, metaphorically, a "place of dying." Initiates are stripped not
only of status attributes but of personal identity. Moreover, looking at
such rituals I fail to see the "sentiment for humanity" expressing itself
in some of the ordeals, nor can I see the "spontaneous, immediate and
personal nature" of these rituals. Turner's contention that communitas
is neither normative nor institutionalized seems equally misleading; indeed, it is highly inaccurate. Ritual behavior is highly structured, involving patterns of authority and specific role expectations. The
relationships that are expressed are not "unmediated relationships between person and person." One could say much the same about the
religious mystics, who, although they may be outside the formal structures of society, are also alleged to exemplify communitas. For such
mystics salvation is not an exemplification of a philosophy of personalism

but rather a denial of the existential self. When the Islamic mystic Mansur exclaimed, "I am God," he highlighted an important truth.

What is striking about Turner's study *The Ritual Process* (1974b) is that it seems to contradict the general premises of his earlier work. In these studies Turner had suggested that during rituals, social categories, particularly the sexual division, were emphasized during the rite, so that the ultimate unity of Ndembu society would be sustained. This was pure Gluckman, and the studies indicated the intimate and complex relationship between ritual symbolism and sociopolitical relationships. These two aspects – the cultural structure and social relationships – are clearly separated and held to be contrasting aspects of social life. Ritual is deemed to efface the role structure and, in fact, to be antistructure. Yet Turner's writings on communitas betray an occasional acknowledgment that ritual has an ideological function. For instance, he writes that "in this no place and no-time that resists classification, the major classifications and categories of the culture emerge within the integuments of myth, symbol and ritual" (1974a: 259). He notes, too, that the individual undergoing the transition rite may learn about social structure; in fact, he suggests, it is an occasion when "a society takes cognizance of itself " (240). This indicates that what is usually reflected in ritual is not simply jural relationships nor an egalitarian "sentiment for humanity" that is antistructural but rather a wider system of values, "a global view of man's place in the cosmos," as Turner himself expresses it.

Turner contends that communitas is characterized by egalitarian personal relationships, whether manifested in religious movements or utopian ideologies, and that the routinization of relationships represents a deviation, a decline into the domain of structure. Apart from the fact that a number of utopian conceptions postulate a stratified order, it is surely untenable to equate religion with communitas. Religious institutions, often highly bureaucratized and with a hierarchy of ritual roles, are social facts of fundamental importance in many societies. Yet where do these fit in Turner's analysis? Gandhi's harijans, it is worth noting, were untouchables to orthodox Brahmins. The caste system, the Ethiopian churches of South Africa, and the Shona spirit cults are all phenomena that do not fit easily into the structure–communitas paradigm. Turner also fails to stress that his conception of communitas involves the notion of authority and hierarchy, for the criterion of "total obedience" is listed as one of its properties. Communitas is therefore virtually equivalent not to Buber's community but to the Weberian notion of ritual or charismatic authority. Thus when Turner suggests that both social modalities (structure and communitas) are indispensable for human continuity, the choice we are given is between secular authority (at

261

its extreme a despotism or a regimented bureaucracy) and a moral community in which personal integrity is subsumed under the authority of a ritual elder or prophet or lost in a mystical union. It reminds me of the Japanese peasant who had a poster that read "Which road is the correct one: Is it the way of Confucius, the Buddha, Jesus Christ or Genghis Khan and Hitler?" Communitas and structure? This is really no choice at all. Turner, of course, assuming that what these individuals represent constitutes social life, does not insist that we make a choice but rather that we maintain a balance, appropriate to the historical circumstances, between the two. *Homo hierarchicus* (which Turner equates with structure) and the religious mystic (exemplifying communitas) seem to divide the world between them. Turner leaves no scope, either in terms of his theoretical concepts or in terms of his political credo, for secular patterns of mutual aid and reciprocity.

But what is seminal in his discussion of communitas is the distinction he draws between varying patterns of religious authority. He notes two distinct patterns.

The first is the distinction between political and ritual authority. He cites the Shilluk of the Sudan, who had a system of ritual localities that were important in the staging of various national ceremonies, such as the installation of the king. Such sites were quite distinct from the political centers and divisions, and thus ritual and political authority were "polarized" (1974a; 184). In an interesting essay on Thomas Becket (1974a; 60–97), a discussion focused on what he calls the "root paradigm of martyrdom," Turner notes that many of the conflicts during the period (the twelfth century) drew cultural support from two divergent theories. The first was that a papal monarchy should direct all the spiritual and temporal affairs of Christendom and therefore advocated a theocracy. The other was that society should be dualistically organized into separate spheres of church and state – the dichotomy under discussion.

Since political authority in tribal cultures is invariably ritualized, the distinction between political and ritual authority is closely linked with a second distinction that Turner explores. This second one emerges from Meyer Fortes's account (1945) of the Tallensi of northern Ghana. The Tallensi kinship system involves an opposition between patrilineal descent (which is associated with property, political allegiance, and jural authority and ritual privileges and obligations) and what Fortes calls the "submerged" line, namely the uterine links through the mother. The links between a person and his or her mother's kin involve spiritual characteristics and mutual interests and concerns. This distinction, Turner felt, exemplified his structure–communitas paradigm. But the Tallensi also articulate a further dichotomy, for like other African communities they have two types of cults, one focused on earth shrines, situated outside local settlements, the other on ancestral shrines, located within the village. The former are associated with the original inhabitants of the country and are under the control of the indigenous priests, whereas the invading conquerors, the Namoos, are identified with chieftainship and the ancestral cults. Turner notes that this ritual duality is common in other African communities, for example among the Shona, and that what we essentially have are ancestral and political cults that represent crucial power divisions and sectional interests, and earth and fertility cults that represent ritual bonds and shared values of a wider community and that are basically inclusive and "universal" (1974: 185). The latter cults, Turner implies, are associated with stateless societies, and he sees them as "homologues" of the pilgrim centers in politically centralized, high-agricultural cultures; both, of course, are examples of communitas. But the political cults, and cults like those of the Aztecs, which were organized around the symbolism of the center, hardly seem to fit, as I have noted, into the communitas paradigm.

Turner's career, as he described it, was a personal voyage of discovery from traditional anthropological studies of ritual (which I reviewed earlier in this book) to an interest in modern theater. In a way it was the "return of the repressed," for he was born into a theatrical family (1982; 7). Its not surprising, therefore, that Turner's work reflects a strongly humanistic perspective, particularly in his later writings, which show the influence of Dilthey. But his concept of ritual as "social drama," though it did indeed lead him to put a focal emphasis on meaning, social action, and processual analysis, nonetheless inevitably implied that he saw social life outside the ritual context as essentially static and inhuman. For Turner, humanity seems to flourish only in ritual and through religion and art. Generalizing from the economic and political structures of his own time, he offered a bleak vision. He chides structuralists for interpreting religious symbolism in terms of rigid, atemporal cognitive structures, but his own conception of social structure is equally atemporal and lacking in movement.

6

Religious thought: structure and hermeneutics

Lévi-Strauss and totemism

Claude Lévi-Strauss has been described as an "institution," a "modern Heraclitus" who has painted a "delibinized version" of Freud, and as a "beacon," a kind of light to guide us clear of the rocky shores of empiricism – the latter reflecting the standpoint of Malinowski and Radcliffe-Brown. Clearly Lévi-Strauss is a complex intellectual figure, whose "structuralist" approach to anthropology was embraced more than a decade ago with almost religious enthusiasm by many anthropologists. His mode of analysis has had a profound influence on psychoanalysis, Marxism, and literary studies, as well as on anthropology, and effectively ousted existentialism from the French intellectual scene. Structuralism and Lévi-Strauss are inextricably linked. Indeed Lévi-Strauss has been described as the "father" of the movement and the present decade as the "age of structuralism," so pervasive has been his influence. (For useful accounts of structuralism and its various forms, see Gardner 1972, Rossi 1974, Sturrock 1979, and Kurzweil 1980.)

Born in Belgium in 1908, Lévi-Strauss studied law and philosophy at the University of Paris, but feeling dissatisfied with purely intellectual pursuits he accepted a teaching post in sociology at the University of São Paulo. This gave him the opportunity to make occasional trips to the interior of Brazil.

The outcome was not only the gathering of a wealth of empirical detail on Amerindian communities – though Lévi-Strauss's fieldwork experiences have usually been unfairly disparaged by other anthropologists – but eventually led to the writing of a fascinating and memorable travelogue, *Tristes Tropiques* (1955) (*The Sad Tropics*). In describing these early journeys, the book conveys the feeling of a vision quest, a romantic search for the untouched "primitive." The book is indeed, as Geertz suggests (1975: 347), one of the finest ever written by an anthropologist. Inevitably, what Lévi-Strauss found was no pristine state but "our own filth, thrown into the face of mankind" (1955: 43). The experience, it seems, had two important effects on Lévi-Strauss; it led him to sense that behind the empirical diversity of human societies there was an underlying unity, that the mind of mankind was fundamentally the same everywhere. And second, as a reaction, as it were, to a "disappointed romanticism," he came to adopt an approach to social life that was detached and scientistic. Diamond goes so far as to suggest, in a rather hostile critique, that Lévi-Strauss made a fetish of the scientific mode of cognition (1974: 302), but Lévi-Strauss's whole tenor of thought, it seems to me, is metaphorical and concrete – almost poetic, rather than abstract. He has, as he put it, "a rather neolithic kind of intelligence" (1955: 64; cf. Leach 1970: 7–20).

In 1939 Lévi-Strauss returned to Paris, but owing to the vicissitudes of war he soon moved to New York, and he spent the war years teaching at the New School for Social Research. Through his contact with Roman Jacobson he began to develop an interest in structural linguistics as well as delving into the American anthropological literature, particularly the writings of Boas, whose influence on Lévi-Strauss tends to be ignored by most commentators.

Lévi-Strauss, in his theoretical work, has been concerned, as Badcock (1975) points out, with some of the key issues in sociological theory, unsolved problems bequeathed by Durkheim: the relationship of the individual to society, and the origin of social facts. Lévi-Strauss describes himself as an "inconstant disciple of Durkheim" and like his compatriot, is a philosophical rationalist (Scholte 1966), but he deviates substantially from Durkheim's sociology in presenting, in the final analysis, a form of psychological reductionism – or rather, he is a sort of psychologist who employs cultural facts in a search for the underlying "structures of the mind." "Ethnology," he wrote, "is first of all psychology" (1966: 131). But the relationship between collective representations and the "unconscious structures" is not reductionist in any simple sense; the structures of the mind are, as it were, "immanent" in the cultural data – in myths and symbolism. In what manner the unconscious can be seen to "generate" empirical data (Coward & Ellis 1977: 21) remains problematic.

One's understanding of Lévi-Strauss is hampered perhaps by his style of writing, which is scholastic in flavor. Although his studies reveal outstanding erudition (few anthropologists have such a good knowledge of ethnography *and* philosophy) and refreshing subtleties of thought, they are essentially ambiguous and esoteric, "full of diversions, false trails, metaphoric asides and inconclusive perorations," as Maybury-Lewis (1969) says. This is especially true of his work on totemic classifications. Edmund Leach, with his usual candor, admitted that he had read *The*

Savage Mind through three times and on each occasion had obtained a different impression of the argument, and that he found the last chapter virtually incomprehensible.

Lévi-Strauss's writings radiate, as Leach intimated (1970), like a three-pointed star, around his autobiographical travelogue *Tristes Tropiques* and thus can be roughly divided into three broad theoretical concerns: kinship theory, the logic of myth, and the theory of totemic classifications. I am primarily concerned here with this last category, specifically with his study *The Savage Mind*, a work that, Lévi-Strauss suggested, was a "kind of pause" in the development of his theories. "I felt the need for a break," he wrote, "between two bursts of effort." That this work is considered by its author as a temporary diversion between his study *The Elementary Structures of Kinship* and his more recent work on mythology is surely indicative of Lévi-Strauss's intellectual vigor.

Before examining Lévi-Strauss's work on totemism, some general remarks on his theoretical approach may be apposite. It has often been said that contemporary anthropology and sociology are largely a confrontation between two rival paradigms. The first, characteristic of German idealism and the French anthropological tradition, generally assumes the primacy of the intellect or of culture and approaches social phenomena along structuralist lines. Such an approach is largely rationalist and takes a "collectivist" or "holistic" approach to society. The second paradigm, largely characteristic of the Anglo-American anthropological tradition, assumes the primacy of behavior or social action and adopts an approach that is inductive and empiricist. Adherents of this approach tend to have an individualistic orientation toward social phenomena. Durkheim and Mauss stand in the first tradition, whereas Malinowski belongs to the second. Lévi-Strauss adopts, as I have noted, the rationalist approach of Durkheim. This is clearly evident in the two basic postulates that underpin his work.

The first is that social phenomena can be understood if viewed as systems of communication; in fact, he defined anthropology as a semiological science that took as its guiding principle the notion of "meaning." In his study of kinship structures, specifically of prescriptive marriage rules, he therefore viewed these rules in terms of exchange theory and argued that underlying these institutions is the notion of reciprocity, a concept he derived from Mauss. The value of these exchanges, he wrote, "is not simply in the goods exchanged. Exchange... has in itself a social value. It provides a means of binding men together" (1969: 480). There are overtones here of a functionalist interpretation, but as Ekeh (1974) notes, Lévi-Strauss had a nonutilitarian approach, for what is important about exchange is not the intrinsic value of the items exchanged but their symbolic value. Like Mauss, Lévi-Strauss saw gift giving as symbolic behavior, and like Freud (though for very different reasons) he sees the incest taboo and exogamic rules as key factors in the emergence of human society. He recognized that there were problems in approaching cultural practices as systems of communication. As he said, "In admitting the symbolic nature of its object, social anthropology does not thereby intend to cut itself off from *realia*" (1973: 11). But this is precisely what his programmatic writings entail, for, as Ioan Lewis notes, his approach is thoroughly asociological. By denying that social phenomena can be understood in functional or historical terms, Lévi- Strauss, Lewis says, "cut the link which binds religion to its social base, thus dealing a savage blow to the sociological tradition in the study of religion pioneered by ... Durkheim" (1971: 14) – and, one might add, Marx and Weber.

It is important to realize, therefore, that Lévi-Strauss defines anthropology in rather narrow terms, as the study of "collective representations" – "thought-of " orders of myth and religion. The "real situation," or the "lived-in" orders (1963: 313), the economic infrastructures of Marxist theory, are best left to history, with the help of other empirical sciences. Thus Lévi-Strauss does not doubt the primacy of the social infrastructures (1966: 130) but, like Kardiner, he places the operations of the unconscious mind as a mediator between praxis (primary institutions) and cultural beliefs and practices (Kardiner's projective systems). But whereas Kardiner's basic personality structure was culturally specific, Lévi-Strauss's "mind" is panhuman. For Lévi-Strauss, then, anthropology is fundamentally the study of "thought" (Geertz 1975: 352).

In an important sense, therefore, Lévi-Strauss did not apply the theoretical paradigm of structural linguistics to culture as a totality but only to those aspects of social life that constituted ideological forms: myth, religion, totemism, and, as he implied, modern political ideology. As he clearly denoted, he looked upon his work in *The Savage Mind* as contributing to the Marxist "theory of superstructure" (1966: 130). Marx, it may be noted, looked upon the economic categories of capitalism as essentially constituting a religious system, whose meaning could be both interpreted and explained. He did so, of course, not by reference to invariant structures of the mind, which are virtually beyond the grasp of empirical science, but by elucidating the nature of productive relationships (Godelier 1977: 169–85; Novack 1978: 181).

The second postulate underlying Lévi-Strauss's theoretical work is that cultural facts are the manifestation, at the conscious level, of fundamental structures inherent in the human mind. He writes,

> If . . . the unconscious activity of the mind consists in imposing forms upon content, and if these forms are fundamentally the same for all minds – ancient and modern, primitive and civilized – it is necessary and sufficient to grasp the unconscious structure underlying each institution and each custom, in order to obtain a principle of interpretation valid for other institutions. (1963: 21)

This led Lévi-Strauss to define social structure in a manner quite different from that of Boas and Radcliffe-Brown. Whereas for these writers social structure is largely a descriptive concept reserved for observable relations and interactions, for Lévi-Strauss social structure "has nothing to do with empirical reality but with models which are built up after it" (279). Regrettably, as many writers have noted, Lévi-Strauss is none too clear about the epistemological status of the "unconscious structures." Are they culturally specific, as he implies in his discussion of Zuni symbolism, the "structures" referring to the unconscious ritual classifications that underscore and unify within a community the other more "empirical" aspects of culture? This kind of "structural" analysis is no different from that of scholars in the Oxford phenomenological tradition, who have largely followed Evans-Pritchard (eg., Hicks 1976). Or do the structures refer to socioeconomic relationships (and ecology), which, as some of his myth analyses imply, are "masked" or concealed by the mythical discourse? In this, as Augé has discussed (1982: 3), Lévi-Strauss is close to the perspectives of Marx (cf. Larrain 1979: 141–50). Lévi-Strauss suggested in his early essay on social structure that the basic problem for the anthropologist was to determine the relationship between the way a society conceives its orders and their ordering and the "real situation" – the relationship, that is between the "thought-of" (religion and myth) and the "lived-in" orders. He never explored this theoretical trail, however, despite his frequent allusions to Marx.

Then, again, are the unconscious structures panhuman, substantive patterns or categories that simply provide meaning or "order" to a diversity of empirical data, as the "principle of reciprocity" is seen to explain a variety of kinship systems? Or, finally, are the structures entirely abstract, and devoid of "meaning" in the ordinary sense of the term? (cf. Augé 1982: 57–8).

Interestingly, both Harris (1980: 166–9) and Jenkins (1979: 14–21) rightly argue that the concept of the unconscious mind or structures is vague and is not operational from a scientific standpoint. Yet whereas Harris chides Lévi-Strauss for his humanistic orientation and his general disdain for empirical validation, Jenkins accuses Lévi-Strauss of following an empiricist epistemology. Most writers have not agreed with Jenkins and have in fact, applauded Lévi-Strauss for his antiempiricist stand (e.g., Rossi 1982). Ricoeur, in a well-known comment, even suggested that Lévi-Straussian structuralism was "Kantianism without a transcendental subject" (1963: 599). This, I think, is misleading: A more accurate description of Lévi-Strauss's theory is "transcendental materialism," a label that he himself coined. Jenkins's definition of empiricism is so broad that he describes even Lévi-Strauss as an empiricist (as well as an essentialist). Jenkins, in reacting, like other structural Marxists, against a crude form of theory that took "facts" as given and unmediated (the standpoint of classical empiricism, reflected in behaviorism, positivistic sociology, and the writings of such anthropologists as Radcliffe-Brown), seems to offer a Kantian epistemology which suggests that "raw data" (objective reality, whether of a physical or cultural form) has no existence at all apart from the concepts.

This kind of epistemology, denying that conceptual structures have any connection with empirical reality – the "real object" – since they have "only a theoretical existence" (1979: 36) seems to me not only pre-Marxist but pre-Hegelian, echoing the Kantian thesis. It is a form of idealism – masquerading as Marxism – which suggests that the world, culture, or empirical facts, or what have you, are essentially unknowable, never "grasped" by concepts or thought. By this epistemology not only can Lévi-Strauss be dubbed an empiricist, but so could Marx and Hegel. Did not Hegel himself say that "whatever is true must be in the actual world and present to sensation" and that all analysis "starts from the concrete"? (Weiss 1974: 141–3). Lévi-Strauss neither has a disdain for empirical data nor did he give them theoretical priority or take them as given, for his essential standpoint was to deny any simple "continuity between experience and reality" (1955: 71). Hence his polemics against the phenomenologists. Nor did he expunge the human subject or the human "essence" from the theoretical discourse – quite the contrary. He offers only a critique of "subjectivism" and of the transcendental subject outside of nature and society. But unlike Marx he conceptualizes the human "subject" in terms of thought – the human mind *l'esprit humain*) (Leach 1970: 112; Shalvey 1979: 36), rather than in terms of human praxis, and hence as not only transempirical but ahistorical. Taking their bearings from Lévi-Strauss's critique of empiricism and existentialism, some structural Marxists seem to have gone overboard the other way and to have almost renounced both empirical knowledge and the human subject entirely. Also, by applying his methodology to the totality of culture, they have implied that all social life can be reduced to thought or language (Seve 1978: 398–405).

Before discussing Lévi-Strauss's seminal work *The Savage Mind*, let me briefly outline his short essay on totemism (1962), for this constitutes both an introduction to his larger study on totemic classifications and a critique of earlier studies.

The word *totem* is taken from the Ojibwa, an Algonquin people of Canada. The expression *ototeman* means roughly, "He is a relative of mine," and expresses membership in the exogamic group. Ojibwa clans were named after animal species, so that people might say *makwa nintotem*: "My clan is a bear." Subsequent researchers applied the term *totemism* liberally to similar phenomena elsewhere, and it came to be used as a general concept, referring to any situation in which a special relationship was thought to exist between a social group and one or more classes of material objects, specifically animals and plants. Frequently the relationship is a ritual one, the animal is considered sacred, and there are specific taboos associated with it, and the members of the group may even believe themselves to be descended from the totemic species. As Frazer (1903) put it, "Totemism is ... both a religious and a social system. In its religious aspect it consists of relations of mutual respect between a man and his totem; in its social aspect it consists of relations of the clansmen to each other and to men of other clans" (15).

Totemism was therefore seen as a unitary phenomenon, a type of primitive religion, and, as we have seen earlier, many attempts were made to explain it. McLennan, whose article is, significantly, entitled "The Worship of Animals and Plants" (1869–70), initially set the problem, and Robertson-Smith, Durkheim, and Radcliffe-Brown all viewed totemism as a ritual relationship between man and certain natural species, and hence as a form of religion.

The initial task Lévi-Strauss set himself was both to question the unitary nature of the concept of totemism – hence he refers to it as an "illusion" – and to disentangle the ritual from the social aspects of the phenomenon. He quotes with approval the American anthropologist Alexander Goldenweiser, considering his short articles on totemism as of more theoretical value than Frazer's monumental study *Totemism and Exogamy* (1910), a work that ran to over two thousand pages. Goldenweiser questioned whether it was sensible to define totemism in terms of a combination of three different kinds of social phenomena – the organization of a society into clans, the attribution of natural species to clans as names or emblems, and the belief in a ritual relationship between the clan and certain animal species – since these seemed to vary independently of one another. Moreover, Lévi-Strauss stresses that the relationship between humans and animals and plants takes on various forms. A group may hold a particular animal, a sacred crocodile perhaps, in veneration, or it may have a special relationship with a natural category. The group in question may be a society, a kinship group, a cult group, or a sexual category. Likewise an individual may have a special ritual association – that involving the guardian spirit – with either a particular species or a specific animal or plant.

Thus in speaking of totemism Lévi-Strauss suggests that there has been a tendency to confuse and confound two quite separate problems. On the one hand there was the problem posed by the frequent identification of human beings with animals and plants. This aspect was part of a general problem dealing with the relations between humans and nature, and involved art and magic as well as religion. On the other hand, there is the problem of symbolism, the designation of groups based on kinship by animal and vegetable terms. The term *totemism* covered both problems, and Lévi-Strauss's aim is to separate them and to argue that totemism is best understood not as a primitive form of religion but as a particular illustration of a certain mode of thought. The reason why totemism was placed in the category "religion," he held, was that this served a purpose for Victorian writers like Frazer in separating and distancing their own beliefs from those of preliterate peoples.

In the chapter on the "totemic illusion," Lévi-Strauss examines two ethnographic cases, that of the Ojibwa and that of the Tikopia. In both cases he suggests that the society's religious ideas and their totemic classifications form separate systems.

The Ojibwa Indians were organized into patrilineal and patrilocal clans of which five enjoyed a particular prestige. According to one of their myths, these Indians originally had five clans – catfish, crane, loon, bear, and martin – but Lévi-Strauss shows that there were any number of totemic species, mostly animals. He notes that we may discern a tripartite division of the totemic species into water (sturgeon, catfish, pike), air (eagle, loon and crane) and earth (caribou, moose, martin) categories but questions whether the Ojibway believe that members of the clan are descended from the totemic animal. Moreover, there is no simple association of one clan with one animal but rather a relationship between two orders, the classification of people and the classification of natural species. The relationship is homologous and metaphorical.

In examining their religious ideas, Lévi-Strauss stresses that this collective naming system is not to be confused with the Ojibway notion of a guardian spirit, the idea that an individual may enter into a special relationship with a specific animal. Such a spirit is acquired by individual enterprise and acts as a supernatural protector. In fact, the Ojibwa have a hierarchy of spirits (or *manido*) – the great spirit, the sun and moon, thunder spirits, the four cardinal points – and a host of lesser spirits, both benevolent and malevolent. All food taboos are derived from this religious system and are related to individual experiences, the specific

271

prohibition being communicated to the individual by a particular spirit, mostly in dreams.

Thus the totemic system and the manido or religious system, Lévi-Strauss argues, are quite separate, and only a few natural species are common to both.

Similarly, among the Tikopia, a Polynesian-island community who are the subject of an important series of monographs by Raymond Firth, Lévi- Strauss was anxious to show, by an examination of the ethnographic material, that their religious ideas and their group symbolism could not be equated as a unitary system.

A reanalysis of the Ojibwa and Tikopia material leads Lévi-Strauss to suggest that totemism does not constitute a phenomenon sui generis; it is not an institution but rather an aspect of a classificatory mode of thought. This leads him to critically analyze Elkin's writings on Australian totemism.

Though Lévy-Strauss clearly admires Elkin as an ethnographer, he points out that in his essay on totemism (1933) Elkin reduced totemism to irreducible variants: individual, sex, cult, moiety, section, clan, and even dream totemism. Starting with a healthy reaction against the traditional amalgam, Elkin, by stressing its diversity, ends up, Lévi-Strauss suggests, preserving its reality: "Elkin chops it up and comes to terms with the pieces. But it is the very idea of totemism that is illusory, not just its unity" (1962: 115). Lévi-Strauss admits that in the conclusion to his article Elkin defines totemism in rather broad terms as being a ritual attitude toward nature, not merely a method of classifying nature "but an expression of the idea that man and nature form one corporate whole." But this formula, Lévi-Strauss writes, is altogether too vague and general, and, of course, a characteristic of all religious systems.

Having established in these initial chapters that totemic phenomena are ill understood if taken as an institution or a form of religion, Lévi-Strauss proceeds to examine various functionalist explanations. Durkheim's symbolic approach is, in a sense, bypassed, for Durkheim was interested in the relation between the totemic species and a specific group, or, as Lévi-Strauss would put it, in relating the two series contiguously. And, as I have noted, Durkheim saw the totemic species as a symbol, the deification of the social group. But Lévi-Strauss sees totemism essentially as a kind of code that expresses a homology between two cultural domains – a system of social categories and a natural classification – that expresses an awareness of the empirical discontinuity of biological species. Thus Lévi-Strauss generally evades any discussion of the category "religion," and, unlike Durkheim, does not attempt to explain religious phenomena. Rather he draws a distinction between two modes of thought, scientific thought and what he calls "savage" or un-tamed thought, totemic classifications being a particular modality or illustration of the latter mode. His main disagreement with Durkheim is that Durkheim concentrated too much on the relationship between beliefs and symbols and the social structure and ignored the relationship between society and nature. It is the latter that is Lévi- Strauss's primary concern, but the human interest in the natural world that he denotes, though perceived as proto-scientific, is metaphorical and symbolic rather than pragmatic and utilitarian.

"It is the obsession with religious matters," he wrote,"which caused totemism to be placed with religion." The latter category, however, he refuses to consider as an autonomous order that can be approached scientifically. To make an objective study of religion, only psychological (or organic) and sociological approaches are open to us, he suggests, and these "do no more than circle around the phenomena" (177).

But although hostile to Durkheim's treatment of totemism, Lévi-Strauss was equally critical of explaining totemism in naturalistic terms. Malinowski, as we have seen in Chapter 4, thought of magic and religion as having a cathartic function. His explanation is basically an emotionalist one. Talcott Parsons took a similar view but broadened the perspective, relating magic and religion to the problem of meaning; he writes, "Cor-relative with the functional need for emotional adjustment to such ex-periences as death is the cognitive need for understanding" (1954: 63). Malinowski's specific interpretation of totemism was essentially natur-alistic, utilitarian, and affective – and Lévi-Strauss is against all three perspectives.

Regarding explanations in terms of emotion, he writes, "As affectivity is the most obscure side of man, there has been the constant temptation to resort to it, forgetting that what is refractory to explanation is *ipso facto* unsuitable for use in explanation" (1962: 140). And criticizing both Freud and Malinowski in this context, as well as Durkheim, he continues, "Men do not act as members of a group in accordance with what each feels as an individual; each man feels as a function of the way in which he is permitted or obliged to act. Customs are given as external norms before giving rise to internal sentiments ... They are consequences, never causes" (141–2).

In his hostility to the role of the individual in the explanation of social phenomena, Lévi-Strauss is closely following Durkheim. But curiously, in suggesting that the causes of social phenomena can be found only in the "organism which is the exclusive concern of biology, or in the in-tellect, which is the sole way offered to psychology and to anthropology as well" (142), Lévi-Strauss was essentially suggesting a mode of interpretation that was psychologistic. He assumes all through his writings that the key to understanding social phenomena lies in the collective attributes of the human mind. But his hostility to affectivity leads him to disregard biopsychological factors in more general terms. As Marvin Harris has written (1969), Lévi-Strauss considers hunger, sex, fear, and love to be peripheral concerns, of little interest to the anthropologist. Moreover, like some behavioral psychologists he does not appear to conceive of anything that mediates between culture and the human organism, or rather the human intellect.

However, one can see that in attempting to move, as it were, between Durkheim's symbolist and sociological perspective and Malinowski's naturalism, Lévi-Strauss puts human thought as a mediating element between the two series, nature and culture. This is indeed how Leach (1965) has interpreted him in suggesting that Lévi-Strauss, like Freud, has a conceptual triad: "nature, culture and a mediator which is mostly a structural aspect of the human brain." But on this issue the writings of Lévi-Strauss are difficult to decipher. For instance, he writes, "The connexion between the relation of man to nature and the characterization of social groups, which Boas thought to be contingent and arbitrary, only seems so because the real link between the two orders is indirect, passing through the mind" (1962).

Here the mediation of the mind (however conceptualized) is not between nature and culture but between those aspects of culture that imply an empirical approach to the natural world (natural taxonomies) and those aspects of culture that relate to patterns of social organization. Thus whereas Malinowski reduced totemic ideas to basic human needs – to our pragmatic concerns with the world – Durkheim reduces such ideas to the social order and leaves nature out of account. Lévi-Strauss is trying to steer between Malinowski's pragmatism and Durkheim's sociologistic rationalism. This is why he called himself a "transcendental materialist" (1966: 246).

But to return to his essay on totemism. Radcliffe-Brown had, like Durkheim and Boas, thought of totemism largely in terms of a relationship between humans and natural species, as these denoted a ritual dimension. He held, according to Lévi-Strauss, that anything that exercised an important influence on the material or spiritual well-being of society tended to become an object of the ritual attitude. Thus if natural species came to serve as emblems of social groups, this is because these species were already objects of ritual value before totemism. Thus Radcliffe-Brown, as Lévi-Strauss remarks, reversed the Durkheimian interpretation according to which the totems are considered sacred because they are symbols of the group. Lévi-Strauss, unfairly ignoring

Radcliffe-Brown's symbolist approach, suggests that like Malinowski Radcliffe-Brown held that an animal "only becomes 'totemic' because it is first good to eat" (1962: 132).

To summarize the discussion so far, it can be seen that Lévi-Strauss takes his departure from earlier approaches in several senses. First, for Lévi-Strauss totemism, as Fortes and Leach have both remarked, does not belong to the domain of ritual beliefs and practices but rather is an aspect of a mode of thought that mediates between natural and social classifications.

Second, and coupled with this, Lévi-Strauss, though positing a distinction between the two series social relations and natural categories, sees them as mutually exclusive and the relationship between the "orders" as homologous and metaphorical. He defines totemism in these terms.

An important aspect of Lévi-Strauss's approach is that it emphasizes that totemic elements cannot be understood in isolation. In discussing the work of Firth and Fortes, for instance, Lévi-Strauss writes that in adopting an animal or plant as an eponym, a social group does not make an "implicit assumption of affinity of substance" between the symbol and itself, as myths would often suggest, nor is the totem merely a diacritical symbol, the emblem of the group. The connection he suggests is not arbitrary, nor is the relation based on a perception of resemblance. And in saying this he recapitulates Henri Bergson's discussion written many years before. For the latter writer, rejecting Lévy-Bruhl's notion of a prelogical mentality, had written "If the primitive man does not identify himself with his totem, does he simply take it as an emblem? This would be going too far the other way ... The truth must be somewhere between these two extremes" (1935: 184). Although the interpretation the two writers offer of totemism is dissimilar, Lévi-Strauss nevertheless takes over this perspective, aiming to guide his thesis between these two extreme hypotheses – the one of "mystical participation" (Lévy-Bruhl), the other of reducing the totem simply to the role of group emblem (166). Again Lévi-Strauss attempts to steer a middle course.

In his discussion of Tallensi symbolism, Meyer Fortes had suggested that animal species were considered particularly apt symbols for the ancestral spirits because they symbolized the "potential aggressiveness of the ancestors as the supreme sanction of Tale cultural values." And thus it was contended that men's relations with animals in the world of common-sense experience provided the symbolism of the "relations of men with their ancestors in the sphere of mystical causation" (1945: 145). Firth is also thought to hold a similar theory with regard to Tikopia totemism, but Lévi-Strauss, although considering these explanations

275

more satisfactory than those of the earlier writers on totemism, nevertheless thinks their interpretations too limiting in that they focus on the resemblances between the two series, and their "solutions" have a limited field of application. What is to be done with the other totems?, he asks. Among the Tallensi, how is one to interpret the symbolic significance of grasshoppers, rodents, squirrels, turtledoves, and many other totemic species by such procedures? As he succinctly put it, both Fortes and Firth have taken a great step "in passing from a point of view centered on subjective utility (Malinowski) to one of objective analogy. But this progress having been made, "it remains to effect the passage from external analogy to internal homology" (1962: 150). This step, Lévi-Strauss suggested, had been initiated by Evans-Pritchard, and especially by Radcliffe-Brown's paper on the comparative method in anthropology.

The Nuer of the Sudan speak about natural species by analogy with their own social segments, specifically lineages, and thus, like scientific taxonomists (who also take their terms from social categories) think of animals in terms of the social world. For instance, carnivorous animals (*cieng*) have as one of their lineages (*thok dwiec*), the mongooses, which in turn are divided into a number of lineages. Such theoretical classifications, Lévi-Strauss maintained, are the basis of totemic ideas, and he quotes Evans-Pritchard, who writes, "An interpretation of the totemic relationship is here, then, not to be sought in the nature of the totem itself, but in an association it brings to mind" (1956: 82).

In noting that the totem selected by the Nuer had no marked utilitarian interest, Evans-Pritchard had stressed that totemism could not be interpreted as a "ritualization of empirical interests," a comment specifically directed against Malinowski. But though sympathizing with Evans-Pritchard's contextual or metaphorical interpretation of Nuer totemism, Lévi-Strauss had certain reservations about it, namely that theological elements are brought into the interpretation, hence making it a "culture-specific" explanation, again limiting its scope. Lévi-Strauss is searching for a more general approach.

I have outlined in an earlier chapter Radcliffe-Brown's interpretation of totemism, specifically his second paper on the subject, in which he suggests that a structural principle, the "union of opposites," elucidates totemic classifications associated with moiety systems. For example, the bat and the tree creeper are dissimilar but both inhabit hollow trees and, by analogy, express social relations. It is an example of a symbolic dualism widespread elsewhere, and, according to Lévi-Strauss, embodies ideas and relations conceived by speculative thought on the basis of empirical observations of the natural world. It is an example of associative logic, which has been all too readily and unnecessarily discredited, for it represents a common denominator of all thought and a direct expression of the structures of the mind.

Lévi-Strauss hailed these suggestions of Radcliffe-Brown's as something of a breakthrough and as a key that would unlock the door of totemism. It was a theory, he suggested, that Bergson had anticipated some twenty years before, though it is well to note that Bergson had an antipathy toward intellectualist interpretations. As he wrote, "We shall say it over and over again; before man can philosophize man must live; it is from a ritual necessity that primaeval tendencies and convictions must have originated. To connect religion with a system of ideas, with a logic or pre-logic, is to turn our remote ancestors into intellectuals" (1935: 176).

Not surprisingly, Bergson found the theories of Tylor and Marett unacceptable and postulated that religion originated through humans' attributing "purposes to things and events." Distinguishing between animal cults and that "strange thing" totemism, Bergson attempted to explain totemism by avoiding the extremes I have already noted. And in so doing he writes, "To express the fact that two clans constitute two different species, the name of one animal will be given to one, that of another to the other. Each of these designations, taken singly, is no more than a label; taken together they are equivalent to an affirmation. They indicate . . . that the two clans are of different blood" (1935: 176).

Linking totemism with exogamy, Bergson considered that this institutional form prevented intermarriage between kinship groups, thus reflecting an instinct that disposed the tribe to split up into clans. But, as Lévi-Strauss indicated, if such an instinct existed a recourse to institutions would be superfluous, and furthermore, since animals are endogamous the natural series could hardly serve as a model for the social organization. In spite of these criticisms, Lévi-Strauss felt that Bergson, like Radcliffe-Brown, had offered some seminal thoughts on the interpretation of totemism.

In his introduction to an edition of Lévi-Strauss's *Totemism*, Roger Poole, with some eloquence, claimed that it was "a sort of guided tour towards a point of vantage from which we may stare down on the whole terrain of the subject of symbolic codes" (Lévi-Strauss 1962: 28). In reality, Lévi-Strauss's aim is more modest; it is to indicate that totemism is neither an institution nor a religion but a mode of thought (Lévi-Strauss, significantly, hardly ever uses the terms *symbol* or *symbolism*) – a "classificatory device" that mediates between social categories and relations and our conceptions of the natural world.

277

The savage mind

Earlier I noted the curious paradox evident in Durkheim's classic study of religion, for though the book is largely devoted to stressing the symbolic and functional aspects of religion, Durkheim was nevertheless appreciative of the logic and intellectual nature of religious thought. And in chapter 3, in the section entitled "Cosmology and Social Structure," I quoted a key extract which indicated that Lévi-Strauss's structuralist perspective constitutes a development of Durkheim's "hidden thesis" (1964b: 235–7).

Like many of his contemporaries, Durkheim postulated a bifurcation of thought. On the one hand, we have "primitive thought," equated with religion, myth, and a "considerable part of contemporary literature." But unlike Lévy-Bruhl, Durkheim considered this mode to be proto-scientific and essentially logical. On the other hand, we have science, which has come to be associated with Western thought generally, with rather misleading implications. Lévi-Strauss is essentially concerned with this issue, with understanding the nature of so-called primitive thought.

The Lévi-Straussian concept of the "savage mind," or thought untamed, is a vague, intangible notion, more of a metaphor than a scientific concept. To come to terms with essential tenets of Lévi-Strauss's thesis is therefore not an easy task. Badcock admits that the book *The Savage Mind* is largely incomprehensible at a first reading. But if we approach it through Durkheim, the essential ideas of the book seem to me fairly straightforward.

Although Lévi-Strauss was anxious to separate religion from classificatory symbolism and to ground the latter not in social categories but in natural taxonomies, he follows Durkheim, rather than Lévy-Bruhl, in the way he contrasts "primitive" and scientific thought. "Nothing is more dangerous," he once remarked, "than for anthropology to build up two categories, the so-called primitive peoples and ourselves" (Steiner 1966: 35). Thus he came to argue that what we find in comparing preliterate cultures with our own is essentially two types of scientific thought and that the "savage mind" evident among preliterate people is in no sense inferior or defective, let along prelogical. Like Durkheim, he stresses that the religious symbolism of preliterate communities is "prior" or primary rather than primitive. But the focus of this symbolism, Lévi-Strauss maintains, is the natural world, or external reality. He thus largely ignores, as I have intimated, those elements and beliefs focusing on spiritual agencies. Moral ideas, too, Lévi-Strauss tends to bypass.

His concept the "savage mind" seems to loosely cover myth and magic, as well as totemism and symbolic classifications, though to what extent

278

this mode of thought is evident in Western culture he does not explore. But as Sahlins (1976) has suggested, much symbolism of Western culture is of a totemic nature, especially in relation to clothing habits. Durkheim and Radcliff-Brown were more explicit, both suggesting that Western religions belong to the same category as the mythological conceptions of preliterate people.

The crucial point, however, is that Lévi-Strauss avoids the sort of dichotomy advocated by Lévy-Bruhl and by Ernst Cassirer in his conception of mythopoeic thought, although there are marked similarities between Lévi-Strauss and Cassirer in their evaluation of symbolic thought.

Lévi-Strauss attempts to avoid a rigid dichotomy between science and "untamed" or savage thought for a number of reasons. First, he feels it necessary to stress that preliterate people are neither ignorant nor childish nor illogical in their general thought. The first pages of *The Savage Mind* are largely devoted to demonstrating that preliterate people have a detailed knowledge of the natural world and that their thinking is not solely governed by organic or economic needs.

Second, following Durkheim, he is concerned to show that religious thought is primarily concerned, like science, with intellectual understanding. As Durkheim and Mauss wrote with respect to symbolic classification, "Their object is not to facilitate action but to advance understanding, to make intelligible the relations which exist between things. Such classifications are thus intended above all, to connect ideas, to unify knowledge; as such they may be said without inexactitude to be scientific, and to constitute a first philosophy of nature" (1903: 81). *The Savage Mind* is a development and an elaboration of these thoughts.

It would be a mistake, however, in countering the pragmatic orientation of earlier anthropologists like Malinowski, who conceived of preliterate people as being solely concerned with primary needs – propagation and nutrition – to imply that classificatory schemata are devised only as intellectual enterprises, as merely a demand for order. Lévi-Strauss is certainly correct in suggesting that systematic knowledge of the environment "cannot relate just to practical purposes"; nevertheless, symbolism often serves an ideological function, and natural taxonomies, like science, have a pragmatic value. This is why taxonomies tend to be more complex and systematized around the more fundamental pragmatic concerns, such as game animals and domesticated crops.

Third, and again following Durkheim, Lévi-Strauss is concerned to show that there are fundamental similarities between science and magico-religious thought. But whereas Durkheim saw science as superseding "primitive classifications" (he notes that the latter "exists today only as a survival"), as well as being its progeny, Lévi-Strauss postulates two modes of scientific thought and writes, "These are certainly not a function of different stages of development of the human mind, but rather of two strategic levels at which nature is accessible to scientific enquiry; one roughly adapted to that of perception and the imagination; the other one at a remove from it" (1966: 15).

It will be noted at once that this conception is widely at variance with that of another "intellectualist" theorist, Robin Horton (1967), who saw traditional African religion as postulating theoretical and explanatory constructs (gods, spirits, and witches), and thus, like science, putting events into a causal context wider than that provided by common sense. Lévi-Strauss's conception of science, on the other hand, largely ignores the notion of causality; he sees magico-religious thought as focusing on the level of the "concrete" and, by relating specifically, as a mode of understanding, to the natural world, as having little connection with normative structures. In contrast, for Horton, as I shall discuss later, magic and religion are explanatory schemata that relate misfortune to social morality.

By postulating "two parallel modes" of acquiring scientific knowledge, Lévi-Strauss felt he had solved a paradox, namely the gap between the neolithic revolution and the rise of science over the past hundred or more years. Since modern science is comparatively recent, the invention of metallurgy, weaving, and the domestication of animals and plants during the neolithic period seemed to Lévi-Strauss problematic. These latter techniques were based on centuries of active and methodical observation, and this was provided by the "savage mind." But the postulation of two modes of scientific thought hardly provided an adequate answer as to why there was a period of "stagnation" between the neolithic and scientific revolutions, and the former seems to me to have been based on procedures and experiments akin to those of a practical science rather than to analogical thought characteristic of primitive classifications – the savage mind.

Edmund Leach, I think, cogently summarizes the distinction between traditional science and the "science of the concrete"; it is one, he writes,

> between a logic which is constructed out of observed contrasts in the sensory qualities of concrete objects, e.g., the difference between the raw and the cooked, wet and dry, male and female – and a logic which depends upon formal contrasts of entirely abstract entities ... The latter kind of logic, which, even in our own society, is used only by highly specialized experts, is a different way of talking about the same kind of thing. (1970: 84)

Lévi-Strauss certainly implies this sort of distinction, for he writes, "Both science and magic require the same sort of mental operations and they differ not so much in kind as in the different types of phenomena to which they are applied" (1966: 13).

Valid though this distinction may be, the concept of the "savage mind" gives rise to some conceptual difficulties. The first limitation is what I have stressed earlier, namely that Lévi-Strauss sees myth and magico-religious phenomena largely in terms of their articulation with the natural environment. He thus not only underemphasizes the importance of animistic beliefs in the culture of preliterate people but largely ignores the relation between religion and symbolism, on the one hand, and the social structure, seen as a moral order on the other. His definition of religion as the "anthropomorphism of nature" reflects this onesided viewpoint.

Second, in order to give substance to his concept of the savage mind Lévi-Strauss focuses his discussion on two elements that are common to both science and magico-religious phenomena, namely, classification and their articulation with nature. But just as magic, myth, and religion cannot be adequately defined in terms of their relationship with the natural world alone, so science is more than classification. Even Durkheim saw causality as the basic paradigm of scientific knowledge.

Third, it remains problematic as to what extent magic and myth can give us valid knowledge of an external reality (which is what science is concerned with) over and above that of ordinary common-sense experience. Lévi-Strauss gives the savage mind (exemplified in a practical sense by the handyman, or *bricoleur*) the status of science on the grounds that

(a) It articulates with the natural world, though the suggestion is that it is at the perceptual level "halfway between percepts and concepts," even though the elements of folk taxonomies pertain to the level of concepts. Only symbolism fits the image of the bricoleur and kaleidoscope.

(b) It is logical. Since science and logic have usually been considered different aspects of thought – the one synthetic, the other analytical (in Kant's terms) – to demonstrate that myth and magic are logical hardly suggests that they are scientific.

Fourth, what is one to make of this logic? Piaget suggested that it may be a prelogic, operating at the level of "concrete operations" (1971: 116), whereas Worsley quoting Vygotsky, implied that totemic classifications were based on a cognition that employed congeries or complexes rather than abstract concepts (1967: 151–2). Perhaps all three scholars are saying essentially the same thing, but, significantly, Lévi-Strauss raises concrete thinking, expressed in divination and magic, to the status of science.

And finally, Lévi-Strauss seems to equate symbolic classifications that unite various aspects of experience and have an essentially religious function with folk taxonomic systems that order a specific domain and correspond to what Durkheim and Mauss called "technological classifications." These are best termed "protoscientific taxonomies," as Worsley suggested. Moreover, under the rubric "savage mind" Lévi-Strauss also includes magic and divination and sees totemism as an aspect of this general systematic activity.

For example, in discussing the Navaho system of classification he notes that they classify animals into various general categories, and he notes later that these are based on carefully built up theoretical knowledge, so that these classifications are comparable with biological classifications. But then following this extract he alludes to the system of "correspondences" reflected in Navaho myth and ritual, which relate specific species to a natural element – crane to sky, or cornbeetle to earth – and then goes on to discuss the symbolic classifications of the Hopi, which, like those of the Zuni, have a "vast system of correspondences." Indeed, following Durkheim's lead, he suggests that many preliterate cultures have a "conceptual scheme" or master plan that unites the various classifications. He writes, "The societies which we call primitive do not have any conception of a sharp division between the various levels of classification ... Commonly zoological and botanical classifications do not constitute separate domains but form an integral part of an all-embracing dynamic taxonomy" (1966: 138–9).

Clearly it is misleading to equate folk taxonomic and symbolic classifications, and it is an open question as to whether all preliterate cultures have a complex system of "correspondences." (Cf. my papers on the Hill Pandaram and Navaho taxonomies, 1976, 1979.) Moreover, the classificatory systems of the Chinese and certain astrological systems associated with early theocratic states can hardly be deemed primitive. Worsley, indeed, suggested, in discussing Groote Eylandt totemism, that there was a need to separate the totemic classification, or "compendium," as he prefers to call it, from the protoscientific classifications and the symbolic order imposed upon them.

Prompted by Boas, Lévi-Strauss tries to answer the question as to why animals and plants were so regularly used by preliterate people in mythical tales and in totemic systems:

> If it is the case that zoological and botanical typologies are employed more often and more readily than other typologies, this can only be by reason of their intermediate position as logically equidistant from the extreme

forms of classification; categorical and singular . . . The importance of the notion of species is to be explained by its presumptive objectivity; the diversity of species furnishes man with the most intuitive picture at his disposal and constitutes the most direct manifestation he can perceive of the ultimate discontinuity of reality. (1966: 136–7).

The "specific" level thus not only serves as an objective model that is utilized in the "creation of new taxonomies" – thus Lévi-Strauss completely reverses Durkheim's formulations – but it serves as a medial classifier, as a logical operator, that lies midway between the concrete and the individual, on the one hand, and the abstract and the system of categories on the other. "The species, level," he writes, "can widen its net upwards, that is in the direction of elements, categories and numbers, or contract downwards in the direction of proper names" (149).

In an absorbing discussion, Lévi-Strauss goes on to describe how the "specific" level articulates with other classificatory schemata; how species categories are utilized in organizing territorial space and conceptions of disease; and how parts of the body and systems of proper names can serve as terms for a classification.

In his discussion of totemism in *The Savage Mind* Lévi-Strauss was anxious, given his theoretical bias, to separate totemism from ideas about taboos and sacrifice. Significantly, as Leach remarked, Lévi-Strauss "considerably plays down the importance of food customs as cultural indicators" (1970: 198) and seems to consider food taboos as cultural ideas that are independent of totemic classifications. They are extratotemic; the prohibition of eating the totemic animal is simply a particular case of food prohibitions. The latter he interprets as having a "denoting significance" in a scheme of classification. On the other hand, he sees the institution of sacrifice as diametrically opposed, in its underlying conception, to that of totemism. Whereas totemism is based on a homology between two classificatory domains, such that species are not interchangeable, sacrifice postulates a connection between a social group and a deity, the sacrificial animal being simply a mediator. As such, the species sacrificed can be substituted – a cucumber instead of an ox. The Intichiuma ceremonies discussed by Durkheim are, he argues, in no sense a form of sacrifice but are rites of increase, which are widespread, and their presence in a community varies independently of totemism.

In a discussion of dual organizations, Lévi-Strauss lists various historical interpretations as to why moieties may be instituted – for example, the fusion of adjacent groups for various reasons (economic, demographic, ceremonial), or the crystallization in institutional form of norms designed to ensure marriage exchanges within a group – and he indicates quite clearly a dissatisfaction with such historical explanations. Thus, although he does not question the validity of historical interpretations as to why certain cultural elements are utilized in myth or in symbolic classifications, he does seem to demote this type of explanation. As one writer has suggested, for Lévi-Strauss history is no more than an "auxiliary science," merely a source of materials (Gaborian 1970: 161). Lévi-Strauss's principal aim is to provide a structural explanation, although this approach would seemingly be applicable only as a theory of superstructure.

Then again, because his writings are focused on symbolic systems and he uses a linguistic model, many empiricist anthropologists have tried in vain to interpret his work in an orthodox Durkheimian fashion. Thus Maybury-Lewis ends a review of his myth analyses with the words, "After all of Lévi- Strauss's dialectical ingenuity we still do not know who is supposed to be saying what, and in what language, to whom" (1969: 121).

But since Lévi-Strauss is concerned with discerning the "grammar" of a culture, in a sense nothing is being said. His "meaning" is syntactic, not semantic, and this is why he so rarely uses the terms *symbol* and *symbolism*. As Sperber cogently puts it, for Lévi-Strauss "everything is meaningful, nothing is meant" (1979: 28). (For useful discussions of "analogic" thought, see Godelier 1977: 204–20, and Sperber 1979: 25–33.)

The final chapter of *The Savage Mind* is hardly the concern of most anthropologists, for it is addressed largely to French intellectuals and contains a polemic against Sartre's *Critique of Dialectical Reason* The chapter is concerned with disputing the privileged position that Lévi-Strauss feels Sartre has accorded historical explanations in the social sciences. Sartre had made an absolute distinction between analytical thought, on the one hand, which describes and characterizes, and dialectical thought, a mode of consciousness that attempts to account for changes in preconceptions, and he intimated that preliterate people were incapable of dialectical reasoning, because they had no conception of history. Although not disputing the distinction between these two modes of reasoning, Lévi-Strauss feels that they are not absolute opposites but that dialectical reasoning is complementary and "something additional to analytical reason" (246). He criticizes Sartre on two counts: that Sartre's own study is the result of the mode of thought that Sartre devalues, analytical reasoning; and that he takes an ethnocentric viewpoint. But Levi-Strauss's main criticism, which indicates his essential relativism, is that Sartre's distinction between two modes of consciousness gives them, respectively, an inferior and superior status, according to a historical context and position. Lévi-Strauss himself, as we have seen, postulates two forms of logic, one related to conventional science and the modern period, and "supremely abstract"; the other related to mytho-logical thought, and, being "analogical," "supremely concrete." But whereas "domesticated thought" has, as one of its aspects, "historical knowledge," the characteristic of the savage mind is its "timelessness." He rejects the idea that the former mode of thought is somehow superior. As he writes, "Some special prestige seems to attach to the temporal dimension, as if diachrony were to establish a kind of intelligibility not merely superior to that provided by synchrony, but above all more specifically human (256).

Thus, like Boas and Radcliffe-Brown, Lévi-Strauss makes a distinction between historical and comparative studies, the latter approach being specifically anthropological and structural. This distinction leads him to trace a contrast between what he terms "cold" societies, which, as it were, encapsulate history in terms of myth or classificatory schemata, and "hot" societies, which admit the notion of flux as a part of their self-image and therefore explain themselves with history. Thus Lévi-Strauss writes that there is a fundamental antipathy between "structure" and "event" and between systems of classification and history, which accounts for the "totemic void" in modern industrial societies.

Although rebuking Sartre for his ethnocentricity, he admits that "internality," namely the viewing of the world from a specific sociohistorical standpoint, is inevitable, and he writes "I am not suggesting that man can and should sever himself from this internality. It is not in his power to do so and wisdom consists . . . in seeing himself live it, while at the same time knowing (but in a different register) that what he lives so completely and intensely is a myth" (255). Mary Warnock has suggested that the French are inclined to believe that there is only one sort of knowledge: "Descartes certainly thought there was. Sartre has reached the position where there is none but historical knowledge. Lévi-Strauss perhaps thinks that there is only anthropology" (1966: 586).

But it is an anthropology that focuses on society as a cultural system, for Lévi-Strauss sees man's essential humanity expressed in Cassirer's designation of man as an *animal symbolicum*. "Man," Lévi-Strauss explains, "has been described as Homo Faber, the maker of tools, and this characteristic has been accepted as the essential mark of culture. I confess that I do not agree and that one of my essential aims has always been to establish the line of demarcation between culture and nature, not in tool-making, but in articulate speech. It is with language that the leap forward occurs" (Charbonnier 1961: 149).

Lévi-Strauss's whole approach is one that attempts to combat what Sahlins calls "practical reason." In a sense he attempts to synthesize Marx and Durkheim, using Durkheimian sociology to combat the pragmatism of much Marxist theory, while using Marx as a means of resituating Durkheim's "society" within nature. Like Evans-Pritchard, he hardly ever mentions Weber.

Apart from two seminal essays on shamanism (1963: 167–205) Lévi-Strauss wrote little on specifically religious topics, and his later years have been largely devoted to the writing of his important studies on the "Science of Mythology." In these studies Lévi-Strauss adopts a theoretical position similar to that outlined in *The Savage Mind* and in his early essay on the structural study of myth (1963: 206–31). He thus explicitly follows the kind of structural analysis pioneered by Ferdinand de Saussure, the Swiss linguist. Saussure had argued that for linguistics to become truly scientific it had to adopt a "synchronic" approach and treat language as a system independent of the human subject and the natural world in which people are situated. It had to treat language as a network of structural relations existing at a given point in time and thus could suspend historical interpretations. Defining *sign* as an arbitrary – that is, conventional – relationship between a sound image (*signifier*) and a concept (*signified*), Saussure thus made an important shift in emphasis away from semantics. As Rossi put it, the Saussarian perspective produced a shift from the traditional sociological approach "according to which the meaning of a symbol is determined on the basis of the cultural content or subjective meaning it conveys, to the semiotic perspective, according to which the meaning (or rather the value) of a sign is determined from its position" within a system of relationships (1983: 135).

In his approach to myths, Lévi-Strauss adopts Saussure's semiotic perspective, and, as I noted in the last section, this involved the search for "invariant structures" or elements within the myths. Such structures are not evident at the empirical level. As in his writings on totemism, Lévi-Strauss advocates an approach to mythical thought that neither treats it as simply determined by the basic necessities of life nor as a kind of mythopoeic thought. Thus, on the one hand Lévi-Strauss is against the utilitarian functionalism that postulates a direct relationship between economic infrastructures and cultural institutions and beliefs, and on the other he is unsympathetic to the view put forward by writers like Lévy-Bruhl and Cassirer that primitive thought is determined by emotion and mystical representations. "What I have tried to emphasize," he wrote, "is that ... the thought of people without writing is on the one hand disinterested – and this is a difference in relation to Malinowski – and on the other hand, intellectual – a difference in relation to Lévy-Bruhl" (1978: 16). His basic hypothesis, therefore, is that mythical thought implies disinterested thinking and a need or a desire by preliterate people to understand the world around them. He argues that the human mind is everywhere one and the same, though different mental capacities may be developed in different cultural circumstances. He likewise argues – and in his myth analyses attempts to demonstrate – that although mythical stories may seem arbitrary, absurd, meaningless, and fanciful, the very fact that certain motifs reappear all over the world indicates that behind the apparent disorder there is some kind of order or logic – the logic of the concrete. And he writes, "If this represents a basic need for order in the human mind and since, after all, the human mind is only part of the universe, the need probably exists because there is some order in the universe and the universe is not a chaos" (1978: 13).

In a series of detailed and scholarly studies devoted to exploring and analyzing the myths of American Indian cultures, Lévi-Strauss offers a structural analysis based on these premises (1969, 1973a, 1978, 1981). Thus he suggests that the elements of the myth, like the elements of language, are meaningless if taken in isolation, and he is therefore critical of Jung's idea of archetypal patterns. For Lévi-Strauss the elements of myth – the *mythemes* – become meaningful only in relation to other elements. Using this linguistic analogy, Lévi-Strauss shows in an analysis of various myths how a structure can reveal itself at different levels, though he does not necessarily see a preexistent harmony or homology between the various codes or orders – ecological, economic, sociological, cosmological; in fact, he stresses the varied transformations that may occur between them. Like Marx, Lévi-Strauss views social reality as consisting of multiple levels, and, though not questioning the primary of the infrastructures, he sees the relationship between them, though expressed in logical terms, as complex, variable, even contradictory. Lévi-Strauss puts a focal emphasis on binary oppositions and appears to see the function of myths as essentially that of mediating or resolving structural oppositions that are evident in the natural and cultural world, as well as reconciling contradictions between mythical and experiential knowledge (see P. S. Cohen 1969: 347–9; Rossi 1983: 145). This leads Lévi-Strauss to play down the significance of the narrative and at times to imply that myths have an ideological function in concealing inherent contradiction. Significantly, of course, in view of my earlier discussion, Lévi-Strauss seems to suggest that the "message" of the myth is conveyed by the structure as a whole. Kirk and others have questioned Lévi-Strauss's use of the model of structural linguistics, suggesting that the function of language is to convey the content rather than to convey its

287

own structure (its grammatical and syntactical rules) and that it is there-fore misleading for Lévi-Strauss to suggest that the "meaning" of the myth is conveyed by its own structure (1970: 43).

It seems quite clear that Lévi-Strauss not only saw his advocacy of a structural approach to myth as akin to the approach of Freud and Marx – who, along with geology, he described as having had a formative influence upon his work (1955: 68–71) – but that he looked upon struc-turalism as essentially constituting the scientific method of analysis. Struc-turalism was therefore nothing new or novel, simply a "pale and faint imitation" of what the physical and biological scientists had been doing for a very long time – since the Renaissance. It is not surprising, there-fore, that he embraced cybernetic functionalism, with its emphasis on "system," with some enthusiasm. In an early review of structuralism, W. G. Runciman (1969) had already stressed that Lévi-Strauss's struc-tural method was phrased in such a way that it was in no way distinct from scientific explanations in general. The problem, as I indicated earlier, is the status and explanatory value of the "invariant structures" that Lévi-Strauss postulates. Is his method applicable only to cultural represen-tations such as totemism, kinship rules, and mythology, and does it imply a denial of the fundamentally historical nature of social phenomena?

Lévi-Strauss's structuralist theory has given rise to a plethora of critical studies and commentary, and this has established and affirmed his rep-utation as one of the most seminal social thinkers of the present decade (see Leach 1970, Shalvey 1979, Sperber 1979). Yet in spite of his im-portant and stimulating contributions to the study of kinship, myth, social structure, and folk classifications, there is an underlying feeling among many scholars that his overall theoretical approach is limiting, even stultifying, to our understanding of social life. Three points of criticism have been highlighted. The first is that although Lévi-Strauss is certainly a materialist or realist, in that he conceptualizes the "struc-tures" of the mind as existing apart from the anthropologist (Keat & Urry 1975: 124–32), in nature, as it were, as well as in the mind, such structured models, Piaget (1971: 106) and others have noted, are neither functional, nor historical, nor genetic. Lévi-Strauss's structuralism is es-sentially synchronic and ahistorical. Although Lévi-Strauss has fre-quently been compared to Freud, as the psychoanalyst of collective dreams (Shalvey 1979: 145), the whole tenor of his thought is undialect-ical. When Harris describes Lévi-Strauss as an "idealist" involved in a search for "meanings" through Hegelian "dialectics" (1980: 165–8), he seriously misrepresents Lévi-Strauss's position. But his conclusion – namely that structuralism is a "stationary dialectic," though a contradic-tion in terms, certainly conveys this limitation of Lévi-Straussian theory.

As Diamond put it, with Lévi-Strauss's theory, "The significance of human action is read out of existence" (1974: 305).

The tendency of defenders of Lévi-Strauss, such as Ino Rossi, to see this "static structuralism" as the only alternative to phenomenology (subjectivism) and behaviorism (objectivism) – both forms of empiricism – is highly parochial. And to equate humanistic, historical, and critical thinkers (Rousseau, Vico, and Marx) with the latter approach, as Rossi does, is quite misleading (1982: 3–4).

Second, the "nondialectical antinomies" that Lévi-Strauss emphasizes and that he sees as characteristic of human thought – particularly the opposition between nature and culture – may, as Diamond suggests, involve the imposition of Western dualistic concepts onto the thought of preliterate people. Not only are the categories "nature" and "culture" problematic as universal categories (MacCormack & Strathern 1980: Leacock 1981: 246–7), but the thought of tribal and "ancient" communities tends to be organismic and synthetic rather than mechanistic and dualistic (I have explored this issue elsewhere in my essay on changing conceptions of nature, 1981). The writings of Lee and Whorf clearly seem to imply that a nondualistic perspective is evident in the world views of many preclass societies.

Finally, Lévi-Strauss's many writings, divorced as they are from social and political problems, tend inevitably to be scholastic in style and substance. Not only do they tend to eliminate in a radical way all interest in history and human praxis, as well as in the problem of meaning (Goldmann 1969: 12), but his structuralism "avoids all mention of social processes such as exploitation, alienation, the extreme division of labour, modern war and the character of the state. His thirst for the ultimate evades our realities" (Diamond 1974: 300) – a harsh judgment, given his commitments at a personal level, but not, I think, unfair (cf. Leacock 1981: 209–22). Yet whenever Lévi-Strauss does write on political and economic issues, his writings have a critical and radical impulse, and his essay on cultural discontinuity (1973: 312–22), suggesting an intrinsic relationship between economic development and the underdevelopment of third world societies, is similar to that of Gunder Frank and anticipates his perspective.

In the final volume of his *Introduction to the Science of Mythology* (1981), Lévi-Strauss responds to the various criticisms of his work, and I conclude this section with a brief summary of his defense. First, he denies that his mode of analysis is formalist. Certainly Lévi-Strauss stresses that the "truth" of the myth does not lie in any special content; rather it consists of "logical relations which are devoid of content (1969: 240). This has led writers like Ricoeur to accuse Lévi-Strauss of discovering little more than "a sterile syntactic arrangement of a discourse that tells us nothing" – an assessment that is hard to gain from a reading of his mythological studies, which contain a wealth of empirical detail. For Lévi-Strauss there is no privileged order or code that forms the basis of the myth, but this does not imply that his analyses lack meaning. He stresses, to the contrary, that his studies are "packed with meaning " but warns us that we have to resign ourselves to the fact that myths tell us nothing instructive about the order of the world, the nature of reality, or the origin and destiny of mankind. It is latent mysticism to assume that they do. But he argues against the notion that form can be set against content, the concrete against the abstract, or the intellect against the senses, suggesting that structure "is content itself, apprehended in a logical organization conceived as property of the real" (1973: 115). There is, indeed, a latent Hegelianism running through Lévi-Strauss's writings, which leads him to pen such statements as "My work gets thought in me unbeknown to me" (1978:3).

Second, Lévi-Strauss has been criticized for his antihumanist stance and accused of "demolishing the human person." He has indeed been a critic of phenomenology and existentialism, with its "illusions of subjectivity," as his debate with Sartre suggests. His own shafts of criticism, however, are not aimed specifically at human agency per se but at the Cartesian notion that human consciousness has priority in cultural understanding. Like Hegel, Freud, and Marx he is antiempiricist, rather than antihumanist. Thus his response to this kind of criticism is to say, "The social sciences, following the example of the physical sciences, must grasp the fact that the reality of the object they are studying is not wholly limited to the level of the subject apprehending it" (1981: 638). But to recognize that "consciousness is not everything" is no reason, he writes, for abandoning it, anymore than Freud or Marx suggested abandoning reason. All three were rationalists.

Third, and linked with this attitude toward consciousness, Lévi-Strauss defends himself against the criticism that he underestimates or even ignores the importance of the emotions and the lived experiences of individual subjects. He denies that he does this but reiterates his position, first expressed in his essay on totemism, that the emotions are secondary to the intellect and have no explanatory priority. In an important critique of Turner's writings on Ndembu ritual symbolism, Lévi-Strauss argues that "ritual is not a reaction to life; it is a reaction to what thought has made of life. It is not a direct response to the world, or even to experience of the world; it is a response to the way man thinks of the world" (1981: 681).

Finally, just as Lévi-Strauss's failure to give subjective meaning analytical priority did not necessarily imply that he was antihumanist, so his tendency to give structural analysis priority over historical explanations did not imply, as many have suggested, that he was "antihistory." He certainly drew a distinction, like Boas, between anthropology and history, and, as his debate with Sartre suggests, he was reluctant to give priority to historical knowledge. But Lévi-Strauss clearly saw diachronic studies as an adjunct to structural analysis, the latter engaging in a "transformational" rather than a "fluxional" method (1973: 18), and he applauds the writings of Evans-Pritchard, which, he noted, showed the reciprocal influence of history and structure (239). Certain developments of social life require a diachronic analysis, and even synchronic studies demand a constant recourse to history. By showing institutions in the process of transformation, he wrote, history alone makes it possible to abstract the structural patterns (1963: 22).

Lévi-Strauss suggested that his studies were an attempt to reintegrate anthropological knowledge into the Marxist tradition, and he always affirmed that they had a deterministic and realistic inspiration (1969: 27). Yet their main emphasis was never on human praxis as such but always on the "thought-of" orders of myth and cultural representations (1963: 313). The human mind, for Lévi-Strauss, seems to mediate between these orders and the economic infrastructures, the "lived-in" orders. Thus anthropology for Lévi-Strauss is more a philosophy of knowledge than a comparative sociology. Whereas Hegel, Marx, Weber, Freud, and Evans-Pritchard express an uneasy tension between the humanistic and scientific dimensions of social thought, Lévi-Strauss, following Durkheim, takes his bearings by reference to the aspirations and methods of the natural sciences. In an important sense, therefore, Lévi-Strauss remains true to the heritage of the Enlightenment.

Modes of thought

In the decade after the publication of *The Savage Mind* in 1966, and under the combined influences of Evans-Pritchard and Lévi-Strauss, a renewed interest in religious thought emerged within anthropology and this took two forms. One was an interest in symbolic classifications; the other was a debate into the nature of religious thought. In a sense they represent the hermeneutic and comparative dimensions of Evans-Pritchard's work. Both interests are reflected in two important symposium studies.

The collection of articles on dualistic symbolic classifications, edited by Rodney Needham (1973), is largely of a structuralist orientation, though each article focuses on a specific ethnographic context. Two examples will be considered here. The first is a seminal essay written by a student of Durkheim's, Robert Hertz. Entitled "The Pre-eminence of the Right Hand: A Study in Religious Polarity," it was originally published in 1909 and forms the leading essay in the collection.

Every social hierarchy, Hertz suggested, claims to be founded on the nature of things and accords itself eternity. Thus men who are affronted by feminist claims allege that women are naturally inferior. The right hand is the symbol and model of all aristocracies. Is its preeminence, Hertz asks, based on biological factors? He thinks not. How closely the two hands resemble each other, yet, almost universally, they are accorded unequal value. Such ideas, Hertz suggests, have their genesis in religious beliefs and emotions and thus can be understood only by a comparative analysis of social institutions.

The fundamental opposition that dominates the spiritual world of preliterate communities, Hertz writes, is that between the sacred and the profane. This dualism so dominates their social organization that the two moieties that constitute a tribe are reciprocally opposed as sacred and profane, a person's own moiety being considered sacred. With the evolution of social systems, this reversible dualism is replaced, according to Hertz, by a hierarchical structure made up of classes or castes, those ranking high being considered sacred and superior. But the principle remains the same: "Social polarity is still a reflection and a consequence of religious polarity" (8).

Durkheim's influence is clear here, though Hertz appears to give the religious categories priority. Hertz notes that this dualism is reflected in other symbolic oppositions: light and dark, sky and earth, high and low, and that the sexual categorization is often extended to all beings in the universe, even to inanimate objects. He cites the Maori and their division between *tama tane*, "male side," which designates a diversity of things – men's virility, patrilineal descent, creative force, offensive magic – and *tama wahine*, the "female side," which covers everything that is contrary to these. Such cosmic distinctions, he suggests, rest on a primordial religious antithesis that marks the "entire thought" of preliterate people. The human body is simply a microcosm, a reflection of this "law of polarity which governs everything." The different symbolic values associated with the right and left hand, which are common in many societies and reflected in most Indo-European languages (right expressing the ideas of strength, activity, rectitude, moral integrity, and good fortune, and left signifying most of the ideas contrary to these) are seen therefore as being based on the fundamental opposition between the sacred and the profane. The meaning and source of this polarity, which dominates religious life and is "imposed on the boy itself," Hertz does not explore.

But he recapitulates the basic ideas that form the basis of Durkheim's sociology of knowledge, namely that symbolic dualisms are linked to the structure of social thought, rather than being innate or derived from individual experience.

A second example is the essay by Rodney Needham. Influenced by Evans-Pritchard, his work has essentially been concerned with outlining the basic intellectual principles by which a society's values and ideas are ordered. His structuralism is therefore more empiricist and sociological than that of Lévi-Strauss, and it is interesting that in his brief introduction to his study *Symbolic Classification* (1979) he makes no reference to this important scholar.

One of Needham's early essays (1961) was devoted to an ethnographic puzzle, namely why the left hand of the Mugwe, a religious leader among the Meru people of Kenya, was considered to have ritual power. In a study of this prophet, B. Bernardi (1959) had written that his left hand, which was kept covered, was considered sacred, a source of spiritual power. Such observations were counter to Hertz's notion of the universal preeminence of the right hand. In an examination of the ethnographic record of the Meru, Needham discerned a dualistic classificatory symbolism. The various subtribes, for instance, were divided into two divisions associated with the north and south, and the age-set system too was seen as a dichotomous organization. In fact a good deal of Meru social life and thought was consistent with a symbolic classification in which each binary pair is analogically related by the principle of complementary dualism.

The Meru scheme may be outlined as follows:

Right	Left
East	West
North	South
White clans	Black clans
Day	Night
Senior	Junior
Light	Dark
Political power	Ritual authority
Cultivation	Honey-gathering
Male	Female

Needham stresses that this systematic ordering of experience is based on analogy; that the terms, like the Yin–Yang classification, are complementary; and that context is important. For example, the Mugwe, the ritual expert, was superior to the elders in a ritual context, but in a profane context he was not. Thus Needham suggests that the reason why the left hand of the Mugwe was considered sacred was that it was in accordance with this symbolic ordering and consistent with the total scheme of relations between the particular terms.

In concluding this essay, Needham stresses the validity and usefulness of this type of structural analysis and suggests that the near universality of this sort of dualistic symbolism may indicate the "natural proclivities of the human mind" (1973: 123). He is aware, however, that symbolic classifications are not everywhere of a dualistic kind; more complex symbolic classifications may be evident in other societies, and the "range" of symbolic structures may be variable. He notes too that we have among the Meru an interesting example of dual sovereignty, the distinction between the elders and the Mugwe reflecting a complementary division, found in many oriental states, between secular power and religious authority, between the functions of king and priest.

Needham's article on Nyoro symbolism (1967) replicates the form of analysis that he used with reference to the prophet Mugwe. For he poses the question as to why the Nyoro diviner uses his left hand in casting cowrie shells (given the notion of the pre-eminence of the right hand and the fact that left-handed people are "hated" by the Nyoro) and answers the question by outlining the dualistic classification system of the Nyoro which is similar to that of the Meru.

Right	Left
Man	Woman
Heaven	Earth
White	Black
Purity	Impurity
Classified	Anomalous
Life	Death
Security	Danger
Hard	Soft

And he notes too the secular–mystical diarchy, or complementary governance, that is evident in the Nyoro political system, as well as the importance of ritual reversals.

The kind of analysis suggested by Needham has been criticized by various scholars. Indeed Needham's introduction to the collection of essays *Right and Left* is largely devoted to countering a critique of his own analysis of the Nyoro by John Beattie. This ethnographer had questioned whether "all the terms listed in the column headed by the word 'right' ... are thought of as good, auspicious and esteemed" by the Nyoro people (1968: 435). For Beattie, Nyoro symbolic dualism did not form a totality, or a systematic body of ideas, but rather related to a very much narrower range of Nyoro collective representations. Needham's response was that the "two-column" schema he had outlined was simply a mnemonic or suggestive device, and, because it was based on analogy, did not imply that all the terms in either column were necessarily associated. Moreover, Needham stressed that context was of overriding importance in ascertaining the structural position of the contrasting values.

The issue is this: What degree of consistency must there be, both in the structural oppositions and in the analogous links, for such symbolism to be termed a classification? In his analysis of both the Meru and the Nyoro, Needham suggests that there is a coherence in the dualistic schema, such that it forms a symbolic order. Beidelman too (1973) considered the symbolism to form a "consistent whole," whereas one writer who has followed this type of analysis closely goes even further in asserting (with respect to Tetum symbolism) that the "dyads contained in the matrix cohere into a set," thus forming a symbolic "unity" that brings together all aspects of cultural experience into a "meaningful whole" (Hicks 1976: 108).

Jack Goody has offered some further and cogent criticisms of Needham's structural approach and has suggested

(1)   that a strictly contextual approach (advocated by Needham) renders a tabulation of symbols as a fixed matrix simplistic and crude and obscures the ambivalent and polysemic nature of many symbols (as stressed by Turner).

(2)   rather than providing a "key" for the understanding of preliterate cultures, such analyses often confound folk and Western categories.

(3)   that the classifications do not represent a basic cultural code, for the schemata are either derived from ritual specialists or are evident only in the ritual context.

(4)   that the type of dualistic thinking these schemata exemplify is more characteristic of literate communities, particularly societies in the early phases of literacy, than of preliterate communities. Dualistic symbolism may therefore be the product of "our tables," Goody suggests, "rather than [of] their thoughts" (1977: 65).

This final criticism may be debatable, but Goody is clearly on the right track in suggesting that there is a close relationship between the elaboration of classificatory symbolism and the advent of literacy. Since the latter was linked to the rise of theocratic states, such symbolism, the product of a specialized literati, undoubtedly had an ideological function. Goody notes, however, the similarity between the classificatory symbolism of the Zuni and Dogon and what is indicated in Culpeper's *Herbal* – a point made by Lévi-Strauss. But Lévi-Strauss was keen to stress that although we are willing to attribute a natural philosophy to astrological herbalists, there is some reluctance to credit preliterate cultures with such theoretical knowledge. Douglas, Lévi-Strauss, and Hertz – all Durkheimian sociologists – took an extreme view in implying that all preliterate communities had complex symbolic classifications that "unified" experience. Goody's writings seem to suggest the opposite extreme and to deny that preliterate communities have integrated symbol systems – or rather that the classificatory symbolism that has been recorded is held to be a literary elaboration, a function of the ethnographer's own search for order. The truth probably lies between the two extremes.

Complex classificatory symbolism has, of course, been noted in many tribal societies. I have, in earlier chapters, already discussed the triadic symbolism of the Ndembu and the Zuni system of ritual classification. Indeed, many of the cultures examined in Needham's text have a more complex symbolism than the dualistic pattern outlined. Both the Gogo of Tanzania (Rigby 1966) and the Mapuche Indians of Chile (Faron 1962), for instance, have a symbolic classificatory pattern based on six directions that is identical, in structure at least, with that of the Zuni Indians. Different cultures, as Douglas has indicated, may employ different aspects of experience in developing a symbolic code: color among the Ndembu, space among the Zuni (1975: 125).

One could mention, of course, the best-known symbolic classification of all – astrology, which is steeped in the history of all the early literate civilizations. The term *zodiac*, in fact, is derived from the ancient Greek word *zodiakos*, meaning "having to do with animals," which suggests a totemic origin. Greek medicine, too, was based on a symbolic classificatory system, organized around the four humors of the body and the four seasons (Seznec 1953: 46–9). Neither of these is mentioned by Needham, who sees the task of anthropology as essentially that of delineating the indigenous criteria by which things are defined and classified in a particular society (1979: 15). (For other interesting studies of symbolic classifications, cf. Griaule 1965, Granet 1973.)

I turn now to the debate on the nature of so-called primitive (that is, religious) thought.

In their introduction to the important symposium *Modes of Thought* (1973), Horton and Finnegan suggest that in Evans-Pritchard's classic study of the Azande Lévy-Bruhl's early theory is being tested, even though, as I have said, he is not mentioned in the text. In fact Evans-Pritchard notes that he is going to avoid theoretical issues relating to the sociological explanation of ritual and mystical notions and will let his interpretations emerge as part of the description (5). Yet, as Horton and Finnegan note, many features of the book reflect the stimulus of Lévy-Bruhl's work. There is the insistence that people's beliefs are determined

296

by the culture they belong to and that the people of an alien culture think neither more nor less rationally than ourselves but simply live out their lives in the light of different theoretical premises. And finally, Evans-Pritchard accepts Lévy-Bruhl's contrast between empirical (in which he lumps together, like Malinowski, both common sense and science) and mystical beliefs. Unlike Lévy-Bruhl, however, he argues that the Azande spend much of their time at the level of common sense, adopting a mystical stance only in times of crisis or misfortune.

Many of those who have written recently on the relationship between science and religious thought have attempted to exorcise the ghost of Lévy-Bruhl, and though they may differ widely in their approaches they have frequently taken Evans-Pritchard as a point of reference. Leaving aside Lévy-Bruhl's own theory of "primitive mentality" and such theories, which maintain that religious thought (specifically that of preliterate people) is unintelligible to Europeans, one may, I think, delineate three approaches to the question of the rationality of religious thought. These are the *contextual*, the *symbolist*, and the *intellectualist* approaches.

The first approach, the *contextual*, has been advocated by a number of writers and derives in a sense from Evans-Pritchard's treatment of the Azande and Nuer material. This approach suggests that we adopt an attitude of sympathy and charity toward alien beliefs, no matter how strange and illogical they may appear to be. In his distinction between empirical and ritual behavior, Evans-Pritchard suggested that the latter involved "no objective nexus between the behaviour and the event it is intended to cause" (1937: 12). Such behavior therefore can be made intelligible only by knowing the mystical notions associated with it and by exploring the context and background of the beliefs. The essay by Martin Hollis entitled "Reason and Ritual" (1970) exemplifies this approach, for Hollis argues that ritual can be identified and understood not by looking for empirical truth conditions nor by recourse to metaphor but only by an appeal to "our own criteria of rationality" (227). Like Evans-Pritchard, he suggests that although religious beliefs may be empirically invalid, they are rational, or at least can be understood and rendered meaningful only if they are assumed to be so. He argues, however, against the view of Peter Winch, who, in his well-known text *The Idea of a Social Science* (1958), had taken an extreme relativist position, considering the notions of reality and rationality as relative to a particular community's conceptual scheme. For Hollis, Winch's theoretical position, like that of American linguist Whorf, was simply untenable, for without the existence of a "bridgehead" – shared assumptions about empirical perception and empirical truth – even translation, he holds, would be impossible. "Interpretative charity" is the mode of approach Hollis advocates, though he is aware of the dangers of collapsing into relativism. (For more recent discussions of this issue, see Hollis & Lukes 1982.)

The philosopher Ludwig Wittgenstein has had an enormous influence on some empirical anthropologists, particularly Needham, and it is one of Wittgenstein's classic phrases – "The limits of my language mean the limits of my world" – that forms the crux of Winch's approach. In a later essay (1970), Winch even criticizes Evans-Pritchard for not taking seriously enough his own premise that the "concepts used by primitive people can only be interpreted in the context of the way of life of those people." Assuming that for the Azande magical beliefs are one of the principal foundations of their whole social life, Winch argues that Evans-Pritchard assumed that the scientific conception of reality is the correct one and that the Azande magical beliefs are mistaken. This, Winch appears to suggest, is inadmissible. Evans-Pritchard, of course, linked science with common sense – "Science has developed out of common sense" (12) – and did not assume that the Azande lacked empirical beliefs (in fact, he stressed the contrary), so the dichotomy Winch makes between Evans-Pritchard's own conception of reality and that of the Azande is not as stark as he implies. Nonetheless Winch takes the contextual approach to extremes, suggesting that preliterate conceptual ideas can be understood only in their own terms. In doing so he implies that there are no universal or context-free criteria of truth and validity; no evaluative judgments can therefore be made regarding the cognitive status of such beliefs.

Numerous critiques of this form of relativism have been made. Lukes (1973), for example, has stressed that the existence of a common "reality" is a necessary precondition for understanding another culture or even for learning another language, and he argues pervasively that there are universal criteria of truth and logic. The danger lies, he suggests, in confusing such fundamental criteria with the current content of European beliefs and using the latter as a yardstick for classifying other people's beliefs. An anthropologist should therefore, Luke suggests, be critical of his or her own beliefs without embracing any form of epistemological relativism. By adopting the latter one fails to see any disjunction, he writes, between social consciousness or ideology and social realities and is thus unable to raise any "questions about the ways in which belief-systems prevent or promote social change" (243).

The same general criticisms have been made by another social philosopher, Ernest Gellner, who in a series of trenchant essays has consistently argued against the type of conceptual relativism espoused by Winch. Gellner began his academic career as a philosopher at Oxford, but having published a devastating critique of Wittgenstein's philosophy

(*Words and Things*, 1959), he was, as it were, ceremonially expelled from the tribe, for the journal *Mind* refused to review his book. He therefore took up social anthropology and did some important research among the Berbers of Morocco (1969). Since then he has written an endless stream of critical essays and reviews on contemporary intellectual trends, particularly with respect to the idealist perspectives of Leach and Needham (Gellner 1973). What is of interest in the present context is Gellner's rejection of relativism and the "charter of toleration," and of the contextual approach that this theory implies.

Gellner notes that what most people deem to be a problem – that truth is different on the other side of the Pyrenees – the relativist takes as a solution. To the relativist, truth is that which is locally believed, and this can be determined only by an examination of the "forms of life" (a phrase taken from the later Wittgenstein) that a particular language or culture exhibits. Such a stance, taken by Winch, allows no universal, independent criteria of truth. The problem is, as Gellner stresses, that there are numerous, diverse, and overlapping forms of life, many of which are contradictory or undergoing change. Which one of them is to be accepted? A consistent relativist like Winch seems to suggest that all of them are acceptable and to imply that witchcraft and science are equally valid. Leaving aside the important problem, noted by Gellner, that Winch gives us no warrant to apply his relativism to his own argument, Gellner's main criticism is that relativism as an intellectual recipe is both empty and worthless (1974: 50). It is like a signpost that is unhinged. What sane person would take guidance from it, Gellner asks? But, significantly, such a philosophy leads to an overvaluation of cultural tolerance and contextual interpretations, against which Gellner makes some cogent criticisms.

First, Gellner feels that the "charter of tolerance" granted by relativism is suspect. Genuine toleration, he writes, does not presume that everything and anything may be true; it merely says that only arguments, rather than force or pressure of any kind, may be used in persuasion. It distinguishes between social toleration and logical toleration, for the latter (relativism) implies the abandonment of reason. If nothing is universally true, who are you to defy local custom or authorities? (48).

Second, the notion of contextual interpretation itself is more problematic than its proponents realize. Gellner indicates that the amount and kind of context, and the way the context itself is determined, depend on a priori assumptions about the kind of interpretation one wishes to find. The assumption that all beliefs are rational and logical, and thus that beliefs that seem contrary to common sense in terms of their social context or their place in a conceptual scheme are also rational and logical, Gellner suggests, is going too far. Such all-embracing logical charity, he argues, may lead us into thinking that there are no societies with absurd or inconsistent beliefs, yet the approach adopted ensures that it could not be otherwise. He examines Evans-Pritchard's analysis of the Azande and Nuer material, and notes "how Evans-Pritchard takes Nuer statements which, on the face of it, violate common sense, and also others which go counter to a dualistic theology ... and how, by holding these statements to be metaphorical and elliptical, he squares them with common sense and an acceptable theology" (1973: 36–7).

The trouble with the "excessive indulgence in contextual charity," Gellner holds, is that it not only evades theoretical issues relating to social change and to conflicts between contending doctrines and paradigms, but it also blinds us to the possibility of examining the social role of absurd or inconsistent beliefs as a form of social control – that is, as ideologies. Contextual interpretation, Gellner concludes, is valuable, but at the same time liable to disastrous abuse (44).

This contextual approach to the rationality of the religious beliefs of preliterate people is frequently linked with what has been termed the "intellectualist" approach to ritual, stemming from Tylor and Frazer. Skorupski (1976) gives a basic outline of this approach in four propositions or stages. The first poses the question Why do people in traditional cultures perform magical and religious actions? They perform them, Tylor and Frazer suggest, because they believe them to be the means of achieving certain ends that they seek. The actions are rational in terms of such beliefs. Second, Why are such beliefs accepted? Here the intellectualist answer, according to Skorupski, is that the believer grows up in a culture where religious and magical beliefs are theoretical postulates that are socially legitimate. A third question arises: Why do people go on believing such doctrines when, on the anthropologist's reckoning, these are clearly untenable? The answer to this, which Tylor discusses in detail, is that there are structural and attitudinal doctrines that act as "blocks to falsifiability" (5): improper performance of rites, counter-magic, and the like. Thus far, Evans-Pritchard's approach is consistent with that of Tylor, but the intellectualist poses a further question, namely, How did the beliefs originate in the first place? And the answer given is that they arose out of a need to understand and control the natural environment. Hence preliterate religion is to be seen as rational and intellectual, as a crude natural philosophy – even if it now seems faulty and erroneous. As Frazer put it, "Their errors are not wilful extravagances or the ravings of insanity, but simply hypotheses ... which a fuller experience has proved inadequate" (1976: 348).

300

A writer who has consistently followed Frazer and combined an intellectualist approach with one advocating situational (contextual) logic is I. C. Jarvie. In an early study on cargo cults (1964), Jarvie argued that religious beliefs are essentially rational in that they offer theoretical explanations for events in the world. This idea, as Jarvie admits, is in the "Frazerian tradition." But Jarvie also argues (primarily against Lucy Mair's contention that cargo cults were nonrational) that, given their frame of reference, members of cargo cults in their rituals, which were goal-directed, were acting perfectly rationally (131). He developed these ideas in a further paper on the rationality of magic, written in conjunction with the philosopher Joseph Agassi (1967). This essay is specifically directed against the symbolist approach to ritual advocated by Beattie (which I discuss later) and hinges on a distinction between two forms of rationality, namely, rational action, seen as goal-directed behavior, and rationality in terms of rational beliefs. Jarvie and Agassi waver ambiguously between equating rational beliefs with science and assuming that magic, like science, is also rational. They rebuke Beattie for his parochialism in assuming that science is the mark of rationality and for failing to admit that error can be based on rational thought. In rejecting Frazer's idea that ritual action is erroneous (for this would imply a derogatory evaluation of preliterate people) and in stressing that all cultures have technical knowledge, Jarvie and Agassi maintain that Beattie is ethnocentric and has a naive, empiricist view of science. Marred by such polemics, their essay lacks a certain clarity, but nonetheless they provide a good illustration of the intellectualist approach to religion.

The *symbolist* approach to religion has been discussed in earlier chapters, for it is represented by such writers as Leach, Turner, and Douglas and reflects a particular interpretation of Durkheim's work. This approach tends to avoid any discussion regarding the seeming irrationality of magical and religious beliefs, for it argues that these beliefs are to be interpreted as symbolic. Douglas regarded Frazer's interest in the efficacy of rituals as an intellectual "blind alley" (1966: 30) that could only lead to preliterate people's being considered childish and irrational, as she felt Frazer viewed them. Leach, on the other hand, regarded as "scholastic nonsense" all theoretical discussions about the content and rationality of religious beliefs (1954: 13). To him, as we have seen, "ritual action and belief are alike to be understood as forms of symbolic statement about the social order" (14). But as Skorupski notes (1976: 21), it was not Tylor and Frazer who regarded religious beliefs as irrational but Leach himself. And the same may be said of Douglas's criticisms of Frazer: Magical beliefs for Frazer were rational, and the flaw was not in the reasoning but in the premises, which led to erroneous conclusions.

Although both Frazer and Lévy-Bruhl may have implied derogatory attitudes toward preliterate people, it is worth stressing that they held very different theoretical orientations. Frazer implied a similarity between the intellectual procedures of science and magic, where Lévy-Bruhl postulated an intellectual gulf between them, for science was rational and logical, magico-religious beliefs mystical and nonlogical. The symbolists, like Lévy-Bruhl, view religious beliefs as essentially nonlogical. Talcott Parsons expressed this view succinctly when he remarked that "ritual actions are not ... simply irrational, or pseudo-rational, based on pre-scientific erroneous knowledge, but are of a different character altogether and as such are not to be measured by the standards of intrinsic rationality at all" (1968: 431). Likewise Firth held that religious beliefs belong to the "same order of creative imaginative reality as the arts, sharing the same general kind of non-empirical assumptions" (1964: 238).

Although it has been a long-standing approach to religion, the symbolist mode of interpretation has come to be closely associated with John Beattie, whose essay on ritual and social change (1966) was a careful and explicit statement of what this type of theory implied. It was also a response to what he felt was a "back-to-Frazer" movement in social anthropology. Three writers were seen by Beattie as exemplifying the latter.

The first was Jack Goody, who defined ritual as behavior in which the "relationship between the means and the end is not intrinsic, i.e., is either irrational or non-rational" (1961: 142). Though Beattie does not directly refute this, he feels that to define ritual in terms of unintelligibility leads us nowhere. The second was Robin Horton, who had argued in an early paper (1964) that the religious concepts of the Kalabari implied a "passionate interest in explanation" and were comparable to scientific theories. And finally, there was I. C. Jarvie, whose analysis of Melanesian cargo cults, noted earlier, implied that the ritual response to social change was the result of a "purely intellectual craving" (1964: 166).

Beattie felt that all three perspectives were misleading and that ritual could be more fruitfully understood if seen as essentially expressive behavior. There is, he argues, a "crucial difference" between scientific and practical procedures, on the one hand, and ritual procedures on the other; the latter is rather like art or drama, a kind of language. Thus cargo rituals are not explanatory or intellectual activities but "recourses, in times of stress, to the consolations of rite and drama; in a very fundamental sense to the consolations of make-believe." Linking technology with science, Beattie quotes with approval Malinowski's assertion that magic is a "sober, prosaic, even clumsy art, enacted for purely practical reasons," and defends the validity of Durkheim's sacred–profane dichotomy.

In a later essay, responding to the criticisms of Jarvie and Agassi, Beattie develops these ideas and gives a lucid account of the symbolist approach, noting the similarity between his ideas and those of Firth and Leach. Again there is the distinction between "practical," empirically based procedures, "which can be understood when the ends sought and the techniques used by the actor are grasped," and ritual acts, which can only be understood, he feels, by a comprehension of their meanings as symbolic statements. Following Leach, he suggests that this distinction usually refers to aspects of social actions rather than to specific acts, but insists that the distinction is analytically important.

Thus for Beattie, to quote from his earlier paper,

> the sensible student of myth, magic and religion will . . . be well advised to recognize that their tenets are not scientific propositions, based on experience and on a belief in the uniformity of nature, and that they cannot be adequately understood as if they were. Rather, as symbolic statements, they are to be understood by a delicate investigation of the levels and varieties of meaning which they have for their practitioners, by eliciting, through comparative and contextual study, the principles of association in terms of which they are articulated, and by investigating the kinds of symbolic classifications which they imply. (1966: 72)

Beattie admits that in seeking specific goals through ritual a person is behaving rationally, and he regards Jarvie and Agassi's stress on this as somewhat puzzling. "No present-day social anthropologist," he writes, "denies so obvious a truism" (1970: 246). But to stress this as an explanation, Beattie feels, hardly advances our understanding of magical behavior. He is even more puzzled by their criticisms of scientific thought and resolutely maintains that magical beliefs are not rational, reserving the notion of rationality for scientific procedures: the formulation of hypotheses (no matter at what level of abstraction and complexity), and their testing against experience. This sort of intellectual procedure, evident in science as well as in the building of a grass hut, differs fundamentally, Beattie argues, from symbolism, whether in the context of magic, religion, or art. And it is because these two modes of thought have to be understood in different ways that it is important to distinguish them.

With respect to the rationality of magico-religious beliefs, Beattie suggests that they are irrational in the sense that they are not of the same order as the empirically grounded and testable hypotheses of science or common sense, but they are by no means irrational in the sense that they lack coherent organization or rationale (257). There are, then, two kinds of "truth," those of practical experience and those of religion, myth, and poetry (symbolism). Thus Beattie suggests that if the terms *mystical* and *prelogical* are interpreted as applying to symbolic procedures, then the "symbolist" approach was foreshadowed by the writings of Lévy-Bruhl (259). Significantly, the dichotomy is to be viewed not as distinguishing different types of cultures but aspects of all societies.

It is against this sort of approach that the important writings of Robin Horton have been largely directed. He has, in a series of essays, consistently advocated an *intellectualist* approach to the study of religion. His classic paper "African Traditional Thought and Western Science" (1967) succinctly outlines his basic ideas.

Horton's essential thesis is that African traditional thought can be best understood if it is seen as a theoretical activity that has affinities with science. He enumerates what he thinks are the essential similarities.

First, the question for theoretical explanation, he suggests, is basically a quest for unity underlying apparent diversity, and for ordered regularities underlying the apparent complexity and disorder of the world. Adopting an approach that is not specifically empiricist but that concedes the reality of both common-sense things and theoretical entities, he argues that African religious cosmologies form an underlying schema that interprets a diversity of everyday experience in terms of a limited number of entities. He notes that among the Kalabari three types of spirits – ancestors, heroes, and water spirits – are seen as causal agents relating to many aspects of Kalabari life. Such spirits, he suggests, are equivalent to scientific entities like atoms and molecules and introduce conceptual order. Seen this way, the puzzles raised by Lévy-Bruhl, such as the question of how a person could literally see a spirit in a stone – come to make sense.

Second, and this is an important point, theory places things in a causal context broader than that provided by common sense. Horton notes that an idea widespread throughout Africa is that affliction is caused by spiritual agencies and that divination invariably involves reference to some event in the world of visible, tangible happenings. Thus a causal link is postulated between disturbed social relations and disease or misfortune, and this, Horton thinks, has affinities with scientific theories, which also link events in the phenomenal world. It can be seen, then, that Horton, unlike the symbolists, links religion with science and sees them both as theoretical activities and as distinct from common sense. though accepting that the nexus between social disturbance and individual affliction postulated by traditional religion is expressed in a personal idiom, he feels that it is misleading to describe it as "nonempirical." Indeed he suggests that some of the connections made might be substantiated by medical science and points to some interesting similarities between the concepts of psychoanalytic theory and West African theories of the soul.

Third, Horton suggests that common sense and theory have complementary roles in everyday life. For much of the time, he suggests, people in all cultures "live" in the everyday world of common sense, and it is only in certain circumstances that there is a need to "jump" from common sense to theoretical (mystical) thinking. Among the Kalabari, for example, the treatment of illness by herbal medicines takes place in an atmosphere of common sense, it is only when the sickness fails to respond to treatment that recourse is made to spiritual agencies as explanations.

Horton makes several other interesting points relating to the nature of theory: that the level of theory varies with the context, and that there is a frequent use of analogies drawn from familiar phenomena and experience.

In treating traditional African religious systems as theoretical models akin to those of science, Horton sought to stress the continuities between religion and science and to question the usefulness of some familiar dichotomies – rational versus mystical, empirical versus nonempirical, for example. But he did not mean to imply that traditional thought was a kind of science and indeed sought to delineate some of the crucial differences between the two modes of thought. These hinge on two issues.

First, Horton suggests that traditional cultures, unlike science, have no developed awareness of alternatives to the established body of theoretical tenets. These tenets are in a sense held sacred and constitute something of a "closed" system of thought. He quotes from Evans-Pritchard's study of the Azande to illustrate this absence of alternatives.

Second, and a consequence of this, any challenge to the established beliefs with regard to traditional religion is seen, Horton suggests, as a "threat of chaos, of the cosmic abyss, and therefore evokes intense anxiety." There are "secondary elaborations" that protect the major theoretical assumptions, and "taboo-reactions" with respect to events that seriously defy the established lines of classification. Moreover, through rites of renewal and through symbolic classifications, the passage of time tends to be encapsulated within the conceptual system, and in this Horton echoes the writings of Eliade and Lévi-Strauss. Horton is also aware, citing Kuhn's important study (1962), that scientists often become entrenched in their attitudes toward established paradigms, but, as he writes, "The picture of the scientist in continuous readiness to scrap or demote established theory contains a dangerous exaggeration as well as an important truth" (1967: 163).

To summarize: African traditional thought, Horton therefore maintains, is akin to science in being a theoretical activity that has explanatory functions. It differs from science in that its theoretical concepts are expressed in a personal idiom (spirits, witches) and in being a closed system of thought. He admits, however, that the scientific method is the most efficient means of ascertaining valid causal connections.

Some cogent criticisms of this thesis have been made by many writers, and they have given rise to some interesting discussions on modes of thought. First, as Beattie and Douglas have both suggested, science is largely grounded in the concept of a mechanistic universe, and this implies that there is always an important moral component to religious explanations.

Second, spiritual agencies are clearly more than a set of explanatory concepts, for they are propitiated and are treated as having volition. Moreover, certain magical beliefs have the status of empirical knowledge for the people concerned, with no theoretical mediation – for example, the Nuer belief that incest causes leprosy.

Third, as Beattie stresses in an important and sympathetic critique of Horton, Horton equates African traditional thought with religion (1970: 259–68). It is not immediately obvious, Beattie asks, why African rather than Western religion should be compared with science, and writes, "If religious beliefs are to be compared with 'scientific' ones, it might be thought more instructive to compare them in the same cultural context" (260).

And finally, although writers like Tambiah and Barnes have followed Horton in stressing the important role that analogy plays in both magic and science, many writers have questioned the distinction Horton makes with respect to the "openness" of science. Barnes, for instance, citing Kuhn, asks whether so much explanatory weight can be attached to the openness of the individual scientist, who may often cling tenaciously to established paradigms (1973: 189–91). This is reminiscent of the earlier writings of Polanyi (1958), who argued persuasively that scientific thought was comparable to that of the Azande not only in its logical structure but in its secondary elaborations and in its treatment of anomalies or of experience that ran counter to a particular scientific theory. On the other hand, Gellner argues that Horton's choice of quotations from Evans-Pritchard's work on the Azande is selective and that there are many passages in that study denoting a skeptical and open attitude toward their own beliefs by the Azande (1973: 167).

In a later essay (1973), Horton makes an interesting comparison between Lévy-Bruhl and Durkheim. He notes that these two scholars were essentially agreed in arguing that individual thought was socially deter

mined and that preliterate thought was basically religious, but that they
parted company in their descriptions of the relationship between science
and religion. For Lévy-Bruhl the distinction was one of contrast and of
historical change in terms of intellectual movements – the "great transition" – a pattern of inversion, with science replacing religion. For Durkheim, on the other hand, Horton argues, there is an essential continuity
between these two modes of thought, science developing out of religious
thought, for both are seen as intellectual activities. The intellectual history of humankind has been one of evolution and increasing specialization rather than of inversion, with one mode of thought giving way
before its opposite. Horton goes on to discuss how even writers who
have been most critical of Lévy-Bruhl – for example, Malinowski and
Lévi-Strauss – have tended to fit into the contrast/inversion school. Although seemingly deriving inspiration from Durkheim rather than Lévy-
Bruhl, Lévi-Strauss nonetheless considered that there were two modes
of thought that were incommensurable: Wild thought attempts to grasp
the world through symbol and metaphor and is essentially nonpractical;
domesticated thought (science) aims at achieving practical goals, and its
development is controlled by success and failure in achieving these goals.
Lévi-Strauss, Horton suggests, evades any discussion of religion, seeing
it as the domain of confusion and emotion. Thus there is no great
difference between Lévi-Strauss and the more prosaic symbolists of the
Anglo-Saxon tradition like Leach and Beattie when it comes to a discussion of science and religion, for they all take a particular interpretation of Durkheim's work that ignores his main thesis, namely that
religion is an intellectual precursor of science. This has come about,
Horton contends, by their focusing on the sacred–profane dichotomy
of Durkheim rather than on his discussion of the relationship between
science and religion, from which Horton quotes extensively (cf. Durkheim 1915: 236–9). Horton contends, rightly I think, that Durkheim's
main ideas about religion were intellectualist rather than symbolist in
orientation and that most contemporary anthropologists, though claiming to be disciples of Durkheim, have ignored the main theme of *Elementary Forms of the Religious Life* regarding the theoretical content and
aspirations of preliterate thought.

In a review of recent ethnographic monographs on African religion,
Horton suggests that these give the impression that traditional religious
concepts can best be understood not as "symbolic substitutes for literal
discourse, nor as expressions of emotions, nor yet as manifestations of
some mystical communion between man and nature, but simply as theoretical concepts couched in a slightly unfamiliar idiom" (1973: 278).
This is a reassertion of his earlier theory. In addition he argues that

both the history and the philosophy of science support his own and Durkheim's perspective. For recent writings on science have stressed the inadequacy of the Baconian idea that science is nothing more than the expansion and systematization of common sense and have noted the continuities and parallels between science and traditional religious thought. The writings of Polanyi and Popper and other philosophers of science, Horton feels, support Durkheim's main thesis.

Why, then, have contemporary anthropologists and sociologists, though acclaiming Durkheim's intellectual stature, ignored his insights and theoretical attitudes? Horton suggests that two influential ideological trends have been responsible for this.

The first is what he calls *liberal romanticism*. Reacting against the dominant trends of Western culture that have been the outcome of industrial technology – the depersonalization of social life in the name of efficiency, the increasing anxiety and uncertainty in emotional life, the encouragement of an impersonal theoretical idiom – Western intellectuals have gone from one extreme to the other. No longer the spokesman for an aggressive imperialism that lauded progress and science, the Western intellectual is now filled with pessimism and self-doubt. The ethnocentric disparagement of non-Western peoples evident in the nineteenth century has given way to an idealization of such cultures, reflected in such social movements as surrealism. Thus, much contemporary thought is "romantic" and sees preliterate cultures as exemplifying a "lost heritage." They represent an image of an organic community in which the individual is reunited with the group and where there is "communion with nature." Reason and science are suspect, and so feelings and symbolism are given priority as ways of understanding the world. In short, Horton writes, "The romantic search for a 'lost world' has given rise to an image of traditional culture which can be understood entirely as a reaction to the stresses and strains of life in the modern West" (293). Thus the symbolist anthropologist has a romantic tendency that leads him to deny that religion has a theoretical and intellectual dimension.

The second intellectual trend that has had a debilitating effect on anthropology Horton identifies as *positivism*. He notes that Durkheim has often been labeled a positivist but suggests that *Elementary Forms of the Religious Life* has essentially an antipositivist bias. By positivism Horton means a philosophical outlook that exalts science as providing the only valid means of acquiring knowledge of the world and has, in addition, a specific conception of the scientific method, namely that theoretical knowledge is based on inductive generalizations about the visible, tangible world. By accepting this inadequate conception of science, anthropologists have, Horton maintains, been led far astray, for it encouraged writers like Evans-Pritchard, Leach, and Beattie to regard science as simply an extension of common sense and as being concerned only with questions of "how" observables behave.

Thus Horton argues that contemporary anthropologists have been influenced by two important though baneful intellectual trends: the ideologies of liberal romanticism, and positivism. The first ideology is based on a disillusionment with science, the second on an excessive enthusiasm for science – a seeming paradox that Horton feels is more apparent than real. The right approach to the issues we have examined in this chapter is then, for Horton (and with this I concur), to have a conception of science sufficiently wide to enable us to see the continuities and similarities between science and magico-religious thought without necessarily collapsing into a denunciation of science and rationality. Moreover, as both Horton and Jarvie stress, an erroneous explanation proves nothing about the intellectual capacity of those who put it forward. In this respect the magical notions of the Azande and some redundant theories of distinguished scientists have much in common.

In all these discussions an implicit distinction is made between two modes of thought. On the one hand there is "magical" or mythopoeic thought, reflected in myth, ritual, and symbolic classifications – a mode of thought misleadingly associated only with preliterate communities and erroneously labeled "primitive." It is a mode of thought in need of some explanation. On the other hand there is scientific thought, a mechanistic paradigm usually assumed – and this again rather misleadingly – to be associated with Western culture. Radcliffe-Brown put this distinction neatly when he suggested that

> in every human society there inevitably exist two different and in a certain sense conflicting conceptions of nature. One of them, the *naturalistic*, is implicit everywhere in technology, and, in our twentieth-century European culture, has become explicit and preponderant in our thoughts. The other, which might be called the mythological or *spiritualistic* conception, is implicit in myth and in religion, and often becomes explicit in philosophy. (1952: 130)

The essential dispute, therefore, centers not on the presence of this kind of distinction but rather on the nature of religious thought. For Horton, religious consciousness is abstract, theoretical, and offers explanations of phenomena, and is therefore akin to science: For Freud, Lévy-Bruhl, and the symbolists it is expressive of the emotions, the unconscious or the sociocultural order, and, in a sense, as Freud suggested (1938b: 44), rather like art. There is, I think, truth in both positions.

The issue of "modes of thought" has continued to interest anthropologists. Hallpike (1979) has attempted to argue, drawing on Piaget's theories of cognition, that there has been an evolution of systems of thought and representations of reality from thought that is context-bound, concrete, affective, and ethnocentric (*animism*) to thought that is abstract, specialized, impersonal, and largely objective (*science*). This is essentially a restatement of Lévy-Bruhl's schema, as Hallpike admits in a footnote (1976: 269), but Hallpike agreed with Horton in seeing pre-literate thought largely in cognitive terms. To conclude this section, let us briefly examine Hallpike's controversial thesis, beginning first with a summary of Piaget's position.

Although in an earlier paper Piaget had hinted at the possibility that adult thinking, in many cultures, may not "proceed beyond the level of concrete operations" (1966: 13) and had noted the "parallels" between Greek science and child animism, he was generally wary about making unsubstantiated claims. But clearly Piaget's distinction between concrete and formal operational thought brings to mind similar distinctions that scholars have made in attempting to understand human thought: With Freud we have the distinction between the "primary processes" (fantasy, dreams, neurotic symptoms) and their cultural manifestations in religion, myths, and symbolic thought and the "secondary processes" reflected in conscious, logical thought and science. With Ernst Cassirer (1944) we have the distinction between science and mythopoeic thought. Like Lévi-Strauss, Cassirer suggested that the thought of preliterate people did not divide life into different spheres or domains, but for Cassirer this unity was synthetic and one of feeling, rather than analytical and cognitive. Finally, with Lévy-Bruhl we have the distinction between science and prelogical thought. All three scholars, like the "symbolic" anthropologists and Boas, essentially see "symbolic" thought as nonrational and associated with the emotions. It is therefore, for these scholars, fundamentally acausal and nontheoretical. With Freud, as with Spinoza and Malinowski, such thought is also seen as having an adaptive function in coping with stress, cognitive uncertainty, and fear (cf. Jahoda 1969: 127–37).

The writings of Lévi-Strauss represent an essential break and departure from this kind of interpretation. "Analogical" or untamed thought, the "science of the concrete," is interpreted as proceeding "through understanding, not affectivity" (1966: 268) and as being logical, rather than non- or pre-logical.

Piaget notes the affinities between his own concept of "concrete" operations and both Lévy-Bruhl's "prelogical thought" and Lévi-Strauss's "thought untamed," but true to his own developmental theory he insists that such thought is prelogical and preparatory to explicit, or scientific logic (1971: 116).

The question, therefore, inevitably arises as to whether preliterate people think primarily in terms of a concrete logic, as Freud, Lévy-Bruhl, and Vygotsky implied. Piaget's response to this is ambiguous, but he appears to stress two points. First, he asserts that the kinship systems of preliterate people imply an advanced logic beyond that of concrete operations. Second, he insists that a radical distinction must be made between cultural representations and the "reasoning" of individuals in a society (1971: 116–17).

In spite of these warnings and Piaget's own hesitancy to equate infantile thought with that of preliterate people, Hallpike, as Shweder put it, rushes in "where even Piaget feared to tread" (1982: 354). For Hallpike argues, in terms that are akin to those of Lévy-Bruhl, that preliterate people's thought is prelogical and that they are unable to engage in operational thinking.

In an incisive review of Hallpike's study, Richard Shweder has outlined a number of important criticisms, but in the context of the present study one major criticism of the work is worth making. In collapsing the distinction between collective representations and individual cognition, Hallpike employs the former data to infer or "deduce" that preliterate people lack operational thought, and then, in circular fashion, he sees such representations as "reflecting" or "manifesting" their cognitive processes. But in exploring the nature of their collective representations in his discussion, for instance, of time, space, and classification, Hallpike puts the focus almost entirely on their religious cosmologies and on their ritual classifications, and though in theory he eschews the idea of making any stultifying contrast between science and primitive thought (33), this, in fact, is precisely what he does. Consider, for instance, his discussion of classification. Hallpike argues, rightly I think, that folk classifications have a functional bias, are prototypical, and are not conceptualized into logical hierarchies. But, interestingly, his whole analysis (169–235) is largely concerned with symbolic classifications, and he ignores the nature of those empirical taxonomies that have interested ethnoscientists.

Yet he compares such ritual classifications not with European totemic ideas and folk classifications but with scientific taxonomies and highly abstract notions of logic classes. Rather like Lévy-Bruhl, therefore, he interprets preliterate thought as essentially symbolic and European thought as abstract and logical. Hallpike admits, of course, that Europeans operate on several levels of thought but seems to imply that creativity and imagination involves some kind of "regress" to a more

311

elementary level of thought (33) and that European religious ideas – if thought by a theologian rather than a peasant – cannot possibly be at the preoperational level. In bypassing the practical and concrete operational logic of preliterate people and the symbolism inherent in European collective representations, Hallpike errs in the same way as Lévy-Bruhl, and he is open to the same kind of criticisms that Boas and Radin (1957: 12) long ago leveled at the French philosopher.

Religion as culture

In discussing anthropological studies of religion in earlier chapters, I have noted that the influence of Marx and Weber has been either muted or negligible. Lessa and Vogt's important reader in comparative religion (1972) makes no mention of either scholar, focusing largely on tribal cultures. In the last decade, however, the writings of Weber and then Marx have been increasingly utilized by anthropologists and sociologists in an attempt to go beyond the structural-functionalist paradigm. These "new directions" tend not to be new but rather to draw on perspectives and ideas that were formulated at the end of the nineteenth century. Such critiques of functionalism have tended to move in two contrasting directions, the one tendency drawing on Dilthey's and Weber's writings and advocating a phenomenological or hermeneutical approach, the other drawing on Marx. But, interestingly, the influence of Lévi-Strauss has meant that the latter tendency has stressed the positivist and structuralist dimension of Marxism to the neglect of the humanist and historical dimension, whereas with respect to the first tendency Weber has been viewed essentially as an interpretative sociologist, not as an advocate of historical sociology. Thus in both tendencies the dialectical and historical emphasis that stemmed from Hegel and German idealism has been either neglected or downplayed. But equally important is the fact that Durkheimian sociology has remained central to both these recent currents of thought.

The first tendency is represented by Clifford Geertz, who has, like Berger (1973), consistently argued that religion should be approached from the standpoint of interpretative sociology. The influence of Weber is apparent both in Geertz's substantive study of the religion of Java (1960) and in his more programmatic theoretical statements on religion. We may initially consider his more general theory, as Geertz advocates a style of analysis that has found favor, under the rubric "semantic anthropology," among many contemporary scholars. It is worth noting at the outset, however, that in its stress on interpreting religion as the locus of meaning, Geertz's anthropology has close affinities with the kind of approach suggested by Jung and Eliade.

In his classic article "Religion as a Cultural System" (1975) Geertz bewailed the fact that no recent theoretical advances of major importance had occurred in anthropological studies of religion, and that scholars in this field were essentially living off the conceptual capital of its founding ancestors, Durkheim, Weber, Freud, and Malinowski. This is undoubtedly true; however, biologists are still living off the conceptual capital of Darwin and Mendel, but they do not seem too upset about this, the developments and "empirical enrichment" of their theories being accepted as valid. Geertz does not suggest abandoning the important insights of these four scholars, but rather the need to widen the perspective and to accept that religion is essentially a cultural system that gives meaning to human existence. He defines religion in these terms, implying that it has a universal function to provide such meaning. He writes,

> A religion is a system of symbols which acts to establish powerful, pervasive, and long-lasting moods and motivations in men by formulating conceptions of a general order of existence and clothing these conceptions with such an aura of factuality that the moods and motivations seem uniquely realistic. (1975: 90)

He suggests, therefore, that religious symbols formulate a "basic congruence" between a particular style of life and a specific metaphysic and so function to synthesize a people's ethos – the aesthetic style, tone, and quality of their life – and their world view, their most comprehensive ideas of order. Such symbolic structures, he continues, have an intrinsically double aspect, being a model *of* "reality" and a model *for* "reality," or, as he graphically expresses it, "They both express the world's climate and shape it" (95). Geertz therefore views religious beliefs as essentially functioning to provide meaning, in offering explanations for anomalous events and experiences (Tylor), in giving comprehension and emotional support for human suffering (Weber and Malinowski), and in providing a workable set of ethical criteria to explain the discontinuity between things as they are and as they ought to be. He therefore views religious symbolism as intrinsically linked to what he calls "the problem of meaning". A few short extracts will succinctly give the tenor of his argument:

> There are at least three points where chaos – a tumult of events which lack not just interpretations but interpretability – threatens to break in upon man; at the limits of his analytic capacities, at the limits of his powers of endurance, and at the limits of his moral insight . . . The existence of bafflement, pain, and moral paradox – of the Problem of Meaning – is one of the things that drives men toward belief in gods, devils, Spirits,

313

totemic principles, or the spiritual efficacy of cannibalism ... Religious concepts spread beyond their specifically metaphysical contexts to provide a framework of general ideas in terms of which a wide range of experience – intellectual, emotional, moral – can be given meaningful form. (1975: 100–23)

Geertz is aware that the elaboration and systematization of such symbolic structures is variable, and he draws a distinction between the religious perspective and the other perspectives that people employ to construe their world – the commonsensical, the scientific, and the aesthetic (1975: 110–12; 1983: 73–120). Whereas common sense is a form of naive realism, science a mode of understanding based on disinterested observation and formal concepts, and the aesthetic perspective a kind of suspension of naive realism and practical interest in favor of sensory contemplation, the religious perspective "moves beyond the realities of everyday life" to correct and complete them. "Rather than detachment, its watchword is commitment; rather than analysis, encounter." Through ritual, Geertz suggests, the world as lived and the world as imagined are fused through the agency of symbolic forms (1975: 112). In an earlier essay he had likewise argued that the essential element of all religions was to demonstrate a meaningful relationship between the values a people hold and the general order of existence within which it finds itself.

Geertz thus concludes that the anthropological study of religion is a two-stage operation: first, an analysis of the system of meanings embodied in the religious symbolism, and second, the relating of these systems to social-structural and psychological processes. The first of these, he felt, had been neglected by anthropologists, but he warned that he was not advocating a "kind of jejune cabalism." Although Geertz obviously felt that he was suggesting a "whole new approach" to the analysis of religion, his plea for the interpretative understanding of cultural phenomena had, of course, been suggested long ago by Dilthey and Weber. Moreover, this tradition was not wholly alien to anthropology, for Benedict's classic introductory study is in the *Versehen* tradition (see Harris 1969, Morris 1984), and Gladys Reichard's study of Navaho religion (1950) exemplifies this approach.

Apart from the cultural relativism that this kind of analysis implies, Geertz's definition of religion is open to a number of criticisms, and these have been explored by Talad Asad in a review article on the essay. First, in suggesting that religious symbols induce certain psychological dispositions – a suggestion similar to Radcliffe-Brown's theory of sentiments – Geertz not only assumes a one-to-one relationship between beliefs and specific dispositions but ignores "social and economic insti-

314

tutions in general, within which individual biographies are lived out" (1983: 241).

Second, in equating the two levels of discourse (symbols that induce dispositions and those that place those dispositions in a cosmic framework), Geertz, Asad suggests, assumes a theological standpoint, ignoring the "discursive processes" by which meanings are constructed.

Third, in separating religion from science, common sense, and aesthetics, Geertz gives religion a distinctive perspective and a universal and unique function: to establish meaning. The issue as to whether religion is true, illogical, an illusion, or false consciousness is therefore bypassed, and it is of interest that in his essay on ideology Geertz not only does not consider religion as a form of ideology but argues for a genuinely nonevaluative conception of ideology. Such a standpoint somewhat contradicts his suggestion as to the social function of science vis-à-vis ideologies, namely to understand them – what they are, how they work, what gives rise to them – and to criticize them (1975: 232). This is clearly not his approach to religion.

Fourth, there is no suggestion in Geertz's essay that religion is ever affected by experiences in the common-sense world, for he always starts from the notion of a religious culture – a symbolic structure – which is sui generis, and largely divorced from socioeconomic processes and power. In Geertz's essay, Asad suggests, there is a "hiatus" between the cultural system and the social reality, and a failure to explore the historical conditions necessary for the existence of particular religious practices and discourses (1983: 252).

This assessment of Geertz's well-known definition of religion has, I think, some substance, but it is a limited critique in that Asad does not take into account Geertz's more substantive studies. One wonders what criticisms Asad would have made of Marx's well-known definition of religion quoted in Chapter 1. During the 1950s, Geertz, like many of his contemporaries – Gluckman, Leach, and Firth, for example – was clearly dissatisfied with the static, ahistorical implications of functionalist theory, whether of the sociological (Radcliffe-Brown) or sociopsychological (Malinowski) variety. Sensing that the relationship between cultural forms and social organization was neither "derivative" nor simply one of "mirror-image," Geertz, in his essay "Ritual and Social Change," explored the possibility of a more dynamic functionalist theory. He argues that the distinction between culture and the social system, and between meaning and function, implies two forms of integration. "Culture," he suggests, involves "logico-meaningful" integration whereas, "causal-functional" integration is, following the organic analogy, char-

315

acteristic of the social system. The influence of Talcott Parsons is evident in this formulation and implies a union of Weberian and Durkheimian modes of analysis. Examining certain Javanese rituals in which the ceremonies become a focus of political debate and conflict as well as of religious propitiation, Geertz suggests that this is due to an "incongruity" between the cultural framework of meaning and the patterning of social interaction (1975b: 169). Even so, it is clear from his analysis that there is no integration at either the cultural or social level. But in attempting to understand religion within a specific sociopolitical context, Geertz certainly provides a more dynamic approach to religion than that evinced by anthropologists who have not been influenced by Weberian sociology – Douglas and Turner, for example. His studies of the religious systems of Java and Bali, in fact, indicate the pervasive influence of Weber, and though Geertz accepts the notion that his own approach is one of cultural hermeneutics, these studies go beyond that of simply interpreting the religious symbolism. As with Durkheim and Weber, there is a discrepancy in Geertz between his theoretical intent, specified in general programmatic statements, and his substantive analyses.

In *The Religion of Java* (1960) Geertz outlines not a simple religious system but three distinctive "world views" or traditions. The study is based on two years' research (1952–4) undertaken in the small town of Modjokuto in east central Java (now Indonesia). It was a small, shabby sort of place, he wrote: "Land was short, jobs were scarce, politics was unstable, health was poor, prices were rising, and life was altogether far from promising, a kind of agitated stagnancy." Yet in the midst of this depressing scene, he continued, there was an astonishing intellectual vitality, and peasants and others were continually engaged in philosophical debate and in discourses about religious doctrine and practices (1983: 60). *The Religion of Java* gives a detailed account of such beliefs and practices, which Geertz suggests fall into three distinctive "cultural types" that are associated with the three main social institutions of Java: the village, the market, and the government bureaucracy.

The first, the Abangan religious tradition, is focused on a ritual feast called the Slametan and involves an intricate complex of beliefs concerning spirits and a whole set of theories and practices relating to curing, sorcery, and magic. This system, evident among peasants as well as among the urban poor, consists of a "balanced integration of animistic, Hinduistic and Islamic elements, a basic Javanese syncretism which is the island's true folk tradition, the basic substratum of its civilization" (1960: 5).

The second subtradition, which Geertz refers to as Santri, is associated with the market and the trading classes and represents a more pantheistic version of Islam that is common in Java. Besides consisting of the regular execution of the basic rituals of Islam – the prayers, the fast, and the pilgrimage to Mecca – the santri tradition also involves a whole complex of social and political Islamic institutions. Though mainly associated with the Javanese trading element, this tradition is also adopted by the richer peasants.

Finally, there is the Prijaji tradition. This term originally referred to the hereditary, ruling aristocracy that was once the dominant elite in Java but had been transformed by Dutch colonial rule into a salaried civil service. The religious tradition of this aristocracy stressed neither the animistic nor Islamic elements but rather the Hinduistic, developing a kind of "Far Eastern Gnosticism," with its classical art forms and its intuitive mysticism. This religious tradition is now associated with the bureaucratic elite.

Setting a descriptive analysis of these three religious traditions within the historical and sociopolitical context of Java, Geertz's study is reminiscent of Weber's studies of India and China, though it lacks Weber's overall concern with ethical rationalism and economic factors. Geertz's main conclusion is that though religion may indeed express common values and have an integrative function, it is also a means whereby political conflicts and disputes are aired and enacted. Political conflict, he writes, which is often intense in present-day Indonesia, tends to "focus around ostensibly religious issues" (364). Thus, like Weber, Geertz associates specific religious traditions with certain social strata, though he does not discuss in detail the nature of this "affinity," simply noting that "traders and richer peasants are seen ... as more or less 'naturally' Santris, civil servants as 'normally' Prijaji, and poorer peasants and town proletariat as 'typically' Abandan" (374).

In his essay on the religion of Bali, where he undertook research in 1957–8, Geertz is specifically concerned with Weber's concept of religious rationalization, the notion that the systematization by religious intellectuals of the so-called world religions was provoked by specific and radical social changes. This essentially implied the "disenchantment" of the world, greater formalization and integration of religious symbols, and a more explicit sense of ethical doctrine. Although the Balinese are, in a broad sense, Hindus, Geertz suggests that their religious system showed little rationalization. It is "concrete, action-centered, thoroughly interwoven with the details of everyday life" and shows little philosophical sophistication (1975: 175). Yet the traditional elite of Bali, Geertz suggests, faced with a populist ideology and with the undermining of their position by the economic and political changes of republican Indonesia, are in the process of rationalizing the rituals, beliefs, and doctrines of

317

Hindu-Balinese religion through encouraging religious literacy and the reorganization of religious institutions. What happened in Greece and China after the fifth century B.C. seems to be happening, Geertz writes, in mid-twentieth century Bali. And interestingly, he sees this rationalization on the part of the ruling nobility as largely a way of maintaining their political dominance (186). In his empirical analyses, at least, Geertz does not see religion as wholly divorced from politics.

In his excellent comparative and historical study *Islam Observed* (1968), Geertz explores religious developments in Indonesia and Morocco, having undertaken researches in the ancient walled city of Sefran (1964–66) (see Geertz 1979). He explicitly describes the study as an exercise in macrosociology, both historical and comparative in the style of Weber, thus avoiding, he suggests, the "pallid mindlessness" of cultural relativism (the kind of interpretative understanding he had earlier advocated) and the "shabby tyranny" of historical determinism (by which he presumably means the kind of analysis suggested by Marx and Engels). He begins the book by suggesting that the aim of a systematic study of religion is not just to describe ideas and institutions but to determine how these sustain or inhibit religious faith and to ascertain "what happens to faith when its vehicle alters" (2). His focus therefore is specifically on religious beliefs and institutions, rather than upon the relationship between religion and social life.

After describing the history and culture of the two countries and their "classical styles" of religious expression – maraboutism, in Morocco, with its emphasis on saints and Sufism, and illuminationism in Indonesia, with its concept of the "theatre state" and its Prijaji tradition – Geertz attempts to describe and explain the religious changes that have taken place during the last century. He expresses dissatisfaction with the four main theories of social change – indexical, typological, world-acculturative, and evolutionary – and suggests that attention must be paid not to indexes, stages, trails, or trends but to the processes and mechanisms of social transformation. To understand, therefore, why the classical religious styles in both countries are now besieged by other currents of thought, specifically secularism and Islamic scripturalism, Geertz suggests that three related developments have to be taken into account. The first is the establishment of Western domination, the impact of colonialism being primarily economic, with the establishment of banks, roads, railroads, and an enclave economy. Second there was the crystallization of an integrated, activist nation-state, which produced a bifurcated society. And finally, in reaction to the Western intrusion, a scriptural form of Islam developed, scholastic and legalistic, and stressing a return to the Koran and the hajj. This scripturalist tendency was directed not only against the colonial powers, Geertz writes, but also against the "classical" forms of religion, which in Indonesia were not specifically Islamic. Significantly, this Islamic fundamentalism was not only a dissident religious ideology and a rebellious political creed but involved a "determined modernism." As Geertz wrote, "Stepping backward in order better to leap is an established principle in cultural change; our own Reformation was made that way" (1968: 69). Ultimately, in both countries, on independence the classical traditions were renovated and reaffirmed, though scripturalism still remains a powerful force. Geertz explores the personalities of the two important political figures in these countries at the time and concludes, "With Sukarno the theater state returned to Indonesia; and with Muhammed V maraboutic kingship returned to Morocco" (74).

In his concluding chapter, Geertz advocates two contrasting approaches to the study of religion. One is the semantic or hermeneutic approach, which suggests that religion is concerned with meaning, functioning to give unity to experience and to overcome the "felt inadequacies of commonsense ideas." Whatever else Islam – maraboutic, illuminationist, or scripturalist – does for those who are able to adopt it, he writes, "it surely renders life less outrageous to plain reason and less contrary to common sense" (101). This is the viewpoint expressed in his essays. He notes, however, widespread skepticism evident in both Indonesia and Morocco and discusses the relationship between religion and modern science in the two countries (103–6). The other approach that Gertz advocates is comparative and "scientific"; it involves, he writes, the description of the wide variety of forms in which religion appears, "the uncovering of the forces which bring these forms into existence, alter them or destroy them; and the assessment of their influences . . . upon the behaviour of men in everyday life" (1968: 96).

Given his stress on religion as a symbol system and his tendency to see religion as an inner state – a "faith" – Geertz never fully explored the social forces that produced the religious beliefs and practices. Geertz's whole outlook remained close to the German idealist tradition.

Structural Marxism

As a student-novitiate of anthropology in 1971, I was asked by my tutor to prepare a paper on the alternatives to functionalism. The outcome was an essay entitled "Fourteen Alternatives to Structural-Functionalism." Besides structuralism and structural Marxism, the essay surveyed a plethora of theoretical strategies that were then being broached: games theory and generative models; various forms of "symbolic" and hermeneutic understanding; cultural ecology; cultural materialism; network and transactional analysis; and the "new" ethnography (ethnoscience and cognitive anthropology). I mention this here because there has been a noticeable tendency in the last decade to reduce theoretical discussion to essentially three paradigms – functionalism, structuralism, and structural Marxism (Godelier 1977, Augé 1982), or, if the study has a sociological bias, another classical paradigm – interpretative sociology (hermeneutics, phenomenology, and ethnomethodology) – is added (cf. Bleicher 1982, Rossi 1983). Although such divisions are not without their validity and usefulness, they do tend to unnecessarily highlight the contrasts between the various approaches, thus glossing over the continuities of social thought, and to ignore the complexity not only of the specific theoretical styles but of the individual scholars themselves. To interpret Marx as an economic determinist, Weber as an interpretative sociologist, Durkheim as a classic functionalist and positivist, and Evans-Pritchard as simply a student of hermeneutics is, as we have seen, to seriously underestimate the complexity and value of their work. It is, then, somewhat misleading to see recent anthropological studies as involving a kind of dialectical progression from functionalism to structural Marxism, via Lévi-Strauss. Structural Marxism is only one tendency within the anthropological tradition, and a recent one at that, which, as I noted in Chapter 1, represents only one particular interpretation of Marx's writings.

Structural Marxism is indubitably connected with the writings of Louis Althusser, a French Marxist philosopher, who, in the early 1960s, wrote a number of trenchant and critical essays advocating a structuralist interpretation of Marx (1969, 1972). Althusser's concerns were primarily epistemological, namely to offer a scientific theory of history and society based on a reading of Marx's mature work *Capital*. Althusser suggested that an "epistemological break" had occurred in Marx's writings around 1845–6 and that this involved a radical new conception of history, based not on the "essence of man" but on the notion that history was a process without a subject. In contrast to the ideological and Hegelian implications of his early writings, Marx had formulated in *Capital*, Althusser argued, a novel and essentially scientific approach to history. This new theory involved the idea of "structural causality" and utilized such concepts as mode of production, relations of production, social formation, and ideology. Althusser's formulations gave rise to much heated debate and critical comment (cf. Callinicos 1976, Clarke et al. 1980, Benton 1984), but his work was only a part of a much broader current of thought known as structuralism. For in his critique of empiricism and in his repudiation of the humanistic, subjectivist, and historicist emphasis of Sartre's Marxism, Althusser's philosophy has affinities with that of Lévi-

Strauss. By the end of the decade the combined influence of these two scholars led to a resurgence of interest in the relationship between Marxism and anthropology, and a number of French Marxists – Terray, Rey, Godelier, and Meillassoux – began to explore the possibility of interpreting precapitalist societies in terms of a structural Marxist paradigm (see Kahn & Llobera 1981 for an excellent discussion of French Marxist anthropology). Since only one of these scholars has addressed himself to the issue of religious ideology, we can, I think, usefully focus on the writings of Maurice Godelier.

Although Godelier was undoubtedly influenced by Althusser's writings – for Godelier began his "strange itinerary" as a philosopher and was a much younger scholar (born in 1934) – it is clear from his early essays that Godelier's work had its own originality and that Althusser had simply anticipated his ideas. It is of interest, however, that Godelier rarely cites Althusser in his own work, in spite of the close affinities between their theories. In 1958, Godelier suggests, he began a research program with two questions uppermost in his mind: "Is there a *hidden* logic in the economic systems" that appear and disappear in the course of history? and "What are the epistemological conditions for a rational understanding of these systems?" To answer this question he was led from philosophy to economics, and in 1965 he published an essay on economic anthropology, concluding negatively that there was "no exclusive economic rationality" (1972: 317). Within this essay he criticized both the "formalist" and "substantivist" approaches to economic anthropology, suggesting that in the end the idea of "rationality" simply obliges us to analyze the basis of the structures of social life. Thus, under the guidance of Lévi-Strauss he turned to anthropology and set forth to serve his appenticeship as an anthropologist, undertaking fieldwork (1967–9) among the Baruya of New Guinea, an isolated group of shifting cultivators. Since then Godelier has outlined, in a number of important and seminal essays (1972, 1977), the nature and scope of what he envisages as the most viable paradigm for social science. Essentially it constitutes a structural reading of Marxism. Let me briefly outline some of the key features of the social theory he proposes.

As a fundamental premise, Godelier follows Lévi-Strauss in strongly advocating a nonempiricist standpoint. In a well-known article (1972) he argues that both Marx and Lévi-Strauss shared a common epistemology; for these scholars, he writes, "a structure is not a reality that is directly visible, and so directly observable, but a level of reality that exists beyond the visible relations between man, and the functioning of which constitutes the underlying logic of the system" (1972: xix).

Science, he suggests, cannot take the individual and his or her "immediate" experience of the world and of other people as its point of departure. He even implies that scientific thought, and Marx, not only do not take the "appearances" – the collective representations of a community – as a "starting point" but "must ignore them" (1977: 3). This is quite erroneous. Can you imagine any scientific scholar who "ignored" the world ever discovering anything about it? Science always begins with empirical reality; it simply does not take this reality as "given." There is nothing novel or startling about this suggestion: It is the standpoint of all science, and it was suggested by Hegel at the beginning of the nineteenth century. But it is important in the context of anthropological theory, for Radcliffe-Brown's functionalism – which Lévi-Strauss criticized – took social relations to be a given reality, which could be understood simply by inductive generalizations. Godelier argues that this was a radical theoretical defect of functionalism, for in conflating structure with the visible social relations it precluded adequate explanation of such phenomena. But he stresses that both Marx and Lévi-Strauss adopted a materialist standpoint, seeing the "structures" as a part of reality, existing independently of the human mind. Leach's notion that structure is an ideal order that the mind brings to bear on the flux of reality (implied in his article on taboo), Godelier suggests, is idealist, and he quotes Lévi-Strauss's response to Maybury-Lewis's criticisms of his work to stress that Lévi-Strauss was essentially a realist: "Ultimate proof of the molecular structure is provided by the electron microscope, which enables us to see the *actual* molecules ... It is hopeless to expect that structural analysis will change the *perception* of concrete social relations. It will only explain them better" (Lévi-Strauss 1973: 80).

Thus Godelier argues that Marx and Lévi-Strauss share a common affirmation that science must be materialistic and deterministic, and that scientific understanding essentially consists of discovering the internal structure hidden behind the visible functioning of the social system. Godelier argues that Marx's analysis of capitalism essentially follows a structuralist method, or at least a nonempiricist one. But Godelier alludes to the crucial difference between the two scholars when he writes that the radical originality of Marx's thought, which opposes it to both structuralism and functionalism, is that Marxism "assumes that this inner relation, which provides the underlying logic of the functioning of societies and of their history, is determined, in the last analysis, by the conditions of production and reproduction of their material basis, or, to use his terminology, their mode of production" (1972: xxviii).

The important point, of course, is that for Marx the "internal structure" is not some invariant structure but the "material conditions of existence" and that rather than being determinant in the "last instance," they are determinant in the "first instance," for Marx assumes that these conditions are the basis of social life and prior to human consciousness. Moreover, this "reality" is an ever-changing process that terms like *structure* and *logic* tend to obscure. As I indicated in the first chapter, the tendency to situate Marx's analysis in a causal-mechanistic framework is highly misleading and creates intractable problems about the degree to which the infrastructures are determinant.

Several interesting points emerge from this. One is that in taking the "mode of production" as the underlying "logic of a social system," Godelier argues consistently against all forms of "reductionist" materialism that attempt to explain cultural life by reference to either technology or biological adaptation. The neofunctionalism of Marvin Harris (1978: 143–70), for example, which attempts to explain the cultural significance of food taboos concerning animals by reference to the animals' utility is cited (but compare Rappaport's interesting analysis of the ritual regulation of environmental relations among the Tsembaga of New Guinea, 1967, 1968). Godelier is critical of such "vulgar" materialism, which reduces all social relations to the status of epiphenomena associated with economic relations that are themselves reduced to biological adaptation (1977: 42).

Second, although Godelier advocates a "science that aims to account for structures without forgetting their origin or their evolution" (1972: 246) and suggests rescuing this science not only from functionalist empiricism but from the "helplessness of structuralism in [the] face of history," his whole approach, like that of Althusser and Lévi-Strauss, gives historical understanding a secondary role in cultural understanding. In his programmatic statements, Godelier advocates a structuralist interpretation of culture, not the kind of historical sociology suggested by Marx, Weber, and Evans-Pritchard or by such contemporary Marxists as Wolf, Worsley, and Wallerstein. His plea for combining history and anthropology (as well as economics, sociology, and political science) to create a genuinely holistic social science is laudable, but this is done at the expense of historical understanding. Like Althusser, he conflates history as an object of study with history as a mode of understanding. Thus he writes that for a Marxist, "history" is not a category that explains; it is a category that has to *be* explained, and he continues,

> Historical materialism is not another "model" of history. It is primarily a theory of society, a hypothesis about the articulation of its inner levels and about the specific hierarchical causality of each of these levels. And when it is able to discover the types and mechanisms of this causality and articulation, Marxism will show its ability to be a true instrument of historical science. (1977: 49)

323

But Marx was as much concerned with the genesis and evolution of capitalism as with its structure and functioning, and it is quite misleading to imply that he gave "priority to structures" or that the study of the "internal functioning of a structure" must precede an analysis of its genesis and evolution. In *Capital*, both anthropology and history are combined. To suggest that all societies are in history and change is a truism, is no reason at all for ignoring this fact, for social analysis is concerned with understanding structural changes as well as a system's functioning. It is debatable whether Marx had a linear conception of social evolution, but it can hardly be contested that he was an evolutionary thinker concerned with the understanding of social transformations, not simply the functioning of social systems. As E. P. Thompson argues in his imprudent but important critique of Althusser's structural Marxism, Marx was concerned with both process and structure and continually affirmed the objectivity of historical analysis (1978: 217). The same kind of criticisms may be addressed to Godelier, whose style of analysis is functional and mechanistic rather than historical and substantive, although in his empirical analyses the vocabulary of structural Marxism largely gets left behind. As Kahn and Llobera suggest, Godelier either focuses on synchronic structural-Marxist studies or uses traditional, grandiose evolutionary schemes; "Real, concrete history is always avoided or postponed" (1981: 316).

Third, to distance himself from classic functionalism Godelier argues that the limitations of this mode of analysis was that it denied the existence of contradictions, either within a structure or between structures, and so had to look beyond the social system for the cause of evolutionary change. However, his suggestion that the old principle of "unity of opposites" had two variants, one scientific (Marx and Godelier), the other unscientific and idealistic (Hegel), is, I think, a misreading of the relationship between Hegel and Marx (discussed in Chapter 1).

Godelier's social theory is based on the notion of "structural" relationships between "levels." These so-called levels – by which he seems to mean the various institutional orders recognized by functionalist anthropologists (such as economy, politics, kinship, religion) – designate, he writes,

> some articulate aspect of one and the same social process and are related to the unique and complex logic of this articulation or structure or order among the social structures which compose the whole society ... By relationship of "causality" we therefore mean an order of priority, not chronological but of structural linkage, a hierarchical order of functions all of which are simultaneously necessary for a society to exist but which have an unequal importance in the reproduction of this society. (1982: 241)

This is reminiscent of Parsonian functionalism, apart from the fact that Godelier speaks of structural contradictions and follows Marx in giving causal priority to the mode of production. But Godelier stresses that there is no simple relationship between structure (used as an empirical concept in the manner of Radcliffe-Brown) and function. Thus in some interesting analyses he suggests that a structure may be multifunctional, so that religion, for example, may serve in the organization of production (as among the Inca) and kinship may perform the functions of both in infrastructure and ideology (see Bloch 1975 and 1983: 165–7). Following a suggestion of Marx that in different societies different cultural institutions may be dominant – kinship in tribal societies, politics in the Greek city-states, religion in medieval Europe – Godelier argues that what gives these structures predominance is not simply that they are integrative or multifunctional but that they "take on the function of relations of production" (1977: 36). I think such abstract formulations are highly questionable; the fact that religion or the economy or kinship may function to organize production does not make it any less ideological. Another limitation of Godelier's approach is that not only does he take these structural levels as universal categories – and is thus open to the charge of ethnocentrism (cf. Baudrillard 1975: 70–81 for a critique of Godelier's "productivist" and "functionalist" discourse) – but he largely follows, like Douglas, the traditional Durkheimian approach that takes the concept of society or social system as the basic unit of analysis (cf. Kahn & Llobera 1981: 298).

Given this structural-Marxist approach, it is not surprising that he follows Marx in interpreting religion as an "ideological" system. Two of his discussions – one general, the other empirical – are worth outlining here.

Implying that the concept of "fetishism of commodities" is almost a casual by-product of Marx's thought, Godelier nevertheless gives a succinct discussion of Marx's theory of ideology, indicating that social relations and economic categories have a "phantasmic" character that conceals the underlying productive relations, the "commodity" forms concealing the actual extraction of the surplus value (1977: 169–71). Godelier rightly suggests that for Marx religion in precapitalist societies performs a similar function, and he quotes Engels's statement that "all religion is nothing but the fantastic reflection in men's minds of those external forces which control their daily life." This leads Godelier to ask a very general question, similar to that posed by early Victorian anthropologists: namely, What is the nature of mytho-religious thought? He suggests that Marx and Engels gave an answer similar to that suggested by modern anthropology, and Godelier himself seems to follow this line of reasoning. He makes the following points.

(1) "Primitive" – that is, mytho-religious thought, is essentially analogical thought, a logic expressed in metaphor and metonym. Thus people picture the natural world as being analogous to the human world, and they represent the invisible forces and realities of nature as "subjects" – that is, as beings endowed with consciousness.

(2) These "illusory" representations of the world are treated as having an objective, independent existence.

(3) Religion exists spontaneously in a theoretical form (representation – explanation of the world) and a practical form (magic and ritual, influence over the real). Religious thought derives its impulse from a desire to know reality (though in an illusory way), and magic is a way to change the world (in an imaginary way).

(4) Religion is the dominant form of ideology in preliterate communities. Philosophical thought was a new mode of speculative thought that emerged in the sixth century B.C. in Ionia, and, like religious thought and science, answered the same human need: to explain the world, and to discover the causes and connections relating to phenomena.

(5) The importance of imaginary kinship relationships in myths has its origin not in "pure principles" of thought nor from "models" in nature but from social relations and the fact that kinship relationships are dominant in preliterate communities.

(6) In summary, therefore, Godelier views the genesis of religion as arising from two sources: the effect *in* consciousness of a specific type of historical relation of humans being with each other and with nature, and the effect of analogous thinking itself on the content of its representations.

Although Godelier explicitly draws on the writings of Marx, Engels, and Lévi-Strauss in the essays that I have just summarized (1977: 176– 85, 204–20), such ideas are reflected, as we have seen, in the writings of many earlier scholars: Feuerbach, Tylor, Comte, Frazer, and Van Gennep. They essentially represent an intellectualist interpretation of religion that was challenged by Durkheim and Freud long ago. It seems somewhat incongruous that a Marxist scholar should be concerned with trying to explain the origin of "religion," but hardly surprising that he comes up with statements that merely echo those of late-Victorian anthropologists.

Godelier's discussion of Mbuti religion is more substantive. Religious practices among the Mbuti take the form of a forest cult, the forest being viewed by these foragers of Zaire as an animate, divine being, who protects them and provides them with all the necessities of life. The Mbuti "personify the forest," and, as Colin Turnbull records, "The perennial certainty of economic sufficiency, the general lack of crisis in their lives, all lead the Mbuti to the conviction that the forest, regarded as the source of Pepo (life)...is benevolent" (1965: 254). The two major rituals are the *Elima*, the puberty ritual for girls, and the *Molima*, the funerary ceremony for a respected adult, though a lesser Molimo may be held for poor hunting or sickness. Death is associated with the forest's sleeping, and the need is thus felt to "awaken" the forest. The Molimo festival, which may last a month, should ideally be a time of sheer joy, with singing and dancing, and the band spends every day hunting. Refusal to hunt or sing is thought to disrupt the vital cooperation of the band. Godelier suggests that the forest represents for the Mbuti an "ideological instance" where the conditions of their mode of production and their society are represented in inverted, mythical fashion. "It is not the hunters who catch game, it is the forest" that provides. The forest represents the totality of the material and social conditions for the reproduction of Mbuti society. There are echoes here of Durkheim's functionalism, but Godelier goes on to suggest that during the Molimo rite there is "an intensification of the process of production." It is therefore a form of symbolic labor that at the same time intensifies and exalts group cooperation. He thus concludes that far from having nothing to do with material culture, as some idealists hold, the religious rite has both a material and a political function. The Mbuti are an egalitarian community, but Godelier suggests that in this intensification of labor we can understand why, when circumstances permitted, certain men or groups came to personify the common good themselves or to gain exclusive access to the supernatural powers that were supposed to control the world. What began as domination without violence could develop into ideological oppression and economic exploitation (1977: 9–10, 51–61).

Godelier is primarily concerned with offering a New Marxist theory of religion, his main suggestion being that one should explore the relationship between religion and the symbolic systems of a particular society and its mode of production. But since this relationship is conceived as ideological, does it follow that religion has a universal political function, as Godelier seems to imply? Or, if symbolic systems are seen more specifically as "instruments of domination" serving to legitimate group interests (which is not specifically Marxist), is this mode of analysis more usefully applied to those societies characterized by class struggle and a state apparatus? (cf. Feuchtwang 1975, Bourdieu 1979). Godelier's reply would seem to be a negative one.

All in all, it seems that Godelier does not have much to offer in the way of an anthropology of religion – nothing to compare with Geertz, Turner, and Douglas. Yet in adopting Marx's materialism as the epistemological horizon for critical work in the social sciences, Godelier's writings are important and salutary. He offers a way forward, whereas hermeneutics and symbolic anthropology lead only to interesting cul-de-sacs. It is, then, a pity that he failed to incorporate in his work the dialectical, historical, and humanistic dimension of Marx's thought – the dimension that derives from Hegel, with whom we began this study.

Selected monographs for
further reading

Aberle, D. F. 1966. *The Peyote Religion among the Navaho*. University of Chicago Press. An important study, covering all aspects of the Peyote cult among the Navaho Indians of New Mexico.

Ahern, E. M. 1981. *Chinese Ritual and Politics*. Cambridge University Press. An interesting study, based on fieldwork in Taiwan, of popular Chinese ritual behavior toward the gods. Such ritual communications, she argues, are metaphors for political transactions.

Ahmed, A. S. 1976. *Millennium and Charisma among Pathans: A Critical Essay in Social Anthropology*. London: Routledge & Kegan Paul. A theoretical treatise on the Swat Pathans of northwestern Pakistan, largely devoted to a critique of Barth's earlier study, which adopted an equilibrium model and games theory to explain Swat politics. Ahmed offers a more dynamic approach and in doing so provides some interesting material on Islam.

Appadurai, A. 1981. *Worship and Conflict under Colonial Rule: A South Indian Case*. Cambridge University Press. Using the insights of Geertz and Turner, Appadurai offers a careful and important ethnohistorical analysis of a South Indian temple over a two hundred–year period. The study explores the cultural system of the temple and the changing political relationships between the temple and the colonial state, from the eighteenth century to the present.

Babb, L. A. 1975. *The Divine Hierarchy: Popular Hinduism in Central India*. New York: Columbia University Press. Focusing on the Brahmanic tradition, the study offers a structuralist analysis of Hindu rituals, specifically life-cycle rituals and the concepts of purity and pollution. It has a wealth of interesting data on Hinduism.

Barley, N. 1983. *Symbolic Structures: An Exploration of the Culture of the Dowayos*. Cambridge University Press. The book combines an essay on symbolism with a detailed analysis of the symbolism and rituals of the Dowayos of northern Cameroon.

Barnes, R. H. 1974. *Kedang: A Study of the Collective Thought of an Eastern Indonesian People*. Oxford University Press. Focusing entirely on the collective thought of the Kedang, Barnes demonstrates, through an examination of their myths, social structure, religious beliefs, and rituals, that there is a unifying metaphysics. A dense but interesting ethnography.

Barrett, L. 1977. *The Rastafarians: The Dreadlocks of Jamaica*. Kingston: Sangsters Heinemann. A useful and readable study of this contemporary socioreligious movement. Barrett gives a good account of its history, beliefs, rituals, and symbolism.

Bartels, L. 1983. *Oromo Religion: Myths and Rites of the Western Oromo of Ethiopia: An Attempt to Understand.* Berlin: Dietrich Reimer. A sympathetic and well-written study of the traditional religion of the Oromo of the Wallaga Province of Ethiopia. Based on ten years of research, it is mainly ethnographic.

Bastide, R. 1978. *The African Religions of Brazil: Toward a Sociology of the Inter-penetration of Civilizations.* Baltimore: John Hopkins University Press. A wide-ranging synthesis and sociological interpretation of the Afro-American religious cults of Brazil, based on nearly twenty years of research. Bastide attempts to provide a dynamic framework for the understanding of these cults. It is an impressive study.

Bastien, J. W. 1978. *Mountain of the Condor: Metaphor and Ritual in an Andean Ayllu.* New York: West. An ethnographic account of rituals among a Qulla-huaya community of the Bolivian highlands. Bastien indicates the presence of an underlying symbolic pattern, a mountain/body metaphor that links the several villages and hamlets that are situated on the mountain slopes.

Bateson, G. 1936. *Naven.* Stanford University Press. A classic study of the Naven ceremony of the Iatmul of Papua New Guinea. Bateson situates the ceremony within its cultural context, relating it to the structure and ethos of the society.

Bellah, R. N. 1957. *Tokugawa Religion: The Values of Pre-Industrial Japan.* New York: Free Press. A valuable study of the importance of religious factors in the political and economic development of Japan. Using a Weberian frame-work, Bellah examines the feudal Tokugawa period.

Berglund, Axel-Ivar. 1976. *Zulu Thought-Patterns and Symbolism.* London: C. Hurst. Born of Swedish missionaries serving in Zululand, Berglund is a mis-sionary and a theologian as well as an anthropologist. The study is the result of twelve years' research and is a rich and detailed analysis of Zulu religion. It discusses in detail their concepts of divinities and spirits and their various rites: sacrifice, initiation, witchcraft, healing. Berglund reveals their subtle symbolism and their underlying logic and meaning.

Berndt, R. 1974. *Australian Aboriginal Religion.* Leiden: E. J. Brill. A compre-hensive survey of Australian aboriginal religion, divided into four cultural areas. It usefully summarizes a wealth of ethnographic material and contains an extensive bibliography. A useful introductory text.

Beyer, S. 1973. *The Cult of Tara: Magic and Ritual in Tibet.* Berkeley: University of California Press. Based on data collected in a monastic community of Ti-betan refugees in Hamachal Pradesh, where Beyer spent more than a year, the study focuses on the cult of the goddess Tara. He describes in great detail the organization of the Drugpa Monastery and gives a good description and analysis of the Tibetan religious practices.

Bjerke, S. 1981. *Religion and Misfortune: The Bacwezi Complex and the Other Spirit Cults of the Zinza of Northwestern Tanzania.* Oslo: Universitets Forlaget. Primarily focusing on the Bacwezi Complex, a phenomenon well known among the other interlacustrine Bantu, and basing his analysis on a year's intensive field-work (1966–7), Bjerke presents an interesting study of an African religion.

330

He argues that the growing significance of this spirit cult among the Zinza is associated with the imposition of colonial rule and the rapid social changes that have taken place during the past century.

Buxton, J. 1973. *Religion and Healing in Mandari.* Oxford University Press. A fine ethnographic study of a small group of Nilotic people living in the arid regions of the southern Sudan. Based on fieldwork done primarily in 1952–3, the study gives a sensitive account of Mandari religion and cosmology and of their medico-religious practices. She indicates the underlying significance of vertical and color symbolism.

Calley, M. J. C. 1965. *God's People: West Indian Pentecostal Sects in England.* Oxford University Press. Based on two years' intensive study, this is a useful early account of Pentecostal sects, with discussions of the dynamics of sect formation and of the congregational rituals.

Carrithers, M. 1983. *The Forest Monks of Sri Lanka: An Anthropological and Historical Study.* Oxford University Press. Based on fieldwork conducted in 1972–5, Carrithers gives a fascinating account of the forest-dwelling monks of Sri Lanka. The study contains a wealth of biographical material on the life of these solitary monks.

Cohn, N. 1957. *The Pursuit of the Millennium: Revolutionary Millenarians and Mystical Anarchists of the Middle Ages.* London: Secker & Warburg. A scholarly and important study of millenarian movements in western Europe between the eleventh and sixteenth centuries.

Cohn, N. 1975. *Europe's Inner Demons: An Enquiry Inspired by the Great Witch Hunt.* London: Heinemann. A highly readable account and interpretation of European witch beliefs and the "witch hunt" of the sixteenth and seventeenth centuries.

Crapanzano, V. 1981. *The Hamadsha: A Study in Moroccan Ethnopsychiatry.* Berkeley: University of California Press. A comprehensive study of a religious brotherhood in Morocco, the Hamadsha, which is associated primarily with the lower classes of urban areas, specifically the city of Meknes. Tracing its ancestry back to two Muslim saints of the late seventeenth century, the brotherhood is renowned for its cult rituals, which involve head slashing and other forms of self-mutilation. Crapanzano gives a good account of the forms of therapy associated with the cult.

Das, V. 1977. *Structure and Cognition: Aspects of Hindu Caste and Ritual.* Oxford University Press. A monographic study of two Sanskrit texts, the Dharmaranya Purana and the Grihya Sutra, in which Das offers an interpretation of Hindu theories of caste and ritual. Primarily structuralist in her approach, she offers an analysis of the categories of Brahman, King, and Sanyasi, and their relationship to the Jati system. The study also includes useful discussions of pollution and sacrifice.

Deren, M. 1975. *The Voodoo Gods.* London: Granada. A reissue of the study *Divine Horseman,* published in 1953, it gives a clear account of the folk religion of Haiti by someone who was both an anthropologist and a cult participant.

Droogers, A. 1980. *The Dangerous Journey: Symbolic Aspects of Boys' Initiation among the Wagenia of Kisangani, Zaire.* The Hague: Mouton. An excellent ethno-

331

graphic description of boys' initiation rites among the Wagenia of Zaire. Its theoretical import is limited, Droogers tending to follow Turner's approach to ritual symbolism.

Dumont, J. 1976. *Under the Rainbow: Nature and Supernature among the Panare Indians.* Austin: University of Texas Press. A stimulating structuralist analysis of the culture of the Panare, a small hunting-horticultural society living in the forests of southern Venezuela.

Eickelman, D. F. 1976. *Moroccan Islam: Tradition and Society in a Pilgrimage Center.* Austin: University of Texas Press. This book is a study of popular beliefs and practices of Muslims in an urban pilgrimage center of Morocco. It focuses on one "Cult of the Saints," that of the Sherqawi. The study concludes with a general discussion of the maraboutic tradition and the effects of French colonialism on the various cults.

Endicott, K. 1979. *Batek Negrito Religion: The World View and Rituals of a Hunting and Gathering People of Peninsular Malaysia.* Oxford University Press. An excellent study of the religion of the nomadic Batek, focusing on their beliefs in supernatural beings who control the processes of nature, such as thunderstorms. Endicott gives an interesting analysis of their cosmology, shamanism, prohibitions, and rituals.

Favret-Saada, J. 1980. *Deadly Words: Witchcraft in the Bocage.* Cambridge University Press. A detailed account of witchcraft beliefs and practices among a contemporary peasant population living in the Bocage region of western France. Taking a subjectivist approach, Favret-Saada presents an interesting analysis of the relationship between the accused witch, the victim, and unwitcher.

Fernandez, J. W. 1982. *Bwiti: An Ethnography of Religious Imagination in Africa.* Princeton University Press. An extremely rich and detailed study of the religious culture of the Fang, a Bantu people of West Equatorial Africa, based on twenty years of research studies.

Firth, R. 1940. *The Work of the Gods in Tikopia.* London School of Economics Monographs, nos. 1–2. London: Percy Lund. A classic functionalist account of the religion of the people of the Tikopia, a small island in the Pacific. Firth stresses the unity of their complex ritual system.

Fry, P. 1976. *Spirits of Protest: Spirit Mediums and the Articulation of Consensus among the Zezuru of Southern Rhodesia (Zimbabwe).* Cambridge University Press. Based on fieldwork carried out in 1965–6 in a rural area near Salisbury (Harare), the study explores the relationship between African nationalism and the new emphasis on traditional institutions, especially spirit mediumship. The analysis is based on a number of detailed case histories of spirit mediums.

Fuchs, S. 1965. *Rebellious Prophets: A Study of Messianic Movements in Indian Religions.* Bombay: Asia Publishing House. A descriptive analysis of the various millenarian cults that have appeared throughout the Indian subcontinent, dealing mainly with those movements that have arisen among the tribal communities.

Fuller, C. J. 1984. *Servants of the Goddess: The Priests of a South Indian Temple.* Cambridge University Press. A detailed study of the religious organization and administration of the Minakshi Temple at Madurai in South India and of the social functions of the Brahman priests who serve the temple. It also throws important light on Hinduism in practice.

Gell, A. 1975. *Metamorphosis of the Cassowaries: Umedia Society, Language and Ritual.* London School of Economics Monographs SE. London: Athlone. A fascinating study of a small village in the West Sepik province of lowland Papua New Guinea. Giving a good outline of the social structure of the village and its pervasive dualism, the study contains a rich analysis of a public dance ritual, Ida, which is held annually and combines a *rite de passage* with a fertility ritual.

Gellner, E. 1981. *Muslim Society.* Cambridge University Press. An important collection of essays on Islam and Islamic society, including several reviews of other studies. The central essay develops Gellner's "pendulum swing" theory of Islam, the notion of an oscillation between a tribal, ecstatic, and personalized religious form and one that is urban and scriptural.

Gilsenan, Michael. 1973. *Saint and Sufi in Modern Egypt.* Oxford University Press. A fine study of the rise and sociological significance of an Egyptian Sufi order, Hamidiya Shadhiliya, founded in the first decades of the present century. The study includes a biography of its founder Salama and interesting descriptions of the order's main rituals.

Goldman, I. 1975. *The Mouth of Heaven: An Introduction to Kwakiutl Religious Thought.* New York: Wiley. The Kwakiutl, an Indian community of the Northwest coast of America, are well known through the studies of the pioneer ethnographer Franz Boas. This important study presents a rich and detailed analysis of Kwakiutl religious beliefs and rituals, showing how their cosmological beliefs united the entire universe – people, animals, plants, spirits, and objects – into a cosmic whole.

Granet, M. 1976. *The Religion of the Chinese People.* (1922) New York: Harper & Row. First published in 1922, this is a classic study of chinese religion, which includes an introduction by Maurice Freedman. The book is a significant sociological analysis in the tradition of Durkheim and Mauss. Although weak ethnographically, it is an important historical document.

Greenberg, J. 1981. *Santiago's Sword: Chatino Peasant Religion and Economics.* Berkeley: University of California Press. Their social and religious systems (the Fiesta Complex and closed corporate organization), having to adapt both to local ecological conditions and to the wider political-economic system, are a two-edged sword, Greenberg argues. It both defends community interests and is an instrument of domination by church and state.

Griaule, M. 1965. *Conversations with Ogotemmeli: An Introduction to Dogon Religious Ideas.* Oxford University Press. For over twenty years Griaule directed ethnographic studies in western Africa. The present text records the conversations with a blind ritual elder, Ogotemmeli. It gives a sensitive outline of Dogon myths and cosmology.

Hammond-Tooke, W. D. 1981. *Boundaries and Belief: The Structure of a Sotho World View.* Johannesburg: Witwatersrand University Press. A study of the cosmology of a group of Sotho-speaking peoples of southern Africa, the Kgaga of the Lowveld. Hammond-Tooke gives a detailed account of their religious beliefs and practices, as well as of their initiations, witchcraft, and pollution beliefs, and attempts to delineate the underlying symbolic patterns.

Harris, Grace. 1978. *Casting Out Anger: Religion among the Taita of Kenya.* Cambridge University Press. An interesting study of the religion of the Taita people of eastern Kenya, focusing on the Butasi belief and ritual complex. Based on research studies carried out between 1950 and 1952, the work show how anger and the threat of anger affect many aspects of Taita social life.

Hicks, D. 1976. *Tetum Ghosts and Kin: Fieldwork in an Indonesian Community.* Palo Alto, Calif.: Mayfield. An ethnographic study of the Tetum, a group of swidden cultivators living on the island of Timor. Taking the ritual relationship between ancestral ghosts and their human kin as a starting point, Hicks shows how the different facets of Tetum culture are united into a comprehensive system.

Howell, S. 1984. *Society and Cosmos: Chewong of Peninsular Malaysia.* Oxford University Press. A perceptive study of a small group of Malaysian aboriginal people who inhabit the tropical rain forests of Pahyang. The focus of the study is on Chewong cosmology and their indigenous psychological concepts and classifications.

Hugh-Jones, S. *The Palm and the Pleiades: Initiation and Cosmology in Northwest Amazonia.* Cambridge University Press. A study of a men's secret cult, Yurupary, that is widespread throughout northwestern Amazonia. A structuralist study.

Jensen, E. 1974. *The Iban and Their Religion.* Oxford University Press (Clarendon Press). Based on extensive fieldwork carried out between 1959 and 1966 in the Lubok Antu district of Sarawak, the study gives a good account of the religious beliefs and practices of these swidden cultivators. Its strengths are ethnographic rather than theoretical.

Jules-Rosette, B. 1975. *African Apostles: Ritual and Conversion in the Church of John Maranke.* Ithaca: Cornell University Press. A study of the church of John Maranke, which was founded in Zimbabwe and has since spread to Zaire, where Jules-Rosette undertook her main researches (1971–2), studying one congregation in detail. She became a member of the church, and the study is highly personalized and contains a stimulating discussion of the apostolic ritual. It is weak in theoretical insights.

Junod, H. A. 1927. *The Life of a South African Tribe.* London: Macmillan. A sympathetic study by an early missionary of the religious beliefs and practices of the Thonga of Mozambique. It gives a good account of their ancestral rites.

Kapferer, B. 1983. *A Celebration of Demons: Exorcism and the Aesthetics of Healing in Sri Lanka.* Bloomington: Indiana University Press. An analysis of the rites of exorcism among a community in southwestern Sri Lanka, it gives a detailed account of possession and exorcism and of how such phenomena are to be understood in terms of Sinhala-Buddhist culture, particularly focusing on their aesthetics.

Karim, W. 1981. *Ma'Betisek Concepts of Living Things.* London School of Economics Monographs No. 54. London: Athlone. An important and well-written structural analysis of the myths and rituals of a Malaysian aboriginal community.

334

The author outlines the coexistence of two opposed and apparently incompatible conceptions of the relationship of humans to the plant and animal world. In the Tulah view, animals and plants are seen instrumentally as sources of food, whereas in the Kemali view they are seen as possessing spirits that, if they are killed or destroyed, can subject humans to misfortune or death.

Katz, R. 1982. *Boiling Energy: Community Healing among the Kalahari !Kung.* Cambridge, Mass.: Harvard University Press. A vivid and detailed account of the !Kung trance dance, a curing ritual that activates the *num* or magical energy within the bodies of the dancers. The study gives numerous descriptions by !Kung men and women about the experience of this boiling energy.

Keesing, R. M. 1982. *Kwaio Religion: The Living and the Dead in a Solomon Island Society.* New York: Columbia University Press. An ethnographic account of the religious practices and beliefs of the Kwaio, an isolated community living in the interior mountains of Malaita in the Solomons. Keesing combines a number of approaches to the subject matter: Marxism, structuralism, symbolic analysis, as well as depth psychology.

Kessler, C. S. 1978. *Islam and Politics in a Malay State: Kelantan, 1838–1969.* Ithaca: Cornell University Press. An important study tracing the social and political history of the Kelantan state from the early nineteenth century and exploring the way in which religion – specifically Islam – articulates peasant interests.

La Barre, W. 1975. *The Peyote Cult.* (1938) Hamden, Conn.: Shoe String. First published in 1938, this is a classic psychoanalytic study of the peyote cult. It is highly informative and contains a very detailed bibliography. It is perhaps the best introduction to the cult.

Lambek, M. 1982. *Human Spirits: A Cultural Account of Trance in Mayotte.* Cambridge University Press. A description and analysis of trance behavior among the Malagasy speakers of Mayotte, an island off eastern Africa. The study is primarily concerned with a category of spirits known as *patros*, and it explores the interaction between these and human beings in the context of curing rituals. Women are the main participants in these rituals, although Lambek found no linkage between possession and the women's low status.

Lawrence, P. 1964. *Road Belong Cargo: A Study of the Cargo Movement in the Southern Madang District New Guinea.* Manchester University Press. A detailed and important case study of a cargo cult, that associated with the Madang district and the prophet Yali. Besides outlining indigenous cosmological beliefs and the impact of the colonial order, Lawrence gives a very precise and lucid account of the history and beliefs associated with the cult movement.

Leacock, S., and R. Leacock. 1975. *Spirits of the Deep: A Study of an Afro-Brazilian Cult.* New York: Doubleday. A comprehensive account of a contemporary Afro-Brazilian religious cult found in Belem, Brazil. Based on researches undertaken during 1962–3, it gives a lucid description of the possession rites (Batuque) and of the cult organization and includes an account of the life history of a medium.

Lewis, G. 1980. *Day of Shining Red: An Essay on Understanding Ritual.* Cambridge University Press. Primarily a study of initiation rites among the Gnau of Papua New Guinea, Lewis offers some important theoretical reflections of structuralist analysis of ritual, tending to suggest that a more phenomenological approach is needed.

Lienhardt, G. 1961. *Divinity and Experience: The Religion of the Dinka.* Oxford University Press. Complementing the work of Evans-Pritchard on the Nuer, this important study gives a sensitive analysis of the religion of the Dinka, a pastoral people of the Sudan. Primarily focused on their cosmological ideas and their concept of divinity.

MacGaffey, W. 1983. *Modern Kongo Prophets: Religion in a Plural Society.* Bloomington: Indiana University Press. A comparative study of prophetic movements of the lower Congo. Focusing primarily on the Kimbangu, the Black Church of Mpadi Simon, and the Universal Church of the Twelve Apostles, MacGaffey details their distinctive responses to the colonial and postcolonial situations.

Martin, C. 1978. *Keepers of the Game: Indian–Animal Relationships and the Fur Trade.* Berkeley: University of California Press. A stimulating and controversial study by a historian of the Algonkian Indians of eastern Canada. Drawing on ecological, historical, and anthropological studies, Martin explores the paradox between, on the one hand, the well-documented accounts of Indian religious cosmology that required a reverential attitude toward animals and, on the other, the seemingly wanton slaughter of game that occurred with the inception of the fur trade.

Martin, M. 1975. *Kimbangu: An African Prophet and His Church.* Oxford: Blackwell Publisher. A historical account and analysis of the Church of Christ according to Simon Kimbangu, a prophet who was arrested in 1921 by the Belgian authorities and spent the remaining thirty years of his life in prison. Martin discusses the establishment of the church, its symbolism, and its relationship to contemporary Zaire.

Mauss, M. 1978. *Seasonal Variations of the Eskimo: A Study in Social Morphology.* (1906) London: Routledge & Kegan Paul. A reprint of the classic study of Inuit social life first published in 1906. Contrasting the communal winter organization with that of the family-based summer pattern, Mauss shows how other social institutions – kinship usage, religious rituals, food taboos – reflect and express the basic seasonal dualism.

Metcalf, P. 1982. *A Borneo Journey into Death in Berawan Eschatology from its Rituals.* Philadelphia: University of Pennsylvania Press. A rich analysis of mortuary rituals among the Berawan of northern Borneo, who live in longhouse communities. The study examines the detail their funeral ceremonies and eschatological beliefs.

Metraux, A. 1959. *Voodoo.* London: Deutsch. A useful account and sociological analysis of voodoo in Haiti by a pioneer ethnographer.

Middleton, J. 1960. *Lugbara Religion: Ritual and Authority among an East African People.* Oxford University Press. An exemplary study in the tradition of sociological functionalism, giving a rich analysis of the place of ritual and belief in the social life of the Lugbara of Uganda. Focused on the cults of the dead and their role in maintaining lineage authority.

Mooney, J. 1965. *The Ghost-dance Religion and the Sioux Outbreak of 1890.* (1896)

University of Chicago Press. An abridged reissue of Mooney's classic account of the Ghost Dance Religion, first published in 1896.

Morioka, K. 1975. *Religion in Changing Japanese Society*. University of Tokyo Press. The book contains several articles, rich in empirical detail, on the main religions of Japan: Shinto, Buddhism, and Christianity. It deals with the relationship of religion to many aspects of contemporary Japanese life and has a useful bibliography. A good introductory text.

Myerhoff, B. G. 1974. *Peyote Hunt: The Sacred Journey of the Huichul Indians*. Ithaca: Cornell University Press. On the basis of fieldwork that she did in the 1960s, Myerhoff discusses the ritual journey of some 170 miles made by the Huichol Indians of the Sierra Madre, Mexico, in order to obtain a year's supply of peyote: Drawing on Turner's studies of symbolism, she gives a lucid account of the symbolic significance of hunting among the Huichul.

Nadel, S. F. 1954. *Nupe Religion: Traditional Beliefs and the Influence of Islam in a West African Kingdom*. London: Routledge & Kegan Paul. A full and detailed description by a pioneer ethnographer of the religious beliefs and practices of a Nigerian people. The study has a concluding discussion of the influence of Islam.

Nelson, R. K. 1983. *Make Prayers to the Raven: A Koyokon View of the Northern Forest*. University of Chicago Press. An ethnographic description of the knowledge and beliefs relating to the natural world of the Koyokon Indians, a group of Athapaskan speakers of the interior forests of Alaska. Nelson outlines the material in respect to specific types of animals and plants, thereby revealing their Koyokon Indians' shamanistic world view.

Obeyesekere, G. 1981. *Medusa's Hair: An Essay on Person Symbols and Religious Experience*. University of Chicago Press. Combines a rich ethnographic account of the Kataragama cult in Sri Lanka with a theoretical essay on the meaning and significance of religious symbolism. Obeyesekere attempts an interpretation of symbols and ritual that uses the insights of both Weber and Freud.

Ortiz, A. 1969. *The Tewa World: Space, Time, Being, and Becoming in a Pueblo Society*. University of Chicago Press. An important study by a member of the Pueblo. Ortiz describes Tewa mythology, cosmology, and ritual in relation to its moiety system and traces the wider significance of this symbolic dualism in the society.

Ortner, S. B. 1978. *Sherpas through Their Rituals*. Cambridge University Press. A study of Tibetan Buddhism, stressing the individualistic orientation of the Nepalese villagers. Adopting Geertz's approach to ritual symbolism – that it offers a model of society, and for social life – Ortner presents a useful analysis of Sherpa rituals and a good discussion of their style of Buddhism.

Peacock, J. L. 1978. *Muslim Puritans: Reformist Psychology in Southeast Asian Islam*. Berkeley: University of California Press. Based on fieldwork studies undertaken in 1969–70 in Indonesia and Singapore, the study attempts to place Muslim reformism within a wider cultural context. Using the insights of Weber and Geertz and incorporating statistical and historical data into his analysis, Peacock attempts to provide a psychological dimension to this important study of reformism.

Pocock, D. 1973. *Mind, Body and Wealth: A Study of Belief and Practice in an Indian Village*. Oxford: Blackwell Publisher. A study of the beliefs and practices of the Patidars, a dominant caste of central Gujarat, India. A well-written study, including interesting discussion of various Hindu sects.

Rabinow, P. 1975. *Symbolic Domination: Cultural Form and Historical Change in Morocco*. University of Chicago Press. The study focuses on a group of Muslim holy men, descendants of a Sufi saint, who live in the villages of the middle Atlas Mountains of Morocco. In recent years these religious leaders have been losing their political dominance, and Rabinow explores the reasons for this and the interrelationship between the core symbols of Moroccan culture – like baraka – and changes in social and economic life.

Reichard, G. A. 1963. *Navaho Religion: A Study of Symbolism*. Princeton University Press. An important symbolic analysis of the religion of Navaho Indians of New Mexico. Reichard reviews a lot of ethnographic material and demonstrates that the many elements of their complex religious system have an underlying order and coherence.

Reichel-Dolmatoff, G. 1971. *Amazonian Cosmos: The Sexual and Religious Symbolism of the Tukano Indians*. University of Chicago Press. An important study based solely on the information provided by one informant, a Tukano Indian living in Bogota. It gives a sophisticated account of Tukano cosmology that puts a central focus upon sexual symbolism and on the intimate relationship between humans and nature.

Richards, A. I. 1982. *Chisungu: A Girl's Initiation Ceremony among the Bemba of Zambia*. London: Tavistock. A reissue of a classic study first published in 1956, with a useful introduction by Jean la Fontaine. It contains an absorbing account and interpretation of a girl's initiation ritual among the Bemba.

Roe, P. G. 1982. *The Cosmic Zygote: Cosmology in the Amazon Basin*. New Brunswick, N.J.: Rutgers University Press. Drawing on the ethnography of the Shipibo and of the peoples of the northwestern Amazon, Roe argues that underlying their myths and rituals there is a basic "metacosmology" built out of animals and other natural symbols. Such a metacosmology, he suggests, is best expressed in the image of a cosmic egg, that symbolizes an endless cycle of death and rebirth.

Scharer, H. 1963. *Ngaju Religion: The Conception of God among a South Borneo People*. The Hague: Martinus Nijhoff. A classic study of religious cosmology of the Ngaju, which expresses both a complex unity of all beings and a pervasive dualistic symbolism.

Shirokogoroff, S. M.1935. *The Psychomental Complex of the Tungus*. London: Kegan Paul. A classic monograph of the spirit beliefs and possession rites of the Tungus, a group of Siberian reindeer herders. It gives interesting details on shamanism – the social position of the shaman and the psychological aspects of the possession rites.

Simpson, G. E. *Black Religions in the New World*. New York: Columbia University Press. A monumental study, based on over forty years' research and fieldwork, describing Afro-American cults in detail.

Singer, M. 1972. *When a Great Tradition Modernizes: An Anthropological Approach to Indian Civilization.* University of Chicago Press. An important collection of essays on Indian culture and Hinduism, following the tradition of Redfield and his concept of the great and little traditions. Includes some illuminating discussion of bhakti religious cults in Madras.

Southwold, M. 1983. *Buddhism in Life:The Anthropological Study of Religion and the Sinhalese Practice of Buddhism.* Manchester University Press. A lively and perceptive study of Sinhalese Buddhism, which attempts to assert the authenticity of village Buddhism, with its stress on the ethical norms of goodness and gentleness, as against the interpretations of Buddhism offered by Western scholars, middle-class elites, and the clerics.

Speck, F. G. 1935. *Naskapi: The Savage Hunters of the Labrador Peninsula.* Norman: University of Oklahoma Press. A pioneering study of the religion of the hunting bands of Labrador, Canada. It has important discussions of their myths, divination, and spirit concepts, as well as of their ritual relationships to animal life.

Spiro, M. E. 1972. *Buddhism and Society: A Great Tradition and Its Burmese Vicissitudes.* New York; Harper & Row. An important and substantial study of Burmese Buddhism, combining functionalist, historical, and psychoanalytic approaches. Spiro identifies three distinct ideological systems within Buddhism and offers important discussions of the relationship between the textual and practical conceptions of Buddhism and of the relationship of the Sangha, an order of monks, to the state and Burmese society.

Srinivas, M. N. 1952. *Religion and Society among the Coorgs of South India.* London: J. K. Publishers. A classic study of the religious beliefs and rituals of a high-caste community of South India, interpreting the religion with respect to its social context. Srinivas introduces the concept of Sanskritization, the adoption by low-caste communities of Sanskritic rituals in order to enhance their social status.

Sundkler, B. G. M. 1948. *Bantu Prophets in South Africa.* Oxford University Press. A missionary with wide experience of southern Africa, Sundkler presents a sympathetic and detailed account of the independent churches of South Africa, making a distinction between the Ethiopian and Zionist types.

Tambiah, S. J. 1970. *Buddhism and Spirit Cults in North-East Thailand.* Cambridge University Press. An excellent and substantial ethnographic account of religious beliefs and practices of people in a village in northeastern Thailand. Tambiah relates the village religion to classical Buddhism as well as to the social context, identifying four main ritual complexes.

Tambiah, S. J. 1976. *World Conqueror and World Renouncer: A Study of Buddhism and Polity in Thailand against a Historical Background.* Cambridge University Press. A well-documented account of the relationship between Buddhism and politics in Thailand, focusing on the Sangha, an order of monks. Highly readable, the final chapter has an important comparative discussion of Buddhism and politics in Sri Lanka, Burma, and Thailand.

Tambiah, S. J. 1984. *The Buddhist Saints of the Forest and the Cult of Amulets.* Cambridge University Press. Complementing his other studies on Thai Buddhism, this volume deals with modern Thai forest saints and their associated cult of amulets. Tambiah explores the relationship of these forest monks to other aspects of the society: the state, village monks versus urban monks, and the Buddhist laity.

Tanner, A. 1979. *Bringing Home the Animals: Religious Ideology and Mode of Production of the Mistassini Cree Hunters.* New York: St. Martin's Press. Based on eighteen months' research among the Cree Indians, hunters and trappers living in the boreal forest, east of James Bay, Quebec, this study examines their hunting ideology and provides an exciting account of their ritualization of space, hunting divination, and the respect that they show toward the game animals.

Taussig, M. T. 1980. *The Devil and Commodity Fetishism in South America.* Chapel Hill: University of North Carolina Press. Combining ethnographic description with a penetrating analysis of capitalist development in Latin America, Taussig attempts to relate the social significance of the devil in the folklore of plantation workers in western Columbia and of tin miners in Bolivia to their proletarianization.

Tonkinson, R. 1978. *The Mardudjara Aborigines: Living the Dream in Australia's Deserts.* New York: Holt, Rinehart & Winston. A perceptive study of the Mardudjara people of the arid Western desert. Rich in ethnographic data, it aims to give an ethos of their daily life and has good accounts of their initiations and the religious system (the dreaming).

Van Binsbergen, W. M. J. 1981. *Religious Change in Zambia: Exploratory Studies.* London: Routledge & Kegan Paul. A collection of several important essays on religious movements in Zambia. Written from a Marxist standpoint, it includes discussions of spirit cults, cults of affliction, and the Lumpa church.

Walker, J. R. 1980. *Lakota Belief and Ritual.* Lincoln: University of Nebraska Press. An important collection of ethnographic materials on Oglala religion and ritual obtained by Dr. James Walker, who held the position of physician at Pine Ridge Agency for eighteen years. It records the thoughts of old Oglala Sioux as set down by Walker.

Williams, F. E. 1977. *"The Vailala Madness" and Other Essays*, ed. E. Schwimmer. Honolulu: University Press of Hawaii. Williams served as a government anthropologist in Papua New Guinea from 1922 to 1943. He was a functionalist, and his essays throw important light on early cargo cults.

Worsley, P. 1957. *The Trumpet Shall Sound: A Study of "Cargo" Cults in Melanesia.* London: MacGibbon & Kee. An important pioneering work, with clear descriptions of the early millennial cults in Melanesia. A Marxist analysis, but clearly and vividly written.

References

Abercrombie, N., S. Hill, and B. S. Turner. 1980. *The Dominant Ideology Thesis.* London.

Abraham, J. H. 1973. *The Origins and Growth of Sociology.* Harmondsworth: Penguin Books.

Acton, H. B. 1958. The Marxist-Leninist theory of religion. *Ratio* 1:136–49.

Adorno, T., and M. Horkheimer. 1973. *Dialectic of Enlightenment,* trans. J. Cumming. London: Lane.

Allen, D. 1978. *Structure and Creativity in Religion.* The Hague: Mouton.

Althusser, L. 1969. *For Marx.* Harmondsworth: Penguin Books.

1972. *Politics and History.* London: New Left Books.

Althusser, L., and E. Balibar. 1970. *Reading Capital.* London: New Left Books.

Altizer, T. J. J. 1963. *Mircea Eliade and the Dialectic of the Sacred.* Philadelphia: Westminster Press.

Aron, R. 1967. *Main Currents in Sociological Thought.* Vol. 2. Harmondsworth: Penguin Books.

Asad, T. 1983. Anthropological conceptions of religion: reflections on Geertz. *Man* 18:237–59.

Augé, M. 1982. *The Anthropological Circle.* Cambridge University Press.

Avineri, S. 1968. *The Social and Political Thought of Karl Marx.* Cambridge University Press.

Ayer, A. J. 1936. *Language, Truth and Logic.* London: Gollancz.

Badcock, C. R. 1975. *Lévi-Strauss: Structuralism and Sociological Theory.* London: Hutchinson.

Baker, S. 1867. *The Races of the Nile Basin.* London: Transactions of the Ethnological Society of London.

Barnes, B. 1973. A comparison of belief systems: anomaly versus falsehood. In Horton and Finnegan 1973, pp. 182–98.

Barnes, H. E. 1948. Herbert Spencer and the evolutionary defence of individualism. In H. E. Barnes, ed., *An Introduction to the History of Sociology.* University of Chicago Press, pp. 81–108.

Barth, F. 1964. *Nomads of South Persia.* London: Allen & Unwin.

Baudrillard, J. 1975. *The Mirror of Production.* St. Louis: Telos Press.

Beattie, J. 1966. Ritual and social change. *Man* 1:60–74.

1968. Aspects of Nyoro symbolism. *Africa* 38:413–42.

341

1970. On understanding ritual. In Wilson 1970, pp. 240–68.

Beetham, D. 1974. *Max Weber and the Theory of Modern Politics*. London: Allen & Unwin.

Beidelman, T. O. 1966. Swazi royal ritual. *Africa* 36:373–405.

1971. Nuer priests and prophets: charisma, authority and power among the Nuer. In T. O. Beidelman, ed., *The Translation of Culture*. London: Tavistock, pp. 375–416.

1973. Right and left hand among the Kaguru: a note on symbolic classification. In Needham 1973, pp. 128–66.

1974. *W. Robertson-Smith and the Sociological Study of Religion*. University of Chicago Press.

1975. Review of R. Willis, *Man and Beast*. *Man* 10:328–30.

Bellah, R. N. 1964. Religious evolution. *American Sociological Review* 29:358–74.

Bendix, R. 1959. *Max Weber: An Intellectual Portrait*. London: Methuen.

Bennett, E. A. 1966. *What Jung Really Said*. London: MacDonald.

Benoit-Smullyan, E. 1948. The sociologism of Emile Durkheim and his school. In H. E. Barnes, ed., *An Introduction to the History of Sociology*. University of Chicago Press, pp. 205–43.

Benton, T. 1984. *The Rise and Fall of Structural Marxism*. London: Macmillan.

Berg, C. 1951. *The Unconscious Significance of Hair*. London: Allen & Unwin.

Berger, P. L. 1973. *The Social Reality of Religion*. Harmondsworth: Penguin Books.

Bergson, H. 1935. *The Two Sources of Morality and Religion*. New York: Henry Holt.

Berlin, I. 1963. *Karl Marx: His Life and Environment* (1939). 3d ed. Oxford University Press.

Bernardi, B. 1959. *The Mugwe: A Failing Prophet*. Oxford University Press.

Berndt, R. M. 1951. *A Study of an Australian Aboriginal Religious Cult*. Melbourne: Cheshire.

Birnbaum, N. 1953. Conflicting interpretations of the rise of capitalism: Marx and Weber. *British Journal of Sociology* 4:121–41.

Blackham, H. J. 1952. *Six Existential Thinkers*. London: Routledge & Kegan Paul.

Bleicher, J. 1982. *The Hermeneutic Imagination*. London: Routledge & Kegan Paul.

Bloch, M. 1975. Property and the end of affinity. In M. Block, ed., *Marxist Analyses and Social Anthropology*. London: Malaby Press, pp. 203–28.

1977. The past and present in the present. *Man* 12:278–92.

1983. *Marxism and Anthropology*. Oxford University Press (Clarendon Press).

Boas, F. 1938. *The Mind of Primitive Man* (1911). New York: Macmillan.

Bocock, R. 1976. *Freud and Modern Society*. London: Nelson.

Bohannan, P. 1969. *Social Anthropology*. New York: Holt, Rinehart & Winston.

Bottomore, T. 1984. *Sociology and Socialism*. Brighton: Harvester Press.

Bottomore, T., and R. Nisbet. 1979. Structuralism. In *A History of Sociological Analysis*. London: Heinemann, pp. 557–98.

Bourdieu, P. 1979. Symbolic power. *Critique of Anthropology* 13:77–85.

Brome, V. 1978. *Jung*. London: Macmillan.

Brown, J. A. C. 1961. *Freud and the Post-Freudians*. Harmondsworth: Penguin Books.

References

Brown, R. H. 1978a. History and hermeneutics: Wilhelm Dilthey and the dialectics of interpretative method. In Brown and Lyman 1978, pp. 38–52.

1978b. Symbolic realism and sociological thought: beyond the positivist–romantic debate. In Brown and Lyman 1978, pp. 13–38.

Brown, R. H., and S. M. Lyman, eds. 1978. *Structure, Consciousness and History*. Cambridge University Press.

Buber, M. 1947. *Between Man and Man*. London: Collins.

Burrows, J. W. 1966. *Evolution and Society*. Cambridge University Press.

Callet, M. J. C. 1965. *God's People: West Indian Pentecostal Sects in England*. Oxford University Press.

Callinicos, A. 1976. *Althusser's Marxism*. London: Pluto Press.

1983a. *Marxism and Philosophy*. Oxford University Press (Clarendon Press).

1983b. *The Revolutionary Ideas of Marx*. London: Bookmarks.

Campbell, J. 1949. *The Hero with a Thousand Faces*. New York: Pantheon Books.

Cansdale, G. 1970. *Animals of Bible Lands*. Exeter: Paternoster.

Capra, F. 1982. *The Turning Point*. London: Fontana.

Carver, T. 1981. *Engels*. Oxford University Press.

Cassirer, E. 1944. *An Essay on Man*. New York: Bantam Books.

Centre for Contemporary Cultural Studies. 1978. *On Ideology*. London: Hutchinson.

Chalmers, A. F. 1978. *What Is This Thing Called Science?* Milton Keynes: Open University Press.

Charbonnier, G., ed. 1961. *Conversations with Claude Lévi-Strauss*. London: Jonathan Cape.

Chaudhuri, N. C. 1974. *Scholar Extraordinary: The Life of Friedrich Max Müller*. Delhi: Orient Paperbacks.

Clarke, S., et al. 1980. *One-dimensional Marxism*. London: Allison & Busby.

Cohen, A. 1974. *Two-dimensional Man*. London: Routledge & Kegan Paul.

Cohen, P. S. 1968. *Modern Social Theory*. London: Heinemann.

1969. Theories of myth. *Man* 4:337–53.

Colegrave, S. 1979. *The Spirit of the Valley*. London: Virago.

Colletti, L. 1973. *Marxism and Hegel*. London: New Left Books.

Collingwood, R. G. 1945. *The Idea of Nature*. Oxford University Press (Clarendon Press).

1946. *The Idea of History*. Oxford University Press.

Copleston, F. 1963. *A History of Philosophy*. Vol. 7, pt. 1. *Fichte to Hegel*. New York: Doubleday.

Cornforth, M. 1980. *Communism and Philosophy*. London: Lawrence & Wishart.

Coward, R., and J. Ellis. 1977. *Language and Materialism*. London: Routledge & Kegan Paul.

Cullen, B. 1979. *Hegel's Social and Political Thought*. London: Gill & MacMillan.

Cushing, F. H. 1883. Zuni fetishes. *Annual Report of the Bureau of American Ethnology* 2:1–45.

1896. Zuni creation myths. *Annual Report of the Bureau of American Ethnology* 13:321–447.

343

De Coulanges, F. 1900. *The Ancient City: A Study of the Religion, Laws and Institutions of Greece and Rome* (1864). London: Lee & Shepherd.

Descombes, V. 1980. *Modern French Philosophy*. Cambridge University Press.

Diamond, S. 1974. *In Search of the Primitive*. New York; Transaction.

Dilthey, W. 1976. *Selected Writings*. Ed. (with Introduction) H. P. Rickman. Cambridge University Press.

Dimock, E. C. 1966. Doctrine and practice among the Vaisnavas of Bengal. In M. Singer, ed., *Krishna: Myths, Rites and Attitudes*. University of Chicago Press, pp. 41–64.

Douglas, M. 1970a. *Natural Symbols*. Harmondsworth: Penguin Books.

1970b. *Purity and Danger* (1966). Harmondsworth: Penguin.

1975. *Implicit Meanings*. London: Routledge & Kegan Paul.

1980. *Evans-Pritchard*. London: Fontana.

1982a. *Essays in the Sociology of Perception*. London: Routledge & Kegan Paul.

1982b. *In the Active Voice*. London: Routledge & Kegan Paul.

Dubos, R. 1980. *The Wooing of Earth*. London: Athlone.

Dumont, L. 1975. Preface to the French edition of Evans-Pritchard 1940. In J. H. M. Beattie and R. G. Lienhardt, eds., *Studies in Social Anthropology*. Oxford University Press (Clarendon Press), pp. 328–42.

Durkheim, E. 1938. *The Rules of Sociological Method*. University of Chicago Press.

1964a. *The Division of Labour in Society* (1896). Glencoe, Ill.: Free Press.

1964b. *The Elementary Forms of the Religious Life* (1915). London: Allen & Unwin.

Durkheim, E., and M. Mauss. 1963. *Primitive Classifications*, ed. R. Needham (1903). University of Chicago Press.

Ehrenfeld, D. 1978. *The Arrogance of Humanism*. Oxford University Press.

Eisenstadt, S. N. 1968. *The Protestant Ethic and Modernization*. New York: Basic Books.

Ekeh, P. 1974. *Social Exchange Theory*. London: Heinemann.

Eldridge, J. E. T., ed. 1972. *Max Weber*. London: Nelson.

Eliade, M. 1958. *Patterns in Comparative Religion*. London: Steed & Ward.

1959a. Methodological remarks on the study of religious symbolism. In M. Eliade and J. M. Kitagawa, eds., *The History of Religions*. University of Chicago Press, pp. 86–107.

1959b. *The Sacred and the Profane: The Nature of Religion*. New York: Harcourt, Brace.

1968. *Myths, Dreams and Mysteries*. London: Collins/Fontana.

1969. *The Quest: History and Meaning in Religion*. University of Chicago Press.

1974a. *The Myth of the Eternal Return (Cosmos and History)* (1949). Princeton University Press.

1974b. *Shamanism: Archaic Techniques of Ecstasy*. Princeton University Press.

Elkin, A. P. 1933. Studies in Australian totemism. *Oceania* 4:114–31.

1964. *The Australian Aborigines*. New York: Doubleday.

Engels, F. 1956. *The Peasant War in Germany*. Moscow: Progress.

1968. Ludwig Feuerbach and the end of classical German philosophy (1886). In Marx and Engels 1968, pp. 586–622.

References

Evans-Pritchard, E. E. 1937. *Witchcraft, Oracles and Magic among the Azande.* Oxford University Press (Clarendon Press).

1940. *The Nuer.* Oxford University Press (Clarendon Press).

1949. *The Sanusi of Cyrenaica.* Oxford University Press (Clarendon Press).

1951. *Social Anthropology.* London: Routledge & Kegan Paul.

1956. *Nuer Religion.* Oxford University Press.

1962. *Essays in Social Anthropology.* London: Faber & Faber.

1965. *Theories of Primitive Religion.* Oxford University Press (Clarendon Press).

1981. *A History of Anthropological Thought.* Ed. E. Gellner. London: Faber & Faber.

Fackenheim, E. 1967. *The Religious Dimension of Hegel's Thought.* Bloomington: Indiana University Press.

Faron, L. C. 1962. Symbolic values and the integration of society among the Mapuch of Chile. *American Anthropology* 64:1151–64.

Feuchtwang, S. 1975. Investigating religion. In M. Bloch, ed., *Marxist Analyses and Social Anthropology.* London: Malaby Press.

Feuerbach, L. 1957. *The Essence of Christianity,* trans. George Eliot (1841). New York: Harper.

Firth, R. 1964. *Essays in Social Organization and Values.* London: Athlone.

1966. Twins, birds and vegetables: problems of identification in primitive religious thought. *Man* 1:1–17.

1973. *Symbols: Public and Private.* London: Allen & Unwin.

1975. The sceptical anthropologist? social anthropology and Marxist views on society. In M. Bloch, ed., *Marxist Analyses and Social Anthropology.* London: Malaby Press, pp. 29–60.

Fletcher, R. 1971. *The Making of Sociology.* London: Nelson.

Fordham, F. 1953. *An Introduction to Jung's Psychology.* Harmondsworth: Penguin Books.

Fortes, M. 1945. *The Dynamics of Clanship among the Tallens.* Oxford University Press.

1959. *Oedipus and Job in West African Religion.* Cambridge University Press.

1966. Totem and taboo. *Proceedings of the Royal Anthropological Institute.* 5–22.

Fox, J. J. 1975. On binary categories and primary symbols: some Rotinese perspectives. In Willis 1975, pp. 99–132.

Fox, R. 1967. Totem and taboo reconsidered. In E. Leach, ed., *The Structural Study of Myth and Totemism.* London: Tavistock, pp. 161–78.

Frank, A. G. 1984. *Critique and Anti-Critique.* London: Macmillan.

Frazer, J. G. 1903. *Encyclopaedia Britannica,* 9th ed., S.V. "Taboo: totemism."

1976. *The Golden Bough* (1922). London: Macmillan.

Freeman, D. 1969. Totem and taboo: a reappraisal. In W. Muensterberger, ed., *Man and His Culture.* London: Rapp & Whiting, pp. 53–80.

Freud, S. 1920. *Beyond the Pleasure Principle.* London: Hogarth Press.

1930. *Civilization and Its Discontents,* London: Hogarth Press.

1938a. The history of the psychoanalytic movement. In A. A. Brill, ed., *The Basic Writings of Sigmund Freud.* New York: Random House.

1938b. *Totem and Taboo* (1913). Harmondsworth; Penguin Books.

1953. *Introductory Lectures on Psychoanalysis* (1915–17). New York: Doubleday.

1978. *The Future of an Illusion* (1928). London: Hogarth Press.

Freund, J. 1979. German sociology in the time of Max Weber. In T. Bottomore and R. Nisbet, eds, *A History of Sociological Analysis*. London: Heinemann, pp. 149–86.

Fromm, E. 1942. *The Fear of Freedom*. London: Routledge & Kegan Paul.

1949. *Man for Himself*. London: Routledge & Kegan Paul.

1950. *Psychoanalysis and Religion*. New Haven: Yale University Press.

1970. *The Crisis of Psychoanalysis*. Harmondsworth: Penguin Books.

1980. *Beyond the Chains of Illusion* (1962). London: Sphere Books.

Gaborian, M. 1970. Structural anthropology and history. In M. Lane, ed., *Structuralism: A Reader*. London: Jonathan Cape, pp. 156–69.

Gardner, H. 1972. *The Quest for Mind*. New York: Knopf.

Geertz, C. 1960. *The Religion of Java*. University of Chicago Press.

1968. *Islam Observed: Religious Developments in Morocco and Indonesia*. New Haven: Yale University Press.

1975. *The Interpretation of Cultures*. London: Hutchinson.

1979. Suz: the bazaar economy of Sefron. In C. Geertz et al., eds., *Meaning and Order in Moroccan Society*. Cambridge University Press, pp. 123–244.

1983. *Local Knowledge*. New York: Basic Books.

Gellner, E. 1964. *Words and Things*. Harmondsworth: Penguin Books.

1969. *Saints of the Atlas*. London: Weidenfeld & Nicolson.

1973. *Cause and Meaning in the Social Sciences*. London: Routledge & Kegan Paul.

1974. *Legitimation of Belief*. Cambridge University Press.

1981. *Muslim Society*. Cambridge University Press.

Geras, N. 1972. Marx and the critique of political economy. In R. Blackburn, ed., *Ideology in Social Science*. London: Fontana/Collins, pp. 284–305.

Gerth, H., and C. Wright Mills. 1948. *From Max Weber: Essays in Sociology*. Routledge & Kegan Paul.

Giddens, A. 1971. *Capitalism and Modern Social Theory*. Cambridge University Press.

1978. *Durkheim*. London: Fontana/Collins.

1979. Positivism and its critics. In T. Bottomore and R. Nisbett, *A History of Sociological Analysis*. London: Heinemann, pp. 237–86.

Giddens, A., ed. 1974. *Positivism and Sociology*. London: Heinemann.

Glacken, C. 1970. Man against nature: an outmoded concept. In H. Helfrich, ed., *The Environmental Crisis*. New Haven: Yale University Press, pp. 127–38.

Glover, E. 1950. *Freud or Jung*. New York: Norton.

Gluckman, M. 1963. Rituals of rebellion in South East Africa. In *Order and Rebellion in Tribal Africa*. London: Cohen & West, pp. 110–37.

Godelier, M. 1972a. *Rationality and Irrationality in Economics*. London: New Left Books.

1972b. Structure and contradiction in capital. In R. Blackburn, ed., *Ideology in Social Science*. London: Fontana/Collins, pp. 334–68.

1977. *Perspectives in Marxist Anthropology*. Cambridge University Press.

1982. Myths, infrastructures and history in Lévi-Strauss. In I. Rossi, ed., *The Logic of Culture*. London: Tavistock, pp. 232–62.

Goldenweiser, A. 1964. Religion and society: a critique of Durkheim's theory of religion (1917). In Lessa and Vogt 1964, pp. 70–84.

Goldman, L. 1969. *The Human Sciences and Philosophy*. London; Jonathan Cape.

Goody, J. 1961. Religion and ritual: a definition problem. *British Journal of Sociology* 12:142–64.

1977. *The Domestication of the Savage Mind*. Cambridge University Press.

Gould, R. A. 1969. *Yiwara: Foragers of the Australian Desert*. London: Collins.

Gouldner, A. W. 1973. *For Sociology*. Harmondsworth: Penguin Books.

1980. *The Two Marxisms*. London: Macmillan.

Granet, M. 1973. Right and left in China. In Needham 1973, pp. 43–58.

Gray, J. G. 1970. Introduction. In J. G. Gray, ed., *G. W. F. Hegel: On Art, Religion and Philosophy*. New York: Harper & Row.

Green, R. W., ed. 1961. *Protestantism and Capitalism: The Weber Thesis and Its Critics*. Boston: Heath.

Griaule, M. 1972. *Conversations with Ogotemmeli: An Introduction to Dogon Religious Ideas* (1965). Oxford University Press.

Hall, S. 1977. Rethinking the "base-and-superstructure" metaphor. In J. Bloomfield, ed., *Class, Hegemony and Party*. London: Lawrence & Wishart, pp. 43–72.

Hallpike, C. R. 1969. Social hair. *Man* n.s. 4:256–64.

1976. Is there a primitive mentality? *Man* 11:253–70.

1979. *The Foundations of Primitive Thought*. Oxford University Press (Clarendon Press).

Harris, M. 1969. *The Rise of Anthropological Theory*. London: Routledge & Kegan Paul.

1977. *Cows, Pigs, Wars and Witches*. London: Fontana/Collins.

1978. *Cannibals and Kings*. London: Fontana/Collins.

1980. *Cultural Materialism*. New York: Random House (Vintage Books).

Hawton, H. 1956. *Philosophy for Pleasure*. Greenwich, Conn.: Fawcett.

Hayley, A. 1968. Symbolic equation: the ox and the cucumber. *Man* 3:62–271.

Hegel, G. W. F. 1942. *Philosophy of Right*, trans. and ed. T. M. Knox. Oxford University Press (Clarendon Press).

1948. *Early Theological Writings*, trans. T. M. Knox. Philadelphia: University of Pennsylvania.

1956. *The Philosophy of History* (1840). New York; Dover.

1970. *On Art, Religion, Philosophy*, trans. and ed. J. Glenn Gray. New York: Harper & Row.

1977. *Phenomenology of Spirit*, trans. A. Miller (1807). Oxford University Press.

Hertz, R. 1909. The pre-eminence of the right hand: a study in religious polarity. In Needham 1973, pp. 3–31.

References

Hiatt, L. R. 1969. Totemism tomorrow: the future of an illusion. *Mankind* 7:83–93.

Hicks, D. 1976. *Tetum Ghosts and Kin: Fieldwork in an Indonesian Community*. Palo Alto, Calif.: Mayfield.

Hindess, B., and P. Q. Hirst. 1975. *Pre-Capitalist Modes of Production*. London: Routledge & Kegan Paul.

Hirst, P. 1975. *Durkheim, Bernard and Epistemology*. London: Routledge & Kegan Paul.

Hirst, P., and P. Woolley. 1982. *Social Relations and Human Attributes*. London: Tavistock.

Hobsbawm, E. J. 1963. *Primitive Rebels*. Manchester University Press.

   1965. Introduction. In E. J. Hobsbawm, ed., *K. Marx Pre-Capitalist Economic Formations*. New York: International Publishers.

   1972. Karl Marx's contribution to historiography. In R. Blackburn, ed., *Ideology in Social Science*. London: Fontana/Collins, pp. 265–83.

   1982. Marx, Engels and pre-Marxian socialism. In E. J. Hobsbawm, ed., *The History of Marxism*. Brighton: Harvester Press, vol. 1, pp. 1–28.

Hodges, W. 1974. *The Philosophy of Wilhelm Dilthey* (1952). Westport, Conn.: Greenwood Press.

Hollis, M. 1970. Reason and ritual. In Wilson 1970, pp. 221–39.

Hollis, M., and S. Lukes. 1982. *Rationality and Relativism*. Oxford: Blackwell Publishers.

Homans, G. C. 1941. Anxiety and ritual: the theories of Malinowski and Radcliffe-Brown. *American Anthropology* 43:164–72.

Home, H. J. 1966. The concept of mind. *International Journal of Psychoanalysis* 47:42–9.

Hook, S. 1962. *From Hegel to Marx*. Ann Arbor: University of Michigan Press.

Horton, R. 1964. Ritual man in Africa. *Africa* 34:85–104.

   1970. African traditional thought and Western science (1967). In Wilson 1970, pp. 131–71.

   1973. Lévy-Bruhl, Durkheim and the scientific revolution. In Horton and Finnegan 1973, pp. 249–305.

Horton, R., and R. Finnegan, eds. 1973. *Modes of Thought*. London: Faber & Faber.

Hubert, H., and M. Mauss. 1964. *Sacrifice: Its Nature and Function*. London: Cohen & West.

Hughes, H. S. 1958. *Consciousness and Society*. New York: Random House (Vintage Books).

Hume, D. 1956. *The Natural History of Religion* (1757). London: Adam & Black.

Hunn, E. 1979. The abomination of Levitians revisited. In R. F. Ellen and D. Reason, eds., *Classifications in Their Social Context*. New York: Academic Press, pp. 103–14.

Jahoda, G. 1969. *The Psychology of Superstition*. Harmondsworth: Penguin Books.

James, W. 1971. *The Varieties of Religious Experience* (1902). London: Fontana.

Jarvie, E. C. 1964. *The Revolution in Anthropology*. London: Routledge & Kegan Paul.

348

References

1970. Explaining cargo cults. In Wilson 1970, pp. 50–61.

Jarvie, I. C., and J. Agassi. 1970. The problem of rationality of magic (1967). In Wilson 1970, pp. 172–93.

Jenkins, A. 1979. *The Social Theory of Claude Lévi-Strauss*. London: Macmillan.

Jones, E. 1944. The psychology of religion. In S. Lorand, ed., *Psychoanalysis Today*. New York: International Universities Press, pp. 315–25.

1964. *The Life and Work of Sigmund Freud*, abridged, ed. L. Trilling. Harmondsworth: Penguin Books.

Jones, R. J. 1977. On understanding a sociological classic. *American Journal of Sociology* 83:279–319.

Jung, C. G. 1921. *Psychological Types*. New York: Harcourt, Brace.

1933. *Modern Man in Search of a Soul*. London: Routledge & Kegan Paul.

1938. *Psychology and Religion*. New Haven: Yale University Press.

1963. *Memories, Dreams, Reflections*. London: Collins.

1971. *The Portable Jung*, ed. J. Campbell. Harmondsworth: Penguin Books.

1972. *Synchronicity, An Acausal Connecting Principle*. London: Routledge & Kegan Paul.

Jung. C. G., ed. 1964. *Man and His Symbols*. London: Pan Books.

Kahn, J. S., and J. R. Llobera 1981. Towards a new Marxism or a new anthropology. In Kahn and Llobera, eds., *The Anthropology of Pre-Capitalist Societies*. London: Macmillan, pp. 263–329.

Kardiner, A., and E. Preble. 1961. *They Studied Man*. New York: New American Library (Mentor Books).

Katz, R. 1982. *Bailing Energy: Community Healing among the Kalahari Kung*. Cambridge, Mass.: Harvard University Press.

Kaufman, Y. 1961. *The Religion of Israel*, trans. M. Greenberg.

Kaufmann, W. 1965. *Hegel: A Re-Interpretation*. Indiana: University of Notre Dame Press.

Kaufmann, W., ed. 1971. *The Portable Nietzsche*. London: Chatto & Windus.

Kautsky, K. 1972. *Foundations of Christianity* (1908). New York: Monthly Review Press.

Keat, R., and J. Urry. 1975. *Social Theory as Science*. London: Routledge & Kegan Paul.

Kirk, G. S. 1970. *Myth: Its Meaning and Functions in Ancient and Other Cultures*. Cambridge University Press.

Kojeve, A. 1980. *Introduction to the Reading of Hegel* (1969). Ithaca: Cornell University Press.

Kolakowski, L. 1973. Ideology and theory. In T. Bottomore, ed., *Karl Marx*. Englewood Cliffs, N.J.: Prentice Hall, pp. 119–22.

1981. *Main Currents in Marxism*. Vol. 1. *The Founders*. Oxford University Press.

Kovel, J. 1978. *A Complete Guide to Therapy*. Harmondsworth: Penguin Books.

Krader, L. 1972. *The Ethnological Notebooks of Karl Marx*. Assen.

Kroeber, A. L. 1972a. Totem and taboo: an ethnologic psychoanalysis (1920). In Lessa and Vogt 1972, pp. 20–3.

1972b. Totem and taboo in retrospect (1930). In Lessa and Vogt 1972, pp. 24–7.

349

References

Kuhn, T. S. 1962. *The Structure of Scientific Revolutions*. University of Chicago Press.

Kuper, A. 1973. *Anthropologists and Anthropology*. Harmondsworth: Penguin Books.

Kuper, A., ed. 1977. *The Social Anthropology of Radcliffe-Brown*. London: Routledge & Kegan Paul.

Kuper, H. 1947. *An African Aristocracy*. Oxford University Press.

Kurzweil, E. 1980. *The Age of Structuralism: Lévi-Strauss to Foucault*. New York: Columbia University Press.

Larrain, J. 1979. *The Concept of Ideology*. London: Hutchinson.

1983. *Marxism and Ideology*. London: Macmillan.

Lavrin, J. 1971. *Nietzsche: A Biographical Introduction*. London: Studio Vista.

Leach, E. R. 1954. *Political System of Highland Burma*. London: Athlone.

1958. Magical hair. *Journal of the Royal Anthropological Institute* 88:147–64.

1961. Two essays concerning the symbolic representation of time. In *Re-Thinking Anthropology*, London School of Economics Monograph No. 22. London: Athlone Press, pp. 124–36.

1964. Animal categories and verbal abuse. In E. H. Lenneberg, ed., *New Directions in the Study of Language*. Cambridge, Mass.: MIT Press, pp. 28–63.

1969. *Genesis as Myth and Other Essays*. London: Jonathan Cape.

1970a. The epistemological background to Malinowski's empiricism. In R. Firth, ed., *Man and Culture*. London: Routledge & Kegan Paul, pp. 119–38.

1970b. *Lévi-Strauss*. London: Fontana/Collins.

1971. Kimil-A category of Andamanese thought. In P. Maranda and E. K. Maranda, eds., *Structural Analysis in Oral Traditions*. Philadelphia: University of Pennsylvania Press.

1976. *Culture and Communication*. Cambridge University Press.

1983. Why did Moses have a sister? In E. Leach and D. A. Aycock, eds., *Structural Interpretation of Biblical Myth*. Cambridge University Press.

Leacock, E. 1981. *Myths of Male Dominance*. New York: Monthly Review Press.

Leeuw, G. van der. 1963. *Religion in Essence and Manifestation* (1938). 2 vols. New York: Harper & Row.

Lefebvre, H. 1968. *The Sociology of Marx*. Harmondsworth: Penguin Books.

Lessa, W. A., and E. Z. Vogt, eds. 1972. *Reader in Comparative Religion*. New York: Harper & Row.

Lévi-Strauss, C. 1955. *Tristes Tropiques*. Harmondsworth: Penguin Books.

1962. *Totemism*. Harmondsworth: Penguin Books.

1963. *Structural Anthropology*. Harmondsworth: Penguin Books.

1966. *The Savage Mind*. London: Weidenfeld & Nicolson.

1969a. *The Elementary Structures of Kinship*. London: Eyre & Spottiswoode.

1969b. *The Raw and the Cooked*. Vol. 1 of *Introduction to a Science of Mythology*. New York: Harper & Row.

1973a. *From Honey to Ashes*. Vol. 2 of *Introduction to a Science of Mythology*. New York: Harper & Row.

1973b. *Structural Anthropology*, vol. 2. Harmondsworth: Penguin Books.

References

1978a. *Myth and Meaning*. London: Routledge & Kegan Paul.

1978b. *The Origin of Table Manners*. Vol. 3 of *Introduction to a Science of Mythology*. New York: Harper & Row.

1981. *The Naked Man*. Vol. 4 of *Introduction to a Science of Mythology*. London: Jonathan Cape.

Lévy-Bruhl, L. 1926. *How Natives Think*. London: Allen & Unwin.

1949. *The Notebooks on Primitive Mentality*, trans. P. Riviere. Oxford: Blackwell Publications.

1965. *The Soul of the Primitive* (1928). London: Allen & Unwin.

Lewis, I. 1971. *Ecstatic Religion*. Harmondsworth: Penguin Books.

Lewis, I., ed. 1977. *Introduction to Symbols and Sentiments: Cross Cultural Studies in Symbolism*. New York: Academic Press.

Lewis, J. 1975. *Max Weber and Value-free Sociology*. London: Lawrence & Wishart.

Lichtheim, G. 1961. *Marxism: An Historical and Critical Study*. London: Routledge & Kegan Paul.

Lienhardt, G. 1969. Edward Tylor, 1832–1917. In T. Raison, ed., *The Founding Fathers of Social Science*. Harmondsworth: Penguin Books, pp. 84–91.

Ling, T. 1980. *Karl Marx and Religion*. London: Macmillan.

Llobera, J. 1981. Durkheim, the Durkheimians and their collective misrepresentation of Marx. In Kahn and Llobera 1981, pp. 214–40.

Lomas, P. 1966. Psychoanalysis – Freudian or existential. In Rycroft 1966, pp. 116–44.

Lowie, R. 1937. *History of Ethnological Theory*. New York: Farrar & Rinehart.

1948. *Primitive Religion* (1924). New York: Liveright.

Lowith, K. 1960. *Max Weber and Karl Marx*, trans. T. B. Bottomore. London: Allen & Unwin.

Luethy, H. 1970. Once again: Calvinism and capitalism (1964). In Wrong 1970, pp. 123–34.

Lukes, S. 1973a. *Emile Durkheim: His Life and Work*. Harmondsworth: Penguin Books.

1973b. On the social determination of thought. In Horton and Finnegan 1973, pp. 230–48.

McCarney, J. 1980. *The Real World of Ideology*. Brighton: Harvester Press.

MacCormack, C., and M. Strathern, eds. 1980. *Nature, Culture and Gender*. Cambridge University Press.

McGuire, W., ed. 1974. *The Freud/Jung Letters*. London: Hogarth Press.

MacIntyre, A. 1964. Is understanding religion compatible with believing? In J. Hicks, ed., *Faith and the Philosophers*. London: Macmillan.

1970. *Marcuse*. London: Fontana.

McLellan, D. 1973. *Karl Marx: His Life and Thought*. London: Granada.

MacQuarrie, J. 1973. *Existentialism*. Harmondsworth: Penguin Books.

MacRae, D. G. 1974. *Weber*. London: Fontana.

Malinowski, B. 1935. *Coral Gardens and Their Magic*. London: Kegan Paul.

1944. *A Scientific Theory of Culture*. Chapel Hill: University of North Carolina Press.

351

References

1963. *Sex, Culture and Myth*. London: Hart Davies.

1974. *Magic, Science and Religion, and Other Essays* (1925). London: Souvenir Press.

Mandel, E. 1962. *Marxist Economic Theory*. New York: Monthly Review Press.

Marcuse, H. 1941. *Reason and Revolution: Hegel and the Rise of Social Theory*. London: Routledge & Kegan Paul.

1969. *Eros and Civilization* (1955). London: Sphere Books.

Marshall, G. 1980. *Presbyteries and Profits: Calvinism and the Development of Capitalism in Scotland*. Oxford University Press (Clarendon Press).

1982. *In Search of the Spirit of Capitalism*. London: Hutchinson.

Marshall, L. 1969. The medicine dance of the !Kung bushmen. *Africa* 39:349–81.

Martindale, D. 1961. *The Nature and Types of Sociological Theory*. London: Routledge & Kegan Paul.

Marx, K. 1847. *The Poverty of Philosophy*. Moscow: Progress.

1957. *Capital* (1867), trans. E. Paul and C. Paul, ed. G. D. H. Cole. Vol. 1. London: Dent.

1959. *Economic and Philosophic Manuscripts of 1844*. Moscow: Progress.

1973. *Grundrisse*, trans. and ed. Martin Nicolaus. Harmondsworth: Penguin Books.

Marx, K. and F. Engels. 1957. *On Religion*. Moscow: Progress.

1965. *The German Ideology* (1846). London: Lawrence & Wishart.

1968. *Selected Works*. London: Lawrence & Wishart.

Masterson, P. 1973. *Atheism and Alienation*. Harmondsworth: Penguin Books.

Mauss, M., and H. Beauchat. 1979. *Seasonal Variations of the Eskimo*, trans. and ed. J. J. Fox. London: Routledge & Kegan Paul.

Mauss, M., and H. Hubert. 1972. *A General Theory of Magic*, ed. D. Pocock. London: Routledge & Kegan Paul.

Maybury-Lewis, D. 1969. Science or bricolage? *American Anthropology* 71:114–21.

Merleau-Ponty, M. 1964. *Sense and Non-Sense*, trans. H. L. Dreyfus and P. A. Dreyfus. Evanston, Ill.: Northwestern University Press.

Miller, G. 1964. *Psychology: The Science of Mental Life*. London: Hutchinson.

Mills, C. W. 1963. *The Marxists*. Harmondsworth: Penguin Books.

Miranda, J. P. 1980. *Marx against the Marxists*. London: SCM Press.

Mitchell, J. 1975. *Psychoanalysis and Feminism*. Harmondsworth: Penguin Books.

Mitzman, A. 1970. *The Iron Cage: An Historical Interpretation of Max Weber*. New York: Knopf.

Moore, R. 1971. History, economics and religion: a review of "The Max Weber Thesis." In A. Sahay, ed., *Max Weber and Modern Sociology*. London: Routledge & Kegan Paul, pp. 82–96.

Morris, B. 1976. Whither the savage mind? *Man* 11: 542–57.

1978. Ecology and mysticism. *Anarchist Review*. May 9, p. 16.

1979. Symbolism and ideology; thoughts around Navaho taxonomy and symbolism. In R. F. Ellen and D. Reason, eds., *Classifications in Their Social Context*. New York: Academic Press, pp. 117–38.

1981a. Changing views of nature. *Ecologist* 11:130–37.

1981b. Hill gods and ecstatic cults: notes on the religion of a hunting and gathering people. *Man in India* 61:203–36.

1982. The family, group structuring and trade among South Indian hunter-gatherers. In E. Leacock and R. Lee, eds., *Politics and History in Band Societies*. Cambridge University Press, pp. 171–88.

1984. Ruth Benedict: Popular acclaim, academic neglect. *Royal Anthropological Institute Newsletter*.

Müller, F. M. 1889. *Natural Religion*. London: Longmans.

1978. *Introduction to the Science of Religion* (1873). New York: Arno Press.

Nadel, S. F. 1970. Malinowski on magic and religion. In R. Firth, ed., *Man and Culture*. London: Routledge & Kegan Paul, pp. 189–208.

Needham, R. 1961. The left hand of the Mugwe: an analytic note on the structure of Meru symbolism. *Africa* 31:28–33.

1963. Introduction. In Durkheim and Mauss 1963.

1967. Right and left in Nyoro symbolic classification. *Africa* 37:425–52. In Needham 1973, pp. 299–341.

1972. *Belief, Language and Experience*. Oxford: Blackwell Publications.

1979. *Symbolic Classification*. Santa Monica, Calif.: Goodyear.

Needham, R., ed. 1973. *Right and Left: Essays in Dual Symbolic Classification*. University of Chicago Press.

Nelson, B. 1973. Weber's Protestant ethic: its origins, wanderings and the foreseeable future. In C. Y. Glock and P. E. Hammond, eds., *Beyond the Classics? Essays in the Scientific Study of Religion*. New York: Harper & Row, pp. 71–130.

Neumann, E. 1955. *The Great Mother: An Analysis of the Archetype*. Princeton University Press.

Nicolaus, M. 1973. Foreword. In Marx 1973.

Nietzsche, F. 1961. *Thus Spoke Zarathustra*, trans. R. J. Hollingdale (1884). Harmondsworth: Penguin Books.

1968. *"Twilight of the Gods" and "The Anti-Christ,"* trans. R. J. Hollingdale (1889/1895). Harmondsworth: Penguin Books.

Norbeck, E. 1903. African rituals of conflict. *American Anthropology* 65:1254–79.

Nova, F. 1968. *Friedrich Engels: His Contribution to Political Theory*. London: Vision.

Novack, G. 1971. *An Introduction to the Logic of Marxism*. New York: Pathfinder Press.

1975. *Pragmatism versus Marxism*. New York: Pathfinder Press.

1978. *Polemics in Marxist Philosophy*. New York: Monad Press.

Nye, D. A., and C. E. Ashworth. 1971. Emile Durkheim: was he a nominalist or realist? *British Journal of Sociology* 22:133–48.

Ornstein, R. E. 1972. *The Psychology of Consciousness*. Harmondsworth: Penguin Books.

Ortner, S. 1975. God's bodies, God's food: a symbolic analysis of a Sherpa ritual. In Willis 1975, pp. 133–69.

Otto, R. 1917. *The Idea of the Holy*. Harmondsworth: Penguin Books.

Parkin, F. 1982. *Max Weber*. London: Tavistock.

Parsons, A. 1969. Is the Oedipus complex universal? In W. Muensterberger and

S. Axelrad, eds., *The Psychoanalytic Study of Society*. Vol. 3. New York: International Universities Press.

Parsons, T. 1935. H. M. Robertson on Max Weber and his school. *Journal of Political Economy* 43:688–96.

1954. Religion and the problem of meaning. In *Essays in Sociological Theory*. Glencoe, Ill.: Free Press.

1968a. *Sociological Theory and Modern Society*. New York: Free Press.

1968b. *The Structure of Social Action* (1937). 2 vols. Glencoe, Ill.: Free Press.

Passmore, J. 1957. *A Hundred Years of Philosophy*. Harmondsworth: Penguin Books.

Paterson, R. W. K. 1971. *The Nihilistic Egoist: Max Stirner*. Oxford University Press.

Peel, J. D. Y. 1971. *Herbert Spencer, the Evolution of a Sociologist*. London: Heinemann.

Piaget, J. 1966. Need and significance of cross cultural studies of genetic psychology. *International Journal of Psychology* 1:3–13.

1971. *Structuralism*. London: Routledge & Kegan Paul.

Pivcevic, E. 1970. *Husserl and Phenomenology*. London: Hutchinson.

Plekhanov, G. V. 1908. *Fundamental Problems of Marxism*. London.

Pocock, D. F. 1961. *Social Anthropology*. London: Steed & Ward.

1974. Nuer religion – a supplementary view. *Journal of the Anthropological Society of Oxford* 5:69–79.

Poggi, G. 1983. *Calvinism and the Capitalist Spirit*. London: Macmillan.

Polanyi, M. 1958. *Study of Man*. University of Chicago Press.

Popper, K. R. 1945. *The Open Society and Its Enemies*. Vol. 2. London: Routledge & Kegan Paul.

1969. *Conjectures and Refutations*. London: Routledge & Kegan Paul.

Radcliffe-Brown, A. R. 1951. The comparative method in social anthropology. *Journal of the Royal Anthropological Institute* 31:15–22.

1952. *Structure and Function in Primitive Society*. London: Cohen & West.

1964. *The Andaman Islanders* (1922). Glencoe, Ill.: Free Press.

Radin, P. 1957. *Primitive Religion: Its Nature and Origin* (1937). New York: Dover.

Rappaport, R. A. 1967. Ritual regulation of environmental relations among a New Guinea people. *Ethnology* 6:17–30.

1968. *Pigs for Ancestors: Ritual in the Ecology of a New Guinea People*. New Haven: Yale University Press.

Rayner, S. 1982. The perception of time and space in egalisarian sects: a millenarian cosmology. In Douglas 1982a.

Reardon, B. M. G. 1977. *Hegel's Philosophy of Religion*. London: Macmillan.

Reichard, G. A. 1974. *Navaho Religion: A Study of Symbolism* (1950). Princeton University Press.

Ricoeur, P. 1963. Structure et hermeneutique. *Esprit* 11.

1967. *The Symbolism of Evil*. New York: Harper & Row.

1970. *Freud and Philosophy*. New Haven: Yale University Press.

Rigby, P. 1966. Dual symbolic classification among the Gogo of Central Tanzania. *Africa* 36:1–16.

References

Robertson, H. M. 1933. *Aspects of the Rise of Economic Individualism.* Cambridge University Press.

Robertson-Smith, W. 1889. *Lectures on the Religion of the Semites.* Edinburgh: Black.

Rodinson, M. 1974. *Islam and Capitalism.* Harmondsworth: Penguin Books.

Roheim, G. 1930. *Animism, Magic and the Divine King.* London: Kegan Paul.

1950. *Psychoanalysis and Anthropology.* New York: International Universities Press.

1972. *The Panic of the Gods.* New York: Harper & Row.

1974. *The Riddle of the Sphinx* (1934). New York: Harper & Row.

Rosaldo, M. Z., and J. Atkinson. 1975. Man the hunter and woman. In Willis 1975, pp. 43–75.

Rose, G. 1981. *Hegel contra Sociology.* London: Athlone.

Rosen, Z. 1977. *Bruno Bauer and Karl Marx.* The Hague: Martinus Nijhoff.

Rossi, I. 1982. On the assumptions of structural analysis. In *The Logic of Culture.* London: Tavistock, pp. 3–22.

1983. *From the Sociology of Symbols to the Sociology of Signs.* New York: Columbia University Press.

Rossi, I., ed. 1974. *The Unconscious in Culture.* New York: Dutton.

Roth, G. 1971. The historical relationship of Weber to Marxism. In R. Bendix and G. Roth, eds., *Scholarship and Partisanship.* Berkeley: University of California Press, pp. 227–52.

Roth, G., and W. Schluchter. 1979. *Max Weber's Vision of History, Ethics and Methods.* Berkeley: University of California Press.

Runciman, W. G. 1969. What is structuralism? *British Journal of Sociology* 20:253–65.

Russell, B. 1946. *A History of Western Philosophy.* London: Allen & Unwin.

Rycroft, C. 1966. *Psychoanalysis Observed.* Harmondsworth: Penguin Books.

Sahlins, M. 1976. *Culture and Practical Reason.* University of Chicago Press.

Solomon, A. 1945. German sociology. In G. Gurvitch and W. Moore, eds., *Twentieth Century Sociology.* New York: Philosophical Library.

Samuelsson, K. 1961. *Religion and Economic Action*, trans. E. G. French. London: Heinemann.

Sartre, J. P. 1943. *Being and Nothingness* (1909). London: Methuen (University Paperbacks).

Schleiermacher, F. 1958. *On Religion.* New York: Harper & Row.

Schmidt, A. 1983. *History and Structure*, trans. J. Herf. Cambridge, Mass.: MIT Press.

Schoffeleers, J. M. 1971. The religious significance of bush fires. *Cahiers des Religions Africaines* 10:271–81.

Scholte, B. 1966. Epistemic paradigms. *American Anthropology* 68:1192–1201.

Schwartz, B. 1981. *Vertical Classification.* University of Chicago Press.

Seliger, M. 1977. *The Marxist Conception of Ideology.* Cambridge University Press.

Seve, L. 1978. *Man in Marxist Theory.* Brighton: Harvester Press.

Seznec, J. 1953. *The Survival of the Pagan Gods.* Princeton University Press.

Shalvey, T. 1979. *Claude Lévi-Strauss: Social Psychotherapy and the Collective Unconscious.* Brighton: Harvester Press.

References

Sharpe, E. J. 1975. *Comparative Religion: A History.* London: Duckworth.
Shaw, M. 1972. The coming crisis of radical sociology. In Robin Blackburn, ed., *Ideology in Social Science.* London: Fontana/Collins, pp. 32–44.
Sheridan, A. 1980. *Michel Foucault: The Will to Truth.* London: Tavistock.
Shweder, R. 1982. On savages and other children (Review of Hallpike, 1979). *American Anthropology* 83:354–66.
Singer, J. 1977. *Androgyny: Towards a New Theory of Sexuality.* London: Routledge & Kegan Paul.
Singer, P. 1980. *Marx.* Oxford University Press.
1983. *Hegel.* Oxford University Press.
Skorupski, J. 1976. *Symbol and Theory: A Philosophical Study of Theories of Religion in Social Anthropology.* Cambridge University Press.
Sorokin, P. A. 1927. *Contemporary Sociological Theories.* New York: Harper.
Spencer, H. 1876. *The Principles of Sociology.* 3 vols. London: Williams & Norgate.
1966. *Essays on Education.* London: Dent.
Sperber, D. 1975. *Rethinking Symbolism.* Cambridge University Press.
1979. Lévi-Strauss. In Sturrock 1979.
Spinoza, B. de. 1951. *A Theologico-Political Treatise,* ed. R. H. M. Elwes (1670). New York: Dover.
Srinivas, M. N. 1952. *Religion and Society among the Coorgs of South India.* London: J. K. Publishers.
Stace, W. T. 1955. *The Philosophy of Hegel* (1924). New York: Dover.
Stanner, W. E. H. 1965. Religion, totemism and symbolism. In R. M. Berndt and C. H. Berndt (eds.), *Aboriginal Man in Australia.* Sydney: Angus & Robertson, pp. 207–37.
1979. *White Man Got No Dreaming.* Canberra: Australian Nat. Univ. Press.
Stauder, J. 1974. The "relevance" of anthropology to colonialism and imperialism. *Radical Science Journal* 1:51–70.
Steiner, F. 1966. *Taboo.* Harmondsworth: Penguin Books.
Steiner, G. 1966. A conversation with Claude Lévi-Strauss. *Encounter* 26:35.
Stern, J. P. 1978. *Nietzsche.* London: Fontana.
Stirner, M. 1973. *The Ego and His Own,* trans. S. T. Byington (1845). New York: Dover.
Storr, A. 1973. *Jung.* London: Fontana/Collins.
Sturrock, J., ed. 1979. *Structuralism and Since: From Lévi-Strauss to Derrida.* Oxford University Press.
Sulloway, F. J. 1979. *Freud: Biologist of the Mind.* London: Fontana.
Tawney, R. H. 1938. *Religion and the Rise of Capitalism.* Harmondsworth: Penguin Books.
Taylor, C. 1979. *Hegel and Modern Society.* Cambridge University Press.
Taylor, J. V. 1963. *The Primal Vision.* London: SCM Press.
Thompson, E. P. 1978. *The Poverty of Theory and Other Essays.* London: Merlin Press.
Thompson, K. 1982. *Emile Durkheim.* London: Tavistock.
Thompson, L. 1945. Logico-aesthetic integration in Hopi culture. *American Anthropology* 47:540–53.

References

Tillich, P. 1955. Theology and symbolism. In F. E. Johnson, ed., *Religious Symbolism*. New York: Harper, pp. 107–16.
Tiryakian, E. A. 1978. Emile Durkheim. In T. Bottomore and R. Nisbet, eds., *A History of Sociological Analysis*. London: Heinemann, pp. 187–236.
Toren, C. 1983. Thinking symbols: a critique of Sperber. *Man*:260–8.
Toynbee, A. 1976. *Mankind and Mother Earth*. Oxford University Press.
Trevor-Roper, H. R. 1963. Religion, the Reformation, and social change. *Historical Studies* 4:18–44. London: Bowes & Bowes.
Tucker, R. 1965. *Philosophy and Myth in Karl Marx*. Cambridge University Press.
Turnbull, C. 1965. *Wayward Servants*. New York: Natural History Press.
Turner, B. S. 1974. *Weber and Islam*. London: Routledge & Kegan Paul.
    1983. *Religion and Social Theory: A Materialist Perspective*. London: Heinemann.
Turner, V. W. 1957. *Schism and Continuity in an Africa Society*. Manchester University Press.
    1967. *The Forest of Symbols: Aspects of Ndembu Ritual*. Ithaca: Cornell University Press.
    1968. *The Drums of Affliction*. Oxford University Press (Clarendon Press).
    1969. Introduction. In R. F. Spencer, ed., *Forms of Symbolic Action*. Seattle: University of Washington Press.
    1974a. *Dramas, Fields and Metaphors*. Ithaca: Cornell University Press.
    1974b. *The Ritual Process* (1969). Harmondsworth: Penguin Books.
    1975. Symbolic studies. In B. J. Siegel, ed., *Annual Review of Anthropology* 4:145–62. Palo Alto, Calif.
    1982. *From Ritual to Theatre*. New York: Performing Arts J. Publ.
Turner, V., and E. Turner. 1978. *Image and Pilgrimage in Christian Culture*. New York: Columbia University Press.
Tylor, E. B. 1913. *Primitive Culture* (1871). London: Murray.
Underhill, E. 1911. *Mysticism*. London: Methuen.
Van Gennep, A. 1965. *The Rites of Passage* (1908). London: Routledge & Kegan Paul.
Wach, J. 1944. *Sociology of Religion*. University of Chicago Press.
Wallwork, E. 1984. Religion and social structure in *The Division of Labor*. *American Anthropologist* 86:43–64.
Warnock, M. 1966. Review of Lévi-Strauss 1966. *New Society* 584–6.
Weber, Marianne. 1975. *Max Weber: A Biography* (1926). New York: Wiley.
Weber, Max. 1923. *General Economic History*. London: Allen & Unwin.
    1930. *The Protestant Ethic and the Spirit of Capitalism*, trans. T. Parsons (1904–5). London: Allen & Unwin.
    1947. *The Theory of Social and Economic Organization*, trans. A. M. Henderson and T. Parsons. New York: Free Press.
    1949. *The Methodology of the Social Sciences*, trans. and ed. E. A. Shils and H. A. Finch (1904). Glencoe, Ill.: Free Press.
    1951. *The Religion of China: Confucianism and Taoism*, trans. H. H. Gerth. Glencoe, Ill.: Free Press.
    1952. *Ancient Judaism*, trans. H. H. Gerth and Don Martindale. Glencoe, Ill.: Free Press.

References

1958. *The Religion of India: The Sociology of Hinduism and Buddhism*, trans. H. H. Gerth and D. Martindale. Glencoe, Ill.: Free Press.

1965. *The Sociology of Religion*, trans. E. Fischoff, ed. T. Parsons. London: Methuen.

Weiss, F. G. 1974. *Hegel: The Essential Writings*. New York: Harper & Row.

White, L., Jr. 1975. The historical roots of our ecologic crisis (1967). In R. Clarke, ed., *Notes for a Future*. London: Thames & Hudson, pp. 99–106.

White, M. 1955. *The Age of Analysis*. New York: New American Library (Mentor Books).

Whitehead, A. N. 1926. *Science and the Modern World*. Cambridge University Press.

Williams, R. 1958. *Culture and Society, 1780–1950*. Harmondsworth: Penguin Books.

1980. *Problems in Materialism and Culture*. London: Verso.

Willis, R. G. 1974. *Man and Beast*. London: Hart Davis.

Willis, R. G., ed. 1975. *The Interpretation of Symbolism*. London: Malaby Press.

Wilson, B. R., ed. 1970. *Rationality*. Oxford: Blackwell Publications.

Wilson, C. 1981. *The Quest for Wilhelm Reich*. London: Granada.

Wiltshire, D. 1978. *The Social and Political Thought of Herbert Spencer*. Oxford University Press.

Winch, P. 1958. *The Idea of a Social Science*. London: Routledge & Kegan Paul.

1970. Understanding a primitive society (1964). In B. R. Wilson 1970, pp. 78–111.

Wolf, E. R. 1982. *Europe and the People without History*. Berkeley: University of California Press.

Wollheim, R. 1971. *Freud*. London: Fontana/Collins.

Woodcock, G. 1972. *Gandhi*. London: Fontana.

Worsley, P. 1957. *The Trumpet Shall Sound*. London: Paladin.

1967. Groote Eylandt totemism and le totemisme aujourd'hui. In E. Leach, ed., *The Structural Study of Myth and Totemism*. London: Tavistock, pp. 141–60.

1982. *Marx and Marxism*. London: Tavistock.

Wrong, D. H., ed. 1970. *Max Weber*. Englewood Cliffs, N.J.: Prentice-Hall.

Wuthnow, R., R. D. Hunter, A. Bergesen, and E. Kurzweil. 1984. *Cultural Analysis*. London: Routledge & Kegan Paul.

Yinger, J. M. 1957. *Religion, Society and the Individual*. New York: Macmillan.

Zuesse, E. M. 1979. *Ritual Cosmos*. Athens: University of Ohio Press.

Index

359

Index